American Legislative Processes

American Legislative Processes

Jack R. Van Der Slik
Southern Illinois University
Carbondale

Thomas Y. Crowell Company
New York   Established 1834

For Franci, Gary, and Randall—
Bonnie and I have showed them the Way.

Library of Congress Cataloging in Publication Data
Van Der Slik, Jack R   1936–
   American legislative processes.

   Includes bibliographical references and index.
   1. Legislative bodies—United States. I. Title.
JK1001.V36   1977   328.73   76-40259
ISBN 0-690-00870-8

Thomas Y. Crowell Company, Inc.
666 Fifth Avenue
New York, New York 10019

Manufactured in the United States of America

For permission to use copyrighted materials, grateful acknowledgment
is made to the copyright holders listed on the page following the last
page of text, which is hereby made a part of this copyright page.

Contents

III
System Interdependency: Shaping Policy Adoption in the Legislative Subsystem

IV
Inside the Legislative Subsystem

Preface

American political systems are wonderously complex in their structures and processes. Our constitutional tradition requires the governments of this country to be limited in their powers, divided into rival branches, distinguished into local, state, and national levels, and integrated by a two-party mold that shapes electoral processes. My aim in writing this book is to be comprehensive, empirically oriented, and concise in explaining American legislative politics in Congress and in the state legislatures. For aid in organizing my discussion, I have drawn upon David Easton's widely understood model. The model is not a predictive theory, but it admirably organizes analytical thinking about complex political processes. By using this model, comparable findings on legislators, rules of the game, structures, policy outputs, and the like can be brought together, and general patterns of behavior can be observed and explained.

To be comprehensive, my purview includes legislatures in all the states as well as Congress. I take into account the way American political culture shapes the practice of politics, the relationship of legislatures and legislators with the people, other significant actors and institutions in society, while touching on foreign political systems. I discuss intralegislative behavior and differentiate policy outputs.

In emphasizing what legislators are like, how they make decisions, and how they organize themselves, I have made my empirical orientation clear. Rather than comparing actual legislative behavior to how I think they should behave, I compare how legislators think they should behave with how, in fact, they do behave. To support these discussions, I have used a variety of systematic studies of legislative politics.

Withal, I have written to be understood. I have tried to simplify, clarify, and express myself in a readable way. Rather than a source book on legal procedures or a casebook on bill enactments, this is a thorough and concise explanation of the essentials of American legislative politics within a context of contemporary public policy making.

Writing this book has been a happy experience. Scholarship in legislative politics is rich and broad. Each new session of Congress confirms basic generalizations, but reveals new nuances of political behavior. State legislatures are increasingly institutionalized and visible to students. I have written out of what I have learned from countless articles, books, and papers, and from hours of discussion with my students, colleagues, and teachers. I gratefully acknowledge these debts, and many are specifically footnoted. For their intellectual stimulation, I particularly thank Leo Stine, Charles Press, Joseph Schlesinger, Robert Scigliano, Stephen Monsma, Joe Allman, and Eric Carlson. Specific portions of the book were improved in response to ideas and encouragement from Milton Morris, John Jackson, John Baker, Stephen Wasby, Dale Brown, and the anonymous reviewers of my manuscript. Time and resources were made available to me by David Kenney, Roy Miller, William Day, Randall Nelson, and Lon Shelby. Research assistance came primarily from Samuel Pernacciaro, Keith Thornloe, and Thomas Stenger. I benefited from the typing skills of Barbara Bennett, Helen Keller, and Kathy Shannon.

I am most indebted to my wife, Bonnie, and my family. They encouraged and supported me throughout the arduous writing process. Together we thank and praise our heavenly Father for meeting all our needs.

American
Legislative
Processes

Who Cares about Systems and Subsystems?

At first reading, concepts such as *system*, *input*, and *feedback* seem a bit awkward. They stand for abstract ideas. But the abstract ideas are not mere imagination. Implicit in them are actions by real people: T. John Hornblower, ambitious politician; Myron Makemoney, civic booster; Cliff Carney, who could care less about political decision making; Lucinda Rabble, riot raiser and placard painter; Shecky Goodfuture, boy scout and budding environmentalist; and Monte Hooker, pickpocket and cop hater.

The system model defines categories of politically relevant actions and actors. The model, though not original with me, disciplines writing about legislatures and the legislative process. The brief chapter that follows sets forth the model. Subsequent chapters describe the parts and the processes outlined in the introductory chapter. Concern with systems and subsystems provides an overview of the whole, while helping to describe the articulation of the parts.

1

The Legislative Process in the Context of a Democratic Political System

A seven-year-old boy, about to go to bed, concluded his prayer by saying, "This is Gary Johnson at 207 Owens Lane in Springfield, Illinois, U.S.A., North America, Western Hemisphere, planet Earth, of the solar system in the Milky Way, saying amen." This careful identification by a child who had begun to appreciate the particularity of his own existence in a vast universe illustrates how one can systematize information or ideas from the specific to the general.

The process of systematizing ideas can also begin at the general level and proceed to the specific. This is the strategy for explanation that I will use in this chapter. To understand specifics in the legislative process, it will be helpful to view that process in a much more comprehensive context.

A person finds himself in a society. A society is the broadest of all social units.[1] In a society are many *systems.* A system may be defined as *a set of interactions by individuals to achieve shared goals.*

This brief definition suggests several ideas for further comment. First of all, the basic elements of a system are interactions. For example, the routine of activities in which two people engage when one sells the other a used car could be thought of as a system, even though the system is but a fleeting one. The system does not persist, but might occur again. It could become elaborated into a persisting system of car sale interactions. If it did, one could observe the interactions and come to some general conclusions about how car sales are achieved. If this occurred repeatedly, car sale interactions

3

would be institutionalized as a market in which some individuals would have positions of responsibility (sales manager) and position-related patterns of expected behavior, or roles ("your friendly used car salesman"). To understand such a system, it would be useful to know not only the interactions but the rules and norms by which they occur, how one enters these interactions (particularly on a regular basis), and what considerations outside the system of interactions affect what goes on within it, such as increases in the price of new cars or a recession in the general economy.

Systems occur because people are goal oriented. Individuals try to fulfill their needs and desires. When these are known, one can understand the systems of interaction in which they engage. This means that individual personalities explain something about interaction systems. One person's goal orientations may be much stronger than another's. In the used car business, two salesmen of relatively equal ability but differing in drive may have far different sales records. Personality refers to the unique organization of dispositions that each person has as he relates to the people and objects around him. The needs one feels, the compulsions to fulfill them, and the capacities to select ways to satisfy them are all traits of personality.

The *culture* of the people in a society affects their interactions. "As a general term, *culture* means the total social heredity of mankind, while as a specific term *a culture* means a particular strain of social heredity." [2] Men are creatures who learn how to behave. As an individual develops solutions to problems that confront him day by day, he learns that some solutions satisfy more than others. These can be repeated and some often become habitual. Some become imbued with a quality of rightness. Because people are social, the habits of one individual may be adopted by others, and thus become generalized into customs for a set of people. People develop mutual expectations about conforming to customs. Parents pass along the customs, habits, and traditions they learned to their children. In a more generalized way a society develops mechanisms for selectively transmitting its culture to new members. In contemporary American society the school systems constitute an institutional form for preserving and teaching the fundamentals of the culture. A culture has broad relevance to those who have learned its nuances. It includes a common denomination of ideas, perceptions, and stereotypes about people, beauty, progress, power, fortune, wisdom, righteousness, history, and the like. Importantly it constrains men in nearly all aspects of behavior. The specialized relationships of life—husband and wife, mother and child, teacher and student, employer and employee—occur in the context of culture. Of course, what individuals do, see, believe, and create can shape that context, but the context takes on persisting regularities over time and these regularities shape what individuals do, see, believe, and create. In short, the constraints of culture are changeable but, of necessity, they have inhibiting, limiting, disciplining, and ordering consequences.

The interactions of people are also affected and limited by the *environ-ment* in which they take place. The physical characteristics of the interaction situation do not enter into the interaction, but they do set certain constraints upon it. One result may be to change the physical aspects of the situation—to control them or alter the way they affect interactions. The interactions for selling a car could go on in many environments, but in institutionalizing a market those whose goal it is to sell cars would find it advantageous to arrange for a large, attractive lot filled with cars to be sold and office space for negotiations. Some environmental characteristics are easily altered while others are not. They do, however, markedly affect systems of interaction; for example, oil rich nations have foreign policy options unavailable to oil poor countries.

A system is a set of interactions by individuals to achieve shared goals. The system may be fleeting or persisting. It occurs in a society according to cultural constraints, within and limited by characteristics of the environment, and its interactions are by goal-oriented individuals with unique personalities. Systems are not tangible. They are abstractions. To identify a system is to conceptualize interactions in a way which may be helpful for understanding them.

Though the notion of "system" is somewhat vague at this point, let us focus on a smaller area, that of a political system. As the scope of analysis narrows to the interactions that are legislative, the idea of a system may become more sharply etched.

POLITICAL SYSTEM

A political system consists of a set of interactions by individuals to achieve authoritative allocations of values. By values are meant the things, ideas, rewards, and attractions that people desire to have or enjoy and of which they do not wish to be deprived. Harold Lasswell and Abraham Kaplan[3] have suggested a list of eight values (which can be interpreted quite broadly) that all people pursue to some extent. Without trying to specify the meaning of each value carefully, it is helpful to consider their list: wealth, well-being (health and safety), skill, enlightenment, power, respect, rectitude (virtue, goodness, and moral righteousness), and affection. As Lasswell and Kaplan correctly say, individuals and groups differ in the comparative importance that they attach to particular values, but the fact that people pursue them helps bring into focus the purpose of the political system.

Numerous systems of interaction allocate, or distribute, values that people desire. It seems apparent that, for example, an economic system allocates wealth. A medical system distributes services critical for the health and well-being of individuals. The unique goal of a political system is the *authorita-*

tive allocation of values. Social experience through the centuries has clearly taught men that survival is easier to sustain through societal regulation than without it. Perhaps Thomas Hobbes, the seventeenth-century philosopher captured the idea best.

> . . . during the time men live without a common power to keep them all in awe, they are in that condition which is called war; and such a war, as is of every man, against every man. . . .
> *The incommodities of such a war.* Whatsoever therefore is consequent to a time of war, where every man is enemy to every man; the same is consequent to the time, wherein men live without other security, than what their own strength, and their own invention shall furnish them withal. In such condition, there is no place for industry; because the fruit thereof is uncertain: and consequently no culture of the earth; no navigation, nor use of the commodities that may be imported by the sea; no commodious building, no instruments of moving, and removing, such things as require much force, no knowledge of the face of the earth; no account of time; no arts; no letters; no society; and which is worst of all, continual fear and danger of violent death; and the life of man, solitary, poor, nasty, brutish, and short.[4]

In societies men agree to accept binding allocations of values. Putting the matter differently, "An allocation is authoritative when the persons oriented to it consider that they are bound by it."[5]

The political system refers to the set of interactions that are "predominantly oriented toward the authoritative allocation of values for a society."[6] Society is the most inclusive social unit. The political system's allocations are intended to apply to *all those in the society.* This is not true of the allocations made by a church, labor union, or professional association. Of course, not each and every individual takes cognizance of, nor is each touched by, every authoritative allocation. There is, however, exactly that potential. Can it not be shown that because allocations give advantages to some and disadvantages to others, certain individuals refuse to be bound by them? The answer clearly is yes. The risk is implicit in every allocation that those burdened by it may not submit to it. This risk is a real and important one, to which I shall refer again, but it does not preclude authoritativeness. Ordinarily the risk is offset by two considerations. The first is that suggested above by Hobbes. Without a common power to keep men in awe, there is the condition of every man at war with every other; that is, a condition of social chaos. Most men comprehend that such a condition is intolerable. Secondly, and more positively, most men agree to be bound most of the time. Because they do, there is sufficient basis to develop a division of labor in the society providing roles and positions of authority for individuals. Part of the task for those in positions of authority is to promote and encourage society members to accept willingly and to support the authoritativeness of society-wide allocations on a continuing basis. Authorities mobilize and use the resources of society to achieve goals. To preserve the binding character of allocations, this may involve coercion and physical force to compel certain dissidents in the society to accept allocations of values.*

What is and what is not *political* remains a subjective matter. I shall use the term to identify actions associated with authoritative allocations of values. Some acts are obviously political—campaigning, circulating petitions for candidates, lobbying political authorities to enact a particular policy. While other acts are just as obviously nonpolitical—watching a ball game, washing one's hair, worshiping God.† Others may or may not be—serving in the army, not voting, rioting in the streets. Without satisfactorily solving the problem, an action that seems nonpolitical becomes political when it arouses public concern about existing or potential authoritative allocations.‡

A DEVELOPED POLITICAL SYSTEM

Ordinarily political systems are continuing sets of political interaction. For the moment there are three levels of political action to consider: the political community, the regime, and the authorities. The *political community* comprises the set of individuals who accept a common division of labor for the authoritative allocations of values. This is a basic minimum. The motives

---

*E. E. Schattschneider makes this point effectively. He notes that when textbook writers try to explain government, they often speak of it as if it were alone. On the contrary, he says, there are governments and they exist because they are many. Each is an organization of a minority in a world of people that are afraid of one another. Within these minorities, people willingly support and obey their governments, allowing them to use force. The American government, for example, does use force, "but it uses it *marginally* and *incidentally* and *externally* and does not characteristically use force to *govern*." He goes on to add, "Thus the internal relations of American government are not characteristically forceable. Internally the function of the government is to reduce very greatly the amount of force used in the management of the community; the governmental monopoly of force has the effect of denying its use to private persons. As a result very little force is used by anyone. The effect is to diminish the need for force in the community; for 99.9 per cent of the people in the community force is never used at all." See his pithy little book, *Two Hundred Million Americans in Search of a Government* (New York: Holt, Rinehart & Winston, 1969), pp. 3–23. Quotations are found on pp. 18 and 21–22.

†Worshiping God could be political if, as a matter of authoritative policy, it was required (in a theocracy) or was forbidden.

‡For some this definition will raise more questions than it resolves. One may ask, "How aroused must the public be?" or "How much of the public must be aroused?" and "What are the indicators that the public is aroused?" These are empirical questions that a researcher must deal with, but they do not require specification here. Political meaning is highly subjective and what is politically relevant to one person may not be to another. The theorist, of course, must indicate the link between an authoritative allocation and an action which may arouse the public in order to speculate on the *political* character of the action.

of individuals to exhibit such acceptance may be different from one person to another. All sorts of social, cultural, psychological, and economic considerations may encourage individuals to assume the ties of political community. The sense of acceptance will be affected by a great many things including the success enjoyed by individuals in pursuing valued things in the context of the political community. This sense of acceptance can be positive or negative and may be strong or weak. Perhaps it is best characterized as an orientation toward political community. Over generations, it takes shape in a political culture.

The *regime* refers to a complex of principles, rules, procedures, and authority positions. Implicit in the idea of regime are a great many elements that have traditionally been studied in political science—the structure of a government, constitutions, and the basic rights, principles, and beliefs upon which they are based and which they are intended to protect. It also includes the informal rules of the game that participants respect even though these rules may not be written down anywhere. What these elements are, how they have come about, how and why they change—all these aspects of the regime have implications for the capacity of the political system to make authoritative allocations of values.

The *authorities* are those who occupy positions in the regime. Although it is relevant to understand the position of legislator, judge, chief executive, and the like, it is apparent that these positions are abstractions until I suggest individuals such as Senator Edward Kennedy, Representative Julian Bond, Governor George Wallace, Chief Justice Warren Burger, and others. Trying to understand the political system requires consideration of a great many variables that describe the individuals who are authorities in the system. Variables that come to mind include personal characteristics (wealth, education), attitudes, ambition for higher office, abilities.

Each level of political action affects the others. Changes in orientation toward the political community may alter the acceptability of the rules and political structure. New authorities, and how they act, may change the rules and the sense of political community. Defining levels assumes the existence and ongoing interaction of a political system.

Linkage in the Political System

The political system is the one system in society that can respond authoritatively to stress in the society. The stress may be severe—famine, attack from another society—or relatively mild—a disagreement between two property owners about the proper location of a fence, a question of whether or not to permit the sale and use of firecrackers. The political system has two links to the stress in society: by means of *inputs* from the members of society, stress is felt; the political system affects stress with *outputs*.

Inputs are of two types—*demands* and *support*. A *demand* is an expression of opinion that an authoritative allocation of some kind should or should not be made by responsible authorities. Demands are a major form of communication for a political system. Demands energize the authorities. They may be communicated in various ways and some will be considered more seriously than others. They signal stress of some sort in the society.

Support consists of actions and attitudes of society members that are favorable to the goals and policies of the political system. Sometimes support is rather specifically directed toward one or part of the levels of the political system mentioned above. There may be support for a particular authority (President Ford, for example) or for a certain rule (retention of the electoral college). It may be in return for an action of the political system. It may be a learned and relatively uncritical willingness to support all decisions of the political system. More will be said about support as a pattern of learned behavior in the discussion on socialization.

Outputs are political decisions and policies directed at changing aspects of the environment or the political system itself. A policy is "a web of decisions and actions that allocates values."[7]

The political system may mobilize the resources of society to deal with the consequences of famine, war, recession, or the disagreement of two property owners on the location of a fence. It may act to anticipate potential problems—finance research in population control, survey natural energy resources. In a sense outputs are the products of the political system, but because they have impact they are also the instruments for building support for that system. Policies are supposed to have impact. They are the *doing* aspect of the political system. Because they have impact there is change in the environment (a tax increase reduces the money people can spend for consumer goods and services, and thus dampens inflation) or perhaps in the political system itself (a reapportionment redistributes the boundaries for representatives and alters makeup of the constituencies). Thus the outputs, via impact, *feed back* upon the political system in that they affect future inputs of demand and support. Authoritative policies that affect the economic system, for good or for ill, affect the tax base for the regime, the electoral support for incumbent authorities, and perhaps even the general sense of trust people feel in the political system as a whole. A new appointment may encourage new responsiveness among representatives, change the access of certain groups to their representatives, and inspire new confidence in the processes of representation.

The range of decisions and policies of the political system is very broad in a complex industrial society. The political system determines what goals shall be fulfilled. Should the rights of individuals be promoted and, if so, how far? How much effort must the political system exert to produce equal voting rights among society members? Should there be equal rights to work? Should there be equal rights to a guaranteed income?

The political system decides who shall pay the costs. Income tax may have a flat rate (for example, 25 percent regardless of the level of income), progressive rate (the percentage of income taken as taxes rise as the income increases), or a regressive rate (the percentage of income taken as taxes decline as the income increases). The political system may require payment in services—two years of military service, for example. Who must "pay"? Only males between 18 and 26 years of age who are not in college?

The participants in the political system, particularly the authorities, try to promote the continuance of the system. (Whether they are motivated by narrow selfishness or statesmanlike vision is not relevant at the moment.) Policies and decisions are usually intended to reduce stress within the system. This implies distributing values and the opportunities to obtain them in such a way that most people are pacified, if not really satisfied, most of the time.

Besides policies to cope directly with environmental problems, the political system can provide the means for socializing members of the society. In general, *socialization* refers to a process in which individuals learn what others in the society expect of them. The political system can establish an educational program which includes citizenship training. It may even indoctrinate the young to accept the goals of the authorities. Most individuals conform their attitudes and behavior to societal norms. Thus authoritative policies systematically to socialize members of society are means for building support for the political system, for channeling demands, and for obtaining conformity with other policies.

Some of the policies of the political system are for social control since, as I noted earlier, not all men accept all policies as binding. When some members of society refuse to pay the taxes levied upon them, or refuse induction under the draft laws, or totally reject the authority of the political system, the political system is confronted by disruption. After all, allocations are rarely distributed perfectly evenly. Thus if some people reject the authoritative nature of some particular allocations and get away with it, others will be encouraged to do the same with regard to allocations they do not like. If such behavior becomes commonplace, the policies of the political system would have little effect. The policy process would be meaningless and, in fact, by erasing its distinguishing characteristic, authoritativeness, the political system would disappear.

Social control can involve both positive and negative inducements to individuals for behaving in conformity to policies. Often positive inducements are general, vague, and distant. A taxpayer can stop to think about the freeways, national parks, and security from external attack that he enjoys because he pays taxes, but this is hardly in the forefront of his consciousness when he sends in his income tax return each spring. However, when the notion of refusing to pay his taxes crosses his mind, the next thought is likely to be, "But is it worth risking a term in the penitentiary?" Social control implies arrests, fines, and terms in prison along with disgrace, separation from loved ones, and loss of well-being. The political system includes the rules and procedures for depriving society members of life and liberty, and authorities have at their disposal the resources—guns, police, and the like—to make the policies stick. These are powerful negative inducements or coercion. They are particularly important at the moment when a person considers flouting a policy.

Almost no one in a society wants or expects the authorities to rely entirely or even largely upon negative inducement to obtain conformity to policies. It is easier all around if the policies are popular or at least persuasive to most of the people most of the time. Authorities try to use coercion sparingly not only because it costs a great deal for guns and police, but because it can shake the confidence of the people and, in time, actually reduce their willing support. Coercion can be difficult to apply without hurting innocent bystanders. Harm to the innocent is *illegitimate*—not simply impolitic or unwise; it is wrong, immoral, and not imbued with a quality of rightness. Because people are evaluating creatures, they evaluate the actions of their authorities; therefore, it is important for policy effectiveness that the acts of authorities and the policies they adopt be considered *legitimate*—imbued with a quality of rightness. It is clear that authoritative coercion *can* be legitimate, but because it is potentially clumsy, it must be applied with great care and as sparingly as possible.§

It is noteworthy in this regard that policies to carefully socialize members of society to particular values can affect these members' views about what is and what is not legitimate. It would be interesting to compare members of different societies in terms of how seriously criminal they would consider certain classes of crimes. Comparative ratings of treason or particular acts of treason would be very enlightening. Similarly within a society the ratings of various social groups and strata would reveal potential opposition to certain policies and their enforcement. In general it is likely that in most societies and for most individuals treason is considered a high and heinous crime. Where this is true, people will tolerate coercion as a response to treason with

§ Avowed revolutionaries, enemies of the authorities and/or the regime, may desire repressive policies in order to bring the political system into disrepute, and thus make it easier to overthrow. Even they do not wish to shatter the underlying sense of community, however. Presumably they intend to establish a new regime with different authorities.

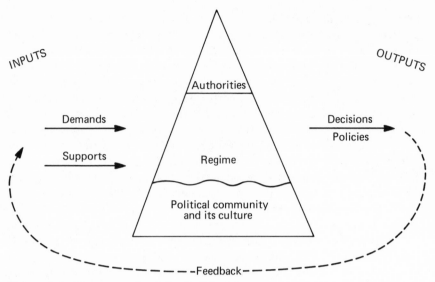

Figure 1.1   Components of the Political System

more patience than coercion as a response to other forms of deviant behavior.

As Figure 1.1 suggests, the political system is a set of interactions for choosing goals and directing policies in response to demands and support from the society. There is a circular flow—the political system processes inputs and produces outputs which affect the systems within and outside the society. People make new demands and vary their support. The process is not static. There are more or less persisting patterns of interaction, but constant changes in the environment mean new and different problems which stimulate and elicit policy innovations.

THE LEGISLATIVE SUBSYSTEM

The discussion thus far has been general, dealing with societal policy making. Implicit however is the idea that authorities are many and, as such, must coordinate activities and divide up the tasks. Likewise there are rules, procedures, and institutions that round out the notion of regime. There is differentiation within political systems. The subdivisions of the political system may be thought of as subsystems. Political subsystems contribute to and take part in the authoritative allocations of values. In this way they are political *subsystems* and not political systems.

The focus of this volume is legislative subsystems. The task of specifying what comprises such a subsystem will be dealt with in detail in future chapters. Obviously the subsystem has a part in authoritative allocations of values. For the moment it will be helpful to summarize this part, which is in no way inevitable or immutable, as that of *policy adoption*. I shall analyze several legislative subsystems and how this part came to be defined for and by them as well as the characteristics within and outside the subsystems that affect policy adoption.

Almost all my attention will be directed toward discussing American legislative subsystems. On the one hand, there is American society with its national political system. However, it is meaningful and analytically useful to think of 50 separate societies in the states. They are comparable and, in many ways, alike. However, there are differences among them that affect authoritative allocations in general and policy adoption in particular. The notion of political system helps to organize the explanation and permits comparative examination of nation and states.

Like the larger political system, the legislative subsystem is a system of interaction mainly for policy adoption. It is an open system, exposed to influences from, for example, the economic system. It is acted upon by individuals and groups active in the larger society. One can best understand its activities by observing regime rules and authorities within it. Because of its enduring character—the agenda of issues for policy adoption is usually crowded for most legislative subsystems—the subsystem is explicitly institutionalized.[8] Its authorities and positions are well known and easily identified. Its organization is complex and differentiated. There is a division of labor and there are distinctive roles to be assumed and expectations to be satisfied. Operational procedures are spelled out in detail; some allow rights to all and some define special privileges. Its authorities include elected members and the supporting staff for the operation of the legislature, its committees, members, and research agencies.

Analytically and structurally distinct are other authorities in the larger political system, such as the chief executive, members of administrative departments, or the like. These authorities interact with legislative authorities. They make demands, supply support, and respond to policy adoption. Their standing with the legislative authorities, because they have positions in the larger regime, is not identical to the standing of citizens and interest group leaders. The latter act in private citizen roles. Nonlegislative government officials have public roles and they are subject to special constraints as they make demands and give support to the legislative subsystem. They have special opportunities to provide inputs—access to the legislative subsystem is easier to obtain and, sometimes, cannot be avoided. Demands that come to the political system may, in the first instance, be directed toward an administrative subsystem, the courts, or the chief executive. As authorities in those subsystems process such demands, perhaps they identify new policy needs. A chief executive, for example, may determine that there should be a new agency to deal with problems identified in demands he has received. His demand for a law to set up such an agency is a special kind of input—a "withinput."[9] It is generated within the political system itself and directed toward a particular subsystem, the legislative subsystem.

Regime Rules in the Legislative Subsystems

The rules in American political systems provide a notable separation among the chief executive, the agencies under his direction, and the legislative subsystem. This is one of the hallmarks of American politics. Legislatures do not apply policy. That task belongs to the agencies of government, most of which are under the direction of the system's chief executive. But legislatures do determine those policies that will be applied. In making this determination, they may vary greatly in their responsiveness to the chief executive, and the extent of such variation is affected by a number of political considerations. However, the rules of the game provide that the legislature is not *required* to be responsive to the chief executive. Legislative authorities have a different base of power than the chief executive, and, as such, are authorized to exercise their judgment on policy questions independently of the chief executive's direction. Both legislators and the chief executive owe their authority to election by the people. All the citizens of the political system may participate together in choosing the chief executive. The legislators, however, receive their authority from small subsets of people. As a group legislators are responsible to all the citizens, but individually they owe their authority to a relatively small portion, or constituency, of the whole society. Thus the executive and the legislators have different parts to play in the policy process because they have different powers to exercise and different bases of authority.

There is a good deal of interaction among the parts of the political system, with the legislative subsystem receiving demands and supports from other subsystems. Because they come from within the political system, these "withinputs" should be distinguished from demands and supports arising from the social environment. Yet in some respects they are similar to demands and supports from society—legislators do not control them nor are legislators controlled by them.

The legislative process is organized and affected by rules of the political system generally and, in particular, those of the legislative subsystem. These rules and structural characteristics need to be reviewed in some detail to understand why they were established and what consequences they have.

Examples include apportionment, bicameralism, veto, committees, unlimited debate, and the like. It is noteworthy that some of the most acrimonious and hard-fought issues in the political process are concerned with changing the rules of the game. To sometimes cynical observers these conflicts demonstrate the worst characteristics of politics—selfish scheming to obtain or preserve advantages in the political process. The rules are not neutral; they *do* give advantages to some and not others. The seniority rule, for example, enhances the opportunities of more experienced legislators to affect policy. Whether or not advantages are right and proper is difficult to determine, and I shall not attempt to make conclusive evaluations. I will try to predict some alternative implications, however. Even this is precarious because it is rarely easy to anticipate all the implications of rule changes. It is this very fact that intensifies conflict about reforms.

Participants in a system must compete to satisfy their goals and, regardless of whether those goals are narrowly selfish or not, competitors can be expected to exploit any advantages available to them. Occasionally particular advantages become associated with certain policy goals and that association complicates the meaning of the advantage. For example, the right to filibuster belongs to every United States senator. Until recently, the rules required a two-thirds majority of the Senate to cut off debate. Because of this rule slightly more than one-third of the senators could prevent a bill from coming to a vote, and possible adoption by a majority vote. Southern senators, with the help of sympathizers from other regions, were able for many years to use this rule to prevent civil rights legislation. They became staunch supporters of the rules preserving filibusters, just as civil rights supporters became opponents of those rules.

Legislators have discretion over most of the rules within the legislative subsystem and many of the rules governing the larger political system— voting rights of citizens, creating agencies and authority positions, even proposing constitutional changes. The nature of the regime rules and the discretion within the legislative subsystem concerning them make these rules an important segment of the substantive matters on the legislative agenda. For the same reason authorities in other subsystems will be highly interested in legislative outputs and will regularly participate in the legislative process.

The Authorities

Rules and titled officials lend an aura of brittleness and artificiality to the legislative process. This is misleading. Governmental institutions are, above all, social entities. Government is an abstract term sometimes used to refer to those who hold authoritative positions in the public policy process. These people fill numerous other positions and roles in society besides their authoritative ones; they are spouses, parents, church members, borrowers, patients, owners, group members, and the like. They are shaped by social, economic, and demographic characteristics. Because titled officials have responsibilities as authorities, the characteristics they possess, which are often thought to influence (or indicate influence) beliefs and behavior of people, attract the interest of those who are concerned about public policy. Are legislators who are lawyers meaningfully different in their political behavior from legislators who are businessmen, teachers, farmers, or something else? Do such characteristics relate to or explain individual styles in representation or do they affect ambition for higher office? What about the authorities of minor rank—staff members who serve committees, individual legislators, or party leaders? These are suggestive questions and require further elaboration. Authorities are and should be the units of analysis in much of political research. Legislators constitute a substantial pool of individuals for analysis. Staff members do as well, but research on them is rather sparse.

Inputs and Outputs

These two terms embrace two large classes of interactions between the legislative subsystems and the larger environment of the political system. On the input side it is perhaps easier to discuss demands than support since demands take more concrete and conspicuous form. Political analysts have paid more attention to demands than support, particularly in relation to the legislative subsystem. It is relevant to know what demands are, what access there is for them, how they are expressed effectively, and who or what agencies specialize in advancing them. Support for the political system may be both specific and diffuse and ought to be distinguished in these terms. Tentatively it appears that support for the legislative subsystem ordinarily may not be differentiated meaningfully from support for the larger political system. Support, and constraints upon support for the political system and legislative subsystem, definitely affects all aspects of the process of making authoritative allocations of values. It affects what demands will be heard, which ones will be ignored, who gets what and who does not, which rules will be preserved and which will be changed, which authorities will remain in office and which will not.

The level and intensity of demands and support are indicators of needs, wants, and priorities in the society. They may bring stress upon the authorities, the institutions, and the rules by which the society operates.

Stress means the "conditions that challenge the capacity of a system to persist."[10] Authoritative allocation is what the political system does and is the function in which the legislative subsystem shares. Authorities respond to stress by making policies. Policies can to some extent affect the environment, alter the support and meet the demands.

The explanation here is, of course, oversimplified. It does not mean that all demands receive an affirmative response. Some demands are mutually contradictory. There is no single measure of just how "loud" a demand must be to achieve a response. Among the response alternatives of authorities is the one of simply ignoring a demand. Responses may be essentially symbolic rather than effectuating policy with real consequences. Authorities may misunderstand and misinterpret demands and support. They may disregard inputs consciously or unconsciously. They may determine policies that do not actually affect the stress-causing issues. In short, to consider the policy process in terms of a legislative subsystem is not intended to suggest anything favorable or unfavorable about it as a just, responsive, fair, or prudent system.

REPRESENTATIONAL DEMOCRACY

Democracy is an important word, one that brings to mind many images. Sometimes people use the word to mean a way of life, a belief system, or a social philosophy. I will use the term in a more restricted way. Democracy is a method of governing. There are four principles that distinguish democratic from nondemocratic methods of rule. These principles may be stated as criteria or standards of measurement.[11] They also help one to understand how the complex regime rules and authority structures are supposed to operate in American political systems. If these criteria are believed to be good, just, and fair, they are a basis for evaluating the goodness, propriety, and openness of the political system to its members.

1. There must be popular control over the makers of public policy. It is the people who must decide who their authorities will be. The mechanics of the selecting may vary, but the heart of that process consists of elections. Note that this principle does not require direct control over policy by the people. But if the people choose rulers to make policy, the policy views of potential authorities can be a relevant consideration in the election process. Popular control means that the collective decision of the people in elections is binding. This principle is violated if some group or agency in the society can superimpose its judgment about who should rule after the fact of an election. The point of elections is to involve contrasting viewpoints, groups, and contestants in the preliminaries to elections, with the election as the final decision-making device in which the people determine their authorities.

2. There must be political equality among adult citizens. All citizens may vote. Each vote carries the same weight as every other vote. There can be honest disagreement about who shall be considered a citizen. If a society undergoes a substantial influx of people from other societies, disagreements tend to emphasize length of residence and avowals of loyalty to the new society. When "foreigners" are not a concern, there may still be distinctions of status and well-being—age, sex, land ownership, literacy, and the like. Opponents of broad citizenship usually argue that the election process must exclude incompetent participants. Except for those excluded on the basis of age (the aging process affects all equally and inexorably), when societies exclude people as "not ready for citizenship," those excluded are often denied the opportunities to gain competence. If a society requires literacy for citizenship but does not teach its illiterates to read and write, the literacy requirement perpetuates the power of an educated elite.

3. Popular control must be available on a continuing basis. It is not sufficient for the people to choose their authorities once. They must have the opportunity to correct mistakes of the past or supply new vigor to the policy process. They must be assured of future opportunities to change their leaders. It is the *definiteness* of future elections that contributes to making the electoral process a competitive one. It encourages the institutionalization of contesting interests into political parties. It urges those who want to become authorities to prepare for a coming election in which they can offer alternatives to the electorate.

4. Elections and policies must be decided by majority rule. It is generally understood that a majority is not necessarily "right" about anything. In decisions that are essentially based on predictions of the future, the majority may decide on the basis of a wrong prediction. In decisions of moral issues, a majority may choose wrongly or inconsistently. The dignity of the majority in a democracy is based upon the equality principle noted above. When a set of individuals choose to make binding decisions by equal vote, the only decision that can have integrity and acceptability for the whole is that supported by more than half of the individuals.[12] This, in brief, is the majority principle.

According to this principle, elections are decided by a majority. If participation is open and unrestrained, the decision of the majority *participating* is usually considered binding. When there are more than two contestants, more than one election may be necessary to produce a majority. By extension, when representatives make decisions, the decision outcomes are selected according to the majority principle.

A majority's decision is binding upon a minority. However, the minority's opportunity to advocate its position must be protected by the majority. Thus, as the people exercise continuing popular control, they have the ongoing opportunity to create a new majority.

Americans consider their state and national governments to be democracies, and in most particulars the rules of the game are consistent with the four principles noted above. There is no point in detailing where there are inconsistencies. Rather, note that the principles are few and relatively simple. Most Americans can easily understand them and identify with them. It is fair, I think, to use these principles to characterize the kind of governing systems Americans expect and to outline the democracy Americans believe they should have. The rules in the American political systems—national, state, and local—are shaped and constrained by these principles.

The *representational* character of American democracy is basic to an understanding of how American legislatures work. A democratic process without representation is *direct* democracy. Under direct democracy the criteria suggested above would hold except that the people would determine policy directly, rather than choosing representatives to do so. An obvious form of "government by the people" is the town meeting, in which each person's voice may be heard and all issues can be decided by majority vote. At first blush the advantages of such an arrangement seem attractive. Each person can have his say, the support and opposition to problems and policies will be well known, and there will not be any officeholders invested with authority who interject their own will in behalf of the people.

The difficulties of such a policy process are important to consider too. Gathering, presenting, and evaluating information is difficult at meetings. The larger the meeting, the harder it is to consider all points of view and resolve issues: the advantages of the process diminish quickly as the size of the group increases. Meetings involving even a few hundred people require organization, a division of labor in which some people have special powers to set the agenda, control debate, call for the votes, and state the decisions. Such division of labor extends to having study committees, position papers, majority reports, and debate techniques that can distort the initial advantages of having everyone participate directly in all decisions. The difficulties of preserving the equal rights of individuals in such decision-making processes are obvious.[13]

Of course, the goal of individuals making policy can be achieved by using referenda. A policy question can be put on a ballot to be voted on by the people. But there are a number of difficulties with such a procedure. Framing the proposition to be voted on is a major difficulty. Imagine the variety of details that could be put into a policy statement concerning the legalization of abortion—the time period from conception, the relation of pregnancy to the physical and/or mental health of the mother, the relevance of a father's preferences in a decision to abort, the discretion of a physician, and the like. Of course the matter could be put simply—"The right of a woman to have an abortion shall not be infringed." But the manner in which the issue is stated will greatly affect its acceptability, and only rarely can policy questions be put into absolute and comprehensive language. Even those who would support the brief proposition above would probably not want a referendum using that statement. The language is so broad that chances for the proposal to pass in Ohio, Massachusetts, or the entire United States would be negligible.

To put the matter in more conditional language—"The right of the mother ... upon the advice of three qualified physicians ... within 120 days of conception ..."—makes discussion of the issues highly complex. The costs of information are high for those people who must decide the issue. For a reasonably intelligent college graduate who is undecided but open-minded, there is a good deal to learn before voting on the referendum. Learning takes time, effort, and some money—to read papers and articles, attend discussion groups, consider the arguments of fact and opinion. But what about the poor and badly educated? How will they consider the decision? Will their votes be won with television and radio campaigns—slogans and ten-second spot advertisements? Or will they simply not participate because they are unsure of the implications of their voting decision?

Once policy is made by direct democracy, it is difficult to change it without going through the whole process again. Policies do not always have the intended consequences and often require refinement with time and experience. Direct democracy inhibits experimenting with policy alterations, pilot projects, and temporary expedients. The role of leadership and creative responses to problems is inhibited by the slowness of the policy-making process in direct democracy.

Advocates of direct democracy see it as a means of achieving authoritative allocations of values that will not be distorted and changed by the authorities and the rules of the game. Obtaining this, they believe that the people of the society will give willing support to the political system. Such advocates underestimate the problems of size, the costs of information for popular decision making on policy, the difficulties of inflexibility, and the likelihood of actually disfranchising those who are least able to comprehend the complexities of policy issues.

Representative democracy introduces a middle man between the people and policy making. Representational democracy involves two basic relationships between the representative and the represented. (1) The decisions made by representatives are binding upon the people represented. (2) The representatives are responsible to the people they represent.

The first relationship is too easily taken for granted. Representational institutions have many tangled historical roots. In the English experience monarchs called upon regional and local influentials for consultation about and endorsement of policies—particularly taxes—in order to obtain compliance by the people. Interestingly those called from the countryside were not all anxious to consult with the king. It was considered a duty to be avoided, if possible, rather than an opportunity to limit the powers of the monarchy.[14] For the king it was a mechanism to obtain support, to attach a new imprimatur of legitimacy. The king did not call upon the people to pay taxes on the basis of his right as sovereign alone. He did it because his judgment had concurrence from those close to the people, the local influentials. But if the endorsement of local influentials imbued the policies with a quality of rightness, increasingly the local influentials had to be involved in developing the policies. A sovereign's decision opposed by the local influentials would no longer carry the imprimatur of rightness. As the legitimating force of the representatives grew, the rules by which representatives were selected and participated became regularized, and increasingly selection involved participation by more and more of the people. By the 1770s the slogan "no taxation without representation" could be asserted with great righteousness and indignation by the Anglo-American colonials. The acts of King George and the British Parliament were deemed illegitimate by people who had no representation in the British policy-making process. If a political system's decisions are not treated as binding, the system has lost its reason for existence.

The second relationship of responsibility, that representatives are responsible to those represented, carries many nuances of meaning. The specific behavioral links and actual patterns of interaction will be discussed in later chapters. The essential cultural and legal aspect of this relationship is that representatives serve at the pleasure of those represented. By winning elections, representatives obtain authority, for a fixed time period, to participate in making policy. During the term of office, the representative's discretion concerning how he will participate in making policy is almost beyond external control. His colleagues can censure him, but those represented are rarely able to "fire" him or recall him from office before his term expires.

Nevertheless, the people do expect their representative to be responsive to their wishes. The expectation is based on the assumption that the representative at least has the ambition to want to stay in his position. To satisfy his ambition, he will try to please his constituents. Even a representative who is ambitious for higher office cannot ignore the folks back home. His standing with his original constituents will be part of the record on which he runs for election to the higher office. Constituents have a basis for expecting that the representative will want to be responsive—to answer requests, "know" the constituency, and protect the interests of those he represents.

The representative and his constituents are in a position of interdependence. Constituents need public policy and an access point for influencing what that policy will be. A representative has policy goals too, but he can only retain his position by winning elections and performing to most people's satisfaction most of the time. This is a balancing act that can be carried on in a variety of ways by different participants. The rich variation that actually occurs is the reason why it is difficult to summarize the meaning of representation and why what seems to be "fair representation" to one person is clearly "unrepresentative" to another.

In summary, then, representative democracy is a method of governing by the consent of the governed. Ordinarily one thinks of elections as the mechanism through which such consent is expressed. However, consent, or the lack of it, is also expressed in rates of conformity to law and support for and trust in political institutions and authorities. Hopefully, if representatives sufficiently relate their policy activities to the wishes of the people they represent, the policies will provide sufficient accommodation to the public weal to obtain continued support.

CHARACTERISTICS OF THE
LEGISLATIVE STYLE

To carry out their function of policy adoption within the constraints of representational democracy, legislatures have developed a particular style of operation. This style is manifest in four characteristics which help explain how legislatures complement the functions of the other subsystems of the American political system.

1. Legislatures are deliberative bodies. If authoritative policies and decisions are important, they ought to grow out of careful consideration. In the American tradition, legislatures are established and characterized as deliberative bodies. Their members hear the facts and implications of decisions that may be at issue. They hear in a general way, as most people do, the voices of the media—reporters, praisers, analysts, complainers, some common people, many prominent people, and the like. As public men they get around, meeting and hearing from specialists at conferences, cabdrivers, cocktail-party goers, political and partisan officials involved in other levels of government. With stakes in the health of the body politic, they are constantly feeling for the public pulse. Thus, they are poll watchers and even amateur poll takers.

They hear in a specific fashion too. Letters, telephone calls, and telegrams are personally addressed to them. Committees of legislators hold *hearings* with great frequency. In such meetings, they can personally carry on a dialogue with individuals who have views on issues in question. Those heard may speak for broad collectives of people or simply for themselves. Spokesmen may include the secretary of defense, the executive director of the United States Chamber of Commerce, the mayor of Cleveland, the president of the Kalamazoo County P.T.A., and the widow of a Vietnam veteran. Often legislators hear from fellow legislators who speak in behalf of themselves, their constituents, or some other person or group. Thus, *hearing* occurs not only in public hearings, floor debates, and other "on the record" proceedings, but also in conversations in the cloakrooms, at social affairs, in offices, on the telephone, and at political party conferences.

Legislators are expected to go to great lengths to hear information relevant to their deliberations. In fact, governments regularly pay for expensive trips to distant places so that legislators can learn firsthand whatever facts are necessary. Congress and many legislatures give committees the power to require (subpoena) witnesses to appear and answer questions. What is less well known is how carefully legislators consider the information directed toward them and what they learn from it. In general, however, legislators are the objects of information and persuasion because of their decision-making responsibilities.

2. Legislatures make decisions. If the political system authoritatively allocates values for a society, obviously decisions are being made somewhere within it. Some of them are made in the legislative subsystem.[15] Legislatures enact laws. This is their most conspicuous duty. But they do not enact every proposal that is suggested. Lawmaking is a selective process that involves making choices. Sometimes there are numerous variations in the form that a law may take and choices must be made among them. The decision may be to reject all the variations and provide no law. The legislators may decide to delay making a law.

Some individuals enjoy making a decision that is consistent with a clear principle of conscience. Legislative decisions are rarely of this kind. In the legislature, decisions are being made constantly by a large number of participants concerning a great variety of affairs. Rules of procedure are elaborate and certain decisions can block consideration of other issues. Participants who seek a particular outcome develop strategies for trading agreements, compromising disagreements, and seeking accommodations. Policies are considered negotiable. When a policy is finally adopted, many participants may agree that it is not entirely satisfactory and that it should be reconsidered later. The enacted policy is simply intended to be a temporary expedient. Many laws are enacted for a specific period of years, often less than five. At the end of the period, they may be reenacted, changed, or allowed to lapse.‖ Budget enactments are regularly decided year by year. Even laws intended to be enduring are constantly subject to amendment.

3. Legislatures relieve societal tensions. New laws can change the relationships men have with one another. When an existing order of things results in frustration and tension in members of the society, the possibility of change may evoke complaints, requests, and public expressions in a variety of forms. An individual can expend a great deal of energy in making an expression that, if pent up, would build to the point of great explosive power. When a person is touched by public policy and says. "They can't do that to me!" and fires off a letter to his congressman, the letter alone may ease his frustration.

It is misleading, of course, to think that the legislative system would have enduring potential for tension release if it were merely a passive punching bag. It is no small matter that the members of the Judiciary Committee of the United States House of Representatives openly debated the abuses of power by the president in a nationally televised forum. Facts were sifted and arguments presented vigorously on all sides. Members not only voted publicly on the articles of impeachment, but they also explained their personal decisions with a mixture of eloquence and agony. This highly public conflict and its resolution made possible a massive release of tension. Conflict in such an open forum obviously is a draining and cathartic experience, both for the leaders who participate directly and for members of the society who identify with the various participants.

4. Legislatures legitimate decisions made elsewhere in the political system. A special case of decision making is that of legitimating decisions made elsewhere. This is a subtle matter, but worth some elaboration. Legitimacy refers to a quality of rightness. Decisions, institutions, and authorities may be characterized as legitimate if people believe they are imbued with a quality of rightness. In an era of growing complexity in public decisions about taxation, foreign policy, defense, civil rights, and the like, it can be satisfying to believe in a decision even if one does not understand it or has not analyzed its implications. Policy makers want to make effective decisions. In their haste to be up and doing, they may not want to engage in long drawn-out explanations about why their policies are wise and proper, but they do want the people to believe in them. It is helpful to get the policy endorsed by a person, a group, or institution whose legitimacy is well established. Such an endorsement may be entirely symbolic, marked by no

‖ For instance, the Universal Military Training and Service Act of 1951 authorized the military draft until 1955. It was extended five times, with a major revision in 1969 establishing a lottery. After a tough political battle in 1971, the law was revised and extended for two years. In 1973 the act was allowed to lapse.

legal authority. Yet the endorsement may aid the policy in that people accept the policy because of the endorsement.

Legislatures sometimes decide to legitimate policies made elsewhere. A conspicuous example in recent American politics was the Gulf of Tonkin resolution, passed by Congress at the time that President Johnson was drastically increasing United States military involvement in Vietnam. Although arguments since that time include overtones about the legal responsibilities and powers of Congress in that expression, it was a resolution (not an act of law) that the president requested from the Congress stating, in part, that

> ... the Congress approves and supports the determination of the President, as Commander-in-Chief, to take all necessary measures to repel any armed attack on the forces of the United States and to prevent further aggression.

On August 7, 1964, the resolution passed 88 to 2 in the Senate and 414 to 0 in the House of Representatives. Undoubtedly this congressional decision, marked by near unanimity, added a quality of rightness to the president's policies in the minds of many Americans. Since that resolution, Congress has struggled long and hard with new resolutions and acts of law to alter the implications of the policies set in motion at that time.

Possibly legislatures will engage in the politics of legitimation more and more. Some social critics argue that legislatures are too clumsy to make complex policies effectively and such policies ought to be made elsewhere. Legislatures could be reduced to making symbolic decisions, "rubber stamping" policies decided elsewhere. The argument is a significant one, but its implications go beyond the purposes of this first chapter.

CONCLUDING OBSERVATIONS

I have outlined a system framework for this text on American legislatures. This system of interaction occurs within the normative requirements of representational democracy. The framework is intended to simplify and organize the chapters that follow. Legislatures and their members are not always easy to understand, nor are they all alike. But the emphasis of this approach is to identify and explain general patterns and order in the legislatures of the states and nation.

NOTES

1. The concepts of this chapter are drawn directly from David Easton. See especially his *A Framework for Political Analysis* (Englewood Cliffs, N.J.: Prentice-Hall, 1965) and *A Systems Analysis of Political Life* (New York: John Wiley & Sons, Inc., 1965).

2. Ralph Linton, *The Study of Man* (New York: D. Appleton-Century Company, Inc., 1936), p. 78.

3. Harold D. Lasswell and Abraham Kaplan, *Power and Society: A Framework for Political Inquiry* (New Haven: Yale University Press, 1950), pp. 55–56.

4. Thomas Hobbes, *Leviathan, Or The Matter Forme And Power Of A Commonwealth, Ecclesiasticall And Civil*, ed. Michael Oakeshott, with an introduction by Richard S. Peters (New York: Crowell-Collier Publishing Company, 1962, originally published in 1651), p. 100.

5. Easton, *A Framework For Political Analysis*, p. 50.

6. Ibid.

7. David Easton, *The Political System: An Inquiry intŏ the State of Political Science* (New York: Alfred A. Knopf, 1953), p. 130.

8. See Nelson W. Polsby, "The Institutionalization of the U.S. House of Representatives," *American Political Science Review* 62, no. 1 (March 1968): 144–68; see particularly p. 145.

9. Easton, *A Systems Analysis of Political Life*, p. 55.

10. Easton, *A Framework For Political Analysis*, p. 90.

11. The criteria are adapted from H. B. Mayo, *An Introduction to Democratic Theory* (New York: Oxford University Press, 1960), especially pp. 61–71.

12. See John Locke, "An Essay Concerning the True Original, Extent and End of Civil Government," often referred to as Locke's "*Second Treatise on Civil Government*" in *Social Contract: Essays by Locke, Hume and Rousseau*, ed. Ernest Barker (New York: Oxford University Press, 1962), pp. 56 ff.

13. See E. E. Schattschneider, *Two Hundred Million Americans in Search of a Government* (New York: Holt, Rinehart & Winston, 1969), especially Chap. 4, "Democracy as a Form of Government," pp. 57–78.

14. See, for example, A. F. Pollard, *The Evolution of Parliament* (London: Longmans, Green and Co., Ltd., 1926), pp. 149–65.

15. Two stimulating studies are Donald R. Matthews and James A. Stimson, "Decision-Making by U.S. Representatives: A Preliminary Model," in *Political Decision-Making*, ed. S. Sidney Ulmer (New York: Van Nostrand Reinhold Company, 1970), pp. 14–43; see also John W. Kingdon, *Congressmen's Voting Decisions* (New York: Harper & Row, Publishers, 1973).

Representational Democracy in Practice: Elections and Legislators

Democratic principles are all well and good. But how do they work out in practice? What are the regime rules by which representatives are chosen? Are the rules neutral in their consequences, or do they affect who will be elected and how the winners actually behave? These are important questions, sometimes difficult to answer. Chapter 2 is a careful look at how representation works in American political systems. You may be surprised to learn that competitive legislative elections are not typical. In fact, there are powerful traditions which discourage competition for legislative positions even at the highest levels. Does that mean there is a conspiracy at work to prevent good men from competing for high office? No, things are not that simple. It is more accurate to say that there are biases in the practice of democratic politics that inhibit wide open competition. Note, too, that the biases are not simply in the rules; they are evident among the political participants—the voters, the party workers, the candidates, and the incumbents. In fact, the biases of the people are their cultural inheritance. Are you from a Democratic family? Is your neighborhood primarily Republican? Are you inclined to support the incumbent rather than the challenger? Do you think legislators should be elected to use their good judgment in policy making or should they follow the will of their constituents? What do legislators think they should take into account in their behavior? Chapter 3 is particularly concerned with the people in the legislature, what they are like and what personal resources they bring to their tasks. By and large, they are a pretty impressive group.

2

Representation, Districting, and Elections

Some cultural characteristics are specified in a formal fashion in rules and structural arrangements of the political system. This is particularly true of procedural matters. A political system may tolerate different views about how a representative ought to be responsible to his constituents. However, the mechanics of electing such a representative have to be defined in detail so that elections can be administered fairly. This chapter describes some basic patterns of American political culture affecting representation that are part of the political system's written rules of the game.

DISTRICT REPRESENTATION

There are many ways that an electorate could choose members to serve in a legislative body. Members could be elected *at large*. Many small and medium-sized cities choose city councilmen in this fashion. Candidates must run citywide. All citizens may vote for as many candidates as there are positions to be filled. Commonly, the voters elect from 5 to 15 councilmen. Legislatures do not conform to this pattern since they are relatively large membership bodies. Congress consists of a 100-member Senate and a 435-member House of Representatives. State legislatures are generally smaller, but even their upper houses range in membership from 20 (Alaska and Nevada) to 67 (Minnesota) and the lower houses from 40 (Alaska and

29

Nevada) to 400 (New Hampshire).[1] Such groups are awkward to elect at large, and with rare exceptions,* legislators are not chosen in this way.

Some societies have experimented with defining particular segments of the population, each of which could choose a certain proportion of representatives. This was the form of the French legislature before 1789 and the French Revolution. Without detailing specific difficulties, suffice it to say that it was a system of representation based upon the inequality of members of society. The different segments, or estates, were intentionally unequally represented. The French Revolution was a movement to achieve equality, and its success discredited representation by social strata. Another French pattern, that of large multimember districts with proportional representation, has not obtained a favorable reception in the American culture. Such an arrangement allows each political party to offer a list of candidates for several legislative positions (perhaps six or eight). Voters cast their votes for a party rather than for individual candidates. A proportion of each party's list of candidates is elected according to the proportion of votes that the party achieved in the election.

There are numerous ways in which a political system's representational arrangements might be structured. The cultural heritage of American society relates most closely to the English tradition in which representation was, originally, representation of the land. In effect, the people belonged to the land. Although most implications of the feudal tradition have passed away, in representation the unit of description remains a district—a defined piece of land—and the people in it choose their representative. When a citizen leaves a district to reside in a different one, he has a different representative. It is true that representational districts are currently drawn to reflect an equal division in the population, but this arrangement is the culmination of a reapportionment revolution that occurred in the 1960s. During that long political struggle there were many who defended representatives of the land; who argued, for example, that each county in a state should have at least one representative in the state legislature. The point to be emphasized here is that whatever whole is to have a legislative body (state or nation), the representatives to that body will be selected from relatively small, geographically defined districts.

A second cultural pattern determines that each district will have a single representative. Thus there will be at least one spokesperson for each citizen. The citizens have but one legislator to keep tabs on and to keep responsive to their interests. It must quickly be said that this is the dominant pattern, but it is far from universal in the American system. All the members of the United

---

*In 1964 Illinois failed to enact a constitutionally acceptable apportionment plan. Without an apportionment, the state constitution required election at large. In the November election the voters confronted a huge ballot on which each major party nominated 118 candidates.

States House of Representatives come from a unique district.† Of course, the U.S. Senate has two members from each of the states, but each is selected in a separate contest. In state legislatures most legislators come from single-member districts; however, more than one-fourth of the state senates (14 of 50) and just over one-half (25 of 49) of the state houses have at least part of their membership chosen from multimember districts.[2]

District representation reflects a cultural tradition in which the elected representatives are expected to be close to the people of their districts. The whole society is represented in the legislative institution of the political system by members from distinct and relatively small geographic/population units. Thus there is an emphasis on localism, local ties, specific interests, and serving district demands. The representative not only represents his constituents to the political system, he represents the political system to his constituents. That is, support and opposition for the political system are registered with him by his constituents. They may call upon him to account for the outputs of the legislative system, even for policies and decisions he himself may have opposed before those policies won adoption.

Because people are spatially distributed in fairly persisting patterns, district representation is adaptable to the requisites of democracy discussed in the preceding chapter. The main requirements of democracy related to representation are that there be regular elections and equal votes for all citizens. The patterned distribution of the people is an important ingredient in the legislative process. People are *not* randomly distributed. If they were, district boundaries could quickly and easily be drawn into equal population units. Individual districts would be random samples of the whole population. Social characteristics such as race, income, and labor union membership would be similar in proportion for the whole society and for every district. Likewise there would be comparable distributions of political attitudes and party identification. Representatives, responsible to highly similar sets of people, would likely pursue similar interests in the process of policy adoption. In the real world of American politics, things are not this way at all. People are unevenly distributed. There are spatial concentrations of rich, old, farmers, blacks, poor, suburbanites, chicanos, Polish, renters, Republicans, union members, and the like. Because of this and because populations in representational districts are relatively small in relation to those of whole states or the nation, they are different from one another and quite different from the states or nation of which they are a part. It is the uneven distribution of people and the political implications of that uneven-

---

†The Ninetieth Congress banned at-large elections in all states entitled to more than one representative, with exceptions for New Mexico and Hawaii. Those states had a tradition of electing both their representatives at large. Both states soon chose to have single-member districts—New Mexico for the 1968 election and Hawaii for 1970.

ness that make apportionment and districting an important concern for representation.

APPORTIONMENT AND DISTRICTING

To begin with, let me make some distinctions in terminology. *Districting* refers to the task of drawing boundaries for representational units according to some defined criteria. *Apportionment* means the process of assigning representation to political units. After each decennial census, the 435 seats in the U.S. House are reapportioned among the states. Each state is apportioned at least one representative regardless of population. Remaining seats are assigned according to population. In 1970 five states received one or more new representatives (California, still growing, added five seats; in 1960 it had gained eight) and nine states lost representatives (New York and Pennsylvania each lost two; seven others each lost one). State legislatures are rarely reapportioned in the same sense, although the battles in certain states have been described somewhat similarly in the newspapers—as if so many seats have been assigned to major cities. A state may reapportion by changing the number of legislators in the legislative body. However, most of the political problems referred to as apportionment matters are really issues of districting—establishing new boundary lines for districts.

Difficulties arise from the need to *re*district. Ongoing legislative systems always have an existing set of districts. The spatial distribution of people occurs in persisting patterns, but in a dynamic society there are changes in population growth associated with social and economic changes in the society. For example there has been conspicuous movement by southern rural blacks to northern cities in this century. Since World War II WASPs have left central cities for the suburbs. Older citizens from northern metropolitan areas have moved to southern "sun belt" cities. Such population changes unevenly affect the various representational units.

When there is a districting scheme and representatives' careers depend upon their particular constituencies, then the prospects of changing the districting seem threatening. Traditionally the legislative system has had the responsibility of adopting public policy affecting governmental structure. Thus legislators typically have found themselves in a conflict-of-interest situation: they could choose to redistrict or they could choose not to, leaving the existing districts in effect. Until the decade of the 1960s began, the second pattern was the more common response. By doing nothing, legislators stirred few people to notice the extent of inequality. However, as census data became available in 1960, many social critics vociferously pointed out how extreme the inequality had become.

The Extent of Inequality

It was easy to show, for example, that two congressmen from Texas, with equal rights to serve in office, represented sharply unequal districts—the Fifth District, with 951, 527, and the Fourth, with 216, 371,[3] a ratio of 4.4 to 1. Ratios in state legislatures were even more uneven; in the California Senate, the ratio of the largest to the smallest district was 422.5 to 1, and in the New Hampshire lower house, the ratio was 1443.3 to 1.[4] In Florida 12 percent of the population could elect a majority of the senate and a somewhat different 12 percent could elect a majority in the house.[5] Population inequality in state legislative districts was so common that in 44 of 50 states, 40 percent or less of the population could elect a controlling majority for the state. The general pattern, dramatized by the extremes noted here, led to speculation by social critics about the discriminatory policies that could be legislated when a small proportion of a state's population could win control of the legislative process. Interestingly, critics did not expend much effort in supporting their arguments by showing that the representatives of popular minorities did act in a cohesive way to take advantage of under-represented majorities. Frequently the ills and difficulties in state governments were simply ascribed to unequal representation. The critics' case was an indictment of the legitimacy of legislatures whose representational base was obviously something other than "one man, one vote." The one man–one vote standard had no explicit status in the U.S. Constitution or in most state constitutions, yet it was implicit in the meaning of democracy for sufficient people to arouse their concern about the propriety of representation based on criteria different from that standard.

Legal Approaches to Redistricting

There were three avenues of approach to the problem with the most obvious one through the legislative process. To obtain change, broad and enduring public demands were necessary. Strong gubernatorial leadership could also prove helpful. But the intended change is in regime rules rather than in outputs of service or regulation. The rules changes would most immediately affect the legislators themselves by disturbing their opportunities for reelection. The immediacy of these political consequences to legislators made them loath to respond. The problem is compounded if the political party that dominates the legislature is the one likely to lose representation because of redistricting. Very few states accomplished redistricting in such politically taut circumstances, and the results in those that did were political compromises.[6] Furthermore, many states had constitutionally established districting formulas either fixing districting or requiring consideration of characteristics other than population.

Another approach to the issue, namely the *initiative*, was available directly to the people in several states. This is a direct democracy mechanism for legislating or amending a constitution. Thirteen states permitted the placing of a constitutional amendment on the ballot, while twenty allowed this procedure for legislation. Thus the people could circumvent the legislative branch to achieve change in districting. However, this method has been used only occasionally in the twentieth century, with the result in several states that formulas other than the population principle were chosen. Typically the opponents of the population principle could polarize opinion outside the major population centers of particular states and defeat proposals seeking districting on population only. In 1952 Michigan voters supported a constitutional amendment freezing districts for the state senate and requiring redistricting of house constituencies after each decennial census primarily according to population.‡ Voters actually had to choose between a "population only" measure and the proposal explained above, which was characterized in the campaign as a "balanced legislature" provision. The population only proposal obtained majorities in the counties of the Detroit metropolitan area. As Jewell noted in 1962, constitutional or statutory initiative offered a mechanism for overcoming inequities, but the mechanism was also available to those who wanted to limit the population principle.[7] In the states where it was available, the costliness of campaigning and divisiveness of the issue seemed to inhibit proponents of the population principle for districting.

A third approach to the problem was through the courts. The judicial subsystem, as a participant in the policy process of the political system, has the part of interpreting authoritative decisions. When there are unreconciled disagreements between agencies of government or citizens and government about the meaning of laws, the arbiter of these conflicts is the judicial subsystem. In a real sense the laws and constitutions mean what the courts say they mean. Two sets of courts were relevant to the apportionment issues: state judicial subsystems and the national judiciary.

State redistricting issues often were questioned in state courts, but their activity usually followed a challenge to a new districting scheme. Typically

---

‡Michigan had a complicated standard for creating 10 of the 110 house districts with populations smaller than the state district average. See Herbert Garfinkel and L. J. Fein, *Fair Representation: A Citizen's Guide to Legislative Apportionment in Michigan* (East Lansing: Bureau of Social and Political Research, Michigan State University, 1960); and Karl A. Lamb, "Michigan Legislative Apportionment: Key to Constitutional Change," Chapter 15 in *The Politics of Reapportionment*, ed. Malcolm E. Jewell (New York: Atherton Press, Prentice-Hall, Inc., 1962), pp. 267–97, especially pp. 268 and 269.

courts would strike down new plans that were grossly inconsistent with principles in their state constitutions, an action that would leave in effect the previously existing districting arrangements. State courts did not take on the task of redistricting nor did they order state legislatures to do so; rather they seemed to accept the conclusion offered by an Illinois court decision: ". . . the people have no remedy save to elect a General Assembly which will perform that duty."[8]

Federal courts were not more sympathetic. Urban voters in Illinois made several attempts to obtain relief from the courts. In 1946 a challenge to Illinois congressional districting was decided by the U.S. Supreme Court in the case of *Colgrove* v. *Green*. District lines had not been redrawn since 1901 and district populations varied from about 112,000 to more than 914,000. The challengers argued that the Constitution required that the U.S. House of Representatives be apportioned by population (Article I, Section 2) and that the existing arrangements violated due process and equal protection under the law, as required in the Fourteenth Amendment. By a vote of 4 to 3, the majority opinion explained that this was a legislative matter and a "political thicket" in which the courts ought not get involved. Both state and federal courts followed the precedent of the Colgrove case, with redress seemingly limited to the two channels noted above.

Comes the Revolution

The constitutional history and politics of the reapportionment revolution have been told in detail by Robert G. Dixon and ably summarized in several other sources.[9] I will only touch upon some highlights and leading cases effecting this major change in the political rules of the game concerning representation. To underscore this point, two subjective assessments are worth mentioning. First, careful review of the U.S. Supreme Court's activities affecting legislative apportionment clearly links the right of equal per capita representation to the matter of fair voting rights generally. It is part of the process of enlarging the electorate and encouraging responsiveness of public authorities to all the people. Richard Claude notes that ". . . the requirements of legitimacy allow for more national and uniform standards of voter qualification and electoral process. In the American political system, voting serves the function of legitimation, that is, as a means to determine which alternatives among leaders or courses of action will be accepted as legitimate and rightful by the entire citizenry. When the electorate and the manner of casting and counting votes differs from one part of the country to the other, the legitimacy of the outcome of various elections is thrown into question. In order to avoid a crisis of legitimacy, it becomes necessary to make qualifications and procedures more uniform so that they are acceptable to all (or at least to the dominant competitors for office and power)." [10] Fair representation is necessary for and implicit in the effort for equality in individual rights.

Secondly, the importance of the apportionment issue is evident from the broad range of responses to it from political authorities at every level. The single comment that points up the significance of the reapportionment issue is that when former Chief Justice Earl Warren was asked to name the most important decision made during his tenure on the United States Supreme Court, he named *Baker* v. *Carr*.[11]

Getting Down to Cases

Baker v. *Carr*[12] will not be known as a conflict-resolving decision. On the contrary, it enlarged the scope of conflict concerning apportionment and districting in every state. Baker was a voting citizen in Nashville, Tennessee, in a legislative district with a population many times larger than that of the smallest legislative district of the state. The Tennessee constitution required districting by population, but the Tennessee General Assembly had not redistricted since 1901. Baker brought his claim to the federal court, noting that other channels of demand were closed. State courts had rejected the case, the legislature refused to act, and the Tennessee constitution allowed no initiative mechanism to solve the problem by direct democracy. Baker claimed that the inequality of the districts deprived him of "due process of law" and "equal protection of the laws," as provided by the Fourteenth Amendment to the U.S. Constitution.

The case was dismissed unanimously by a three-judge panel in federal district court which said it had no jurisdiction over the matter. However, Baker appealed to the Supreme Court and it agreed to decide the case. The decision of the Supreme Court, on March 26, 1962, settled three basic points of law in the case. First, Baker had *standing* in the Court. The Supreme Court recognized that the alleged inequality did injure Baker's voting rights. Second, the Supreme Court accepted *jurisdiction*, meaning that it agreed that there were rights at stake protected by the U.S. Constitution and the Supreme Court has the right to hear and decide the case. Third, there was the matter of *justiciability*. The Court decided that this case was justiciable, that federal courts could decide complaints and provide relief in matters of state legislative apportionment. Thus the Supreme Court set aside the notion that apportionment matters were a "political thicket" that the courts would not enter.

The Baker decision left a great deal undecided since it did not provide relief in the case. In fact the case was returned to the federal district court for resolution. However, the impact of the Supreme Court's decision was broadly felt. Justiciability meant courts would be deciding on fair apportionment, and "equal protection of the laws" was to be spelled out. Dixon interpreted the impact of the decision as follows:

> The strength of pent up pressure for reapportionment was indicated dramatically by the volume of reapportionment activity which had occurred by the end of 1963—the first full year of legislative sessions after the *Baker* decision. Under impetus of *Baker*, reapportionment was on the agenda of most of the forty-seven state legislatures in session that year. Cases were before federal courts in thirty-one states, before state courts in nineteen states, and before both federal and state courts in eleven states. At least one house of twenty-four state legislatures had either been declared unconstitutional, or declared suspect with the court reserving final judgment to allow time for legislative action. Twenty-six states had approved reapportionment plans or state constitutional amendments designed to reduce population disparities in legislative districts—some applying only to one house, some to both houses.[13]

The "one voter, one vote" principle was asserted first by the Supreme Court in the case of *Gray* v. *Sanders*.[14] It was not a legislative apportionment case. Gray challenged the Georgia method of nominating candidates for statewide elected positions, such as U.S. senator and governor. Georgia used a county unit system in which primary candidates would win from two to six unit votes per county. Primary votes were not totaled statewide. To win the nomination, a candidate had to receive the highest total of unit votes, with unit votes obtained on a winner-take-all basis, county by county. The issue raised by Gray was the fact that unit votes were not closely related to population. The largest county, with six unit votes, had more than half a million people, and the smallest, fewer than 2000. The weight of a citizen's vote in the small county was about 100 times as great as for a citizen in the large county. A candidate for nomination could win the most votes in the state for nomination to a statewide office, but fail to obtain the most county unit votes. The Court decided in favor of Gray, and included in its decision, "Once the geographical unit for which a representative is to be chosen is designated, all who participate in the election are to have an equal vote. . . ."[15] In a concurring opinion by Justices Stewart and Clark, the matter was interpreted in these words: "Within a given constituency there can be room for but a single constitutional rule—one voter, one vote."[16]

Another Georgia case raised districting issues; namely, *Wesberry* v. *Sanders*.[17] The issue in this case was the inequality of populations in two congressional districts of the same state. The largest district, containing Atlanta, was three times as large as the smallest district. Wesberry argued that inequality in congressional districts was unequal protection of the laws under the Fourteenth Amendment and violated Article 1, Section 2 of the Constitution, requiring that representatives to Congress be apportioned among the states according to population. The decision of the Court required, "As nearly as is practicable, one man's vote in a congressional election is to be worth as much as another's." [18]

The Supreme Court made a far-reaching decision on state legislative apportionment in *Reynolds* v. *Sims* [19] and five related cases, all decided on June 15, 1964. In each state there were population disparities between districts within the states. Opponents of one voter, one vote especially argued the federal analogy, that even if one voter, one vote were a proper principle, the principle should apply only to one house of a legislature. In Congress, of course, the states, not population, are equally represented in the Senate. The Supreme Court responded by establishing three principles: (1) the equal protection clause of the Fourteenth Amendment does apply to state legislative districting; (2) equal protection means districts of substantially equal population; and (3) the federal analogy does not prevent the equal population principle from applying to both houses of the legislature. The political subdivisions of the states, such as counties, cities, and towns or townships, were never sovereign entities as were states.

One of the companion cases, *Lucas* v. *Colorado General Assembly*,[20] raised a unique question. What about an unequal apportionment plan that had been adopted by popular referendum by the people of a state? Coloradans voted down a straight equal districting plan for both houses of the legislature and approved one in which the House but not the Senate would be districted by population. The Court insisted: "A citizen's constitutional rights can hardly be infringed simply because a majority of the people choose to do so. We hold that the fact that a challenged legislative apportionment plan was approved by the electorate is without federal constitutional significance, if the scheme adopted fails to satisfy the basic requirements of the Equal Protection Clause, as delineated in our opinion in *Reynolds* v. *Sims*."

The Supreme Court's standards of proper districting are not yet altogether clear. The Court has indicated that there should be two distinct standards. One standard applies to congressional districts and was set forth in the case of *Kirkpatrick* v. *Preisler*.[21] After several attempts at redistricting the congressional seats in Missouri, a 1967 plan had reduced variation in each district population to within 3.1 percent of the ideal district population. The plan was challenged in the federal courts, and the Supreme Court said that the plan was unconstitutional. It interpreted the population principle previously outlined in the Wesberry case to mean, "Equal representation for equal numbers of people is a principle designed to prevent debasement of voting power and a diminution of access to elected representatives. Toleration of even small deviations detract from these purposes." In short, practically no deviation from a state's ideal sized district will be allowed in drawing congressional districts.

However, the Supreme Court has indicated that state legislative districting is not to be judged by the same strict standard as congressional districting. In fact, the Court has encouraged states to draw legislative boundaries which respect the boundaries of local subdivisions, such as cities and counties. In its decision in a Virginia case, *Mahan* v. *Howell*, the Court said:

> The policy of maintaining the integrity of political subdivision lines in the process of reapportioning a state legislature, the policy consistently advanced by Virginia as a justification for disparities in population among districts that elect members to the House of Delegates, is a rational one. It can reasonably be said, upon examination of the legislative plan, that it does in fact advance that policy. The population disparities that are permitted thereunder result in a maximum percentage that we hold to be within tolerable constitutional limits.[22]

It is noteworthy that the variation from the ideal constituency was rather substantial, with the smallest district overrepresented by 6.8 percent and the largest underrepresented by 9.6 percent. Since the Mahan case the Court has declared maximum variation of 7.9 percent in Connecticut House districts and 9.9 percent in Texas House districts to be in keeping with the Mahan standard.[23]

CONSEQUENCES OF THE REAPPORTIONMENT REVOLUTION

The most obvious consequence is that reapportionment occurred in every state during the decade of the 1960s. Most states redistricted at three representational levels—congressional districts and districts for both the upper and lower houses of the legislature. Several had to repeat the process at one or more levels during the decade. In short, millions of man-hours were spent poring over population figures, election data, maps, alternative plans by authorities in legislative, judicial, executive, and administrative subsystems at all levels of the American political system. Did it make any difference, and if so, how much? In brief the answers are, yes, it made a difference, but not as much as some people hoped for nor as much as others feared. With that observation, let me briefly review some of the findings and note some reservations about those findings.

Redistricting generally increased the representation of suburban citizens. Although there were gains for some cities in states that had not redistricted in several decades, the prominent growth in population took place in the space adjacent to large urban centers. Losses in representation were particularly evident in the sparsely populated hinterlands—farm and small-town countryside. The common expectation associated with redistricting on a population basis was simply stated by Adrian:

... Undoubtedly, malapportionment, in terms of population, has serious effects upon governmental policies. Rural legislators, for example, will sometimes refuse to vote for legislation needed in large cities, even though the legislation specifically applies only to large cities. . . . The harsh views resulting from rural values relative to crime, its causes and cures, and to mental health also are sometimes imposed upon a state at large by small townsmen who control the legislatures.[24]

Malcolm Jewell argued that:

... The apportionment system does not permit the voters in some states to choose clearly between a Democratic and a Republican government.

One of the least understood implications of malapportionment is its effect on the *internal* structure of the parties, which sometimes discourages growth of a stronger two-party system.[25]

Since reapportionment has been achieved, there have been several studies to measure its consequences both as to public policy and party competition. An early study of the effects of malapportionment tested Adrian's argument by comparing the policies of the 10 best apportioned states to the 10 worst apportioned states (prior to new apportionments following Baker) with regard to old-age assistance payments, distribution of highway funds for urban and rural highways, and spending for public health.[26] The analysis revealed no apparent differences between the best and worst apportioned legislatures. A comprehensive study of all states and their policies on 30 measures of education, welfare, and taxation came to a similar conclusion. "For the most part, variations in public policy can*not* be explained by malapportionment."[27] Both studies acknowledged the need for "before" and "after" studies in the states. A third analysis of state expenditures and measures of malapportionment came to a more mixed conclusion—that malapportionment has affected both policies and political competition.[28]

A study of legislative voting in Georgia during the reapportionment period, 1961–66, discovered that there were numerous splits between urban and rural voters and that the proportion of splits increased and so did the success of the urban legislators in passing legislation.[29] Changes expected due to reapportionment have accompanied actual reapportionment, although there have been other trends of social change in Georgia that may also have caused these changes in legislative voting. Concerning the partisan impact of reapportionment, a recent study examined the pattern of change in party balance for 38 northern state legislative chambers.[30] Results varied for the individual legislative houses, generally to a slight advantage for Democrats. The consistent result, however, was the finding that in 82 percent of the chambers, the partisan impact of reapportionment favored the party that had a pre-reapportionment disadvantage.

California is one of the states whose legislative districts were most sharply reorganized by redistricting. The California Senate had been particularly unevenly districted. In the decade of change, Los Angeles County increased its share of senate seats from 1 ($2\frac{1}{2}$ percent) to $14\frac{1}{2}$ (35 percent), and there were similar increases for other urban parts of the state. Prior to reapportionment the California legislature, particularly the Senate, had often been characterized as a relatively nonpartisan body. However, redistricting was accompanied by a sharp increase in the number of party votes on legislative issues.[31] Moreover, after redistricting, the social and political characteristics of districts won by Republican legislators were much more sharply different than those won by Democrats. After redistricting, the Democratic districts had higher proportions of registered Democrats, more nonwhites, and lower average incomes than previously. In short, the districts of the two parties were more socially and politically distinctive than previously, and the incidence of partisan voting in the legislature increased measurably. From these findings it is difficult to directly link redistricting with public policy changes, but it has evidently affected the partisan picture, both in the electorate and in the internal legislative process.

Redistricting has also loosened the hold of incumbent legislators on their elective positions. Changing boundaries and the partisan complexion of the constituencies have encouraged turnover of officeholders. Some incumbents simply retired rather than campaign in a newly constituted district. Others had to face other incumbents. In numerous constituencies redistricting increases the uncertainty about who and which party can win. Redistricting changes the office opportunities for prospective candidates as new candidates take a chance and enter the competition. Political party organizations are aggregations of groups trying to win particular offices.[32] A candidate for legislative office puts together a nucleus of organization to win the desired nomination and election. New winners mean new organizational elements, individuals, and ideas in state and local party organizations.

One benefit of redistricting is that it has brought the representational arrangements into much closer consistency with the principles of democracy. Those principles are the basis upon which citizens can believe that their rulers are responsible to them. Given that the people believe that the authorities should be responsible to them and that representational bodies should represent people equally, the reapportionment revolution has substantially corrected the inequities of the earlier period. The arguments of social critics that legislative policies ought not be respected because legislatures were unrepresentative of the people have been pretty well laid to rest. Reapportionment has enhanced the legitimacy of the legislatures and encouraged support for them as policy-making institutions.

Finally, it is evident that the one voter, one vote principle for apportionment, having been asserted by the U.S. Supreme Court, is going to be an enduring rule. Affecting officeholders most immediately, it aroused a furor in the states and in Congress. One congressional response was to attempt to remove the matter of apportionment from the Supreme Court's jurisdiction. Another was to protect the federal analogy "that one house of a state legislature could be districted on a basis other than population," with an amendment to the U.S. Constitution. Both efforts received serious support, but eventually failed. The arguments for criteria other than population simply could not attract sufficient support to get the one voter, one vote principle set aside. Failure at the time that change was an issue probably means that the matter has been resolved for a long time to come. Although not all districting difficulties are resolved, the essential principle upon which the new practices are based has general acceptance. All states have reapportioned with varying degrees of closeness to the ideal. Current incumbents have stakes in preserving their opportunities under the present one man–one vote arrangements.

Unresolved Districting Problems

Not all the issues and difficulties associated with redistricting are completely settled. To briefly outline a few:

Gerrymandering. I will define gerrymandering as "the manipulation of district boundaries to the advantage of some political interest." Even when districts are equal in size, there is no unique solution as to how a state may be districted. There are any number of ways to break down a state into units of equal population. But as noted previously, people are not randomly distributed. How the lines are drawn can affect the extent to which people of similar characteristics, such as party identification, wealth, race, and education, are concentrated or dispersed. For example, in a state whose voters usually divide between two parties at 55 percent to 45 percent, the majority party may be able to concentrate supporters of the minority party into a few districts and make the rest quite safe for its candidates. Gerrymandering has always been one of the fine arts of the political process, one that the courts have not dealt with in a definitive way, and for which there is no clearly accepted standard of fairness.

Single-member or multimember districts? Both kinds of constituencies presently exist, and in some states both are represented in the same chamber. The one voter, one vote principle simply requires proportional equality: if a single representative speaks for 50,000 people, four members in a multimember district should represent 200,000 people. The partisan dynamics may work quite differently, of course. For example, if the voters were about evenly divided in their support for two parties, the way in which the districts were drawn could affect the party balance of the elected representatives. The majority party could win all four, win three and lose one, win two and lose two, or win one and lose three. In an at-large contest it would easily win all four.

Of course the example is too formal. Voters do not behave as predictably as the example assumes. Nevertheless, multimember districts tend to give a winner-take-all advantage to the majority party. The question of whether districts ought to be single- or multimember remains open. Arrangements do make a difference and it is an apportionment related matter. Judicial determinations have not decided this matter one way or another.§

Who should draw the districts? In most states the authority for drawing districts remains with the state legislatures. The court decisions have simply made it impossible for states to avoid redistricting. In most states it will be necessary every decade. These considerations do not make redistricting any more pleasant a matter for legislators. It will continue to be a bitterly divisive political issue. During the decisional process, individual legislators do not trust one another, the legislative committeemen handling the matter, their party leaders, the members of the other house, the governor, or the courts. Redistricting is a highly disruptive process because it strains collegial relationships of members. Chances are high that some legislators are going to get hurt; therefore it stimulates a great deal of political infighting.

Several states have experimented with various forms of redistricting commissions, either to originate or to settle upon districting plans after the legislature itself has failed to do so. Such commissions bring new problems: how will the major parties be represented, should there be independents on the commission, would legislators have a place on the commission, who will be able to break tie votes, and the like. No new institutional form has yet emerged as an ideal one for determining districting plans. Regardless of what mechanism is used to establish districting plans, they are appealable to the courts.

§As recently as *White* v. *Regester*, 412 U.S. 755 (1973), the Supreme Court said, ". . . multi-member districts are not per se unconstitutional, nor are they unconstitutional when used in combination with single-member districts in other parts of the State. . . . But we have entertained claims that multi-member districts are being used invidiously to cancel out or minimize the voting strength of racial groups." In that case the Court did insist on single-member districts in two Texas counties because blacks and Mexican-Americans would have been disadvantaged in the multimember situation. The Court contended that single-member districts would help remedy past and present discrimination and bring the Mexican-American community "into the full stream of political life of the county and State by encouraging their further registration, voting, and other activities." Quotations from pp. 765 and 769.

THE PARTISAN ELECTION OF REPRESENTATIVES

Given the mechanisms of apportionment and districting, there is no more significant fact than that the election of members to Congress and state legislatures occurs in regular partisan elections. With few exceptions, candidates contest as Republicans or Democrats.‖ Moreover, most voters vote as partisan identifiers. While this does not mean that all Republican voters can be counted on to support Republican legislative candidates nor that all Democrats will vote for Democrats, there is substantial party voting in legislative elections. The extent of the partisan tendencies varies by place and time, but the tendencies are basic elements in the patterns of American legislative politics.

The Two-Party Mold and Its Significance

The American political system has a remarkably enduring tradition of two major parties. A number of factors combine to make this the case. For one, the two-party alignment dates to the beginning of the United States. The Federalists, those in favor of the new constitution, were opposed by the Antifederalists. After Washington's presidency many of the latter regrouped into what became the Democratic party, which has endured to the present. The Federalists folded, but the societal elements which were its base recombined to produce the Whigs. The Whigs' demise occurred with the onset of the Civil War, when the Republican party emerged from Whig ashes. Policies and appeals have shifted, but these two parties have endured splintering and absorbed new movements to persist until the present day.

The regime rules in the system are significant too. Offices are won with a plurality of votes: the candidate who achieves the most votes is the victor, even if the most votes do not constitute a majority. The argument is that if Jones wins with 25 percent of the vote, then leaders of losing groups will combine to improve their chances of winning next time. Followed to a logical conclusion, aspirants for office make concessions to small clusters of voters until a majority has been achieved. At most, two competing coalitions can seriously and repeatedly contend for majority support. Thus third parties tend to be squeezed out of the competition.

‖ Nebraska has elected legislators on a nonpartisan ballot since 1935. Minnesota used a nonpartisan ballot after 1913, but recently reestablished partisan elections for its legislators. House members were elected on a partisan basis beginning in 1974 and senators in 1976.

Pragmatic considerations have meant that party teams develop for winning elections at all levels of constituency. To win elections at high office levels (president, senator), party leaders aid and encourage candidates and workers at low party levels (counties, precincts) to get the voters out to vote for the party's candidates. Candidates are encouraged to maintain some coherence in their policy appeals. Workers at the lower levels are rewarded with the satisfaction of advancing those policy objectives, enjoying the fun of participating, and perhaps anticipating future opportunities in the party or the regime. Partisans in office can then cooperate to achieve policy objectives and dissolve the checks and balances built into the American political structure.

Partisan beliefs have complemented two broad coalitions. Parties have played down sharp ideological distinctions, separatism, and indoctrination. As distinctive social groups have obtained entry into one party, the other party has attempted to attract participants as well. Cornwell describes his findings on this phenomenon:

[I studied] the members of party ward committees in Providence, Rhode Island, the findings of which may reflect trends elsewhere. Analysis of committee lists or their equivalent going back to the 1860's and 1870's showed initial overwhelming Anglo-Saxon advantages. For Democrats, however, this majority gave way, between the 1880's and 1900, to a roughly 75 percent Irish preponderance, while the Republican committees stayed "Yankee" until after the First World War. Then, in the 1920's both parties simultaneously recruited Italian committeemen to replace some of the Irish and white Protestants respectively. Today, both have varied, and roughly similar, proportions of all major groups in the city population. In other cities, the timing of shifts and the ethnic groups involved may have differed, but the general process and its relation to local patterns of immigration were doubtless similar.[33]

The durability of the two parties has encouraged most people, especially those with office ambitions, to identify with one or the other party. Since 1952 the Survey Research Center has been inquiring of Americans, "Generally speaking, do you think of yourself as a Republican, a Democrat, an independent or what?"[34] With some refinements, the self-identification responses have been taken as the best indicator of partisanship. It has also been shown that partisan identification is the most important single influence upon voting behavior. It is true that the degree of that influence has eroded in the last decade, especially in presidential contests, but its validity for congressional elections remains firm. Arseneau and Wolfinger have shown that the percentage of independents voting in congressional contests is stable, and that there has been only a slight increase in the percentage of defections by party identifiers in congressional contests.[35] The high degree of party loyalty in electorates for legislative contests is the major factor conditioning the campaign behavior of legislators (see Table 2.1).

The dynamic factors in legislative elections that condition the outcomes of individual contests are such things as the popularity of the president, the condition of the economy, and who is on which side of the current political issues. It is interesting to note that legislative contestants seek their political fortunes by running with or against political facts of life which are beyond their control. For example, in every off-year congressional election but one since the Civil War, the president's party in the House of Representatives has suffered a net loss of seats. Close analysis of recent midterm elections suggests that they constitute, in effect, a referendum on how well the president is doing, particularly in managing the economy.[36] If the president is popular, if the economy is prospering, or if both conditions are true, his party's losses are quite small; but if the conditions are contrary, losses are much higher. Yet the distribution of winners and losers depends upon more individualized considerations.

Variability in Electoral Competitiveness for Legislators

Given that legislators' election contests are markedly partisan, it is important to note that the contests are not equally competitive. Despite the two-party mold, the competitive nature of presidential contests, and the fact that the minority party has a monopoly on opposition allowing it to benefit from the errors and misjudgments of majority party incumbents, partisans are unevenly distributed. People vary in party identification in terms of their

Table 2.1   Proportions of Defection and Party-Line Voting in House Elections, 1956–1970

	1956 (%)	1958 (%)	1960 (%)	1962 (%)	1964 (%)	1966 (%)	1968 (%)	1970 (%)
Party-line votes[a]	82	84	80	83	79	76	74	76
Defections[b]	9	11	12	12	15	16	19	16
Independents	9	5	8	6	5	8	7	8
TOTAL:	100	100	100	101	99	100	100	100

[a] Votes by party identifiers for the candidate of their party.

[b] Votes by party identifiers for the other party's candidate.

SOURCE: Robert B. Arseneau and Raymond E. Wolfinger, "Voting Behavior in Congressional Elections" (Paper presented to the Annual Meeting of the American Political Science Association, New Orleans, La., September 4–8, 1973), p. 10. Copyright © 1973, APSA.

earning patterns. Lower income families tend to be Democrats while those of higher income are increasingly becoming Republicans. Ethnic distinctions are relevant. The children of white native Protestants and foreign stock from northwestern Europe tend to be Republican, more so than blacks, Spanish, and Italian or Irish Roman Catholics. Certainly there is a regional bias. Southern whites have traditionally been solid Democrats. The "Solid South" has not been solid for Democratic presidential candidates since 1948, but its regularity in electing Democratic legislators is only gradually declining. In short, partisans of a particular stripe are not randomly distributed. Democrats dominate inner cities, ethnic enclaves, and much of the South. Republicans prevail in suburbs and small towns outside the South, as well as most of the sunny retirement meccas of the South and West.

Legislative districts are not drawn to be competitive. Except for state boundaries, the electoral units for U.S. senators, the constituencies of legislators are drawn (and redrawn) by partisans to obtain partisan advantages. The one man, one vote standard of the U.S. Supreme Court makes distortions of representational strength more difficult, but not impossible.# When one political party dominates the districting process, it usually tries to concentrate voters of the opposite political party in a few districts, while spreading the rest of the opponents in losing proportions in a majority of the districts. Ordinarily few districts are created to be competitive. Turnover and change are not precluded, of course. Population movements, issues, organizational problems, candidate images, and other factors may change. But skillful boundary drawing can be worth several seats to the party that draws the lines.

Incumbency is unlimited. In contrast with chief executives, legislators may be reelected to office as long as a majority of voters are willing to support them. There are no explicit numbers of terms they may serve. On the contrary, the way in which legislatures are institutionalized, seniority enhances a legislator's capacity to serve those who elect him and it facilitates his work within the legislature. Kingdon studied the campaigns of both

---

#Uslander and Weber compared the proportionality of seats won to votes achieved by Democrats for lower houses in 40 state legislatures in "before" (1962) and "after" (1968) reapportionment elections. Contrary to their expectations, they found "that reapportionment had a negative impact upon the overall relationship between votes and seats in the lower houses of the 40 states under analysis" (p. 15). In half of the states, deviations from proportionality increased and in most of those the preapportionment majority increased its advantage. However, looking at 23 states for which more partisan bias data were available, the authors inferred that reapportionment muted the impact of gerrymandering upon deviations from proportionality. See Eric M. Uslander and Ronald E. Weber, "The Electoral Impact of Reapportionment" (Paper presented to the Annual Meeting of the Southern Political Science Association, Atlanta, Ga., November 1–3, 1973).

winning and losing candidates in Wisconsin and noted the marked contrast between challengers and incumbents:

> The campaign period itself is more important to the challenger than to the incumbent. One challenger defined his position in this way:
>
>> We had to overcome the fact that nobody in God's name knew who I was. I'd never been in the papers, had never inherited a million dollars, was never a big athlete. That was the first hurdle—try to get some identification.

The campaign period, then, is often the only opportunity for a challenger to put his name before the voters, and for that reason it is crucial to him. But campaigns are also important to incumbents. Indeed, the opportunity to continue campaign activities throughout his tenure in office is one reason why the incumbent normally has an advantage in an election contest. As one incumbent put it, "I work at it all the time, so campaigns are nothing special." This continuous exposure to the public is something the challenger must overcome.

Incumbents, too, have an opportunity through the years to build up quite an advantage not only in exposure to the public but also in popular confidence in the job they are doing. If the officeholder handles his "cases" with dispatch, returns to the district often, and continually gets himself reported in the mass media, he may build up a considerable reputation as the man who has a genuine interest in the problems of his constituents and who will do his best to see that their complaints are alleviated and that their desires are represented in the councils of government. Some incumbents do so well at this that their opponents are flabbergasted at the disadvantages under which they are obliged to labor. One such hapless challenger remarked, "You're taking on almost a myth." Another said of his incumbent opponent, "He's just a legend."

Being an incumbent and having been actively engaged in the day-to-day affairs of government is also an advantage during the campaign period itself. Several challengers told me that they did not know the issues in any detail, and felt particularly handicapped when campaigning against an officeholder who had been dealing with governmental policy continuously. One incumbent stated his advantage this way:

> I'm sure they don't mean it to turn out this way, but after the League of Women Voters interviews me and my opponent on television, the election is over. This is the best thing they could do, because I always demonstrate my superior knowledge. I hope they continue it.

Another incumbent cited the nonpartisan, politically "neutral" League to make something of the same point:

> The League of Women Voters sends out a questionnaire. . . . On one of their questions they ask candidates to state their qualifications, and this sort of amuses me. I can say I've been in for six terms, and feel qualified for a seventh. This is a real advantage.

As the responses of these two politicians intimate, emphasis on knowledge and experience is not a neutral, nonpartisan factor in politics but confers decided advantages on some and disadvantages on others. For a number of reasons, therefore, many of them having to do with the kinds of campaigning activity in which officeholders engage day in and day out, the incumbent in an election generally holds an advantage.[37]

Competitiveness for legislative seats is concentrated in a few districts. Most state legislators' terms are for two or four years. All U.S. representatives' seats are up for election every two years. These are relatively short terms. The people have frequent opportunities to review the behavior of their representatives and, if unsatisfied, turn them out of office. Legislators seem to be impressed with this potential. For example, Miller and Stokes report that, ". . . the idea of reward or punishment at the polls for legislative stands is familiar to members of Congress, who feel that they and their records are quite visible to their constituents. Of our sample of congressmen who were opposed for reelection in 1958, more than four-fifths said the outcome in their districts had been strongly influenced by the electorate's response to their records and personal standing."[38] Kingdon's respondents indicated to him that they felt a great amount of uncertainty about whether they would win or lose their elections. Fifty-two percent reported feeling uncertain and among those who felt certain, many were headed for defeat. Reflecting on his findings, Kingdon observes that, ". . . the fact that 52 percent of the politicians responded that they were uncertain about the election outcome probably underestimates the actual extent of preelection uncertainty."[39]

Despite the formidable appearance of election contests, most are not close. Table 2.2 reports data on congressional elections since 1952. If elections in which Democrats obtained between 45.1 and 54.9 percent of the vote are considered "close," then only about 40 percent of the Senate contests have been close. In the House the figure is well under 20 percent. What is perhaps more interesting is the percentage of turnovers—seats captured by the opposition party. This happens in about one-fifth of Senate elections, but in less than 7 percent of House elections.

It is instructive to look at the decade of the 1950s for one other aspect of low competitiveness. In five House election years between 1952 and 1960, during which time almost no redistricting took place, there were only 95 districts in which there was a turnover in party control.[40] In short, the party turnover that does occur tends to be concentrated within a small proportion of the existing congressional districts.

Directly comparable data have not been assembled concerning turnovers in state legislatures. Barber points out that in Connecticut, usually considered a competitive, two-party state,[41] incumbents regularly win. In 1201 elections for members of the lower house in which incumbents ran for reelection in the period from 1946 to 1958, they won 982 times, or a resounding 82 percent of the contests.[42]

Table 2.2 U.S. Congressional Elections, by Percent of Democratic Vote of

House of Representatives

	1952		1954		1956		1958		1960		1962	
	cnts.[a]	%	cnts.	%	cnts.	%	cnts.	%	cnts.	%	cnts.	%
80+	91	21.0	99	22.8	80	18.4	113	25.9	93	21.3	68	15.6
79.9–60	54	12.3	74	17.0	72	16.6	106	24.3	94	21.5	105	24.2
59.9–55	25	5.7	29	6.7	30	6.9	20	4.6	38	8.7	46	10.6
54.9–50	45	10.4	30	6.9	52	12.0	45	10.3	39	8.9	40	9.2
50–45.1	38	8.7	61	14.0	38	8.7	60	13.8	47	10.7	35	8.1
45–40.1	53	12.2	62	14.3	61	14.0	47	10.8	65	14.9	54	12.4
40–20.1	118	27.1	78	17.9	99	22.8	44	10.1	58	13.4	86	19.7
20–	11	2.6	2	0.4	3	0.6	1	0.2	3	0.6	1	0.2
Total Seats	435	100.0	435	100.0	435	100.0	436	100.0	437	100.0	435	100.0
Dem. to Rep.	10	2.3	5	1.1	9	2.0	1[b]	0.2	29	6.6	9[b]	2.0
Rep. to Dem.	3	0.6	22	5.1	11	2.6	50[b]	11.4	8	1.8	3[b]	0.6
Total Turnover	13	2.9	27	6.2	20	4.6	51[b]	11.6	37	8.4	12[b]	2.6

Senate

	1952		1954		1956		1958		1960		1962	
	cnts.[a]	%	cnts.	%	cnts.	%	cnts.	%	cnts.	%	cnts.	%
80+	4	11.4	8	20.5	7	20.0	4	11.1	5	14.2	1	2.6
79.9–60	1	2.8	3	7.7	3	8.6	10	27.8	7	20.0	8	20.5
59.9–55	1	2.8	6	15.4	3	8.6	7	19.4	4	11.4	3	7.7
54.9–50	6	17.2	7	17.9	5	14.2	7	19.4	6	17.2	13	33.3
50–45.1	14	40.0	6	15.4	10	28.6	5	13.9	5	14.2	7	17.9
45–40.1	2	5.7	3	7.7	4	11.4	3	8.4	6	17.2	4	10.3
40–20.1	6	17.2	6	15.4	3	8.6	—	—	2	5.8	3	7.7
20–	1	2.8	—	—	—	—	—	—	—	—	—	—
Total Seats	35	100.0	39	100.0	35	100.0	36	100.0	35	100.0	39	100.0
Dem. to Rep.	6	17.2	2	5.1	4	11.4	—	—	2	5.8	1	2.6
Rep. to Dem.	4	11.4	3	7.7	5	14.2	12	33.3	1	2.8	6	15.4
Total Turnover	10	28.6	5	12.8	9	25.6	12	33.3	3	8.6	7	18.0

[a] Cnts. = contests.
[b] Turnovers not associated with changes in district boundaries.
[c] Three-way elections in Connecticut, New York, and Virginia omitted.
SOURCE: Data for the table were drawn from appropriate volumes of Richard M.

Total Major Party Vote

House of Representatives

1964 cnts.	1964 %	1966 cnts.	1966 %	1968 cnts.	1968 %	1970 cnts.	1970 %	1972 cnts.	1972 %	1974 cnts.	1974 %	Av. %
68	15.6	62	14.2	57	13.1	78	17.9	67	15.4	91	20.9	18.5
142	32.7	100	23.1	111	25.5	129	29.7	123	28.3	126	29.0	23.7
25	5.7	54	12.3	38	8.7	28	6.4	33	7.6	33	7.6	7.6
60	13.8	32	7.3	37	8.5	23	5.2	22	5.1	41	9.4	8.9
48	11.1	40	9.2	25	5.7	28	6.4	30	6.9	49	11.3	9.5
54	12.4	22	5.1	33	7.6	37	8.5	36	8.3	37	8.5	10.8
37	8.5	118	27.1	123	28.3	105	24.2	116	26.7	56	12.9	19.9
1	0.2	7	1.7	11	2.5	7	1.7	8	1.8	2	0.5	1.1
435	100.0	435	100.0	435	99.9	435	100.0	435	100.1	435	100.1	100.0
5^b	1.1	25^b	5.7	6^b	1.4	5^b	1.1	15^b	3.5	6	1.4	2.4
49^b	11.2	4^b	0.9	4^b	0.9	21^b	4.8	8^b	1.8	46	10.6	4.4
54^b	12.3	29^b	6.6	10^b	2.3	26^b	5.9	23^b	5.3	52	12.0	6.7

Senate

1964 cnts.	1964 %	1966 cnts.	1966 %	1968 cnts.	1968 %	1970 cnts.	1970 %	1972 cnts.	1972 %	1974 cnts.	1974 %	Av. %
2	5.8	3	8.6	2	5.9	2	6.4	—	—	4	11.8	9.9
13	37.0	4	11.4	7	20.6	8	25.0	5	14.7	10	29.4	18.8
3	8.6	3	8.6	2	5.9	6	18.7	4	11.8	4	11.8	10.9
10	28.6	7	20.0	7	20.6	6	18.7	8	23.5	5	14.7	20.4
6	17.2	3	8.6	7	20.6	6	18.7	7	20.6	6	17.7	19.5
—	—	8	22.8	5	14.7	4	12.5	1	2.9	4	11.8	10.5
1	2.8	7	20.0	3	8.8	—	—	9	26.5	1	2.9	9.6
—	—	—	—	1	2.9	—	—	—	—	—	—	0.5
35	100.0	35	100.0	34	100.0	32^c	100.0	34	100.0	34	100.0	100.0
1	2.8	5	14.2	7	20.6	7	21.9	6	17.6	1	2.9	10.2
2	5.8	—	—	2	5.9	2	6.4	4	11.8	3	8.8	10.3
3	8.6	5	14.2	9	26.5	9	28.3	10	29.4	4	11.8	20.5

Scammon, ed., *America Votes: A Handbook of Contemporary American Election Statistics* [Vols. 1 and 2 (1956–1957): N.Y.: Macmillan, 1956, 1958; Vols. 3–5: Pittsburgh, Pa.: Univ. of Pittsburgh Press, 1959, 1962, 1964; Vols. 6–11: Wash., D.C.: Congressional Quarterly, 1966, 1968, 1970, 1972, 1973, 1975].

Incumbents in Missouri's House of Representatives, operating in a modified one-party Democratic context, were successful in 73 percent of their attempts in 1960–64.[43] There are no sharply contrasting results from nonpartisan Nebraska. A close student of its political history reports that, "Of 416 incumbents running in the years 1936–1962, 341, or 81.5 percent, were successful. If one discards those defeated by former legislators, the result is 341 out of 395 successful, or 86.3 percent."[44]

A last bit of data concerns the fact that most retirements from office by legislators are not due to electoral defeat. Hyneman's findings of 40 and more years ago—25 state chambers between 1925 and 1935—revealed that more than two-thirds of the legislators retired from office on their own rather than because of election defeat.[45] Looking at U.S. senators in 36 northern states between 1914 and 1958, Schlesinger found that in only 19.5 percent of the elections was the incumbent defeated.[46] According to Saloma and Sontag, between 1954 and 1968, "in 3,200 House and 224 Senate primary or general election contests . . . incumbents have won 92 percent and 85 percent respectively."[47]

There are two kinds of circumstances that regularly produce competitive legislative elections. One is the competitive district. There are a few districts in which party turnovers happen, and these persist in being competitive. In every election the incumbent who wants to stay in office must run for his political life. The recent and widespread reapportionment shifts make it difficult to map these out, but for the U.S. House, it is likely that fewer than 100 would be of this type.

The second circumstance occurs when the incumbent retires, leading to increased uncertainty. Usually it results in a two-party contest. Frequently it produces contests in nominating primaries of either or both major parties.

There are additional irregular circumstances that produce contests in legislative elections. New issues arise which cut across conventional partisan divisions (opposition to the American role in the Vietnam war, busing schoolchildren for racial balance) and in which the incumbent takes a stand different from a substantial portion of his constituents. Any legislator may get tagged with the success or failure of a more conspicuous political leader.** As noted earlier, redistricting can change an incumbent's electoral environment, stirring forces for change, increasing electoral uncertainty, and arousing the ambition of competitors.

**Recall the heavy national media attention given in February 1974 to the election to fill the vacancy created by Gerald Ford's appointment as vice-president. The Michigan seat had been held by the Republicans since 1910, and in 1972 Ford won with nearly 62 percent of the major party vote. In the special election, however, the Democratic candidate actually ran against President Nixon and defeated the Republican favorite with more than 53 percent of the two-party vote.

Campaign Strategy for a Legislative Seat

Party organizations usually have relatively weak control over aspirants for legislative and congressional seats. As indicated above, most districts are dominated by one party or the other. Usually too the legislative or congressional district is a unique constituency. The major units of party organization are reserved for constituencies that elect several candidates—typically county, state, and national. Congressional and legislative constituencies are rarely coterminous with such boundaries. They are either smaller or larger, and thus not the chief concern of a significant party chairman. Nevertheless, primary elections tend to attract the participation of party loyalists in the electorate, so that the candidate for nomination ordinarily must give some indication of his loyalty to the party. Often this is done by obtaining the endorsement of some better known party stalwart, for example, the previous incumbent.

Ordinarily, for a challenger to win a nomination, he must organize his own nucleus of supporters and campaign workers. This is very much an individualistic task, one centered around and activated by the candidate. A key advantage for an incumbent is that he has a continuing nucleus and does not have to organize it from scratch each election. It is, thus, especially difficult for a challenger to defeat an incumbent for a nomination. It happens occasionally, but usually only when the incumbent is hurt by a scandal or a suddenly salient issue on which he has taken the "wrong" side in relation to his past supporters. Most contests for nominations occur in the absence of an incumbent.

There are three kinds of election campaigns and some generalizations can be offered about each.

1. Safe incumbent. As indicated earlier, most elections for representatives feature an incumbent standing for reelection. The incumbent may well run "scared" and, indeed, losing would be extremely costly to the career of most incumbents. Nonetheless, their likelihood of victory is usually very high.

The incumbents' tasks remain the traditional ones of getting out the regular supporters (most of whom are identified with the incumbent's party), activating those with stakes in the outcome who may not have a conscious party identification (self-identified independents, young people, those alienated from politics and politicians), and changing the opposition.[48] Most of the effort and priority and resources are spent on the first, with the least on the last. While it might seem reasonable to expect the incumbent simply to spend the resources necessary to obtain a minimum winning coalition, 50 percent plus one of the voters,[49] a big win may have the additional advantage of making him look like an attractive vote getter for a higher office, or scare off competition at a future time. Incumbents tend to keep the discussion of issues general—highly specific discussions are boring, and may invoke needless negative responses. For illustration it is interesting to note one political scientist's observations about an incumbent Massachusetts congressman. The candidate:

> ". . . emphasized his experience as 'a proven public official' and his interest in the Tenth District. . . ." He only discussed issues which were of "immediate interest" to his constituency and "he did not attempt to educate the voters, but rather he presented the appearance of reflecting their views and ideas."[50]

Withal the incumbent was ". . . viewed as an experienced man in Congress, and as a congressman who kept in touch with his constituency."[51]

2. Competitive district. A minority of the constituencies are competitive, but many of them are competitive election after election. Both major parties organize and participate in a more substantial way to compete for such offices. Often party organizations at higher levels—the state party, legislative or congressional campaign committees—provide assistance. If the party balance in the corresponding legislative body is close, these "swing districts" can be the key to majority or minority status in the chamber, with all that it entails for controlling committees and leadership positions.

The party activity takes two forms. First, parties are much more active in selecting the candidate for election. Normally nominating involves the selection of an active worker in the party, someone who has helped in previous contests. The party organization may screen a number of hopefuls and come to a choice which may or may not involve a public preprimary endorsement. Occasionally the party, usually the one trying to upset an incumbent, will seek a "name" candidate who has not been particularly involved in the local organization but who has some party credentials and, more importantly, special personal characteristics that will help him win. (Famous family names help—Robert Taft, Jr., Adlai Stevenson III, Edward Kennedy, and Barry Goldwater, Jr., are beneficiaries.)

In the competitive situation, parties are more active in the campaign than is the case elsewhere. The party organization may provide professional help with media use, professional polling, money for campaign expenses, and workers in the precincts. Party organizations can also create "happenings" for the candidate. A useful one is to have a dinner in behalf of the candidate at which an officeholder of national or statewide stature will come in to praise the party's nominee for the legislature or Congress. Likewise the party can open doors to union halls and executive clubs in ways that would make the typical challenger of a safe incumbent green with envy.††

Issues loom larger in competitive situations. The campaign needs momentum, and the issues provide it. The candidates are more openly cognizant of one another than where there is a safe incumbent. News media are likely to put real pressure on the contestants to respond to the opposition's most recent statement on an issue. Kingdon's data give some verification of the relevance of issues. Looking at both winners and losers in Wisconsin, he asked them whether they presented their issues in a general or a detailed fashion. Typical strategy is to be general. But distinguishing marginal winners and losers from decisive winners and losers, Kingdon found that fewer of them relied on general presentations of issues (see Table 2.3).

3. Irregular circumstances. Sometimes unusual occurrences place a particular incumbent in jeopardy. Divorce from a spouse, immoral conduct by the candidate or someone in his family, a split in the dominant party, redistricting, new salience to an issue for which the incumbent is on record (a few incumbents were embarrassed and then defeated by "doves" in 1968), or being of the same party as an unpopular president (as occurred in both 1966 and 1974). From time to time, a diligent and/or fortunate challenger develops a theme or issue that carries him to an unexpected victory. Occasionally it happens that a complacent incumbent or majority party simply was ambushed, and the challenger developed momentum in the campaign which the incumbent could not stop. Every election provides examples, but the one of Margaret Chase Smith in 1972 is a case in point. At 74 she had served 24 years as senator from Maine. "As usual, she did little campaigning until after Congress adjourned, spent little money on

††Leuthold found this clearly to be the case in the 14 congressional campaigns he studied. "Some winners and competitive candidates were much more likely than sure losers to have their requests granted [for help from party leaders]. Because sure winners did not need or request as much help, a large proportion of the resources went to the campaigns of the competitive candidates. The most widely used indicator of the candidate's chances was the winner's percentage two years before; national party leaders generally designated as marginal the districts in which the winners received 50 to 55 percent of the vote in the last election. . . . The party resource also involves the support of party leaders, especially national and local leaders. Large proportions of the resources that party leaders controlled, such as money, training, research assistance, and workers, were channeled into competitive campaigns." Leuthold, *Electioneering in a Democracy* quotations are from pp. 39 and 46. See also the perceptions of winning 1964 congressional challengers that the contributions of the local party are stronger in competitive than in less competitive races. Curiously, Republicans report "considerable assistance" more frequently than Democrats. See Jeff Fishel, *Party and Opposition: Congressional Challengers in American Politics* (New York: David McKay Company, Inc., 1973), pp. 108–15.

Table 2.3   Type of Race and Issue Presentation

Presentation	Decisive Winners and Losers[a] (%)	Marginal Winners and Losers (%)
General	65	43
Depends	16	30
Detailed	19	27
TOTAL:	100	100
N[b] =	31	30

[a]Decisive winners received 55 percent or more of the two-party vote, and decisive losers, their opponents, received less than 45 percent. Marginal races were those won by less than 55 percent.

[b]N = number of winners and losers for each category.

SOURCE: John W. Kingdon, *Candidates for Office: Beliefs and Strategies* (New York: Random House, 1968), p. 129.

publicity and refused to discuss controversial issues because she said her record spoke for itself."[52] Although rarely mentioned directly by her opponent, a real issue was Mrs. Smith's age. Her challenger, a 48-year-old representative, captured the seat with 20,000 votes to spare. In more of a policy issue campaign in 1970, priest and former law school dean Robert Drinan defeated incumbent Philip Philbin in the Democratic primary on an antiwar campaign. At the time Philbin, a quiet party loyalist who stressed service to constituents and had been in the House since 1943, was also the second-ranking Democrat on the House Armed Services Committee and had supported administration policy in Southeast Asia under both Johnson and Nixon. Beaten in the primary in September by fewer than 6500 votes, Philbin was a write-in candidate in November. He received only 23 percent of the votes cast.[53]

CONCLUDING OBSERVATIONS

An award-winning salesman was asked to explain the secret of his success. His answer: "I have a good territory." The electoral success of most legislators is similar; their elections are mightily affected by the partisan cast of their constituencies. Districts are created in a partisan context, with most drawn to be safe for one party or the other. A few are regularly competitive. Nevertheless, party loyalties among voters are not cast in concrete. Particular changes in circumstances may make an incumbent vulnerable. Age eventually becomes an issue. An incumbent can be defeated by the opposite party, or he may lose in his own party's primary. The retirement or death of an incumbent usually precipitates electoral combat. Withal there is uncertainty because legislative candidates know that until the votes are actually counted, something just might happen to swing the election. And each election year is a circumstance of double jeopardy—first one must win the party primary and then the general election. For candidates, especially incumbents, the career goes on the line each time the voters go to the polls. Even when the likelihood of losing is remote, it is still real.

Regular elections are tests of confidence between constituents and would-be representatives. By their choices, the constituents forge a new relationship of responsibility or renew an old one. Election winners have vast latitude in determining how to behave in office and how to keep voters on their side. I will explore the links among people, representatives, and policy choices later.

NOTES

1. *The Book of the States: 1974–75*, vol. 20 (Lexington, Ky.: The Council of State Governments, 1974), pp. 66–67. Data as of late 1973.

2. Ibid.

3. *Congressional Quarterly Weekly Report*, February 17, 1961, p. 278.

4. From Paul T. David and Ralph Eisenberg, "The Dauer-Kelsay Measures of Representativeness," in *Reapportionment*, ed. Glendon Schubert (New York: Charles Scribner's Sons, 1965), pp. 65–82.

5. Ibid.

6. See, for example, Gilbert Y. Steiner and Samuel K. Gove, *The Legislature Redistricts Illinois* (Urbana: Institute of Government and Public Affairs, University of Illinois, 1956).

7. Malcolm E. Jewell, "Political Patterns in Apportionment," Part 1 in *The Politics of Reapportionment*, pp. 1–48; see particularly pp. 11 and 12.

8. *Fergus* v. *Kinney*, 333 Ill. 437 (1928), quoted in Gordon E. Baker, *The Reapportionment Revolution: Representation, Political Power and the Supreme Court* (New York: Random House, Inc., 1966), p. 115.

9. Robert G. Dixon, Jr., *Democratic Representation: Reapportionment in Law and Politics* (New York: Oxford University Press, 1968). See, for example, Stephen L. Wasby, *The Impact of the United States Supreme Court: Some Perspectives* (Homewood, Illinois: The Dorsey Press, 1970), pp. 116–26; Richard C. Cortner and Clifford M. Lytle, *Modern Constitutional Law: Commentary and Case Studies* (New York: The Free Press, 1971), pp. 425–63.

10. See Richard Claude, *The Supreme Court and the Electoral Process* (Baltimore: The Johns Hopkins Press, 1970), p. 256. In Chapters 7 and 8, he links reapportionment to the forging of a new federalized standard for voting and individual rights.

11. Reported in S. Sidney Ulmer, "Earl Warren and the Brown Decision," *The Journal of Politics* 33, no. 3 (August 1971): 689–702. Ulmer argues that the Brown decision, which Warren ranked second, probably showed more influence by Warren than did the Baker decision.

12. 369 U.S. 186 (1962).

13. Dixon, *Democratic Representation*, pp. 139–40.

14. 372 U.S. 368 (1963).

15. Ibid., p. 379.

16. Ibid., p. 382.

17. 376 U.S. 1, decided February 17, 1964.

18. Ibid., pp. 7–8.

19. 377 U.S. 533 (1964).

20. 377 U.S. 713 (1964).

21. 394 U.S. 526 (1969).

22. 410 U.S. 315 (1973), p. 329.

23. The Connecticut case is *Gaffney* v. *Cummings*, 412 U.S. 735 (1973), and the Texas case is *White* v. *Regester*, 412 U.S. 755 (1973).

24. Charles R. Adrian, *State and Local Governments: A Study in the Political Process* (New York: McGraw-Hill Book Company, Inc. 1960), pp. 306–7.

25. Malcolm E. Jewell, *The State Legislature: Politics and Practice* (New York: Random House, 1962), p. 31.

26. Herbert Jacob, "The Consequences of Malapportionment: A Note of Caution," *Social Forces* 43, no. 2 (December 1964): 256–61.

27. Thomas R. Dye, "Malapportionment and Public Policy in the States," *The Journal of Politics* 27, no. 3 (August 1965): 586–601, quote on p. 595.

28. Allan G. Pulsipher and James L. Weatherby, Jr., "Malapportionment, Party Competition and the Functional Distribution of Governmental Expenditures," *American Political Science Review* 62, no. 4 (December 1968): 1207–19.

29. Ira Sharkansky, "Reapportionment and Roll Call Voting: The Case of the Georgia Legislature," *Social Science Quarterly* 51, no. 1 (June 1970): 129–37.

30. Robert S. Erikson, "The Partisan Impact of State Legislative Reapportionment," *Midwest Journal of Political Science* 15, no. 1 (February 1971): 57–71.

31. See Bruce W. Robeck, "Legislative Partisanship, Constituency and Malapportionment: The Case of California," *American Political Science Review* 66, no. 4 (December 1972): 1246–55.

32. See Joseph A. Schlesinger, *Ambition and Politics: Political Careers in the United States* (Chicago: Rand McNally and Company, 1966).

33. Elmer E. Cornwell, Jr., "Bosses, Machines, and Ethnic Groups," *The Annals of the American Academy of Political and Social Science* 353 (May 1964): 32.

34. The seminal work is Angus Campbell et al., *The American Voter* (New York: John Wiley & Sons, Inc., 1960). The question is quoted in William H. Flanigan, *Political Behavior of the American Electorate*, 2d ed. (Boston: Allyn and Bacon, Inc., 1972), p. 37.

35. Robert B. Arseneau and Raymond E. Wolfinger, "Voting Behavior in Congressional Elections" (Paper presented to the Annual Meeting of the American Political Science Association, New Orleans, La., September 4–8, 1973). Copyright © 1973. The American Political Science Association.

36. This paragraph draws heavily upon the findings of Edward R. Tufte, "Determinants of the Outcomes of Midterm Elections," *American Political Science Review* 69, no. 3 (September 1975): 812–26.

37. John W. Kingdon, *Candidates for Office: Beliefs and Strategies* (New York: Random House, 1968), pp. 110–12.

38. Warren E. Miller and Donald E. Stokes, "Constituency Influence in Congress," *American Political Science Review* 57, no. 1 (March 1963): 45–56; quotation is from p. 54.

39. Kingdon, *Candidates for Office*, p. 87.

40. *Congressional Quarterly Almanac*, vol. 17 (Washington: Congressional Quarterly, Inc., 1961), pp. 1028–32.

41. See Austin Ranney, "Parties in State Politics," in *Politics in the American States: A Comparative Analysis*, 2d ed., (eds.) Herbert Jacob and Kenneth N. Vines (Boston: Little, Brown and Company, 1971), pp. 82–121, particularly p. 87.

42. James David Barber, *The Lawmakers: Recruitment and Adaptation to Legislative Life* (New Haven: Yale University Press, 1965), p. 286.

43. David Leuthold, *Electioneering in a Democracy: Campaigns for Congress* (New York: John Wiley & Sons, Inc., 1968), p. 127.

44. Richard D. Marvel, "The Nonpartisan Nebraska Unicameral," in *Midwest Legislative Politics*, ed. Samuel C. Patterson (Iowa City: The University of Iowa, Institute of Public Affairs, 1967), p. 103.

45. Charles S. Hyneman, "Tenure and Turnover of Legislative Personnel," *Annals of the American Academy of Political and Social Science* 195 (1938): 21–31.

46. Schlesinger, *Ambition and Politics*.

47. John S. Saloma III and Frederick H. Sontag, *Parties: The Real Opportunity for Effective Citizen Politics* (New York: Vintage Books, Random House, 1973), p. 134.

48. See Lewis A. Froman, "A Realistic Approach to Campaign Strategies and Tactics," in *The Electoral Process*, eds. M. Kent Jennings and L. Harmon Zeigler (Englewood Cliffs, N.J.: Prentice-Hall, Inc., 1966), pp. 1–20.

49. The major proposition in Riker's theory of political coalitions; see William H. Riker, *The Theory of Political Coalitions* (New Haven: Yale University Press, 1962).

50. Charles O. Jones, "The Role of the Campaign in Congressional Politics," in *The Electoral Process*, eds. Jennings and Zeigler, pp. 21–41; quotation is from p. 33.

51. Ibid.

52. *Congressional Quarterly Almanac*, 1972 (Congressional Quarterly Inc., 1973), p. 1037.

53. *Congressional Quarterly Weekly Report*, September 18, 1970, pp. 2263–64; *Congressional Quarterly Weekly Report*, November 6, 1970, p. 2774.

3

Legislators: People
and Role Players

The preeminent actors in legislatures are the members. Their rights and prerogatives are defined in constitutions and laws. Products of the political culture, they come to the legislature as winners in the electoral process. Some are new members, a portion of whom are anxious to solve the ills of society; many are old members, and among them are those who have become used to the ills of society and are convinced that tampering with them will probably only worsen conditions.

The members color the institutions in which they serve. Policies, styles of leadership, pace of social change, and responsiveness of government are likely to depend in part upon the kinds of members that serve in legislatures. Certainly the capacity of the members to conduct legislative activity is affected by the assistance they receive in that process. This chapter deals primarily with legislators, the major authorities in the legislative subsystem, and in brief compass with the staff personnel who assist them.

SOCIAL CHARACTERISTICS
OF LEGISLATORS

Contemporary and comparable data on the social characteristics of most legislators is not available. But over time researchers have reported on or described the incidence of certain characteristics among legislators: age, education, profession, and the like. Some of the data is reported here to lend support to generalizations about the characteristics and their meaning.

There are two kinds of social characteristics to take note of: *ascriptive* characteristics and *achievement* characteristics.[1] Ascriptive characteristics are *those to which a person is heir.* They are his by the fact of birth: sex, citizenship, race, language, and time of existence. In contrast, achievement characteristics are *the attributes a person has earned.* Examples include level of education, professional achievements, facility in a language other than the native tongue.

The distinction between these characteristics is analytical; that is, formal and logical. In practice a given trait may be inherited by one person and achieved by another. For example, to most of us our religious identification is an ascriptive matter—we are what we were born: Roman Catholic, Presbyterian, Baptist, Mormon, Jewish, Episcopal, or the like. There is, of course, a measure of achievement involved in maintaining that affiliation—formalizing membership and performing as such. On the other hand, however, one may achieve the status of being a Roman Catholic, Episcopalian, Mormon, or even of "no religious identification." Such a person actively converts from or drops out of an inherited identification to a new, achieved one. The case is similar with social class. If one's parents were "middle class," it is a rather modest achievement to maintain that identification. But to come from working class parents and attain high social standing is certainly a matter of achievement.

Education

Ordinarily educational accomplishment is considered an achievement characteristic. Thus, the data on legislators indicate that they are high achievers, certainly much more educated than the constituents they serve. Table 3.1 reports some selected findings. As the table shows, even in the 1950s and early 1960s substantially more than half of the legislators had college experience, with most of those college graduates. The educational achievements of U.S. House and Senate members are especially impressive with about 80 percent having graduated from college. Substantial proportions of these have done postgraduate work in the professions such as law, medicine, theology, social work, business, and education. Unquestionably, legislators as an occupational group are among the most highly educated in society.

Table 3.1   Educational Level of American Legislators

Education	Calif., 1957 (%)	N.J., 1957 (%)	Ohio, 1957 (%)	Tenn., 1957 (%)
Elementary school only	— (33)[a]	— (47)	4 (43)	4 (60)
Some high school	15 (45)	13 (38)	19 (42)	22 (29)
Some college	31 (11)	24 (6)	19 (7)	28 (6)
College graduate	54 (8)	63 (7)	58 (6)	46 (4)
TOTAL:	100	100	100	100
N[b] =	120	79	162	120

[a]Numbers in parentheses indicate proportions of the total relevant populations in each category.

[b]N = number of legislators polled.

Occupation

Their achievements in occupations are substantial too. Table 3.2 reports occupations in the society for the population, for legislators' fathers, and for legislators. The categories are obviously rather rough distinctions. Traditionally the first two categories would be considered upper or upper-middle status. "Professionals" include lawyers, physicians, educators, journalists, engineers, and the like. "Proprietors and officials" include corporate executives, government officials, and entrepreneurs. Farmers and farm managers may encompass individuals of every social stratum. The "other" designation takes in the bulk of the working class categories, including skilled tradesmen, clerks, industrial workers, and the like. If the first categories are taken as indications of above-average achievement, then several inferences can be made. High occupational achievement in the population was about the same in 1900 and in 1950. Nearly half the state legislators' fathers were above average in occupational achievement and, for U.S. senators' fathers, almost 60 percent were above average. However, high achievement occupations were held by more than 80 percent of the legislators and more than 90 percent of the U.S. senators. In short, more than half of the legislators had fathers with upper-status employment. But most legislators, by the time of their legislative service, had themselves attained that degree of achievement or moved up to it on their own.

Wis., 1957 (%)	Ind., 1961 (%)	Ga., 1961 (%)	Colo., 1957– 1961 (%)	U.S. House, 1966 (%)	U.S. Senate, 1966 (%)
8 (52)	7 (46)	12 (50)	3 (29)	—	— (33)
24 (34)	20 (41)	16 (37)	17 (47)	7	4 (49)
23 (7)	26 (6)	32 (7)	24 (12)	14	13 (9)
45 (5)	47 (5)	40 (6)	56 (15)	79	83 (9)
100	100	100	100	100	100
100	99	259	182	435	100

SOURCE: Malcolm E. Jewell and Samuel C. Patterson, *The Legislative Process in the United States*, 2d ed. (New York: Random House, 1973), p. 80.

Table 3.2   Occupations of Legislators, Their Fathers, and in the Labor Force

Occupation	Labor Force (1900) (%)	State Legislators' Fathers[a] (%)	U.S. Senators' Fathers (%)	Labor Force (1950) (%)	State Legislators (1957) (%)	U.S. Senators (1947–57) (%)
Professional, technical	6	18	24	7	47	64
Proprietor, official	7	29	35	7	35	29
Farmer or farm manager	22	25	32	16	10	7
Others	66	28	9	70	8	—

[a]State Legislators and their fathers refer to the legislators interviewed in New Jersey, California, Ohio, and Tennessee by Wahlke and his colleagues. U.S. senators refers to 180 senators serving in the U.S. Senate for the period indicated.

SOURCES: John C. Wahlke, Heinz Eulau, William Buchanan, and LeRoy C. Ferguson, *The Legislative System: Explorations in Legislative Behavior* (New York: John Wiley & Sons, Inc., 1962), p. 489; Donald R. Matthews, *U.S. Senators and Their World* (New York: Vintage Books, 1960), p. 20.

Political Experience

One form of achievement among legislators should be noted; that is, their previous political experience. First, there is a sharp distinction between national and state legislators. For example, Schlesinger's study of political careers shows that among the 450 senators who served in the United States Senate between 1914 and 1958, only 37 (8.2 percent) held no previous political office; most had more than one previous office experience.[2] State legislators do not have as rich a background in political office as do national legislators. In 1957 the percentage of legislators with no previous governmental experience was 34 in New Jersey, 43 in Ohio, 51 in California, and 51 in Tennessee.[3] Patterson and Boynton report that in 1967, among Iowa legislators, 50.3 percent had not held a previous public office.[4] If these percentages are roughly typical of the states, the legislature is the political office entry point for one-third to one-half of all legislators. Note, however, that legislators are deeply immersed in political activity. As Table 3.3 indicates, by the time of interview, nearly all of the Iowa legislators had engaged in party and campaign activities, and a majority had held party leadership positions.

There is a difference, too, between state legislatures and Congress in the accumulation of experience within the legislature. Table 3.4 shows a rather steady and dramatic increase in the proportion of careerists in the U.S. House. By 1971 one-fifth of the members had spent 20 years or more as representatives—clearly they have made serving in the House their careers.

Table 3.3 Legislators' Adult Political Experiences (in percentages)

Held public office	49.1
Elective office only	(29.8)
Appointive office only	(13.8)
Both	(5.5)
Never held office (except as legislator)	50.3
Made financial contributions	96.7
Attended party meetings	96.1
Served as a party convention delegate	82.9
Campaigned for other candidates	86.2
Helped plan campaign strategy	77.3
Held a formal party leadership position	53.6
N^a =	181

[a]N = number of legislators polled.
SOURCE: Adapted from Samuel C. Patterson and G. R. Boynton, "Legislative Recruitment in a Civic Culture," *Social Science Quarterly* 50, no. 2 (September 1969): 250.

Table 3.4   Congressmen Who Have Won 10 or More House Elections, by Congress

Year	No. of Congressmen	%	Year	No. of Congressmen	%
1911	11	2.8	1943	48	11.0
1913	10	2.3	1945	49	11.3
1915	24	5.5	1947	43	9.9
1917	26	6.0	1949	36	8.3
1919	22	5.1	1951	40	9.2
1921	25	5.7	1953	43	9.9
1923	18	4.1	1955	54	12.4
1925	22	5.1	1957	71	16.3
1927	23	5.3	1959	65	15.0
1929	23	5.3	1961	76	17.4
1931	34	7.8	1963	74	17.1
1933	34	7.8	1965	72	16.5
1935	31	7.1	1967	76	17.5
1937	34	7.8	1969	76	17.5
1939	37	8.5	1971	87	20.0
1941	39	9.0			

SOURCE: Charles S. Bullock III, "House Careerists: Changing Patterns of Longevity and Attrition," *American Political Science Review* 66, no. 4 (December 1972): 1295–1300; table from p. 1296.

Doubtless, by their example we can assume many of the junior members intend to make the House their careers. This contrasts sharply with the findings of Wahlke et al. whose study of state legislators in four states revealed that only 11 of 504 members (2.2 percent) had served in either or both houses of the state for more than 20 years.[5] David Ray reports, however, that membership stability in state legislatures is increasing.[6] He studied senate and house membership in Connecticut, Wisconsin, and Michigan since the end of the nineteenth century. At the beginning of the period, the average prior service by members was a fraction, meaning that there were few members with any seniority at all. In fact, in the Michigan house 80 percent were freshmen, and the average prior service in terms per member was 0.2. By 1925 the average was 1.1, and in 1969 it was 2.6. The average for all six chambers was 0.3 in 1893 and 2.2 in 1969. The rise was somewhat irregular in some parts of the period, but dramatically upward over the entire period. Most legislatures have at least a handful of members who have served 10 years or more and quite a few have one or more veterans of 20 years standing.

Religious Identification

Although Americans tend to think of their political system as open and accessible to people of merit and ability, the opportunity to serve in the legislature is sharply limited to those with the proper ascriptive characteristics. For instance, most legislators have relatively high status religious identifications. Matthews presented data to indicate that the U.S. senators who served in the 1947–57 period were unrepresentative of the religious identifications in the population.

> Protestants are substantially overrepresented, Roman Catholics and Jews underrepresented in the Senate. The same preference for those with high prestige religious affiliations is found among the Protestants. There are about three times the number of Episcopalians and twice the number of Presbyterians among the Protestant senators as would be found in a randomly selected group of Protestants. The Methodists and Congregationalists have about their fair share of the Senate seats, while Baptists and Lutherans are considerably underrepresented.[7]

It is hazardous to estimate with any precision the religious affiliations in the population. Without attempting to replicate Matthews' measure of overrepresentation, let us simply report the identifications of senators as Matthews found them and as they were in 1973. As Table 3.5 indicates, Roman Catholics and Jews are slightly more numerous, but among Protestants, Episcopalians are more numerous than ever. Presbyterians and Methodists are standing steady, and Congregationalists (certainly affected by ecumenical reorganization) are fewer, as are Lutherans and Baptists. In short, the unrepresentativeness of the Senate in terms of religious affiliations is as true of the recent past as it was 20 and more years earlier.

Localism

Another bias is for "local boys," those born and raised in the district where they seek office. Table 3.6 illustrates the point. It is worth noting that most states require by law that legislators reside in the districts they represent. Interestingly, such is not the case for members of the U.S. House. The Constitution only requires that members reside in the state they represent. Politically, however, it is "unthinkable" that, for example, a resident of Cleveland would run for Congress in the Toledo congressional district. Many a mobile citizen has found a ready welcome from the local political party in his newly adopted community. He is encouraged to work in the party organization, serve on its committees, and even hold party office. But if he suggests that he might make a good legislative candidate, the

Table 3.5   Religious Affiliations of U.S. Senators[a]

	1947–1957 (%)	1973 (%)
Roman Catholic	11	14
Jewish	1	2
Protestant	88	83
Methodist	(17)	(17)
Baptist	(12)	(8)
Presbyterian	(14)	(15)
Episcopal	(12)	(17)
"Congregational"[b]	(12)	(8)
Lutheran	(3)	(3)
Morman	(3)	(4)
Quaker	(1)	(0)
Christian Science[c]	(0)	(1)
Unitarian	(2)	(5)
Unspecified, other Protestant	(12)	(5)
Other	0	1
TOTAL:	100	100

[a]Matthews' data are recalculated from Tables 6 and 7, Donald R. Matthews, *U.S. Senators and Their World* (New York: Vintage Books, Random House, 1960), p. 24. Data for 1973 are taken from the *Congressional Quarterly Almanac, 1973* (Congressional Quarterly Service, 1974), pp. 36–38.

[b]I have retained Matthews' classification although some will disagree with it. Because of mergers and changes in names, "Congregational" includes, from Matthews, "Congregational," "Disciples of Christ," and "Christian." For 1973 it includes senators' self-identifications as "Congregational Christian," "United Church of Christ," "Congregational," and "Disciples of Christ."

[c]Less than 1 percent.

arguments in favor of a "hometown candidate" will usually prevail. Obviously there are exceptions, and as Table 3.6 suggests, those exceptions occur especially in environments where nativism is low—California, for example. But the bias toward natives is strong, and the nativism of legislators is typically higher than in the population. Likewise affected by this bias are the foreign-born; typically, those of distinctive foreign stock are underrepresented in legislatures too.

Race is certainly an ascriptive characteristic that has potent social-political meaning in American politics. Table 3.7 shows the percentage of black legislators in both houses of state legislatures as well as the percentage of blacks in the population. Typically, racial minority representatives constitute a smaller percentage in the legislature than the racial minority does in the population, and the index for each chamber shows what that relationship is (that is, Senate Index = percent black in senate/percent black

Table 3.6   Place of Birth of Legislators and State Population

Legislators	Calif. (%)		N.J. (%)		Ohio (%)		Tenn. (%)	
Born in the state	44		71		88		86	
In county represented		(22)		(62)		(71)		(66)
Elsewhere in state		(22)		(9)		(17)		(20)
Born in another state	53		28		10		14	
Foreign-born	3		1		2		0	
N[b] =	120		79		162		132	
Population								
Born in state	42		68		76		80	
Foreign-born	8		12		7		[a]	

[a]Less than 1 percent.
[b]N = number of legislators polled.
SOURCE: John C. Wahlke, Heinz Eulau, William Buchanan, and LeRoy C. Ferguson, *The Legislative System: Explorations in Legislative Behavior* (New York: John Wiley & Sons, Inc., 1962), p. 488.

in state population). For blacks, there are a great number of zeros on the scoreboard.

As noted previously, judicial precedents for districting make it hazardous for a state to draw districts that dilute the voting strength of racial minorities. Increasingly, therefore, blacks concentrated in urban areas have elected black members to state legislatures and the U.S. House. The patterns illustrated in congressional district elections are typical for state legislative seats. As Table 3.8 shows, with few exceptions, it is not until blacks constitute a majority of the electorate in a district that the district is represented by a black legislator. It is noteworthy, too, that the incidence of black legislators is increasing. As recently as the Eighty-third Congress, elected in 1952, there were only two black members in the U.S. House. Change is taking place in state legislatures as well. In 1972 there were 227 blacks elected to the legislatures of 38 states. This is a substantial increase over the mid-1960s when the number was estimated at 90.[8] One of the few nationally recognized state legislators, Julian Bond, is a black representative in the Georgia House.

Family Ties

Finally, it is interesting to notice that family ties are an ascriptive characteristic of declining political value. It is true, of course, that there are some noticeable political dynasties: Robert A. Taft, Jr., senator from Ohio,

Table 3.7   Blacks in State Legislatures: 1972

	Blacks in Senate (%)	Blacks in House (%)	Blacks in State (%)	Senate Index	House Index
Alabama	0	1.9	26.2	0.0	0.1
Alaska	0	5.0	3.0	0.0	1.7
Arizona	3.3	5.0	3.0	1.1	1.7
Arkansas	0	0	18.3	0.0	0.0
California	2.5	6.3	7.0	0.4	0.9
Colorado	2.8	3.1	3.0	0.9	1.0
Connecticut	2.8	2.3	6.0	0.5	0.4
Delaware	5.3	5.1	14.3	0.4	0.4
Florida	0	1.7	15.3	0.0	0.1
Georgia	3.6	6.7	25.9	0.1	0.3
Hawaii	0	0	1.0	*a*	0
Idaho	0	0	0.3	*a*	*a*
Illinois	8.6	7.9	12.8	0.7	0.6
Indiana	0	2.0	6.9	0.0	0.3
Iowa	0	1.0	1.2	0.0	0.8
Kansas	0	2.4	4.8	0.0	0.5
Kentucky	2.6	2.0	7.2	0.4	0.3
Louisiana	0	7.6	29.8	0.0	0.3
Maine	0	0	0.3	*a*	*a*
Maryland	9.3	9.2	17.8	0.5	0.5
Massachusetts	0	1.3	3.1	0.0	0.4
Michigan	7.8	11.8	11.2	0.7	1.1
Minnesota	0	0	0.9	0.0	0.0
Mississippi	0	0.8	36.8	0.0	0.1
Missouri	5.9	8.0	10.3	0.6	0.8
Montana	0	0	0.3	*a*	*a*
Nebraska	2.0	N.A.*[b]*	2.7	0.0	N.A.*[b]*
Nevada	0	2.5	5.7	0.0	0.4
New Hampshire	0	0	0.3	*a*	0.0
New Jersey	2.5	7.5	10.7	0.2	0.7
New Mexico	0	1.4	1.9	0.0	0.7
New York	5.2	6.0	11.9	0.4	0.5
North Carolina	0	2.5	22.2	0.0	0.1
North Dakota	0	0	0.4	*a*	*a*
Ohio	6.1	10.1	9.1	0.7	1.1
Oklahoma	2.1	4.0	6.7	0.3	0.6
Oregon	0	0	1.3	*a*	0.0
Pennsylvania	2.0	4.4	8.6	0.2	0.5
Rhode Island	0	1.0	2.7	0.0	0.0
South Carolina	0	2.4	30.5	0.0	0.1

Table 3.7 cont'd.

	Blacks in Senate (%)	Blacks in House (%)	Blacks in State (%)	Senate Index	House Index
South Dakota	0	0	0.2	*a*	*a*
Tennessee	6.1	6.1	15.8	0.4	0.4
Texas	3.2	1.3	12.5	0.3	0.1
Utah	0	0	0.6	*a*	*a*
Vermont	0	0	0.2	*a*	*a*
Virginia	2.5	2.0	18.5	0.1	0.1
Washington	2.0	2.0	2.1	1.0	1.0
West Virginia	0	1.0	3.9	0.0	0.3
Wisconsin	0	1.0	2.9	0.0	0.3
Wyoming	0	0	0.8	*a*	*a*
TOTAL:	1.9	3.0	11.1		

[a]Indicates that the population of blacks in the state is less than half of the average population in a single legislative district. In Hawaii a state senator stands for 4 percent of the population. Blacks constitute 1 percent of the state population. Even if they were concentrated in one senate district, they would not alone constitute a majority of that district.

[b]N.A.: not applicable.

SOURCE: Research Memorandum, File 8–115, Illinois Legislative Council, July 21, 1972.

is the son of a senator and grandson of a president and chief justice of the Supreme Court. There have been Kennedys, Lodges, and Byrds. But how significant a pattern is this and is it relevant to a proper description of legislators? It is relevant as an indication of modernization. Privileges of birth are marks of traditional society. A society that is achievement oriented will not be dominated by decision makers qualified by their kinship characteristics.

Findings are hardly complete. The study by Wahlke and others reports that the number of legislators with one or more relatives "in politics" was 41 percent for New Jersey, 43 percent for California, 59 percent for Ohio, and 59 percent for Tennessee.[9] A questionnaire sent to a random sample of 200 congressmen in the Ninetieth Congress drew 84 replies, of which 54.1 percent had relatives elected to office—25.9 percent at the local level, 5.9 at the state level, 17.6 at the state and local levels, and 5.9 with relatives who had served in Congress.[10]

The more thorough portion of the study by Clubok et al. was of members of Congress from the First (1790) to the Eighty-sixth, through 1960. They found a regular decline in the percentage of congressmen with relatives (sons, grandsons, nephews, brothers, or first cousins) in Congress. The high was in the First Congress, with 24.2 percent having relatives. The low was in

**Table 3.8 Black Members Elected to the 93d Congress
and Their Constituencies**

Member	District & No.	Black Population (%)
Rep. Ronald V. Dellums	Calif., 7	25.5
Rep. Augustus F. Hawkins	Calif., 21	54.2
Rep. Yvonne B. Burke	Calif., 37	50.7
Rep. Andrew Young	Ga., 5	44.2
Rep. Ralph H. Metcalfe	Ill., 1	88.9
Rep. George W. Collins	Ill., 7	54.9
Rep. Parren J. Mitchell	Md., 7	74.0
Rep. John Conyers, Jr.	Mich., 1	70.0
Rep. Charles C. Diggs, Jr.	Mich., 13	65.8
Rep. William Clay	Mo., 1	54.3
Rep. Shirley Chisholm	N.Y., 12	77.1
Rep. Charles B. Rangel	N.Y., 19	58.7
Rep. Louis Stokes	Ohio, 21	66.3
Rep. Robert N. C. Nix	Pa., 2	65.0
Rep. Barbara C. Jordon	Texas, 18	41.6
Sen. Edward W. Brooke	Mass.	3.1
Del. Walter E. Fountroy	Wash., D.C.	72.1

SOURCE: *Congressional Districts in the 1970's* (Washington, D.C.: Congressional Quarterly Inc., 1973). Percent black is from 1970 census.

the Eighty-sixth Congress when the number was 5.0 percent. There were variations by region. The West had little representation until the middle of the nineteenth century, and the proportion there with relatives was never substantial. The percentage of congressmen in the other regions with relatives—East, Midwest, and South—all declined over time, but the rate of decline was least in the South. By the time of the Eighty-sixth Congress, only 2.9 percent of the members from the East had relatives in Congress. The percentage for the Midwest was 3.6, for the West, 5.7, and for the South, 8.2. Interestingly the authors found that the decline in percentages for the nation corresponded to changes in society relating to birth rates, death rates, education, communication patterns, and certain historic events. In short, this indicator varied with other evidence of social modernization.

There are other behavioral characteristics to consider. Legislative systems include very few female members. Few members of state legislatures are under 35 years of age. Most are well into middle age, although those in state legislatures tend to be younger than members of Congress.

With a democratic selection process it appears that majorities prefer to elect (1) candidates with higher achievement characteristics than are typical of the population and (2) candidates with socially prized ascriptive characteristics. Concerning the first, there is little evidence that blue-collar workers want to choose someone from their own ranks for the legislature, or that housewives seek to vote for a housewife. College degrees, occupational and social success are not liabilities to winning legislative office. Matthews puts the point well: "Voters seem to prefer candidates who are not like themselves but are what they would like to be." [11]

However, it is well to have the ascriptive characteristics typical of one's constituency. To be Roman Catholic may be a real liability in a constituency where the population is mostly Protestant; it is certainly not where Roman Catholics are numerous. How significant are ascriptive characteristics to electoral success? Society gives ascriptive characteristics political meaning. At present whether one is of Irish heritage or not is probably irrelevant in most legislative constituencies, but it was highly relevant at the turn of the century in the Northeast. Until John F. Kennedy shattered the tradition in 1960, it was believed that a Roman Catholic could not win the presidency. Certainly at this point in time the fact of being a female is a liability in most constituencies and to be black is a liability in most constituencies populated by less than an electoral majority of blacks.

In general, it appears that as a society modernizes, it moves away from traditional values which have substance in ascriptive characteristics. Slowly, through cultural change (expressed best perhaps in spatial and social mobility), the ascriptive distinctions of the past are gradually depoliticized. For example, almost anyone can march in the Saint Patrick's Day Parade these days—wear something green and "be" an Irishman for a day. Meantime, among the Irish there are Democrats and Republicans, Catholics and Protestants, suburbanites and city dwellers, upstate and downstate residents, well-to-do and working-class people.

Behavioral Consequences of Legislators' Characteristics

How do the ascriptive and achievement characteristics of legislators affect their behavior as representatives? Findings are far from complete on this point. Several scholars have taken note of the relatively large contingent of attorneys among legislators. Derge studied legislators in Missouri, Illinois, and Indiana. In the first two states he looked generally at roll call voting and concluded that lawyers did not vote in a cohesive bloc.[12] The study of Indiana legislators was narrowed specifically to public policy directly related to the practice of law. Again no lawyers' bloc was found.[13] Eulau and Sprague examined the political activity of lawyers and nonlawyers in California, New Jersey, Ohio, and Tennessee.[14] They concluded that lawyers are numerous in politics generally because politics and the practice of law are convergent professions.* Lawyer legislators did not behave in distinctive ways. Similar findings come from a recent study of Congress. Careful examination of voting records of lawyers and nonlawyers on judiciary-oriented issues revealed no differences.[15]

On the other hand, a recent study of the roll call voting of 12 black members of the U.S. House in 1971 revealed clear deviation from most of their northern Democratic colleagues. However, the researchers reported:

> . . . we found that the Black Caucus members were not alone in supporting these preferences. A total of 29 other non-Black Congressmen regularly supported the Black Caucus. Further analysis showed that the support of these non-Black Congressmen for the Black Caucus policy preferences was only slightly lower than the support the twelve Black members gave to these preferences. The factor that led these non-Black members to support the preferences seems to have been the strength of their liberal convictions rather than characteristics such as racial or economic composition of their districts.[16]

The thrust of these findings, incomplete as they are, is to suggest that the traits of legislators do not clearly dispose them to behave in specific ways. Black legislators, bearing what is currently perhaps the most politically salient ascriptive characteristic present in the American political scene, do behave differently from most of their white colleagues.[16a] Nevertheless, they are accompanied in that different behavior by a number of white colleagues. Put another way, black legislators vote differently from most whites apparently because of their racial identification, but some white legislators vote as the blacks do despite their racial characteristics.

In the absence of clear findings, let me suggest one bit of speculation on this point. Legislators generally bear highly valued ascriptive characteristics, and they are relatively successful achievers. If there is a bias in the political system associated with legislators' characteristics, it is probably in representing those with similar characteristics. In part it may be manifest in a selective bias of legislators to hear from, and treat as reference publics, people like themselves—other high-status, well-educated, achievement-oriented, busily aggressive people. By style and experience, most legislators simply are not in intimate contact with the people of working class or below, who are semiliterate, reared in poverty, have endured inadequate schools, respond casually to petty crime and vice, and live in the midst of a relatively high degree of social disorganization (wife beating, truancy from school and

---

*However, the same career convergence seems apparent in other societies, but without the same high proportion of lawyer legislators. See Mogens N. Pederson, "Lawyers in Politics: The Danish Folketing and United States Legislatures," in *Comparative Legislative Behavior: Frontiers of Research*, eds. Samuel C. Patterson and John C. Wahlke (New York: John Wiley & Sons, Inc., 1973), pp. 25–63.

job, public drunkenness, evictions, being fired or laid off from work, gambling). The legislator is, like many people of middle-class social standing, ambitious, and may not comprehend the lack of ambition, the resigned fatalism, the acquiescence to poverty and public assistance or welfare that he perceives in poor people. The bias is not in the legislator alone. The poor may perceive themselves as too unworthy to trouble the legislator—a "very important person" who is too busy for poor peoples' troubles—or too alienated to try. As Knupfer pointed out, "economic underprivilege is psychological underprivilege: habits of submission, little access to sources of information, lack of verbal facility . . . appear to produce a lack of self-confidence which increases the unwillingness of the low-status person to participate in many phases of our predominantly middle-class culture. . . ."[17]

Certainly one of the forms of participation which the lower status citizen avoids is interaction with political elites. Accurately or mistakenly the "underdog" may well avoid the high-status, achievement-oriented legislator lest he, the underdog, reveal his inadequacy, ignorance, pitiable dependence upon welfare programs, or the like. By contrast, the legislator understands the businessmen, lobbyists, professionals, and bureaucrats who make self-interested demands and who realize that politics is a process of conflict and compromise. The legislator and these constituents "talk the same language," and, even if the legislator does not agree with them on all points, he shares with them a middle- or upper-class perspective on life—an orientation toward the distant future and a willingness to make sacrifices for that future.[18]

If the implications of legislators' high achievement and prized ascriptive characteristics are not altogether clear, many have been willing to conclude that the pattern was both expected and desired. James Madison, considering specifically the proposed U.S. House of Representatives, argued that:

> The aim of every political constitution is, or ought to be, first to obtain for rulers men who possess the most wisdom to discern, and most virtue to pursue, the common good of society; and in the next place, to take the most effectual precautions for keeping them virtuous whilst they continue to hold their public trust.[19]

Tinder observes that the case for representative democracy, in contrast to direct democracy, is supported by the argument that:

> The representative system makes it possible, while allowing the people as a whole to have the final word, to empower those who stand out for their intelligence, their experience, and their interest in political matters. Direct democracy tends to submerge such minorities in the masses.[20]

If educational achievement is evidence of wisdom, high occupational standing means experience, and ambition and broad political participation constitute interest, then American legislators constitute a remarkably qualified, representational elite.

ROLE ORIENTATIONS OF LEGISLATORS

The *position* of legislator is a significant one. In political systems positions are described in the formal rules to have specific obligations, rights, and authority adhere in them. There are rules by which a person may obtain a position in the political regime—minimum age for eligibility, a specific appointment or electoral process, a term of service. These rules are very significant in determining what kind of person will fill the position and what the person can and will do in the position.

The position description of a legislator sets constraints upon his behavior, but does not determine very much. Within their positions, legislators have a good deal of discretion in choosing how they will behave. This is where the concept of role is helpful.

The Concept of Role

A role is a *position-related pattern of expected behavior.*[21] The incumbent of a position may act in numerous roles. There are more definite patterns of expected behavior for some positions than others. The analyst uses the term *role* to specify or distinguish a frequently noted pattern among position incumbents, for instance, legislators. The pioneering study of roles among legislators is that reported in *The Legislative System* based upon the state legislators of Ohio, California, Tennessee, and New Jersey in 1957. The legislators were interviewed and asked, "How would you describe the job of being a legislator—what are the most important things you should do here?"[22] From the answers, two different roles were distinguished: one is the *constituency* role and the other is the *representational* role.† More recently Roger Davidson gathered similar responses from a sample of the members of the U.S. House in 1963 and 1964.[23] The answers to these and related questions are the basis for much of the following description.

---

†The terminology of Jewell and Patterson in *The Legislative Process* is less awkward than that of Eulau et al., who use "focus of representation" and "style of representation."

Constituency Role

The constituency role was manifested in three kinds of orientation. One orientation was primarily toward the *district:* many legislators conceive of their job as one of sponsoring legislation and working for policies that will help the district from which they are elected. Others are oriented primarily toward the *political system.* Such state legislators feel that they should give primacy to the state, rather than their districts, in policy making. In Congress some representatives put the nation ahead of their districts. Between these major alternative types was a mixed orientation called *district–state* or *district–nation* orientation. Among legislators and congressmen were the respondents who mentioned both the district *and* the larger political system.

Representational Role

A little different slant on the job of legislator is brought out by representational role orientations. Instead of the geographic focus that is uppermost in the legislator's mind, this refers to the legislator's conception of how he ought to make his decisions. Three fairly distinct orientations concerning the *how* of representation have been observed. The first is that of the *trustee* —one who acts according to his own conception of what is right, just, wise, and practical. In short, he represents according to his own judgment of what should be done. A contrasting orientation is that of the *delegate*—one who feels he should subordinate his own judgment to an external and superior authority. Generally the superior authority is attributed to his constituency. It is visible in the perspective, "A Representative ought to work for what his constituents want even though this may not always agree with his personal views."[24] If these two conceptions can be thought of as polar opposites, a third type, the *politico*, lies in between. The politico is one who says both perspectives are part of his style. J. William Fulbright, former senator from Arkansas, evidenced this "middle way" in the following statement:

> . . . let us take the poll-tax issue and isolationism. Regardless of how persuasive my colleagues or the national press may be about the evils of the poll-tax, I do not see its fundamental importance, and I shall follow the views of the people of my state. . . . On the other hand, regardless of how strongly opposed my constituents may prove to be to the creation of, and participation in, an even stronger United Nations Organization, I could not follow such a policy in that field unless it becomes clearly hopeless.[25]

Purposive Role

Legislators identify with differing conceptions of the kind of behavior they ought to exhibit in the performance of their duties. Those oriented primarily toward procedure are characterized as *ritualists*. The ritualist makes mastery of legislative routine a major part of his effort. The *tribune* is one whose primary purpose is to be the advocate or defender of popular demands. The *inventor* is one who wants to initiate and pursue new policy solutions to public problems. The *broker* is the legislator who feels he should arbitrate, reconcile, and integrate the demands of competing interests. The *opportunists* are those who put "being reelected" ahead of other objectives.

Interest Group Role

Legislators exhibit distinctive patterns in the way they believe they should relate to interest groups in the political process. Conditioning their attitudes toward interest groups is the degree of knowledge legislators have about interest group activity going on about them. The types of legislators distinguished by these are: *facilitators*, who have both a friendly attitude toward interest groups and a relatively high awareness about that activity; *resisters*, who are hostile toward interest groups and are knowledgeable about group activity; and *neutrals*, those who have no strong attitude toward interest groups or who have very little awareness of them.

Party Role

Legislators have differing conceptions about how they should relate to the party organization. Would people be better served if legislators were elected without party labels? Should people take an interest in government directly, rather than through a political party? If a bill is important to a legislator's party record, should he vote with the party even at the cost of some support in his district? The responses by legislators to such questions have given rise to a typology of legislators. *Superloyalists* feel strongly about the place of parties in the political system and the propriety of their voting with the party. *Loyalists* lean firmly in the direction of parties for organizing political activity, but not with the consistency of the superloyalists. *Neutrals* are in many instances undecided about the place parties and party loyalty should have in the political system. *Mavericks* feel that parties and party loyalty get in the way of popular interests and that legislators should not vote with the party at the cost of support in their districts.

Table 3.9 Legislators' Role Identifications

	Calif., 1957 (%)	New Jersey, 1957 (%)	Ohio, 1957 (%)	Tenn., 1957 (%)	U.S. House, 1963–1964 (%)
Constituency Role					
District	51	39	40	54	45
Political system	29	20	23	24	30
District and political system	20	41	37	22	25
N^b =	78	54	112	46	80
Representational Role					
Trustee	55	61	56	81	29
Delegate	20	17	15	6	24
Politico	25	22	29	13	48
N^b =	49	54	114	78	84
Purposive Role[a]					
Ritualist	58	70	67	72	67
Tribune	55	63	40	58	82
Inventor	36	49	53	30	31
Broker	27	33	48	15	17
Opportunist	—	—	—	—	8
N^b =	113	79	162	120	87
Interest Group Role					
Facilitator	38	41	43	23	29
Resister	20	27	22	40	21
Neutral	42	32	35	37	49
N^b =	97	78	157	116	85
Party Role					
Superloyalist	—	—	—	—	23
Loyalist	—	—	—	—	37
Neutral	—	—	—	—	21
Maverick	—	—	—	—	19
N^b =					86

[a]Respondents could identify with more than one type.

[b]N = number of legislators polled.

SOURCE: Data are taken, and in some instances recalculated to delete respondents who were not placed in these categories, from Eulau et al., "The Role of the Representative"; Wahlke et al., *The Legislative System*; and Davidson, *The Role of the Congressman*.

Role Identifications

Table 3.9 summarizes the role identifications of state legislators and congressmen from two directly comparable studies. Several general observations can be made about these data. First, for each of the roles, legislators come in several types; for example, legislators in each of the political systems studied attach differing priority in their constituency role to the district they represent. There is *no* agreement among legislators that the local constituency has priority over the political system at large. There is variety in each legislature on every role for which comparable data exist. Second, the percentage of each type for the several roles varies moderately from legislature to legislature. The different bodies have their own mix of types. For example, on the representational role, Tennessee has a disproportionately large percentage of trustees, and on the interest group role, U.S. House members are disproportionately neutral. Nevertheless, the percentages in each body do not deviate markedly from those of other bodies. The types appear (or, in the case of the opportunist among the purposive role, fail to appear) in rather similar proportions. Legislatures are arenas of conflict resolution in policy adoption, but some of the conflict between members is likely to grow out of their differing conceptions of what they ought to be doing in the legislature. Third, the differences in role identifications may be a basis for understanding, explaining, or even changing the patterns of behavior within political systems.

Let me briefly illustrate the last point. Consider the distribution of legislators on the representational role. Suppose that we could reorganize the political system and it was our desire to arrange things in order to increase the proportion of "delegate" legislators. As Table 3.10 indicates, there is one other pattern contained within the legislators' responses of which note should be taken. Davidson divided his congressional respondents

**Table 3.10   Marginality of Election and House Members'
Representational Role Types**

Representational Role	Marginal (%)	Safe (%)
Trustee	19	35
Delegate	44	11
Politico	37	54
N^a =	32	52

^{a}N = number of House members polled.

SOURCE: Adapted from Roger H. Davidson, *The Role of the Congressman*, (Indianapolis: Bobbs-Merrill Company, 1969), p. 128.

into two categories: "safe," in which the incumbent won his last election with a 60 percent or greater majority; and "marginal," where the margin of victory was closer than 60 percent. Overall, most congressmen were politicos. But taking the marginal districts by themselves, 44 percent of those congressmen feel they should be delegates. While these data are not sufficient to prove the point, it is plausible to suggest that if legislative districts are drawn to be politically competitive, more legislators elected from them will feel that they should reflect the views of their constituents than would be the case otherwise. Alternatively, safe districts may encourage legislators toward the trustee type of role identification.

Role identifications should be understood as variables.‡ Closer scrutiny should be given to the way role identifications affect, and are affected by, other variables. Constituency orientations may be related to the way a legislator staffs and organizes his office, how he selects his legislative allies, and the seriousness with which he considers his daily mail. Also, there may well be more "position related patterns of expected behavior" to consider. For example, it may be that representational roles should be obtained in relation to specific public issues. A given legislator may assume a trustee role concerning foreign affairs but consider himself a delegate on civil rights matters, as the quotation from former Senator Fulbright suggests. Again, a legislator may see himself as a facilitator in relation to consumer protection interest groups but a resister in relation to economic producer groups.

In short, role identifications are theoretical tools for understanding the constraints legislators feel upon their behavior. Their strength as tools for prediction and explanation have not been fully tested. Knowledge of the variety of role identification enriches the capacity of political analysts to see patterns in the political behavior of legislators and others in the legislative subsystem.

LEGISLATIVE STAFF

Assistants to legislators are members of the legislative subsystem. Although they lack the official prerogatives of legislators (they do not introduce legislation, debate on the floor, vote on bills, or the like), they do have

---

‡Table 3.10 and the discussion above treat identifications with the different types as a dependent variable. Thus competitiveness is taken to be at least part of the explanation for the role identities of legislators. Role identifications can be used as independent variables to explain other kinds of behavior. Friesema and Hedlund expected delegates to have roll call voting records which were more consistent with public opinion in their districts than trustees. They found the opposite to be so. See Friesema and Hedlund, "The Reality of Representational Roles," in *Public Opinion and Public Policy*, ed. Luttbeg.

official standing in the legislature (such as the privilege of going on the legislative floor in many states, the right to call upon executive agencies for information, privileged access to executive sessions of legislative committees, and so on). Legislative staffers are additional eyes and ears for legislators. While legislators vary in the extent to which they use staff, for some members staff people are extensions of their own personalities.

Legislatures in this country vary markedly in the extent and quality of their professional staff. Staff enlarges the capacity of legislators to find, interpret, and use information in order to legislate wisely. It should be noted, however, that there is no inherent value in large legislative staffs. If information is readily and sufficiently available to legislators, staff members may impair the legislative system rather than assist it. Staff members can block, misinterpret, or distort information. They may prevent the flow of information among legislators or from constituents, lobbyists, and outside experts to legislators. The Alaska legislature may be better staffed with 15 professionals than is Ohio with more than 50.

There is a quantum difference between the staffing problems of Congress and those of the states. Also, there is more information available about congressional staffing than there is on state legislatures. Consequently, I will outline staffing patterns at the congressional level in more detail than those for state legislatures.

Congressional Staffing— Organizational Modes

The Watergate hearings and impeachment proceedings made both the members of Congress and the congressional staff more visible to the public than ever before. The quiet assurance of Samuel Dash and John Doar are impressive examples of competent staff personnel. (Dash was chief of staff for Senator Ervin's investigating committee, and Doar was chief of staff for the House Judiciary Committee which held impeachment hearings.) But staff are used in a variety of ways and in several organizational modes.

1. The general staff mode. Congressmen have created agencies to serve Congress with information and expertise. The Library of Congress was created, first of all, to collect and supply information for congressional needs. Although the Library has come to have nationwide services, a substantial part of its staff serves in the Congressional Research Service.§

§Until the Legislative Reorganization Act of October 26, 1970, this unit was known as the Legislative Reference Service.

The CRS staff consists of about 200 research specialists and another 100 clerical and administrative employees. It answers simple factual questions ("When did Hawaii become a state?" "1959.") and conducts in-depth inquiries into complex issues such as "The Supersonic Transport." [26] Each year the CRS responds to more than 100,000 requests, 90 percent of which are highly specific and can be answered within 24 hours. [27]

Each house of Congress has its own Legislative Counsel, a legal staff of about 20 persons, that provides professional assistance to members with bill drafting. A legislator can simply specify the ideas he wants incorporated into his bill and the counsel staff will analyze existing legislation, fit the bill to present law, and put the sponsor's intentions into proper legal language.

A major unit of congressional general staff is the General Accounting Office, usually known simply as the GAO. In 1973 the GAO had a professional staff of nearly 3,250. The task of the GAO is to serve Congress as accountants, to examine the accounts of departments and agencies of the executive branch. [28]

It is helpful to compare the GAO with the Office of Management and Budget (OMB). Both units date back to the Budget and Accounting Act of 1921. The OMB plans and oversees spending with and for the president. The GAO, headed by the controller general, is the watchdog of executive agencies to guard against improper spending. Not only does the GAO check on the legality of spending, it has been authorized since 1970 to do cost-benefit studies intended to evaluate the effectiveness of spending. Such studies attempt to spell out in quantitative terms what benefits are being achieved and how much they cost per unit. Where data are available, alternative approaches to a given problem are compared so that policy makers can choose new programs more wisely. The GAO also analyzes proposed bills for committees, interpreting what proposed policies will cost, what alternative policies will cost, and the like. The GAO makes special investigative reports to Congress, its committees, and its members on request. For example, July 9, 1973, the GAO released a report which concluded that the massive sale of wheat to Russia in 1972 contributed to higher prices for American consumers. It also cited weaknesses in the Agriculture Department's management of the wheat export subsidy program. The criticisms of the Agriculture Department in the report stimulated an amendment to the major farm bill of 1973 which required that the Agriculture Department report within 60 days as to how it would implement the GAO's recommendations for keeping track of conditions in the international grain market. [29]

In short, Congress has a substantial general services staff, whose personnel respond to information and service needs of congressmen on request. This staff is professional and, in varying degrees, specialized and expert.

2. The committee staff mode. Each of the standing committees of Congress is authorized, according to the Legislative Reorganization Act of 1970, to have six professional staff members and six clerical members. The act also gave the minority party the right to choose two of the professionals and one clerical member for each committee. In 1974 the House increased the number to 18 professionals and 12 clerks, with minority control over 10 positions. In practice this authorized number is a lower limit, not an upper one. For example, the *1975 Congressional Staff Directory* shows the House Banking and Currency Committee with 44 staff members, as well as several additional staff members associated with the subcommittees. Committees sometimes have temporary staff members, including specialists "borrowed" from the Congressional Research Service, the GAO, or occasionally from executive agencies.

The number of professional staff members has grown markedly since the Legislative Reorganization Act of 1946. One careful student of Congress recently observed:

> According to the best calculations we can make, House committees employed a total of 51 professional staff people in 1948, but this figure had more than doubled by 1952, reaching a total of 126 professional staff assistants. By 1967 House committees appear to have employed about 270 professional staff members. Since 1967, the total number of employees of House committees appears to have stabilized, and perhaps even declined some. I have not been able to make careful tabulations for the last five years, but it may be noted that the *1972 Congressional Staff Directory* lists only 632 staff members for House committees (but this total does not include investigative staff people borrowed from executive agencies).[30]

Nevertheless most observers believe that committee staffing could profitably be increased to overcome congressional dependence upon executive branch personnel for information and expertise.

There is substantial agreement in Congress and by Congress watchers that committee staffs consist of able people. Their style of action and productivity is substantially affected by informal norms in the Congress and specifically in the committees they serve. Conventionally staff members are loyal to the committee chairman, deferential to the members, moderate in partisanship, and cautious about advocacy. They are expected to remain outside the spotlight of attention and give credit for their work to the legislators they serve. Quotes from chief committee staff men reflect these norms:

> The job of the staff is to be in the background and carry out what the committee decides. The members are elected and have to run for office and the staff has to be a supplement.

Staff people ought not to develop identities of their own. I've seen a lot of staff people who thought they were Senators or chairmen of a committee and that's a short prescription for oblivion.[31]

There are sharp differences among analysts as to whether committee staffs should reflect greater technical competence, partisan distinctiveness, professional detachment, or policy advocacy.[32] There is no reason to expect a single trend. Congressional committees differ from one another in style and temperament. The leadership and eminence of committee chairmen differ, and staff tend to reflect committee characteristics. Because Congress as a whole and individual members do have growing informational needs, committee staffing will continue to develop. It remains to be seen how enduring the self-assertiveness of Congress, vis-à-vis the president and the executive branch, will be, but it presumes the potentiality of stronger information resources than has been the case in the past.

3. The personal staff mode. Each representative and senator has his own office staff. Representatives are allotted approximately $150,000 per year for staff, a maximum of 16 aides. Senators, whose constituencies vary markedly in population, receive between $300,000 and $500,000 per year for their staff, which ranges in size from 10 to more than 50 aides. In 1975 the House employed about 6114 people on personal staffs, while the Senate total was nearly 2600.[33]

Personal staffs, like committee staffs, have been growing rapidly since 1946 and have become increasingly bureaucratized. Each member is free to organize his staff as he wishes. Most House members have a top aide, the administrative assistant, who is general supervisor of the staff. In most offices there is a legislative assistant who does, or manages, policy research and bill analysis and keeps track of legislation in which the congressman has significant interest. Increasingly members have a press aide to handle news releases, produce newsletters for constituents, and generally seek means for publicizing the member's achievements. Many offices have one or more aides with the title of "caseworker." Such a person deals with the range of problems that constituents ask the congressman to handle in their behalf.‖

‖Representative Jim Wright reports the following samples in his book, *You and Your Congressman* (New York: Coward-McCann, 1965), pp. 34–35:

A serviceman, stationed in Greenland, has learned that his father dropped dead and that his mother is on the verge of a nervous collapse. He needs help in getting compassionate leave.

A small industrial firm wants to offer its products to the Federal Government, but doesn't know which agency to deal with or the proper form in which to prepare its bids.

A homeowner with a Federal Housing Authority loan has made payments regularly for eight years. However, because of illness, he has missed the last two payments—the mortgage company has issued instructions for foreclosure. The Congressman will try to get the FHA to intercede.

Table 3.11   Average Staff Work Week for a Congressional Office

Activity	Hours per Week (average)	%
With the member in committee	1.1	0.5
Handling constituent problems (casework)	40.6	18.7
Visiting with constituents in Washington	12.9	6.0
With lobbyists and special interest groups	4.9	2.3
On press work, radio, and television	13.9	6.4
Writing speech drafts, floor remarks	11.2	5.2
On legislative research, bill drafting	13.6	6.3
On pressure and opinion mail	34.2	15.8
On opinion ballots (preprinted by organizations)	4.4	2.0
On requests for information	14.6	6.7
On letters of congratulation, condolence	9.2	4.2
On correspondence other than described	26.2	12.1
Mailing government publications	8.5	3.9
Other	21.4	9.9
TOTAL:	216.7	100.0

SOURCE: John S. Saloma III, *Congress and the New Politics* (Boston: Little, Brown and Company, 1969), p. 185.

Each office has a number of other workers employed as clerks, research assistants, stenographers, receptionists, secretaries, and staff assistants. Most congressmen have one or more district/state offices staffed with aides.

Table 3.11 reports how staff time was allocated in a sample of 60 representatives' offices in 1966. Note that staff time is heavily devoted to constituents and their problems and handling the mail. Speech writing for debates and legislative research really is a small part of the job done by personal staff.

Members' staffs vary in the extent to which they use volunteers and interns. In the summer of 1970, for example, more than 1,250 college students came to Washington to work in the offices of senators or representatives. A variety of *ad hoc* arrangements support others throughout the year. Thus there is a changing population of congressional staff participants.

Let me mention in passing that the party leaders in each house have additional staff in the leadership offices. More will be said concerning that staff in a later chapter.

The Government has lapsed a veteran's GI life insurance policy because he failed to execute and return a certain form. The veteran says he never received the form and he wants his policy reinstated.

Every member of Congress deals with hundreds of similar requests each year.

Congressional Staff in the Legislative Effort

Staff personnel are information buffers for legislators, with much of their effort spent in winnowing out information the legislator would consider unimportant. Others transform technical information into politically meaningful terms. Personal staff also expends a great deal of effort servicing clients of the legislator—constituents, lobbyists, autograph seekers, and term paper writers.

A closer look at legislative effort spent on legislative research, preparation for committee work, and preparation for debate reveals that the capacity of each legislator is greatly expanded by the contributions of staff members. The relative contributions made by the different kinds of staff are illustrated in Table 3.12. According to reports by 160 representatives, their own staffs and committee staffs contribute most to their individual efforts in research and preparation for committee and floor legislative activity. A much smaller contribution comes from the general staff.

Staffing the State Legislatures

Compared to Congress, state legislatures have relatively small professional staff. There is great variation from state to state and little data exist to make specific comparisons. Most of the professionals who serve state

Table 3.12   Sources of Legislative Effort by Congressmen

Work Done by	Legislative Research (%)	Preparation for Committee Meetings and Hearings (%)	Preparation for Floor Debate (%)
The member himself	30.2	61.3	59.6
Members' office staffs	45.6	15.4	28.2
Committee staffs	11.7	20.9	8.7
Legislative reference service	9.0	1.4	2.8
Executive agency staffs	3.3	—	—
Other	0.2	1.0	0.7
TOTAL:	100.0	100.0	100.0

SOURCE: Samuel C. Patterson, "Congressional Committee Professional Staffing: Capabilities and Constraints," in *Legislatures in Developmental Perspective*, eds. Allan Kornberg and Lloyd D. Musolf (Durham, N.C.: Duke University Press, 1970), p. 400; data are drawn from John S. Saloma III, "The Job of a Congressman: Some Perspectives on Time and Information" (unpublished paper, 1967).

legislatures fit the general staff mode. For example, every state legislature has an agency that provides bill drafting service, but the units vary from being independent to that of a subunit in another legislative agency. Most of the professional staff people are lawyers. Nearly all legislatures have a research and policy analysis agency analogous to the Congressional Research Service, but on a much smaller scale. Often it goes under the title of Legislative Reference Service or Legislative Council. Such agencies employ professional researchers with training in the social sciences, law, journalism and, recently, environmental studies. Increasingly legislatures have been strengthening their staff resources in fiscal analysis. In several states this has been done in the general staff mode: Iowa has a Legislative Fiscal Bureau and Louisiana has a Legislative Fiscal Office. Accompanying this development is the increase in legislative audit agencies, loosely comparable to the GAO.

State legislatures increasingly have added professional staffing to their committees. Ordinarily the best staffed committees are the appropriations committees—those that review the budget and spending bills for the legislature. In most states that lack a general services fiscal staff, and even in some that have one, there is a professional staff for budgetary and expenditure review and analysis to serve each house (since 1965 there have been both House and Senate Fiscal Agencies to serve the House and Senate Appropriations Committees in Michigan) or the two houses together (Idaho reorganized its budget analysis staff in 1973 as the Joint Finance–Appropriations Committee). Professional staffing of committees occurs gradually and unevenly in the states. Committees and committee chairmen with prestige are likeliest to have one or more staff experts. Committees may obtain staff during a particularly busy year—an insurance committee, for example, when a complex issue such as no-fault auto insurance is being considered.

Nevertheless, it is striking how modestly legislatures are staffed. An indication of this paucity of professional staff is recorded in a recent study of committee system effectiveness.[34] Using data from 1968, the author divided legislatures into two roughly equal categories: those with "larger staffs," having 15 or more professionals, and those with "smaller staffs," or fewer than 15 professionals.

Personal staff is rare for state legislators. Some states provide expenses to legislators out of which they may hire staff. In Illinois each member may spend up to $12,000 a year. New York allows representatives $6,500 and senators $5,000; Pennsylvania allows $5,000. In such circumstances most aides are clerical rather than professionals with particular competencies related to the legislative process. More typical is the circumstance reported by Duane Lockard, political scientist and former state senator in Connecticut:

I recall that a constituent once wrote asking me to help him obtain an automobile license plate with his initials on it; he apologized for bothering me, but he wondered if my office staff could take care of it for him when I had neither office nor staff. A corner in my hallway at home, piled high with bills, reports, and propaganda, was as near as I could come to an office; and for staff I had a part-time secretary who could barely manage to keep up with the duties assigned to her by the committee of which I was chairman.[35]

In such a context it is not surprising to find that in some states legislators rely very little, certainly much less than do members of Congress, on legislative staff. A recent study of Michigan legislators asked, "What do you do when you must reach a decision and yet do not have enough time to become well informed in legislation outside of the area of your specialization?" Only 3 percent of the responses were "Turn to legislative staff, legislative aides."[36]

On the other hand, in states where the legislature has a sizable staff, the picture is sharply different. A study of the staff of the New York legislature indicates that it has a substantial part in finding, processing, and evaluating information.[37] Interviews revealed that most were active in planning and conducting committee hearings, in drafting bills and memoranda to accompany them, in analyzing and revising legislation under consideration in executive committee sessions, and in helping legislators prepare for floor debates. In short, they engaged in all aspects of bill development except voting on the bills. For a sense of the influence exercised by legislative staff, various participants in the legislative process were asked their views. The data are reported in Table 3.13. Interestingly, legislators and executive

Table 3.13   Views of Legislative Staff Influence

	Proportion Viewing Legislative Staff as		
Group	Very Influential (%)	Influential (%)	Not Influential (%)
Legislators (N[a] = 51)	44	52	4
Executive personnel (N = 20)	55	40	5
Lobbyists (N = 10)	20	70	10
Staffers (N = 62)	27	64	8

[a]N = number of people polled.

SOURCE: Alan P. Balutis, "The Role of the Staff in the Legislature: The Case of New York," *Public Administration Review* 35, no. 4 (July/August 1975): 360.

personnel attribute much more influence to legislative staff than either lobbyists or legislative staff members themselves. Balutis quotes one experienced Democratic senator as saying:

> When the Legislature depends on the executive agencies or private interest groups for research instead of relying on its own sources of information, it makes its choices from the alternatives offered by the interest groups or the executive. Now we have an independent check because we have professional staff. They provide us with alternatives. With adequate staff assistance, we are now able to understand bills as well as come up with legislation of our own.[38]

A comparative study of legislative assistants in Michigan, California, and Virginia, states which now provide legislators with personal assistants, revealed that these aides spent most of their time in research-consultative tasks. These assistants were asked to report the amount of time spent in a variety of activities.[39] The substance of the findings is that they were not used in trivial secretarial functions but that medium to high portions of their effort were spent in discussing ideas, reviewing bills submitted by other legislators, advising the legislator about how particular bills affect his constituency, recommending legislation, conducting research on particular issues, and contacting agencies in behalf of constituents. As Porter's study indicates, the personal assistant provides the legislator with his or her own person, one who may lack some kinds of expertise, but one that is firmly committed to serving the interests and wishes of the employer.

CONCLUDING OBSERVATIONS

This chapter ranges widely to describe the people and roles in the legislative subsystem. Legislators may be viewed as an elite in terms of ascriptive characteristics (attributes to which a person is heir) and achievement characteristics (those attributes one has earned). In a system of democratic elections, voters appear to reward conventional ascriptive characteristics and high achievement characteristics.

Legislators vary substantially in the roles they assume as they pursue their legislative tasks. Some pledge themselves to reflect their constituents' views, while others assert their responsibility to conscience.

While it is easy to find differences in legislators in both characteristics and role identifications, it is difficult to prove that such variables are causally related to legislators' behaviors. Legislators themselves tend to report different kinds of variables affecting their behavior in specific issues. The reason for considering legislators' characteristics and role identifications is to perceive the range of people and backgrounds that are present in the context of legislative policy making.

Legislative staff add another dimension to the legislative process. Here the contrast between Congress and the state legislatures is dramatic. Members of Congress do not lack information for policy making. More likely, the information is overwhelming.# Staff can winnow out information or put it into digestible form for the congressman. This is especially true of committee and personal staff with whom the congressman is familiar and has a trusting relationship. In many states the legislator is more likely to be overwhelmed by the number of snap decisions he must make on the basis of little or no written information. He must vote publicly and on the record many times, often on the basis of what he can see and hear when the bills are debated on the floor of the legislature. He has no staff and few information resources that he can control himself. However, in states such as New York where staff are available, they are highly active, and other legislative participants attribute substantial influence to them.

Personal and committee staff shape the context of policy making in Congress, but they serve very much at the pleasure of the member or committee chairman who appointed them. The staff working in the general staff mode are distantly related to the legislative arena. Their work is available to congressmen on a take-it-or-leave-it basis, and frequently congressmen leave it. In short, congressmen work in an information-rich environment in which staff enlarges the span of the congressman's information. In the legislature, information is much more sparse and the legislator is left to his own devices to search out the information he needs.

NOTES

1. For a theoretical discussion, see Talcott Parsons, *The Social System* (New York: The Free Press, 1951), pp. 65–67 and passim.

2. Joseph A. Schlesinger, *Ambition and Politics: Political Careers in the United States* (Chicago: Rand McNally and Company, 1966), p. 92.

3. John C. Wahlke, Heinz Eulau, William Buchanan, and LeRoy C. Ferguson, *The Legislative System: Explorations in Legislative Behavior* (New York: John Wiley & Sons, Inc., 1962), p. 95.

4. Samuel C. Patterson and G. R. Boynton, "Legislative Recruitment in a Civic Culture," *Social Science Quarterly* 50, no. 2 (September 1969): 243–63.

5. Wahlke et al., *The Legislative System*, p. 491.

6. David Ray, "Membership Stability in Three State Legislatures: 1893–1969," *American Political Science Review* 68, no. 1 (March 1974): 106–12.

#For example, the published hearings of the Select Committee on Committees of the House of Representatives for the Ninety-third Congress runs 2116 pages. This is just one example of the shelves filled with published hearings which include staff reports, witness testimony, and hearing transcripts.

7. Donald R. Matthews, *U.S. Senators and Their World* (New York: Vintage Books, Random House, 1960), p. 23.

8. James Q. Wilson, "The Negro in Politics," in *The Negro American*, eds. Talcott Parsons and Kenneth B. Clark (Boston: Houghton Mifflin Company, 1966), p. 440.

9. Heinz Eulau, William Buchanan, LeRoy C. Ferguson, and John C. Wahlke, "The Political Socialization of American State Legislators," in *Legislative Behavior: A Reader in Theory and Research*, eds. John C. Wahlke and Heinz Eulau (Glencoe, Ill.: The Free Press, 1959), pp. 305–13; see particularly p. 306.

10. Alfred B. Clubok, Forrest J. Berghorn, and Norman Wilensky, "Family Relationships, Congressional Recruitment and Political Modernization," *Journal of Politics* 31, no. 4 (November 1969): 1035–62.

11. Matthews, *U.S. Senators*, p. 45.

12. David R. Derge, "The Lawyer as Decision-Maker in the American State Legislature," *Journal of Politics* 21, no. 3 (August 1959): 427.

13. David R. Derge, "The Lawyer in the Indiana General Assembly," *Midwest Journal of Political Science* 6, no. 1 (February 1962): 49.

14. Heinz Eulau and John D. Sprague, *Lawyers in Politics: A Study in Professional Convergence* (Indianapolis: Bobbs-Merrill Company, 1964).

15. Justin J. Green, John R. Schmidhauser, Larry L. Berg, and David Brady, "Lawyers in Congress: A New Look at Some Old Assumptions," *Western Political Quarterly* 26, no. 3 (September 1973): 440–52.

16. John E. Scharp and Lee Ridgeway, "Black Representation in Congress: An Examination of the 1971 House of Representatives," mimeographed, undated. Bruce W. Robeck draws similar inferences in his study of the Ninety-second Congress, "The Congressional Black Caucus and Black Representation" (Paper presented to the 1974 Annual Meeting of the American Political Science Association, Chicago, Ill., August–September 1974), see especially pp. 11 and 12.

16a. For a discussion of black caucus unity and strategy, see Marguerite Ross Barnett, "The Congressional Black Caucus," in *Congress Against the President*, ed. Harvey C. Mansfield (New York: Praeger Publishers, 1975), pp. 34–50.

17. Genevieve Knupfer, "Portrait of an Underdog," *Public Opinion Quarterly* 11 (1947): 114, quoted in Seymour Martin Lipset, *Political Man: The Social Bases of Politics* (Garden City, N.Y.: Doubleday & Company, Inc., 1960), pp. 111–12.

18. See Edward C. Banfield, *The Unheavenly City Revisited* (Boston: Little, Brown and Company, 1974), chap. 3, "The Imperatives of Class," and passim.

19. Clinton Rossiter, ed., *The Federalist Papers*, no. 57 (New York: New American Library of World Literature, 1961).

20. Glen Tinder, *Political Thinking: The Perennial Questions*, 2d ed. (Boston: Little, Brown and Company, 1974), p. 95.

21. There is massive social science literature on roles. My discussion draws particularly upon the uses of the concept in legislative research. See especially Heinz Eulau, John C. Wahlke, William Buchanan, and LeRoy C. Ferguson, "The Role of the Representative: Some Empirical Observations on the Theory of Edmund Burke," *American Political Science Review* 53, no. 3 (September 1959): 742–56; Wahlke et al., *The Legislative System*, Heinz Eulau and Katherine Hinckley, "Legislative Institutions and Processes," in *Political Science Annual: An International Review,*

Volume One—1966, ed. James A. Robinson (Indianapolis: Bobbs-Merrill Company, 1966), pp. 85–189; Roger H. Davidson, *The Role of the Congressman* (Indianapolis: Bobbs-Merrill Company, 1969); Malcolm E. Jewell, "Attitudinal Determinants of Legislative Behavior: The Utility of Role Analysis," in *Legislatures in Developmental Perspective*, eds. Allan Kornberg and Lloyd D. Musolf (Durham, N.C.: Duke University Press, 1970), pp. 460–500; Malcolm E. Jewell and Samuel C. Patterson, "Legislative Role Orientations," Chap. 16 in their *The Legislative Process in the United States*, 2d ed. (New York: Random House, 1973), pp. 405–37; Ronald D. Hedlund and H. Paul Friesema, "Representatives' Perceptions of Constituency Opinion," *Journal of Politics* 34, no. 3 (August 1972): 730–52; and H. Paul Friesema and Ronald D. Hedlund, "The Reality of Representational Roles," in *Public Opinion and Public Policy: Models of Political Linkage*, (rev. ed.), ed. Norman R. Luttbeg (Homewood, Ill.: The Dorsey Press, 1974), pp. 413–17.

22. See Eulau et al., "The Role of the Representative," p. 749.

23. Davidson, *The Role of the Congressman.*

24. See Davidson, *The Role of the Congressman*, pp. 118–19.

25. Quoted in David J. Vogler, *The Politics of Congress* (Boston: Allyn & Bacon, 1973), p. 62.

26. "The Supersonic Transport" was originally printed as a Library of Congress Multilith paper (HE 9901 U.S.A., 71–78 SP). The multilith version was updated and published as Chap. 3, pp. 685–748, in *Technical Information for Congress*, Report to the Subcommittee on Science, Research, and Development of the Committee on Science and Astronautics, U.S. House of Representatives, Ninety-second Congress, April 15, 1971.

27. Charles A. Goodrum, "The Legislative Reference Service of the United States Congress," *Congressional Research Service* (JF522, 70–930), April 1, 1970: 1–13.

28. Richard E. Brown, *The GAO: Untapped Source of Congressional Power* (Knoxville: The University of Tennessee Press, 1970); and Elmer B. Staats, "General Accounting Office Support of Committee Oversight," *Working Papers on House Committee Organization and Operation*, House Select Committee on Committees, 93d Cong., 1st sess., vol. 2, pt. 3, pp. 692–700.

29. *Congressional Quarterly Almanac, 1973*, (Congressional Quarterly Inc., 1974), pp. 304 and 321.

30. Samuel C. Patterson, "Staffing House Committees," *Working Papers on House Committee Organization and Operation*, House Select Committee on Committees, 93d Cong., 1st sess., vol. 2, pt. 3, p. 673.

31. Richard L. Madden, "Congress Master Mechanics: The Committee Chiefs of Staff," *The New York Times*, March 3, 1974, p. 45.

32. For illustrations of the arguments see, respectively, Walter Kravitz, "Improving Some Skills of Committee Staffing," *Working Papers on House Committee Organization and Operation*, House Select Committee on Committees, 93d Cong., 1st sess., vol. 2, pt. 3, pp. 669–72; John S. Saloma III, "Proposals for Meeting Congressional Staff Needs," Ibid., pp. 681–86; Nelson W. Polsby, "Strengthening Congress in National Policy-Making," *The Yale Review* 59, no. 4 (June 1970): 481–97, especially pp. 495 and 496; and David E. Price, "Professionals and 'Entrepre-

neurs': Staff Orientations and Policy Making on Three Senate Committees," *Journal of Politics* 33, no. 2 (May 1971): 316–36.

33. See Harrison W. Fox, Jr., and Susan Webb Hammond, "The Growth of Professional Staffs," in *Congress Against the President*, ed. Harvey C. Mansfield (New York: Praeger Publishers, 1975), p. 115.

34. Alan Rosenthal, "Legislative Committee Systems: An Exploratory Analysis," *Western Political Quarterly* 26, no. 2 (June 1973): 252–62.

35. Duane Lockard, "The State Legislator," Chap. 4 in *State Legislatures in American Politics*, ed. Alexander Heard (Englewood Cliffs, N.J.: Prentice-Hall, 1966), pp. 98–125; quotation is from p. 114.

36. Two hundred and twelve responses were made by 75 Michigan representatives in 1970. See H. Owen Porter, "Legislative Experts and Outsiders: The Two-Step Flow of Communication," *Journal of Politics* 36, no. 3 (August 1974): 709, Table 2.

37. Alan P. Balutis, "The Role of the Staff in the Legislature: The Case of New York," *Public Administration Review* 35, no. 4 (July/August 1975): 355–63.

38. Ibid., p. 360.

39. H. Owen Porter, "Legislative Information Needs and Personal Staff Resources" (Paper presented at the 1975 Annual Meeting of the American Political Science Association, San Francisco, Calif., September 1975), p. 12.

System Interdependency: Shaping Policy Adoption in the Legislative Subsystem

This book focuses on legislative subsystems. Legislative subsystems play a significant part in authoritatively allocating values for the society. However, they do their job in concert with and in response to other systems and subsystems. The next two chapters discuss the other major systems and subsystems—not exhaustively—*but with particular attention to the ways in which they impinge upon legislatures.*

It is crucial to realize that these systems need the legislature's policy adoptions. Some are more dependent than others. Some are dependent for certain kinds of decisions more than for others. The president, for example, is more dependent upon Congress in domestic matters than he is in foreign affairs. It is also necessary to appreciate the capacities of these systems and subsystems to thwart the legislative subsystem. Interdependence is the basis for interaction and influence relationships.

There are numerous stereotypes about American legislative subsystems. "Poor Congress, it cannot do a thing," wishy-washy "Senator Snort," vacuous and windy "Senator Claghorn," silly state legislators. I think they are misleading. When understood in the context of the political system, legislatures and legislators are significant in the policy process.

4

The Chief Executive Subsystem

At a birthday dinner in his honor, in May of 1954, more than a year after he retired from the presidency, Harry S. Truman observed that ". . . upon the President falls the responsibility of obtaining action, timely and adequate, to meet the nation's needs. Whatever the Constitution says, he is held responsible for any disaster which may come."[1] The observation holds in state political systems for governors too. Two points may be drawn from Truman's observation. First, there is great attention paid to that single, authoritative leader, the chief executive. He can win great acclaim or suffer conspicuous defeat. He exercises broad discretion and wields more power than any other single figure in the political system. Second, he must lead. Leadership means identifying and articulating goals, developing strategies to achieve them, and coordinating other authorities and subsystems fo fulfill those goals.

THE CONTEXT OF LEADERSHIP

Everyone finds himself engaged in leadership in some situation or another. Likewise each person has responded to the leadership of another person. We may accept another person's leadership for several reasons: because we share his desires to fulfill the same goals; because we appreciate his communication skills; because we admire his capacity to perceive a situation as one in which he will succeed at influencing others; and because his willingness to take risks to fulfill goals makes us willing to take similar risks. For present purposes it is sufficient to say that some lead and many follow for a complex of reasons. Because people are social and the work of living is never accomplished, there is a ubiquitous need for leadership in all spheres of interpersonal activity. Part of the political process is the task of defining formal positions, and attaching to them authority and control over instruments to influence others. Then men with the ability and willingness to choose goals and influence others toward those goals will seek the positions as prizes of great worth.

In the American political system there are many leadership positions and many leaders, but in the states and in the nation the position of chief executive is preeminent. He is authorized to use a variety of specific instruments—the budget, the veto, political appointments, personal staff, and many others—to move other people to fulfill his goals. It would be inaccurate to say that the chief executive is *the* controlling leader in the political system, but no other regularly controls him. The speaker of the House, the attorney general, the chief justice of the highest court, the Senate majority leader, the political party chairman, interest group directors, and social critics may rival his influence in particular circumstances, but not on the broad range of issues and decisions dealt with in the political system. The chief executive is the ceremonial head of state, manager of negotiations with other political systems and, usually, the leading partisan in the party through which he won election.

Visibility of the Chief Executive

Associated with positional preeminence is visibility. And visibility has had increasing significance in media-conscious American mass society.[2] Conditioned to understand the chief executive's capacity to *make* news, the news media, particularly television, treat the chief executive *as* news. The national network news pictures the president arriving by limousine, shaking hands with well-wishers, taking off by helicopter, receiving applause, greeting other dignitaries, and the like. Too often the visual news is not accompanied by a discussion of the political problem solving/avoidance that occasioned the visibility. A president can obtain television time by asking for it. So can many governors. News conferences happen at the initiation of the chief executive and are regularly well attended. The chief executive is cast as newsmaker, and he calls on the questioners, he chooses whether or not to answer, and he decides how much detail to offer. Withal, it is his press conference.[3]

The chief executive's visibility is of great significance to him as he promotes his proposals for public policy. He can make strong public arguments for his proposals; he can oppose the arguments of his rivals. More than anyone else, the chief executive can focus the attention of the public upon his explanation of the issues at stake. The chief executive can speak with a single voice. If the president is a hawk, who will receive equal time to speak as a dove? If the governor wants to cut back spending for higher education, who will take front and center in behalf of higher education? When the chief executive vetoes a bill, who is the recognized spokesman for the majorities in the two legislative chambers that passed the bill? The answer in each case is, "It depends; perhaps several people, but maybe nobody." In American political systems there is no single, recognized rival spokesman who is both expected and allowed to contend with the views of the chief executive on an equal footing. No one can preempt public attention to oppose the chief executive in the fashion that he can preempt attention to set forth his views.

The visibility of the chief executive means that he can choose to enlarge the scope of political conflicts if he so desires. Most public policy conflicts do not evoke widespread citizen attention. They are fought out by the relevant political authorities with some advice and pressure from interest groups and spokesmen from affected subsystems. But sometimes particular authorities try to arouse widespread citizen concern to tip the decision in their favor. An example of successful use of this device occurred early in 1970. The appropriation for the Department of Labor and the Department of Health, Education and Welfare was a matter of sharp conflict between the president and his supporters on one hand, and congressional Democrats on the other. The issue was not very visible except to those with rather immediate economic stakes in the outcome of the appropriation fight. The congressional Democrats passed their version of the appropriation. But the president enlarged the scope of the conflict by making a televised address to the nation on January 26, 1970 in which he asserted his reasons for opposing the bill and, in an unprecedented action, he actually vetoed the bill before the cameras. Two days later the House sustained the veto by a large margin.

A president can use his visibility to draw attention away from particular issues or rival leaders. Sickels gives a compact description of several examples:

When Senator Fulbright's Foreign Relations Committee hearings on the conduct of the war attracted a large television audience in 1966, President Johnson made a sudden decision to launch a "peace offensive," flying to meet South Vietnamese officials in Honolulu. When Senator Robert Kennedy was about to address the Senate a year later to propose negotiations in Vietnam and a bombing halt in the North, Johnson delivered an unscheduled speech, called a press conference, announced an agreement with the Soviet Union to discuss arms limitations, produced hopeful statements on the war's progress from General Westmoreland and Secretary of State Rusk, and, when the talk had begun, released a letter to a sympathetic senator, Henry Jackson, defending the bombing program. More recently Senator Jackson, as a candidate for the presidential nomination, on the verge of holding public hearings on the attractive issue of enlarging the Everglades Park in Florida, was upstaged by an announcement from the White House that President Nixon planned a formal recommendation for the same purpose.[4]

The visibility of a chief executive is significant to his opportunity and capacity for leading the people and the other political authorities of the system. But to fulfill his goals, he must have credibility with those he desires to influence. To be caught in a bit of lying braggadocio is perhaps only embarrassing, as when President Johnson told American troops that his "great-great-grandfather died at the Alamo," which reporters found to be untrue. However, in a 1965 news conference after troops had been sent to the Dominican Republic, President Johnson told how ". . . some 500 innocent people were murdered and shot, and their heads were cut off, and as we talked to our ambassador . . . he was talking to us from under a desk while bullets were going through his windows. . . ." Interviewed later, the ambassador told reporters that the events described did not happen.[5]

Furthermore, the persuasiveness of a chief executive is vitally affected by success and failure. Had President Johnson's policies in Vietnam succeeded and a limited victory been won in 1967, it is likely that he would have moved triumphantly to another term in 1968 and probably would have impelled his own chosen successor to election in 1972. Nixon's successes in opening friendly negotiations with China and the Soviet Union and in obtaining release of American prisoners in Vietnam substantially enhanced his persuasiveness throughout government during the first term of his presidency. Success breeds persuasiveness, increasing prospects for future success. With failure, an executive's persuasiveness shrinks, as Johnson's did in 1967 and 1968, and Nixon's did in the aftermath of the Watergate scandal.

Obviously, presidents are not necessarily effective in controlling the scope of attention to issues. Certainly President Nixon worked very hard to prevent broad circulation of the "Pentagon Papers," but this very effort may have stimulated even greater critical attention to the papers by the press. The dramatic unraveling of the White House's attempts to contain the investigation of the Watergate scandal sets a new benchmark for the extent of efforts to control the scope of a conflict and the consequences of an inability to do so.

In American politics leadership is not simply a matter of authority and status. It is accomplished through persuasion. Richard Neustadt argues, in fact, that presidential power is the power to persuade—that the president's position, public prestige, and professional reputation give him the leverage to bend others toward his goals.[6] President Truman put the matter much more colorfully, "They talk about the power of the president, how I can just push a button and get things done. Why, I spend most of my time kissing somebody's behind."[7] If a president loses credibility with the people generally, or with others in positions of power, he loses the capacity to bend them toward his objectives. One of the conspicuous consequences of the Watergate scandal was the decline of public trust in President Nixon in particular, and perhaps in executive leadership more generally.*

Institutionalization in the
Chief Executive Subsystem

The president or governor is at the apex of an institutionalized and hierarchically organized subsystem, with a number of administrative units responsible to him. In the states this means authority over several thousand state employees. A president has nearly 3 million civilian employees subject to his direction. However, in terms of his leadership task, only a few of this number are especially significant to the chief executive.

Those especially relevant to the chief executive in his policy leadership activities are *those who serve at his pleasure to provide information, errands, advice, and service.* For governors in small states, these may number in the tens and twenties. For presidents the number keeps climbing and now exceeds 2000.† The presidency has become increasingly formalized, with organizations and such agencies as the National Security Council, Office of Management and Budget (OMB, formerly the Bureau of the Budget), the Council of Economic Advisers, and others, each having a staff of its own. The inner core of the presidential subsystem is the White House staff. It numbers several hundred, but a reigning group of 20 or fewer senior staffers

---

*It will take some time to sort out the impact of Watergate on the American political system. Short-run implications are apparent from the results of a Harris survey taken September 13–22, 1973, which showed a decline in the proportion of respondents who said they felt "a great deal of confidence" in the executive branch of the federal government from 27 percent (1972) to 19 percent (1973). There was a concomitant rise for the Senate: 21 percent (1972) to 30 percent (1973). For the U.S. House similarly, 21 percent (1972) to 29 percent (1973). *Southern Illinoisan*, December 6, 1973, p. 15.

†In mid-1972 there were 2,206 permanent staff members in the executive office of the president, a number that intentionally excluded "temporary" and "special project" personnel such as those serving the Cost of Living Council and the Council on International Economic Policy. See J. F. terHorst, "White House Staff grows, and grows, and grows . . . ," *Boston Sunday Globe*, July 23, 1972, p. A-3.

("topsiders" as the news magazines refer to them) comprise the inner circle of the "president's men."[8]

A major characteristic of the chief executive's staff is that its members tend not to represent specific interests in the policy process. This is in contrast to the typical appointed department head or the top administrator of a good sized agency. The latter usually have some ties to the industry or segment of society most affected by their department. In states, for example, the director of the insurance department probably has career experience in an aspect of the insurance industry. In the federal government the Treasury secretary has a background in finance. In contrast, staff people may have little or no experience with the policy assignments they receive. More often they are loyalists to the chief executive, known to him as reliable and hardworking at whatever staff assignments they are given. Frequently they have little or no political base, except in association with the chief executive.‡ The Nixon White House staff illustrates these qualities. John Ehrlichman, for example, served for a long time as the president's chief domestic affairs adviser. His experience before joining Nixon's staff was as a Seattle lawyer, specializing in insurance and real estate work. Additionally, he worked in the Nixon political campaigns dating back to 1960, and was a friend and classmate of H. R. Haldeman. He brought few if any connections or loyalties affecting domestic policy other than the desire to help define and achieve the president's own goals in this policy area.

The degree to which the chief executive's subsystem is compartmentalized and jurisdictions are distinguished is at the pleasure of the chief executive. A governor may assign one top staffer as a press secretary, and make media relations totally the press secretary's job. Another governor may allow several staff members to speak to the press concerning whatever "task force" or major project that staff member is organizing in the governor's behalf. So it is with the great range of assignments. Some chief executives want clear lines of jurisdiction and some do not. Some want a detailed hierarchy to organize staff work, while others do not. Among recent presidents, Eisenhower had the most institutionalized staff. Nixon's was hierarchical and provided little access to his person except for a handful of top staff personnel. Johnson's handling of his staff reflected his mood of the moment and was sometimes capricious.[9] To some staff members he was accessible

---

‡This is also true of governors' staff members. Sprengel records these quotes: "Most of us on the staff have known the governor for long periods of time and have developed very close working relationships with him." "We were close friends. I was one of those who urged him to run for governor. I don't think he ever asked me to serve on his staff, it was more or less assumed." Similar responses were given by 30.5 percent of governors' staff members. See Donald P. Sprengel, *Gubernatorial Staffs: Functional and Political Profiles* (Iowa City, Iowa: Institute of Public Affairs, The University of Iowa, 1969), p. 45.

one week and not the next. Kennedy assigned tasks to small informal groups and disbanded them once a policy had been developed or a decision brought to completion.§

Finally, there may be variation within a given chief executive's staff concerning particular kinds of staff jobs. Most chief executives have a highly organized segment of the staff handling budget development. On the other hand policy formulation teams may be very informally organized.

A chief executive creates a staff to serve him. Staff members are observers who report to the chief about what is going on in specific parts of the political system and the society, they supply both information and evaluation, they are negotiators in the chief executive's behalf, they serve as his spokesmen, needling others to do his will. They may be decision makers acting in his name. They serve as buffers, taking the pressure, and sometimes the blame, for the chief executive.[10] A significant portion of staff effort is spent in coordinating and stimulating activities in the agencies and bureaus.[11] Another portion is devoted to maintaining liaison with the legislature.[12] Institutionalized according to his standards for performance and his taste for organizational style, *a chief executive's staff provides him with more control over information than any other actor in the political system.* This is a major resource for leadership.

Nature of the Chief Executive's Position

There are several characteristics of the chief executive's position that affect his capacity for leadership. The first is the matter of tenure. Compared to other political authorities, chief executives hold their positions relatively briefly. Amendment 22 of the Constitution prevents presidents from seeking a third term in office. There is, of course, no assurance of reelection even to a second term. Note, too, that the strain of the office is great and that 8 of 37 presidents before President Ford died in office.

Governors also have short terms.[13] A dozen states have limits similar to that of the national government, while another 11 allow no consecutive reelection. Several states have only two-year terms, and two of those permit but one reelection (New Mexico and South Dakota). An examination of actual terms served by governors in 48 states from 1914–58 indicates that in no state did the average length of service for governors exceed eight years. In 30 states the average was four years or less.[14] While this may may appear to be a long time to students working through four years of college, compared

§Sprengel found clear distinctions among governors. Republican staffs "exhibited more characteristics of a formally structured organization than did Democratic staffs." Sprengel, *Gubernatorial Staffs*, p. 51.

to congressmen, judges, civil servants, and other statewide elected officials (such as the secretary of state), chief executives have a brief tenure. Old hands around the capitol, either state or national, comment on having seen chief executives come and go. J. Edgar Hoover, for example, was director of the FBI, a position filled by presidential appointment, under every president from Calvin Coolidge to Richard Nixon—a "term" of 47 years.

Secondly, because the chief executive has the broadest responsibility of anyone in the political system, he also has the greatest potential for achievement. The chief justice of the Supreme Court is the object of great respect and honor, but no one would equate the responsibility or potential of this office with that of the chief executive. The legislative branch has no single top leader. Thus, the chief executive has, in effect, a preeminent potential for achieving great things.

Third, he is responsible to the whole society, a diverse constituency with numerous and conflicting demands for scarce resources. Others in the political system are encouraged to specialize and narrow the scope of their involvement. Not the chief executive. He can set priorities and assemble particularistic policies into broad programs. The nature of his position allows him to put things together.

Fourth, the chief executive does not have to administer. Despite the fact that he can and occasionally does directly intervene in administrative activities, he does not administer programs and policies. This is done by agency heads and their subordinates in the departments. Most presidents do not even administer their own staffs alone; the staff is organized and institutionalized to meet the chief executive's needs and fulfill administrative necessities. Thus the "doing" end of government does not stop when the president is conducting summit talks or the governor suffers an extended illness.

To sum up, the chief executive has wide responsibilities and powers, a broad constituency, time and opportunity to concentrate upon leadership, and a brief and insecure tenure. His visibility is unmatched in the political system. He commands a loyal and flexible staff. He is a man in a hurry who might be able to achieve great things but who must take his chances with real possibilities of failure. His task is that of moving other men, who share with him the power to make authoritative allocations of values for the society, according to his strategies and to the fulfillment of his goals.

Leadership by the Chief Executive
Means Policy Promotion

The chief executive plays a vital role in the policy process, but he is not superman and the chief executive subsystem *is a subsystem*. It is one that is organized and institutionalized to move policy proposals from initiation to adoption to application and even to interpretation. The way authority is organized in the American system, adoption usually refers to the legislative process, application is the province of the administrators, and interpretation is subject to the authority of the courts.

It is sometimes suggested that the chief executive subsystem initiates the proposals in the policy process. This is a gross exaggeration. In Chapter 1, a demand was defined as an expression of opinion that an authoritative allocation of some kind should, or should not, be made by responsible authorities. While demands may originate with authorities, most originate with others in the society—people who have needs and feel strongly that the authorities ought to do something to fulfill them. I will elaborate on this point later in Chapter 10. Public policy is based on ideas for meeting needs. Ideas circulate, gain support, attract critical analysis and opposition, and the like. Ideas may take shape in editorials, legislative proposals, reports by a chief executive's study commission, proposals by interest groups, or the like.

The chief executive and his people are interested in promoting public policy. Centralized and goal oriented, they can select out and organize ideas and demands into programmatic form. They can dramatize the human needs to be fulfilled, package the proposals to deal with related problems and issues, obtain the expertise to put the proposals into operational form, and offer evidence about what such programs can achieve. The chief executive subsystem is well organized to capture significant ideas, particularly those in written form that have received substantial publicity and attracted broad attention elsewhere.

There are other actors in the political system besides the chief executive who engage in policy promotion. Among those are interest group leaders, eminent social critics (such as Ralph Nader), legislative leaders, and rivals for the position of chief executive. Yet the chief executive is particularly motivated to engage in this activity since his place in history is contingent upon the programs put into effect during his administration. He needs to put the stamp of his administration on public policy and the way to achieve that is by promoting policy proposals.

Instruments of Policy Promotion

There are several methods of promoting policy in the hands of the chief executive, with some relating specifically to his constitutional and legal powers.

Messages and Proposals There are formal occasions for messages to propose and promote policies. A chief executive uses his inaugural address to paint in broad strokes a sketch of his policy programs. Presidents annually make a State of the Union address. Governors usually address the legislatures when they convene. Ceremonial occasions focus attention on the chief executive and provide him with opportunities to exercise leadership. Executives send both formal and informal messages to the legislature in particular: in 1972 President Nixon sent 24 written presidential messages to the Congress, including 116 specific requests for legislation; in 1973 he sent 28 messages and 183 legislative requests; in 1974 there were 161 requests, 97 from Nixon and 64 from President Ford.[15]

There are many less formal ways to make proposals: they are made at press conferences, in meetings with small groups of legislators and legislative leaders, and in the numerous telephone calls between the executive or his staff and legislative members and their staffs. Increasingly presidents have taken advantage of prime television time to promote their policy proposals. So far the only factor limiting the use of such time and access to the people has been the chief executive's own self-restraint. Opponents of the president have largely been frustrated in attempts to get "equal time" to offer alternatives to presidential proposals. Governors have not obtained a similar television advantage in state policy arenas. It can be noted that typically a president combines in his television message pronouncements of how he will exercise his discretionary authority as chief executive, proposals for new authoritative policies, and appeals to the public for support of both his discretionary actions and his proposals. The president's access to the airwaves is justified by the fact that his major discretionary acts are important for the people to know and understand, and appeals for their support are perfectly in order. Such justifications are precisely the ones the president's opponents lack in seeking equal time. What offends the president's rivals is that while he has broad attention from the people he can promote further policies and generate support for them.

Budget The executive budget is a major tool of policy promotion and deserves some detailed description. The capabilities of any government to apply policies to problems is closely associated with what it will spend for those policies. Prior to the 1920s, there was no presidential budget. Heads of governmental agencies requested appropriations on their own initiative. The Budget and Accounting Act of 1921 made the president responsible for creating a coherent budget and transmitting it to Congress. Interestingly, this was a "good government" reform proposal directed more toward obtaining efficiency, economy, and accountability in government than toward strengthening the chief executive. The law created a Bureau of the Budget with a director and assistant director appointed by the president without Senate confirmation. Originally a unit within the Treasury Department, in 1939 this became the first, and for some time the only, agency in the executive office of the president. In 1971 the agency was reorganized as the Office of Management and Budget and it remains as a unit of the president's executive office. It is, in short, the president's immediate staff who create a plan for government spending in the upcoming year.

The mechanics of budget planning for the federal government are complex,[16] but with preliminary guidelines from the president, the Office of Management and Budget in the spring of each year consults with representatives from all government agencies concerning their future spending needs. Agencies estimate their needs according to the tasks assigned them by law; for example, according to law coal mines are to be inspected for conformity to safety standards by the staff of the Bureau of Mines, a unit of the Department of the Interior. Anticipated costs can be estimated fairly easily. The priorities of executives shape expenditures too. J. Edgar Hoover, the long-time director of the FBI, was noted for the priority and resources he directed toward the investigation of Communists. OMB compiles the estimates, analyzes the spending plans, compares agency priorities with the president's intentions, and identifies overlapping and competing functions by separate agencies. With the help of the Council of Economic Advisers and the Treasury Department, it estimates economic trends and the amount of revenue anticipated from taxes. With this information the president, in the early summer, establishes general guidelines and planning figures for the budget. OMB then renders the general guidelines into specific advice to agencies to revise their spending projections. There may be interaction between agency executives and OMB staff about a host of details, including sheer haggling about amounts in the budget requests. By fall the agencies formalize their budget requests. The OMB examines them in detail, reconsiders trends in the national economy and tax revenue income forecasts. In the late fall of the year, the analyses go before the president and he then sets the proposed budgets for the agencies. OMB then communicates the figures to the agencies, and some of them must revise their planning in accordance with the president's decisions. Again there may be a bit of haggling, some revisions and compromises, but final estimates are made for approval by the president about Christmas time. Once all details are finalized, the president prepares his budget message for delivery to Congress and the OMB publishes the proposed budget in a finely detailed report. Thus, for example, on February 3, 1975, President Ford proposed a $349.4 billion budget for fiscal year 1976, with anticipated revenues of $51.9 billion less than he intended to spend.

Until recently the proposed budget had been taken up first in the Appropriations Committee of the House of Representatives, with agency requests divided up among appropriations subcommittees. From there appropriations bills followed a well-worn path of legislative consideration that usually produced enactment of most appropriations bills before July 1, the first day of the fiscal year for which the budget had been proposed.

1976 was the first year of a sharply revised budgetary procedure. The Congressional Budget and Impoundment Act of 1974 reorganized the machinery and timetable for budget enactment.[17] The new format aimed at four objectives: (1) to give Congress better staff for budgetary analysis, (2) to require Congress to coordinate spending with revenue-raising measures, (3) to limit the president's authority to impound (refuse to spend) congressional appropriations, and (4) to make "back door spending" more difficult.‖

Both the House and Senate have new budget committees. For the Senate there is a standing committee of 15 members. The House Budget Committee is unique. It has 23 members selected from among the other committees and party leaders. Selection is done by the two parties separately. Of the 23, 5 are from the Appropriations Committee, 5 from the Ways and Means Committee, 1 from each of the 11 legislative committees, and 1 from the leadership of each party. Membership on the House Budget Committee is to turn over regularly and no person is to serve on the committee more than 4 years of a 10-year period.

The Congressional Budget Office is a new staff unit whose resources are available to all congressional committees, but it gives priority to serving the two budget committees. The CBO, its task mostly analytical, is likely to have a staff of up to 150 people. Besides reviewing the president's budget proposal, it is to issue a report every April 1 discussing national budget priorities and alternative ways to allocate authority and funds to fulfill major national needs. This is a broad assignment and could produce highly creative projections or it could simply increase the amount of words printed at public expense to then be ignored by decision makers.

Important to the new budgetary procedure is a timetable for congressional actions on the budget:

November 10   President projects "current services"—how much would be spent in the coming fiscal year if current federal programs were not changed.

‖"Back door spending" is Washington jargon for procedures that obliged Congress to appropriate money for previously made commitments; in short, procedures that precluded Congress from selecting its own level of spending. Back door spending occurred through contract authority, borrowing authority, and entitlement programs. Some laws give contract authority to agencies of government, meaning that bureaucrats can enter into contracts obliging the federal government to make future payments, payments for which subsequent appropriations will be needed. Borrowing authority is similar, allowing agencies to borrow in advance of appropriations. Entitlement programs are those paying benefits to eligible recipients for such things as welfare, medical assistance, and veterans benefits. Circumstances can change the number of eligible people (recession, war, epidemic) and leave Congress no choice as to how much money to appropriate.

December 31	Joint Economic Committee submits an evaluation of the current services budget outlook.
About January 20	President submits a proposed budget.
March 15	Congressional committees make budget recommendations to the budget committees.
April 1	Congressional Budget Office reports budget priorities and fiscal plans.
April 15	House and Senate Budget Committees send to the floor concurrent resolutions proposing target figures for overall taxing and spending—a tentative budget.
May 15	Legislative committees report all bills authorizing new spending. Also, Congress completes action on the concurrent resolutions establishing the tentative budget.
After Labor Day	Congress completes action on bills authorizing new spending.
September 15	Congress completes action on a second concurrent resolution on the budget affirming or revising the earlier one, and, if necessary, requiring standing committees to revise appropriation, revenue, or debt decisions in a reconciliation measure.
September 25	Congress completes action on the reconciliation measure.
October 1	The new fiscal year begins and budgeted programs go into effect.

The mechanics of this new congressional procedure for adopting the budget are complex and will be altered in practice. It may be that a fair assessment of the procedure cannot be made before 1980. No doubt the timetable will be revised somewhat, with the future significance of the CBO difficult to foretell. The meshing of the traditionally powerful Ways and Means and Finance and Appropriations Committees with the new House and Senate Budget Committees, and especially the directives of the second concurrent resolution on the budget, remain to be seen. New procedures mean new opportunities for wise policy making, but the interdependence of committees and members is apparent; rivalries and competing views could mean delays and missed deadlines. Nevertheless, Congress has enlarged its capacity to review and revise the president's proposals.

The president's role as policy promoter in the budgetary process remains noteworthy. It is evident that he is a key figure, exercising important discretion in selecting and arranging priorities, setting and altering spending proposals, and articulating an overall rationale for the budget. Nevertheless, presidents do not set priorities independently from agencies and then impose the priorities upon them. This would require agencies to adapt and accommodate programs and policies to the president's initiatives. Rather, the numerous parts of the budget well up from the field offices, divisions, and bureaus, through the departments (Defense, Justice, Veterans Administration, and so on) to the budget bureau and the chief executive. The primary outline of the budget has already been formed by initiation of the bureaucrats. Careful empirical analysis of the budgetary process over time indicates that such initiatives are themselves shaped most by appropriations from the preceding year.[18] Although the budget itself is extremely complex, the process has predictable consequences. Distinctive and persisting patterns and trends exist. They are subject to alteration and the sharpest changes occur when there is a change in chief executive, but observers indicate "that alterations in political party and personnel occupying high offices can exert some (but not total) influence upon the budgetary process."[19] Instead of major changes, presidents make marginal changes in budgetary initiatives, altering spending levels up or down, and only occasionally do they cut off programs or initiate major new ones. The president is described variously as "winding down" this program, "stepping up" that one. New departures are not typical.

The task of budget promotion is an important one for the president since he has the need to convince both the Congress and the American people that his budget is a good one. The people, who typically feel that taxes are "too high" and that government spending is generally too high (even though particular sets of people affected by specific policies may feel that spending for their interests is too low), are a potentially critical audience. Congressmen, especially those on the House Appropriations Committee, consider themselves protectors of the national treasury. Representative John Rooney, a senior member of the Appropriations Committee and long the chairman of the State Department subcommittee, characterized his view of the president's budget in his questioning of administration officials defending their requests: "I am questioning you for the taxpayer. I approach [the budget] with the idea that it can be cut. It's an asking price."[20] Richard Fenno quotes another member similarly, "I've been on the [Appropriations] committee for 17 years. No subcommittee of which I have been a member has ever reported out a bill without a cut in the budget. I'm proud of that record."[21] Thus, the president, a man in a hurry to achieve a record, has to press for the money to keep the doing end of government in operation.

The budget bureau and its work supports the president's promotional capacity. It provides him with background information on agency operations in great detail. It allows him to impose some coherence upon both raising revenue and spending. The budget bureau constitutes a spending control agency; thus, the president can in good faith claim to have examined and reduced the spending requests of agencies even before legislative consideration.

There is some variation in the way budgets are assembled in the states.[22] In most states, however, the governor has responsibility for preparing budgetary requests and shares this responsibility only with persons he himself has appointed.[23] Interestingly, in a survey in which governors were asked to report, "What powers, both formal and informal, do you lack which could aid you significantly in effecting your programs?" only a few governors indicated that budgetary powers were missing.[24] Only three of 39 governors who responded felt their lack of power in budgeting to be a significant constraint. If promoting the budget is the chief executive's purpose more so than initiating and creating its shape, the absence of real control noted by some political scientists may not be felt by most governors. Thomas Anton, for example, recently pictured the governor of Illinois as a pathetic figure in the budgeting process:

> The budget document may be compared to a huge mountain, which is constantly being pushed higher and higher by geologic convulsions. On top of the mountain is a single man, blindfolded, seeking to reduce the height of the mountain by dislodging pebbles with a teaspoon. That man is the Governor.[25]

The finding that governors do not feel a lack of budgetary power may indicate more about the promotional role governors play in the policy process than their actual budgetary power.

Appointments and Nominations Important to the chief executive's enterprise of policy promotion are the personnel around him, including those who head the agencies, departments, and administrative units of the political system. Joseph Kallenbach notes that "the chief executive may be captain of the ship of state; but he must function with a crew that is not entirely of his own choosing."[26] The great bulk of public employees, state and national, are civil servants with enduring job tenure. Yet the president and most governors appoint hundreds of agency executives, commission members, and staff personnel. This fact is important because, as noted earlier, the chief executive does not administer policy himself: he effects policies through the agencies by means of the agency executives he has appointed.

The chief executive, frequently affected by political constraints, does not have a free hand in the appointing process. Most governors would not appoint someone as state highway commissioner who was opposed by the state's Good Roads Federation, a federation of road user groups including trucking associations, manufacturers, highway building contractors, along with producers of asphalt, cement, sand, gravel, petroleum products, and perhaps the state police and the state tourism council. Even the president does not appoint an avowed opponent of organized labor to be secretary of labor. Appointees to positions which serve significant clienteles must have some acceptability and credibility among the clients. Also, a chief executive may have to fulfill appointments in response to commitments made during his campaign to win the office.

One of the significant legal rules of the game in executive-legislative relations is the power of the upper chamber of the legislature to consent in executive appointments. The chief executive *nominates* appointees, but they may not assume office until confirmed by a majority vote of the Senate. Kallenbach notes that the degree of influence exercised by the Senate upon presidential appointments falls into four rather distinct categories.[27] First are those in which the president has a relatively free hand. Cabinet level secretaries, deputy and assistant secretaries, bureau heads and diplomatic appointees are rarely rejected by the Senate. In 1959 the Senate rejected Eisenhower's nominee, Lewis B. Strauss, for secretary of commerce. In 1973 the Senate Judiciary Committee refused to recommend Nixon's nominee, Patrick L. Gray for director of the Federal Bureau of Investigation, to the Senate and the nomination was withdrawn. Other nominees have been sharply questioned about some of their policy intentions—thus sensitized to perspectives held by members of the Senate—but then routinely confirmed for office. The unwritten but usually followed rule is that the president should have his own men in control of policy application in offices whose terms of service depend on the president.

A second category of appointments accords the Senate more, but still secondary, influence. The president makes nominations to the Supreme Court, the courts of appeals, and the independent regulatory commissions such as the Federal Trade Commission, Securities and Exchange Commission, and Atomic Energy Commission. These positions have a tenure of office distinct from the president—in the case of judges, for life, and for commissioners, usually five or seven years. President Johnson's nominee for chief justice of the Supreme Court, Abe Fortas, was put off in the Senate until the nomination was withdrawn. Clement Haynsworth and G. Harrold Carswell, two Nixon nominees to the Supreme Court, were denied confirmation by the Senate. More recently, June 13, 1973, the Senate denied confirmation to a Nixon nominee, Robert H. Morris, to the Federal Power Commission. This was the first rejection of a nominee to a major federal independent regulatory agency on the floor of the Senate since 1950.[28] Typically, presidents have enjoyed great latitude in appointments to these tenured positions, but recent events suggest that the Senate may take more seriously its discretion over nominations to offices with terms that extend beyond that of the appointing president.

The third category of presidential appointments really accords discretion to individual senators and is known as "senatorial courtesy" appointments. A number of appointees serve the national government within a particular state, especially in the administration of justice; examples include federal district judges, marshals, district attorneys, and heads of field service offices. The Senate will confirm such a nominee only if the person is acceptable to the senator or senators of the same political party as the president within whose state the nominee must serve. If the president ignores the affected senator, the senator may tell his colleagues that the nominee is "personally obnoxious" to him, in which case most other senators will vote to deny confirmation, out of courtesy to their colleague. The courtesy pattern is well understood to all concerned and rarely needs to be invoked. The president and the affected senator agree on an appropriate candidate prior to public nomination. As recently as 1951, however, Senator Paul Douglas of Illinois successfully appealed to the courtesy of the Senate concerning two nominees by President Truman to federal judgeships in Illinois. Both nominees were defeated.[29] Senatorial courtesy does not guarantee confirmation. In 1965 at the request of Senator Edward Kennedy, President Johnson nominated Francis X. Morrissey, a long-time friend of the Kennedy family, to a district judgeship in Massachusetts. Strong opposition to the nomination developed in the Senate on the grounds that Morrissey was unfit for the office, and after some delay President Johnson, with the acquiescence of Senator Kennedy, withdrew the nomination.

The fourth category consists of appointments requiring confirmation of career civil servants and military officers. For instance, every military officer from second lieutenant and above has his commission as an officer and a gentleman by confirmation. Each promotion is similarly confirmed. Thousands of these are routinely brought forward by the personnel offices of the affected units and acted on by both the president and the Senate with only very rare discretionary consideration.

The power of governors over their administrations through appointments varies widely across the states. Adrian notes, for example, that in Michigan more than 97.5 percent of state positions were under civil service and only four nonclassified positions were allowed in each department. Meanwhile in Pennsylvania, thousands of jobs were appointive.[30] To obtain a quantitative measure of governors' appointive powers, Schlesinger examined the extent to which each governor was free to appoint the heads of major agencies controlling 16 principal functions in state governments.[31] A governor's power was weighted for each of the functions:

5 if governor appoints;
4 if governor and one house of the legislature approves;

3 if governor and both houses of the legislature approve;

2 if appointed by director with governor's approval or by governor and council;

1 if appointed by department director, board, legislature, or civil service;

0 if elected by popular vote.

If a governor rated 5 for all 16 functions, the score would be 100. If all were elected, his score would be 0. If all appointments needed the approval of one house, the score would be 80. In fact, with data drawn from *The Book of the States*, 1968–69, scores varied from 73 (Tennessee) to 17 (Arizona), with most states having scores between 60 and 30. As Table 4.1 indicates, the states with scores lower than 40 are southern states or those with relatively small populations.

Table 4.1   Appointive Powers of the Governor: State Rankings [a]

73	Tennessee	47	Ohio	34	Louisiana
72	Pennsylvania	46	South Dakota	33	New Hampshire
69	Hawaii	46	Vermont	33	North Carolina
68	New Jersey	44	Alabama	32	Kansas
64	Indiana	44	Missouri	31	Wyoming
59	Massachusetts	44	Washington	30	Florida
58	New York	43	West Virginia	29	Texas
56	Maryland	42	Alaska	27	Colorado
56	Virginia	42	Nebraska	26	Georgia
55	Illinois	42	Rhode Island	26	Mississippi
50	Arkansas	41	Utah	25	Delaware
50	California	40	Iowa	25	North Dakota
50	Connecticut	39	Montana	24	New Mexico
49	Idaho	37	Maine	21	South Carolina
49	Kentucky	37	Oregon	20	Oklahoma
48	Michigan	35	Nevada	17	Arizona
48	Minnesota	35	Wisconsin		

[a] The figure for each state is based on the governor's powers of appointment in 16 major functions and offices. It indicates the degree to which the governor can be assumed to have sole power over the 16 functions or offices. The 16 functions are: administration and finance, agriculture, attorney general, auditor, budget officer, conservation, controller, education, health, highways, labor, insurance, secretary of state, tax commissioner, treasurer, and welfare.

SOURCE: Joseph A. Schlesinger, "The Politics of the Executive" in *Politics in the American States: A Comparative Analysis*, 2d ed., (eds.) Herbert Jacob and Kenneth N. Vines (Boston: Little, Brown and Company, 1971), modified from the table on p. 227.

The president has substantial control of his administration by his thorough domination of the appointment process for top political executives. There are significant political constraints upon this control of appointments but, except for appointments subject to senatorial courtesy, these are not because of legislative discretion. Compared to the president, governors typically have more modest control over administrators through powers of appointment. From Deil Wright's study of heads of state agencies, 14 percent were elected.[32] Categorizing nonelected administrators, appointments were as follows:

Governors only	16%
Governor with Senate or council consent	29
Board or commission with governor's consent	11
Board or commission without governor's consent	19
Department head	17
Other and no answer	8

The thrust of these data is to show that ordinarily the governor is a less commanding figure than the president, both in exercising executive leadership and, more particularly, in having the capacity to promote policy to the legislative subsystem and the public.

Vetoes and the Threat of Vetoes   Except for the governor of North Carolina, all chief executives in the states and national government possess the power to veto legislation. Typically a bill passed by both chambers of the legislature needs the chief executive's signature, indicating his approval. If the chief executive does not approve, he returns the bill to the house in which it originated with a veto message indicating his objections. The legislature may take no action in which case the bill is dead; it may amend the bill to meet the objections and pass it again through both houses and re-present it to the chief executive; or it may pass the bill over the chief executive's veto. The last step is a difficult one (as I will explain shortly).

The veto powers of most state governors exceed the president's in that most have an "item veto" power.[33] This means that they may veto parts of bills, particularly bills that appropriate funds for state expenditures. Thus a governor is not put into a "take-it-or-lose-the-whole-thing" position as the president can be. For instance, a state bill may appropriate funds for all of higher education. The governor may approve all but the appropriation for a particular college; thus he does not endanger the funds for all higher educational programs and can narrow down the bargaining process to the

**Table 4.2   Vetoes of Public Bills and Vetoes Overridden:
Recent Presidents**

President	Bills Vetoed	Vetoes Overridden
Eisenhower	93	3
Kennedy	13	0
Johnson	13	0
Nixon	41	5
Ford (through January 2, 1976)	41	7

SOURCES: *Congress and the Nation*, Volume III, 1969–1972 (Washington, D.C.: Congressional Quarterly Service, 1973), p. 101a; *Congressional Quarterly Weekly Report*, January 5, 1974, p. 29; and *Congressional Quarterly Almanac, 1974*, (Congressional Quarterly Inc., 1975), pp. 32–34; *Congressional Quarterly Almanac, 1975* (Congressional Quarterly Inc., 1976), p. 903.

funding level for one particular institution. The item veto provides a governor with a "fine tuning" control which the president lacks.#

There are two noteworthy political patterns in the use of the veto. First, chief executives make only occasional use of their veto powers. Records of recent presidential use are indicated in Table 4.2.

Partisan labels are not consistently the key variable, but it is reasonable to suggest that the veto tends to get greater use by conservative chief executives than liberal ones. If legislative majorities are more liberal than the chief executive, they may extend government authority and initiative to areas of social life which he can prevent by a simple veto. In contrast, the chief executive who is more liberal than the legislative majorities may propose enlarged government authority and initiative which the legislature does not pass, or passes in a watered-down form. A liberal executive, confronted with a watered-down bill, usually signs it. For him it is better that he gets part of what he wants than nothing. The veto is a power to prevent legislation and as such it is a stronger tool for preventing the enlargement of governmental activity than it is for stimulating it.

The second political pattern related to the veto is that vetoes are rarely overridden. Two characteristics help explain why overriding vetoes is uncommon. One is the structural arrangements. An extraordinary majority

---

#Presidents have attempted to counter this lack of control by means of an increasingly controversial technique, namely, impoundment of funds. For an in-depth discussion of the issues, along with arguments pro and con, see the entire issue of *The Congressional Digest* 52, no. 4 (April 1973). Other helpful sources are Louis Fisher's *President and Congress: Power and Policy* (New York: The Free Press, Macmillan, 1972), pp. 122–27, and *Presidential Spending Power* (Princeton: Princeton University Press, 1975), pp. 161–201. The Congressional Budget and Impoundment Act of 1974 sharply limited the president's power to defer, much less refuse, to spend appropriated funds. Either requires congressional consent.

(usually, a two-thirds majority; in some states, three-fifths) is needed in both houses of the legislature to defeat the chief executive. Secondly, in hotly contested issues such extraordinary majorities are very difficult to achieve in a partisan setting. In most states it means getting a substantial proportion of the votes from legislators of the chief executive's party. By a veto, itself an unusual action, the chief executive has placed the spotlight of public attention on a particular bill (about which most citizens were previously unaware) and said "it should not become law." In such an environment it is sometimes difficult to obtain a majority in each house, much less a three-fifths or two-thirds majority including votes from legislators of the chief executive's party.

What the data on vetoes and veto overrides does not tell is also significant. The fact of the veto power and the difficulty in overriding one means that the chief executive may use the threat of veto in bargaining during the legislative process. Sometimes the threat is to the effect, "Pass the bill in the form I want it or I'll kill the whole thing." Sometimes the process is more complicated, such as "Pass Bill A on public health, or I'll veto Bill B on roads and highways that so many legislators want to please their constituents."

For those governors who have the item veto, the second example is particularly relevant. Sharply applied to budget bills, the item veto can be used with good accuracy to punish legislators particularly troublesome to the governor. In short, the veto is a substantial power, one the chief executive can use to encourage legislative response to the policies he wishes to promote.

Foreign Policy Initiative, Executive Agreements, and Treaties

A significant difference between the president and the governors is the fact that the president has such broad authority in foreign policy making. Parallels between governors and the president are numerous (there are parallels in the way they relate to their respective legislative bodies), but the accretion of power in the modern presidency is not matched by that in the governorships because governors do not have a policy area so relatively outside the checking power of their legislatures as does the president. Presidents since Franklin Roosevelt have, with the exception of a few instances, initiated substantial foreign policies and expected loyal and bipartisan congressional support for those policies with legislative authority and appropriations. Until dissatisfaction with Vietnam war policies reached the saturation point, those expectations were met routinely.

Table 4.3   Treaties and Executive Agreements: 1789–1970

Period	Treaties	Executive Agreements	Total No. of Treaties & Agreements
1789–1839	60	27	87
1839–1889	215	238	453
1889–1939	524	917	1441
1940–1970	310	5653	5963
TOTAL:	1109	6835	7944

SOURCE: Louis Fisher, *President and Congress: Power and Policy* (New York: The Free Press, Macmillan, 1972), p. 45.

The legal-constitutional powers of the president are substantial. As commander-in-chief, he directs the military. No congressional authorizations were needed when President Kennedy ordered Cuba "quarantined" by the U.S. Navy in 1962, when President Johnson massively increased troop levels in Vietnam in 1965, or when President Nixon sent troops into "neutral" Cambodia in 1970. The president conducts foreign policy, whether through the formal channels of ambassadors and the secretary of state, or through secret negotiations by presidential assistants. Even the fact of "recognition" of other countries is in the president's control. Thus, foreign policy initiative is substantially in the hands of the president.[34]

An important instrument for formalizing international agreements has, for the United States, been the treaty. According to the Constitution, a treaty does not have force until consented to by a two-thirds majority of the Senate. While most presidentially proposed treaties have been approved,** in a particularly dramatic instance the Senate insisted upon reservations which President Wilson would not accept concerning the Versailles treaty of 1919, thus keeping the United States out of the League of Nations. Since then presidents have increasingly recorded "executive agreements" with foreign countries which have, for all practical purposes, the same binding character as treaties,[35] but do not require Senate approval. The flexibility of the executive agreement, along with the increasing complexity of the United States' role in foreign affairs, has resulted in the pattern suggested in Table 4.3. The great bulk of all policy arrangements with other nations are recorded in executive agreements.

**Kallenbach cites an unofficial compilation by the *New York Times*, August 25, 1963, when the Nuclear Test Ban Treaty was submitted to the Senate, which indicated that 69 percent of all treaties submitted had been unconditionally approved and another 18.4 percent approved with amendments and reservations. See Joseph E. Kallenbach, *The American Chief Executive: The Presidency and the Governorship* (New York: Harper & Row, Inc., 1966), p. 506.

Evidence that the president's role is primary in foreign policy making and that Congress plays a secondary role can be presented in several ways. One bit of evidence relates to that fact that, according to the Constitution, only Congress has the power to declare war. That would appear to be a sharp limit on the president. However, between 1789 and 1970, forces of the United States have gone into military action overseas at least 150 times during an era in which Congress has declared war just five times.†† A second is to note that presidential policies that do receive congressional action usually receive approval.‡‡

A third bit of evidence comes from studies of Congress. The significance of standing committees to the work of Congress is well known. It is often noted that the most prestigious committee in the Senate is its Committee on Foreign Relations.[36] Yet Fenno learned that its members experienced a great deal of frustration in really affecting the conduct of foreign affairs. He quotes the top aide of a senator on the committee as follows:

> My boss is interested in foreign affairs. He broke his back to get on the Committee. It's fine to be interested in something. But unless the Committee does something, you'll just sit there and get ulcers. What good is membership on a committee when it doesn't influence the course of events? The Committee is supposed to have prestige. But I don't understand the prestige bit either. How can you get prestige when you don't do anything? I don't understand why anyone would want to be on that Committee.

He also quotes Senator George Smathers, who, after two years on the committee, resigned, and later said,

> Foreign Relations is the biggest fraud in the Senate. It handles only one big bill a year—foreign aid. And everything I heard in closed-door briefings was no different than I'd read in the newspapers.[37]

The president has broad powers under the Constitution to conduct foreign affairs. The issues are very complex and thus are hammered out primarily by experts in the administration in the Departments of State, Defense, Treasury, and Commerce, along with intelligence personnel and planners on the

††See *CQ Guide to Current American Government*, Fall 1972 (Washington, D.C.: Congressional Quarterly Inc., 1972), p. 91. However, in 1973 Congress enacted a new set of limits on the president's war powers. There is a 60-day limit on any presidential troop commitment abroad without specific congressional authorization. Presidential commitments may be terminated by Congress prior to the 60-day limit by passage of a concurrent resolution, which requires no presidential signature and is, thus, not subject to veto. *Congressional Quarterly Weekly Report*, November 10, 1973, p. 2985.

‡‡In 1973 Nixon's position prevailed in 50.6 percent of the roll calls on which the president took a position. *Congressional Quarterly* reports this score to be the lowest in 20 years of presidential support scoring. Nixon suffered several defeats on the issue of war and bombing in Cambodia. See *Congressional Quarterly Weekly Report*, January 19, 1974, pp. 101-6.

president's staff. On most issues of foreign affairs, there is no direct effect upon a specific part of the electorate. How many Americans feel affected by a decrease in aid to India's agricultural program? In the absence of conspicuous international conflict, great expenditures, or challenges to national patriotism, presidents may conduct foreign relations in a permissive atmosphere of general popular support.

These considerations determine the way in which foreign relations are conducted. There are compelling reasons for secrecy during negotiations. Until a web of agreements can be finalized, particular strands in the negotiations may be fragile. One country does not have full and open debates about the bargains it will or will not strike lest it foreclose valuable alternatives before even negotiating with the other country. For a president to set forth before the American public all his reasons for seeking a particular agreement with another country may only succeed in convincing that country not to conclude the agreement. Finally, the conduct of foreign affairs requires the capacity to act both very slowly and almost immediately. Patience and an enduring commitment to the desirability of nuclear arms limitations have been necessary for success in the SALT (Strategic Arms Limitations Talks) negotiations.§§ On the other hand the president must be able to make a decision which rapidly sets in motion a large part of the government's machinery—to defend West Berlin or to devalue the dollar.

The president has broad authority accompanied by instruments to initiate and promote foreign affairs policy. Domestic political constraints upon the president ordinarily are not exercised in foreign affairs matters. To retain his initiative and flexibility, the crucial problem for the president is to be successful.

Policy Promotion: A High Calling

The preeminence of the chief executive in American political systems is beyond dispute. More than any other, he sets goals, offers policy proposals, and oversees administration. But he needs specific authority to put most policies into effect; this requires legislation and means that he must propose bills to the legislature for education, welfare, defense, taxation, and so on. Similarly he needs funds to make the policies operational; this too requires legislation. To exercise his authority in a creative way, the executive needs to be persuasive in his dealings with the legislature. His office, visibility, and

§§President Nixon's agreements with the Soviet Union in May 1972 were the product of more than 30 months of preparations and negotiations. See *Congressional Quarterly Weekly Report*, June 3, 1972, p. 1252.

instruments impose the task of leadership upon him. The legislature, with its own prerogatives of authority, is his clientele, rival, and institutional near equal. It is not well organized to lead him, but it does not necessarily have to follow his leadership. The level of cooperation and conflict between the chief executive and the legislature depends upon a host of variables, thus helping one to appreciate the complexity of the legislative process.

The capacity of governors for policy promotion is more modest than that of the president. Their visibility is not as great and neither is their eminence. They are more circumscribed by independently elected lower state executives. Significant constitutional limits discourage them from certain policy innovations. In particular, states, and therefore governors, have modest revenue powers. Costly innovations often require a fight for new revenues or state indebtedness. Besides the typical political liabilities associated with taxation or indebtedness, there are the additional barriers of state constitutional limits. In several states long constitutional fights have occurred concerning state sales taxes, income taxes, bond issues, and the like. In brief, the executive may find that he needs to obtain constitutional changes to raise taxes or debt limits in order to raise revenues for initiating new policies. And all this must be achieved before he comes up for reelection. As governors are aware, the barriers to policy leadership are great and reelection is difficult to win.|| ||

CONCLUDING OBSERVATIONS

In the politics of the American states and nation, the political subsystem that most affects the legislative subsystem is that of the chief executive. Note that I have not argued that the executive subsystem is *more* or *less* powerful than the legislative. There has been alarmist talk of late about executives bullying legislatures, dominating political systems, and gaining power at the expense of other subsystems—particularly the legislative subsystem. Such a summary judgment is easier to assert than to demonstrate with a systematic presentation of data. In this chapter I have argued that chief executives are highly visible, they are expected to propose policy, their subsystems are institutionalized to meet such expectations, and that the instruments for policy promotion are readily at hand. In marked contrast to governors, presidents have unique leadership opportunities because of their authority

|| ||Turett has shown that in "Nineteen states with at least moderately competitive gubernatorial elections . . . , and in which a governor could constitutionally succeed himself," the defeat rate for governors in the decade of the 1940s was 34.7 percent; the 1950s, 36.4; and the 1960s, 34.9. See J. Stephen Turett, "The Vulnerability of American Governors: 1900–1969," *Midwest Journal of Political Science* 15, no. 1 (February 1971): 108–32.

and responsibility for conducting foreign relations. In domestic matters, executives have the tools to propose policies and set an agenda for the legislative process. But executives cannot govern by fiat. They need legislative enactments—to legitimize their appointees and to authorize programs and spending. Legislative subsystems have their own resources, broad discretion, and a significant political base. Legislators respond to executive leadership but seldom with mere dutiful compliance.

In Chapter 5, I will describe other systems and subsystems that impinge upon the legislative subsystem, after which I will examine the legislative subsystem more closely.

NOTES

1. See Robert S. Hirschfield, ed., *The Power of the Presidency: Concepts and Controversy*, 2d ed. (Chicago: Aldine Publishing Company, 1973), p. 116.

2. The "mass society" theme is cogently developed in William Kornhauser, *The Politics of Mass Society* (Glencoe, Ill.: The Free Press, 1959). In a mass society, people can escape to a "let's pretend" world through mass communication. See William Stephenson, *The Play Theory of Mass Communication* (Chicago: University of Chicago Press, 1967). For an interesting discussion of the "Indirect Political Effect of the Mass Media," which considers in part, "Radio and the Making of the Presidency," see Harold Mendelsohn and Irving Crespi, *Polls, Television, and the New Politics* (New York: Thomas Y. Crowell (Chandler Publishing Company), 1970), pp. 247–317.

3. For a fascinating discussion by veteran Washington correspondents, see Edward P. Morgan, Max Ways, Clark Mollenhoff, Peter Lisagor, Herbert G. Klein, *The Presidency and the Press Conference* (Washington, D.C.: American Enterprise Institute for Policy Research, 1971).

4. Robert J. Sickels, *Presidential Transactions* (Englewood Cliffs, N.J.: Prentice-Hall, Inc., 1974), p. 161.

5. Quoted in Robert Sherrill, *Why They Call It Politics: A Guide to America's Government* (New York: Harcourt Brace Jovanovich, Inc., 1972), p. 264.

6. Richard E. Neustadt, *Presidential Power: The Politics of Leadership* (New York: John Wiley & Sons, Inc., 1960); see especially Chap. 3.

7. Quoted in Leo Bogart, *Silent Politics: Polls and the Awareness of Public Opinion* (New York: John Wiley & Sons, Inc., 1972), p. 47.

8. See Patrick Anderson, *The Presidents' Men* (Garden City, N.Y.: Doubleday and Co., Inc., 1968).

9. See Eric Goldman, *The Tragedy of Lyndon Johnson* (New York: Dell Publishing Co., Inc., 1968), and George Reedy, *The Twilight of the Presidency* (New York: New American Library, 1970).

10. See Lester G. Seligman, "Presidential Leadership: The Inner Circle and Institutionalization," *The Journal of Politics* 18, no. 3 (August 1956): 410–26.

11. See Robert R. Sullivan for an excellent discussion of variations in this process, "The Role of the Presidency in Shaping Lower Level Policy-Making Processes," *Polity* 3, no. 2 (Winter 1970): 201–21.

12. This process has become exceedingly complex. See Abraham Holtzman, *Legislative Liaison: Executive Leadership in Congress* (Chicago: Rand McNally and Company, 1970). At the national level there has been a decline in the role of the Office of Management and Budget in central clearance in legislative matters. See Allen Schick, "The Budget Bureau That Was: Thoughts on the Rise, Decline and Future of a Presidential Agency," *Law and Contemporary Problems* 35, no. 3 (Summer 1970): 519–39. The enlarged role of White House staff is described by Robert S. Gilmour, "Central Legislative Clearance: A Revised Perspective," *Public Administration Review* 31, no. 2 (March/April 1971): 150–58.

13. Drawn from Joseph A. Schlesinger's discussion of tenure potential for governors. See "The Politics of the Executive," in *Politics in the American States: A Comparative Analysis*, 2d ed., (eds.) Herbert Jacob and Kenneth N. Vines (Boston: Little, Brown and Company, 1971), pp. 210–37.

14. Ibid., p. 222.

15. *Congressional Quarterly Almanac*, Volume 28, 1972, Volume 29, 1973, and Volume 30, 1974 (Congressional Quarterly Inc., 1973, 1974, and 1975), pp. 76, 997, and 943.

16. Aaron Wildavsky, *The Politics of the Budgetary Process*, 2d ed. (Boston: Little, Brown and Company, Inc., 1974) and Ira Sharkansky, *The Politics of Taxing and Spending* (Indianapolis: Bobbs-Merrill Company, Inc., 1969).

17. The discussion draws heavily upon the *Congressional Quarterly Almanac, 1974*, (Congressional Quarterly Inc., 1975), and James J. Finley, "The 1974 Congressional Initiative in Budget Making," *Public Administration Review* 35, no. 3 (May/June 1975): 270–78.

18. Otto A. Davis, M. A. H. Dempster, and Aaron Wildavsky, "A Theory of the Budgetary Process," *American Political Science Review* 60, no. 3 (September 1966): 529–47.

19. Ibid., p. 544.

20. Quoted by Wildavsky, *The Politics of the Budgetary Process*, pp. 47–48.

21. Richard F. Fenno, Jr., "The House Appropriations Committee as a Political System: The Problem of Integration" *American Political Science Review* 56, no. 2 (June 1962): 310–24.

22. See Allen Schick, *Budget Innovation in the States* (Washington, D.C.: The Brookings Institution, 1972).

23. A recent review indicated that 46 of 50 governors had budget-making authority. See *The Book of the States, 1974–75*, vol. 20 (Lexington, Ky.: The Council of State Governments, 1974), pp. 158–61.

24. Thad L. Beyle, "The Governor's Formal Powers: A View from the Governor's Chair," *Public Administration Review* 28, no. 6 (November/December 1968): 540–45.

25. Thomas J. Anton, *The Politics of State Expenditures in Illinois* (Urbana, Ill.: University of Illinois Press, 1966), p. 146.

26. Joseph Kallenbach, *The American Chief Executive: The Presidency and the Governorship* (New York: Harper & Row, Inc., 1966), p. 387.

27. Ibid., pp. 391–95.

28. *Congressional Quarterly Weekly Report*, June 16, 1973, p. 1542.

29. *Congressional Quarterly's Guide to the Congress of the United States: Origins, History and Procedure* (Washington, D.C.: Congressional Quarterly Inc., 1971), pp. 236–37.

30. Charles R. Adrian, *State and Local Governments*, 3d ed. (New York: McGraw-Hill Book Company, 1972), pp. 319–21.

31. Joseph A. Schlesinger, "The Politics of the Executive" in *Politics in the American States: A Comparative Analysis*, 2d ed., (eds.) Herbert Jacob and Kenneth N. Vines (Boston: Little, Brown and Company, 1971), pp. 225–28.

32. Deil S. Wright, "Executive Leadership in State Administration," *Midwest Journal of Political Science* 11, no. 1 (February 1967): 1–26.

33. In 43 states the governor has item veto powers. See *The Book of the States, 1974–1975*, pp. 80–81.

34. For an in-depth discussion of this theme and an interpretation of its implications, see Arthur M. Schlesinger, Jr., *The Imperial Presidency* (Boston: Houghton, Mifflin Company, 1973.)

35. See C. Herman Pritchett, *The American Constitution*, 2d ed. (New York: McGraw-Hill Book Company, 1968), p. 359.

36. For data, see Donald R. Matthews, *U.S. Senators and Their World* (New York: Vintage Books, Random House, 1960), p. 149; and Richard F. Fenno, Jr., *Congressmen in Committees* (Boston: Little, Brown and Company, 1973), p. 150.

37. Fenno, *Congressmen in Committees*, p. 162.

5

The Legislative Subsystem and Its Client Systems

Although the chief executive is the legislature's most conspicuous rival, partner, and client, several other systems and subsystems have relationships of interdependency with the legislative subsystem. There are the numerous bureaucratic subsystems that put legislation into effect. The judicial subsystem interprets and referees the application of public policy in individual cases. There are local and state political systems that have stakes in what public policy is and ought to be. External political systems are interested in and affected by American foreign policy. All these systems and subsystems affect and are affected by legislative subsystems. In the pages that follow, I will describe some general characteristics of these systems and subsystems and show how they relate to legislatures in the making of public policy.

BUREAUCRATIC SUBSYSTEMS

While it makes sense to think of each state political system as having *a* legislative subsystem, *a* chief executive subsystem, and *a* judicial subsystem, each state and the nation have numerous bureaucratic subsystems. Look at the national government. The State Department can be thought of as a subsystem distinct from the other executive departments such as Defense, Treasury, or Commerce. There are independent regulatory subsystems such as the Federal Trade Commission. There are the so-called independent agencies such as the Veterans Administration and the National Aeronautics and Space Administration. Finally, there are governmental corporations such as the Federal Deposit Insurance Corporation and the Tennessee Valley Authority. The states also have bureaucratic subsystems—many of which parallel national ones, at least in organizational patterns. But our concern is not with the organizational or functional details,[1] but rather with those characteristics that typify American bureaucratic subsystems and the way these subsystems relate to legislative subsystems.

Characteristics of Bureaucratic Subsystems

1. *Bureaus are the "doing" part of the political system.* Congress may set up a postal system, but the mailman delivers the mail. The president decides there shall be a military incursion, but the G.I. does the fighting. Bureaus* perform the vast array of services implied in public policy. In a substantial sense *the government*, which most citizens contact from time to time, is manifested in the 2.5 to 3 million civilian employees of the federal government or the more than 6 million employed by state and local governments. Among other things, these employees run the prisons, staff the public universities, distribute the welfare, circulate the library books, catch the criminals, and gather the taxes. Most observers concentrate attention on how policy is made, taking for granted that implementation follows. But in a real sense policy making and policy changing are relevant only because of the vast apparatus that is grinding out public service.

2. *Bureaus are organized and assigned functions by law.* American governments were created to serve the general welfare—a grand but ambiguous goal. Constitutions and charters usually do not spell out the meaning of "general welfare"; instead they specify which authorities and institutions will define, authorize, and implement specific policies directed toward achieving some condition within the general welfare. Americans have adopted a tradition, inaccurately referred to as a separation of powers, of making and overseeing the application of policy through legislatures, executives, and courts. The powers are not really separate (for example, the veto power of the chief executive and the power of the courts to declare laws

---

*I am using the term *bureau* in a nontechnical sense, referring to any governmental administrative unit. Applied to the national government, a more technical use of the term refers to approximately 400 subunits of departments and agencies such as the Federal Bureau of Investigation, a subunit of the Department of Justice; the Office of Education, a subunit of the Department of Health, Education, and Welfare; the Internal Revenue Service, a subunit of the Treasury Department.

unconstitutional involve both of these "branches" in the lawmaking task of the legislature) but the institutions are separate. For example, to become a judge or an executive, a legislator must give up his legislative office. Authorities in the three subsystems, whose powers overlap sufficiently to "check" and "balance" one another, are the primary policy makers. They establish the content of public policy, which is formalized as laws, statutes, and ordinances.

The three major policy-making subsystems of the national government are established in the U.S. Constitution. The bureaus are not. They are defined by law. The pattern is not consistent in state constitutions which, in numerous instances, do establish some bureaus; but the majority of bureaus in the states are, as in the national system, set up by law.

Each bureau is organized by law. For example, it is according to law that the Justice Department is headed by the attorney general who is appointed by the president, with the consent of the Senate. He can appoint a certain number of staff personnel and heads of subunits, with his influence ultimately dependent upon his personal relationship with the president. Others may be appointed by the president, such as the director of the FBI. The subunits are defined by law—the tax division, civil rights division, criminal division, and the like. Most of the positions within these subunits are filled by civil service employees, hired on the basis of merit examinations. There are only a few political executives who serve at the pleasure of the chief executive and/or the attorney general.

The tasks of each bureau are defined by law. The Justice Department, through its relatively new (1957) Civil Rights Division, enforces legislation prohibiting discrimination on the basis of race, color, national origin, or sex. Its particular body of law for enforcement includes the Civil Rights Acts of 1957, 1960, 1964, and 1968 and the Voting Rights Act of 1965, as amended in 1970. In short, bureaus operate under very clear legal mandates.[2]

The tasks of a bureau are likely to be complex and difficult even if the bureau's mandate is clear. The personnel vary in quality, as in any organization, but usually are quite able.[3] This is certainly true in the federal service and is increasingly so in the states. Ability is rewarded and expertise is encouraged by promotion and pay raises. Substantial in size, and hierarchically organized, bureaus tend to maintain regular patterns of turnover and recruitment, providing new blood and ideas.

3. Bureaus are funded by law. In Chapter 4, I described the procedure by which the chief executive develops and proposes his budget. Bureau leaders participate in that development by proposing the budget they hope to obtain for their unit. After the chief executive assembles his grand design, it is proposed to the legislature. There it is divided up again and considered in its various parts by committees and subcommittees. Bureau authorities are called as witnesses to account for past spending and to defend the propriety of proposed spending. Bureaus may spend only what is appropriated through the legislative process.

Consequences of the Characteristics

1. Bureaus are responsible to authorities in the rest of the political system, their constituencies, and their members. The executive, legislative, and judicial subsystems all have authority over the bureaus. The balance of political influence varies with issues, personalities, and events, but all can and do exercise some control. For example, presidents typically dominate the control of the State Department. Congress controls the Corps of Engineers. The courts significantly affect the operation of the criminal division of the Justice Department. In the case of most bureaus, the legislature and chief executive are usually the prime competitors for domination since both are major contributors in the processes of policy formation and fiscal allocation.

Bureaus are also responsible to their constituents. As Allensworth notes, bureaucracies ". . . operate openly in the political process and are constrained by that process. The nature of politics in the United States seems to indicate the building of constituencies. In fact, as interests tend to form around them anyway, they may have no alternative; still, it is a two-way street: bureaucracies generate constituencies, and constituencies are attracted to bureaucracies."[4] The constituencies vary in their visibility, homogeneity, and efficacy. In state and national governments labor departments are close to labor unions, education departments are allied with public school supporters, agriculture departments with farmers, and civil rights agencies with minority group spokesmen. Sometimes relationships are highly specialized and rarely visible, such as between the Bureau of the Mint and coin collectors. Others are volatile and developing, such as those relating to state and national environmental protection agencies. Some constituencies have only marginal standing in the larger society, such as that for a Bureau of Prisons or the United States Information Agency.†

Bureaus are responsible to their members. The external relationships cannot be overlooked, but to be effective a bureau needs high morale. Bureaucrats are achievement oriented[5]; they need to feel successful and obtain rewards. As they grow older, they tend to seek autonomy, wanting to

---

†The United States Information Agency serves people abroad with American propaganda. According to Wildavsky, "Things got so bad that the USIA sought to organize the country's ambassadors to foreign nations to vouch for the good job it was doing." Aaron Wildavsky, *The Politics of the Budgetary Process* (Boston: Little, Brown and Company, 1964), p. 66.

feel self-directed rather than led by others. To enjoy their duties then, bureaucrats must be able to control their tasks, or feel that the duties assigned to them are worthwhile, significant, meaningful, and valuable. Bureau executives, sensitive to such needs, may encourage informal lines of communication and influence, adapting directives from external authorities (the chief executive, legislative committee chairman, department head) to the needs of those in the bureau. These "within subsystem needs" are a significant factor in shaping the way public policies are actually applied to the political community.

2. *Bureaus and bureaucrats are committed to their function.* Obviously there are exceptions, but in general the statement is true. First, most individuals are employed in bureaus that are acceptable to them. Civil servants under merit appointments can move from one bureau to opportunities in another with little loss of tangible job benefits (time in grade, retirement, vacation, insurance) and often with increases. Political executives may take appointments lower than hoped for, but not to positions viewed as presenting little opportunity for advancement or disagreeable responsibility. Secondly, there is a socialization process by which members of a bureau learn and internalize the goals of their unit. Bureau executives often articulate their view of the bureau's task to their staffs and on some occasions to outside groups. When a director gives a talk to the Rotary Club, certainly some of his staff will be there to ensure themselves that they know the director's current thinking about the agency. Typically, bureaus form distinctive rationales to support their activities. The members believe in the policy objectives. They are convinced that they are working in a "good cause," and believe that their achievements will contribute to the bureau's function and goals. These beliefs are intensified by the fact that the bureau cannot measure its value and productiveness by a profit-and-loss statement. Private enterprise corporations have a profit standard; Ford can be compared to General Motors according to an objective standard of net profit relative to investment. This is not true for bureaus. So it becomes functional for bureaucrats to believe they are engaged in doing good work for society. They want others to believe it and, in fact, they want to believe it themselves.

3. *Bureaus and their members want to survive and flourish.* Many a bureau executive has paraphrased Winston Churchill's famous dictum, "I have not become the King's First Minister in order to preside over the liquidation of the British Empire."‡ Typically bureaus seek to grow, expand their programs, enlarge their budgets, and add to their powers. In times of fiscal restraint they try to fight cutbacks and defend the value of their

‡Speech at the Mansion House, November 10, 1942, concerning the Battle of Egypt. Quoted in the *Oxford Dictionary of Quotations*, 2d ed. (London: Oxford University Press, 1953), p. 144.

functions, predicting horrible consequences for government and society if their programs are restricted or their existence terminated. Wildavsky quotes a spokesman for the United States Forest Service in an Appropriations Committee hearing which illustrates this point: "Mr. Chairman, you would not think that it would be proper for me to be in charge of this work and not be enthusiastic about it and not think that I ought to have a lot more money, would you? I have been in it for more than thirty years, and I believe in it."[6]

Implications of the Characteristics and Consequences

1. The responsiveness of bureaus to external policy decisions varies relative to many factors. There is no precise formula for predicting the degree of responsiveness to external authorities that a particular bureau will exhibit in any given situation. In the legal framework in which bureaus operate, they must comply with orders of the chief executive and must fulfill and respect the policies specified in legislation. They are subject to inspection by the chief executive and his staff as well as to investigation by the legislature. The annual budgeting process is a regular, and for heads of bureaus, sometimes a traumatizing procedure.

To speak of the responsiveness of bureaus is to consider only one direction of a two-way flow of influence. Bureaus are subject to influence and they influence others. It is true that the bureaus are obliged to administer laws passed by the legislature, but it is also true that bureaus and bureaucrats sometimes draft the very laws that they later administer. The centerpiece of President Johnson's "War on Poverty" was the Economic Opportunity Act of 1964, the ideas for which were assembled early in that year by a task force headed by Sargent Shriver. A team of legal draftsmen was drawn from several executive departments and was headed by Assistant Attorney General Norbert Schlei, head of the Justice Department's Office of Legal Counsel.[7] Additionally, spokesmen from the bureaus regularly appear before legislative committees to testify on proposed legislation in policy areas related to their functions and expertise. Bureaus and bureaucrats are sources of information to which legislators regularly turn when they wonder "What would be the consequences of such and such a change in the law?"§

§A case study that illustrates this specific point and documents the importance and involvement of bureau experts in the legislative process is that of the Elementary and Secondary Education Act of 1965. Some will recall it as the enactment President Johnson signed outside the one-room schoolhouse where he began his education. "The bill was actually drafted by Chester Relyea of the General Counsel's Office in the Department of Health, Education, and

Legislators are not alone in their dependence upon bureaucratic expertise. Staff workers for both the chief executive and the legislature routinely call upon bureau experts.

Finally, bureaus deal mostly in policy application, with bureaucrats dominating the fleshing out of general policy decisions. They must spell out in detail how actual programs will be put into effect. This means fine print, complexity, and all that is inherent in the term "red tape." Such details are those that policy makers—legislators and top executives—really lack the time or patience to consider at length.

Nevertheless, the authorities in the legislative process have the tools to alter bureaucratic patterns. Prudent bureaucrats, always cognizant of that potential, seek to accommodate themselves and their bureaus to the winds of change. Success is attributed to those who, because of their sensitivity, rarely get into difficulty when routine investigations or annual budget hearings bring them under scrutiny.

2. Policies change incrementally. In American political systems the preeminent method of policy decision making is that characterized by Lindbloom as "continually building out from the current situation, step-by-step and by small degrees. . . ."[8] Incrementalism is understood best by contrasting it with an alternative, the "rationally comprehensive" method. Sharkansky summarizes the latter this way:

1. identifying the full range of available alternatives;
2. identifying the goals of one's organization;
3. ranking the organization's preference for each available alternative;

Welfare. Samuel Halperin, who was acting Deputy Commissioner of Education [in HEW] in 1965, played an important role in the drafting of the bill as well—although Halperin's role became more visible after the bill reached the House. . . ." During debate on the floor of the House concerning the bill, its supporters were not defending it very effectively. A Republican opponent, William Goodell, said, "All right, then we have a nice, clear legislative history to proceed with. Nobody knows what the bill is going to do." The resource people to help explain the bill were a special assistant to the president, Douglas Cater, and bureaucrat Halperin. The case study reports: "While all of this was occurring, the Administration's education strategists were sitting in the gallery of the house, 'scared to hell' as one of them put it. Cater and Samuel Halperin from the Office of Education were sitting together wondering why [Representatives] Carey and Perkins [who were arguing on behalf of the bill] were having such a bad time with a bill they had been with for several months. They went to [Majority floor leader] Carl Albert's office and worked on a statement to rebut the Goodell, Quie, and Griffin attack. The results of their work were delivered a few moments later by Congressman Frank Thompson of New Jersey who told the House that after 'listening with great interest' to the debate about special education services he had 'precisely the answer to the . . . problem,' which he proceeded to offer." In short, Halperin and Cater had coached him on how to answer the opposition. From Eugene Eidenberg and Roy D. Morey, *An Act of Congress: The Legislative Process and the Making of Education Policy* (New York: W. W. Norton & Company, Inc., 1969); quotations are from pp. 89, 128, and 129–30.

4. defining the resources necessary for each available alternative;
5. making the selection on the basis of a comprehensive consideration of alternatives, preferences and resources.[9]

The rationally comprehensive method calls for inclusive and systematic analysis of problems *before* determining policy. Typically, however, policy makers do not confront problems with a freshness that gives rise to such comprehensive consideration. Instead "new" problems are seen as having their roots in "old" problems, for which some solution has previously been found. While even the old problem may not have been fully "solved," it has at least been "handled." That handling is applied to the new problem. While innovation can occur, it is rarely comprehensive. A policy solution may be partially new, and if after implementation it shows promising results, it may be beefed up and made more comprehensive. In short, change advances little by little.

Policy makers claim to lack time to generate policies by the rationally comprehensive method. Top executives and legislators exclaim about their 16-hour work days and the press of wide-ranging and immediate issues. Elected policy makers have short terms of office. Budgets are passed annually in most systems. The process of decision making is accessible to a variety of conflicting interests, and those typically advantaged in the policy process are those who have stakes in "the way we solved this kind of problem last time." American politics and policy making are aptly characterized by phrases such as "the art of the possible," "to get along, go along," and "half a loaf is better than none." The involvement of the bureaus and bureaucrats in the process of policy making encourages continuity and incremental change in American political systems.

3. Career administrators are continuing participants in public policy making. It is not just the top-level political executives who are active in the congressional policy consideration stage. The middle-level program directors, section heads, and unit chiefs are inconspicuous but active participants too. As Gawthrop points out, "In effect, a four-cornered interaction pattern results between the individual administrator, the interest group, the congressional committees, and the policy executive to whom the administrator is nominally accountable, for example, the President, department secretary, or assistant secretary."[10] The bureaucrat helps create consensus on policy proposals and the evaluation of policies already in effect. For example, if he does not like the legislative program of the top executives, he can funnel tough questions to congressional committee members who use them in hearings on administration spokesmen. He can help interest groups anticipate new proposals. The four-cornered game is a complicated political one, but its existence is real. It brings out the fact that bureaucrats, even those at middle levels, are not neutral, insignificant "paper pushers." They are insiders with resources of information and access. They can help other policy participants with views similar to their own, especially lobbyists, legislators and legislative staff, and other bureaucrats in departments with related functions. Bureaucrats cannot be neutral about the policies they administer. Their careers, their intellectual resources, and their day-to-day responsibilities are too materially affected by the substance of public policies for them to ignore them. They can exercise real influence upon the outcome of political conflict.

JUDICIAL SUBSYSTEMS

Controlling neither the purse, as does the legislature, nor the sword, held by the executive, the courts are commonly considered the least powerful branch in American government. Although I concur in this assessment, I think that some elaboration is called for.

What courts and judges can do in policy making is more circumscribed than is the case for legislators and executives, and probably more than for bureaucrats. Although this generalization is broader than I can support with solid comparative data, I do want to present some arguments for it. The primary activity of courts is conducting trials (trials are disputes between two adversaries) and reviewing trials. It is the adversaries who specify the issue about which they are contesting, not the courts. A judge is expected to be neutral toward both the issue between the disputants and the disputants themselves. If he is not, he is expected to disqualify himself from the case so it can be assigned to a judge who satisfies the neutrality criteria. The task of the judge, particularly when there is no jury, is to fit the facts of the dispute to the regulations and remedies of the law, and to decide the issue at stake. In a criminal case the issue is whether or not a defendant has, by proper evidence, been shown to be guilty under the law. In a civil case the question is whether or not one party has injured another, as charged, and what recompense has to be made.

Because judges conduct trials, they necessarily engage in the interpretation of law. It is this interpretational activity that involves them in policy making. In order to make a decision settling a dispute between two parties, the court may have to specify what the law means. It must read into the general language of a constitution or a piece of legislation a precise meaning that applies to the facts of the case at hand. For example, the Civil Rights Act of 1964 opened "public accommodations" to all people, regardless of race, and provided some description of what constituted public accommodations. Nevertheless, a Supreme Court case was necessary to "find" that a privately owned recreational club—in which whites could buy memberships for a nominal fee, but which operated for a profit and served interstate travelers—could not exclude persons on the basis of race.[11] Volumes have been written by the U.S. Supreme Court alone on what the Fourteenth Amendment to the Constitution means by "nor shall any state . . . deny to any person within its jurisdiction the equal protection of the laws."

Judicial Review, Statutory Interpretation, and Case Selection

In the process of trying cases and reviewing trials, two distinct but significant judicial activities can impinge upon congressional policy enactments. The first is *judicial review*. Simply put, judicial review means considering whether or not acts of Congress, the president, national bureaucracies, and the states are appropriate in the light of powers granted to, as well as denied by, the United States Constitution. Probably the general public is overly impressed with the judicial review authority wielded by the Supreme Court. Interestingly, that power is not specifically granted to the Supreme Court in the Constitution. It was established by the Court itself in an interpretation by Chief Justice Marshall in the Court's decision in the case of *Marbury* v. *Madison* (1803). What most people fail to appreciate is how sparingly the Court has exercised the authority to declare unconstitutional statutes enacted by Congress. A review by the Congressional Research Service, Library of Congress, indicates that in the period 1789–1973 only 97 acts of Congress had been held unconstitutional.[12]

The federal courts have, however, been much more aggressive in finding acts of states and local governments that violate the U.S. Constitution. In fact, more critics of the courts, those who charge judges with "legislating" instead of "finding the law," have opposed the decisions which set aside state enactments. In the reapportionment cases, discussed previously in Chapter 2, the Court decided that the way in which states drew legislative districts raised justifiable questions under the equal protection clause of the Fourteenth Amendment.[13] Later it spelled out its standards for congressional, state legislative, and local representation, as I have already explained.

The famous civil rights case, *Brown* v. *Board of Education*,[14] reversed a long-standing precedent of "separate but equal" schools. It set in motion a series of court cases and decisions that declared unconstitutional all state laws separating blacks and whites.

The *Escobedo* and *Miranda* cases were Supreme Court decisions that primarily affected state and local law enforcement agencies in their handling of criminal investigations.[15] The first asserted the right of a suspect to have access to an attorney while being questioned by police. In the second the Court held that a suspect's confession to a crime could not be used against him unless he previously had been informed of his rights.

Another conspicuous Supreme Court decision was that declaring unconstitutional a school prayer written by the Board of Regents of New York for recitation in the classrooms.[16] Closely related decisions forbade the states and their school systems to support, as a matter of policy, Bible reading and recitation of the Lord's Prayer as religious exercises.[17]

As a final example there are the recent cases declaring unconstitutional the Georgia and Texas state laws prohibiting abortion.[18] The Court described standards within which some state regulation could properly occur, but laws such as the ones in Texas and Georgia, which allowed abortion only to save the mother's life and in other such unusual circumstances, were deemed to violate a mother's right to privacy.

All of these cases affected significant policies about which substantial sectors of the public felt strongly. They set aside old standards, laws, and administrative policies and imposed new and different ones. But this aggressive exercise of judicial review by the Supreme Court impinged largely on state and local authorities, not those of the federal government.

Most commentators agree that the courts have greater impact upon public policy by *statutory interpretation* than by comparing statutes to the Constitution. Court decisions allow judges the opportunity to respond to ambiguities and inconsistencies in the law by explaining away the problems. Such opportunities are not uncommon for several reasons. Legislation frequently includes abstract terms such as "nondiscrimination," "affirmative action," and "maximum feasible participation." Some legislative ambiguity is inevitable, while some of it is intentional. The process of legislative compromise produces legal language loaded with "weasel words." Occasionally the problem is simply one of faulty draftsmanship. Nevertheless, ambiguity in the law encourages creative interpretation in the courts. Consider, for example, how the Supreme Court dealt with cases related to the military draft at the height of the Vietnam War. The law provided that inductees could be punished for being delinquent, but in *Gutknecht* v. *U.S.*[19] the Court interpreted that authority as not allowing Selective Service to speed up the induction of a man found delinquent for turning in his draft card as an antiwar protest. Again, the draft law allowed for the status of conscientious objector, one who refused to fight on what traditionally have been called "religious grounds." In *Welsh* v. *U.S.*[20] the Supreme Court interpreted the law more broadly than before, entitling even those who disavowed any religious basis for their beliefs to claim conscientious objector status. All "whose consciences, spurred by deeply held moral, ethical, or religious beliefs, would give them no rest or peace if they allowed themselves to become part of an instrument of war" were said to have the right to conscientious objector status. The examples could be multiplied, but the impact of the Court's power in statutory interpretations is highly significant.

State court subsystems are comparable to that of the nation, but few systematic studies of them are available. All states have a high court of appeals, typically called a supreme court. The principle of judicial review is generally recognized in state constitutions. Commentators indicate, however, that state courts have not aggressively challenged the constitutionality of state statutes, with more than 80 percent having been sustained in the courts. However, findings of unconstitutionality did tend to follow the writing of new state constitutions.[21]

Typically issues of judicial review in the states are relatively trivial, dealing with procedures and technicalities rather than whether or not the social philosophy of the law fits that embodied in the constitution.[22] Sketchy as the findings are, it appears that state supreme courts follow the informal rules scholars ascribe to the United States Supreme Court:

1. Do not decide a constitutional issue unless it is absolutely necessary in order to dispose of the case.

2. Whenever there is a choice, interpret a law in such a way as to render it constitutional.

3. If necessary to make a constitutional ruling, restrict it as narrowly as possible and do not anticipate or decide issues not immediately before the court.[23]

In contrast to the U.S. Supreme Court, however, there is less dissent in state supreme courts. In the former, fewer than half the decisions are unanimous. A comparison of dissents in states for 1966 showed that in 40 states there were dissents on fewer than one-fifth of the cases decided.[24]

One other significant aspect of judicial proceedings is that the courts with the greatest discretion in judicial review and statutory interpretation, the state and U.S. Supreme courts, are also the courts with the broadest leeway in choosing the cases that they will decide. Of the thousands of appeals made to the U.S. Supreme Court, full written opinions are rendered on only about 100 cases each year. State supreme courts are required to deal with appeals in some kinds of cases, but they too can choose to hear appeals or deny them. In short, with more cases appealed than they can possibly give full consideration, courts choose the issues they want to decide. They can duck some issues and go aggressively after others. Thus courts themselves affect the waxing and waning of interest in various kinds of judicial decision making—civil liberties, right to privacy, business regulation, environmental protection, and the like.

Judicial Intervention into
Legislative Behavior

In addition to judicial review and statutory interpretation, the courts affect legislatures and the legislative process by intervening in the inner workings of legislatures. The Supreme Court set aside the conviction of a labor leader who refused to answer certain questions before a hearing of the House Un-American Activities Committee. The Court said the rules defining the committee's duties and powers were "loosely worded" and "excessively broad," and that the questions asked were not shown to be pertinent to the subject of the inquiry.[25] In a later case, however, the conviction of a professor for having refused to answer pertinent questions from the same committee was upheld. The Court said he did not have the right to "resist inquiry in all circumstances."[26]

In *Bond* v. *Floyd*[27] the Supreme Court overruled the Georgia legislature in denying a seat to Julian Bond. After his election to the Georgia House in 1965, Bond endorsed an anti-Vietnam statement. Other members challenged his right to be seated, arguing in part that Bond's statement was inconsistent with a legislator's mandatory oath to support the U.S. Constitution. The Georgia House refused to seat him. The Supreme Court held that the Georgia House could not apply a stricter standard on a legislator's rights of free speech than on any other citizen's, and it could not use denial of his seat to limit his rights of free speech.

In 1969 a congressional seating issue was decided in the case of *Powell* v. *McCormack*.[28] Adam Clayton Powell was a controversial black congressman and chairman of the House Education and Labor Committee, who was elected for a twelfth term to represent New York's Harlem district. Because of charges that Powell had previously filed false expense reports and misused House funds, a select committee was established to decide Powell's eligibility to take his seat. The committee reported to the House that Powell had violated House rules and the law, and the House voted (307–116) to exclude Powell from the Ninetieth Congress. The Court decided that although Congress has a power to maintain its integrity by punishing, even expelling, its members, Congress's power to judge its members' qualifications to be seated extended only to qualifications stated in the Constitution.

Another interesting case expands upon the constitutional immunity of members of Congress. The Constitution says of the members that "for any Speech or Debate in either House, they shall not be questioned in any other Place" (Article 1, Section 6). In 1971 when the Pentagon Papers were a matter of controversy, Senator Mike Gravel called an evening meeting of a public works subcommittee, of which he was chairman, and with no other members present but an audience of press and public he read aloud for hours out of classified documents. Later he arranged for the documents to be published by the Beacon Press. A grand jury, investigating the release of the papers, subpoenaed Gravel's aide, who challenged the subpoena on the grounds that he was protected by congressional immunity. The matter was resolved by the Supreme Court which said that neither Gravel nor his aide could be questioned about the events of the subcommittee meeting because that was a legislative matter. However, both could be questioned about arrangements for the publication of the papers because these were nonlegislative matters.[29]

As these cases indicate, the courts seldom seek to interfere in the legislative branch, but the prerogatives of legislatures and individual members are not determined solely by and within legislatures themselves. As a sidelight, the *Gravel* case points up the fact that legislative prerogatives extend to legislative staff, who hold essential positions in the legislative subsystem.[30]

In trying cases and rendering written opinions, courts are significant checks upon legislatures. The prerogatives of the U.S. Supreme Court extend not only upon the Congress but upon state legislatures as well. State courts interpret state laws and constitutions, circumscribing intrastate subsystems. But courts tend to tread softly, extending and filling in gaps in legislative enactments. Occasionally they do set new policy directions and, in rare instances, confront opposite views from legislatures and executives. But courts respect the authority legislatures have over them as well, so extreme provocations are rare.

Most of the instances for which the courts have been blamed or praised for "legislating" have occurred when the Supreme Court imposed new interpretations of the Constitution upon the states. Defenders of the courts have been cognizant of this pattern and the point is neatly reflected in an observation about the Supreme Court by Justice Oliver Wendell Holmes: "I do not think the United States would come to an end if we lost our power to declare an Act of Congress void. I do think the Union would be imperiled if we could not make that declaration as to the laws of the several states."[31]

STATE AND LOCAL SYSTEMS
AND SUBSYSTEMS

The complex federal structure of the American political system makes it difficult to draw consistently neat analytical distinctions between legislative subsystems on the one hand and their relationships with state and local systems and subsystems on the other, but the range of interrelationships can be illustrated. Let us now consider at some length the relationship of

Congress to subnational systems and then the relationship of state legislatures to their subsystems.

Congress and Subnational
Systems and Subsystems

The United States Constitution recognized two levels of government: national and state. The states were free to create local units. Although initially thought of as distinct and well-bounded layers of government, over time the units have become increasingly involved with one another and have institutionalized policy making in a variety of forms, depending on the particular policy in question. Elazar says:

> From public welfare to public recreation, from national defense to local police protection, the system of sharing has become so pervasive that it is often difficult for the uninitiated bystander to tell who is doing what under which hat. . . . Under this cooperative system, the federal government, the states, and the localities share the burden for the great domestic programs by making the larger governments primarily responsible for raising revenues and setting standards, and the smaller ones primarily responsible for administering the programs. For each program, all governments involved contribute toward making policy in ways that often depend upon the forms of sharing involved.[32]

Because of the partnership aspects of the systems and subsystems, the relationship of states and cities to Congress and the other national subsystems is different from the relationship of interest groups and social critics to Congress. Specific recognition of this difference can be noted in the enlargement of access in planning and discretion in policy application that has been allowed for state and local systems. For example, in 1966 President Johnson required the Bureau of the Budget and other bureau heads "to take steps to afford representatives of the chief executives of State and local government the opportunity to advise and consult in the development and execution of programs which directly affect the conduct of State and local affairs."[33] Subsequent congressional action, notably the Intergovernmental Cooperation Act of 1968 and the Intergovernmental Personnel Act of 1970, has enhanced the capacity of subnational systems to affect shared policy making and application.

Occasionally states use their semisovereign status to raise issues being avoided by the national system. A striking example of such an action was taken by Massachusetts in the spring of 1970 when it challenged the president's authority to conduct war in Vietnam. It passed a law providing that Massachusetts servicemen, in the absence of a declaration of war by Congress, can refuse to take part in "armed hostilities" that are "not an emergency" and "not otherwise authorized in the powers granted to the President as Commander in Chief." The law also directed the state's attorney general to defend and enforce the rights of Massachusetts servicemen, taking the matter into the federal courts in their behalf.[34] The case went directly to the United States Supreme Court under its jurisdiction to hear disputes brought directly before it by the states. But on November 9, 1970, the Court gave a brief order dismissing the suit.[35] The issue was brought to the United States District Court and dismissed again.[36] On appeal, the case went to the United States Court of Appeals, where the dismissal of the district court was affirmed. In brief, the Appeals Court spoke to the issue raised by Massachusetts, saying that the president and Congress have jointly supported the war and "the Constitution has not been breached."[37]

There are formalized mechanisms by which state systems in particular have impact upon the congressional subsystem. According to the Constitution, "on the application of the legislatures of two thirds of the several states, [the Congress] shall call a [Constitutional] Convention for proposing amendments . . ." (Article 5). Although this has never occurred, by the spring of 1967 such application *had* been made by 33 states, one short of the minimum. The issue that aroused state legislatures was apportionment, an issue that no longer inflames concern. Yet the potential for unprecedented change is implicit in the amendment process. It is also true that the state legislatures participate in ratifying amendments. To date, all proposed amendments have come from Congress and required ratification by three-fourths of the states. Typically such adoption is accomplished by passage through the state legislatures.‖ Legislatures sometimes adopt resolutions or petitions which are sent as official communications to Congress, asserting the legislature's position on some issue before the Congress. Legislators, as well as other authorities in state or local political systems, are frequent witnesses before congressional committees.

STATE LEGISLATURES AND OTHER SYSTEMS AND SUBSYSTEMS

State legislatures have enacted laws to involve local authorities in the policy making process too. For example, in 1969 New Jersey created the Hackensack Meadowlands Development Commission to plan the development of a large marshland only five miles from Manhattan, which could ultimately be worth billions of dollars if developed for urban use. In a complex set of checks and balances, a majority of the mayors of the 14 municipalities containing the meadows were given power to veto commission plans. But the

‖Of twenty-six adopted amendments, only the twenty-first, repealing prohibition, was ratified by state conventions.

commission can override the mayors with a five-sevenths vote.[38] The point to be made is that state legislatures are involving substate systems in policy development by state agencies and assigning them authority over state officials.

Legislative subsystems serve one another. Political authorities in states generally and legislatures in particular are sensitive to innovations in other systems. A recent careful study entitled "The Diffusion of Innovations Among the American States"[39] has systematically analyzed the rate at which states adopt policy innovations. By way of example, Walker notes that states sometimes copy the enactments of other states word for word. A fair trade law adopted in California was followed soon thereafter in 20 other states with only minor alterations. In 10 states the legislation even carried two serious typographical mistakes that appeared in the original California enactment. To determine which states lead in innovation, Walker studied 88 specific policies, going back to the nineteenth century, to see which state adopted what policy first, and the time period in which other states followed the innovator. "The state that has been faster, on the average, in responding to new ideas or policies receives the higher innovation score."[40] (See Table 5.1, following page.)

Walker makes some helpful suggestions to explain innovation and its diffusion among the states. It is evident that innovation scores are related to social characteristics of the states, with the more industrialized, urban, and cosmopolitan states tending to have higher scores. However, diffusion is often a regional process; for example, as Lockard reports about fair employment practices acts, once New York had passed such a law, the governor of New Jersey felt he had to urge such a law in his state lest he be considered a "foot dragger" on civil rights.[41] So Walker concluded that state decision makers search for policy cues particularly from those states they perceive to be appropriate sources of comparison, usually those in their own region. However, several states are perceived as national leaders, and they receive requests for advice and information from throughout the nation. Walker refers to California, New York, Wisconsin, Michigan, Illinois, and Minnesota as "national league" states, while states such as Oregon, Colorado, and North Carolina are regional leaders.[42] The interactions of political systems with one another in the policy process is especially significant in American state politics.

EXTERNAL POLITICAL SYSTEMS

Congress has a substantial role in American policy making, with some of those policies vitally affecting external political systems. Defense policies, foreign aid, foreign trade, and the like are matters of concern in the USSR,

Table 5.1   Composite Innovation Scores for the American States[a]

New York	0.656	Kansas	0.426
Massachusetts	0.629	Nebraska	0.425
California	0.604	Kentucky	0.419
New Jersey	0.585	Vermont	0.414
Michigan	0.578	Iowa	0.413
Connecticut	0.568	Alabama	0.406
Pennsylvania	0.560	Florida	0.397
Oregon	0.544	Arkansas	0.394
Colorado	0.538	Idaho	0.394
Wisconsin	0.532	Tennessee	0.389
Ohio	0.528	West Virginia	0.386
Minnesota	0.525	Arizona	0.384
Illinois	0.521	Georgia	0.381
Washington	0.510	Montana	0.378
Rhode Island	0.503	Missouri	0.377
Maryland	0.482	Delaware	0.376
New Hampshire	0.482	New Mexico	0.375
Indiana	0.464	Oklahoma	0.368
Louisiana	0.459	South Dakota	0.363
Maine	0.455	Texas	0.362
Virginia	0.451	South Carolina	0.347
Utah	0.447	Wyoming	0.346
North Dakota	0.444	Nevada	0.323
North Carolina	0.430	Mississippi	0.298

[a]Alaska and Hawaii were omitted from the analysis because data for their years of adoption were often missing.

SOURCE: Jack L. Walker, "Innovation in State Politics," in *Politics in the American States: A Comparative Analysis*, 2d ed., (eds.) Herbert Jacob and Kenneth N. Vines (Boston: Little, Brown and Company, 1971), p. 358.

France, and Germany and also in Nicaragua, Israel, Nepal, and a great many other countries, large and small. Because of their stake in American policies, foreign systems sometimes attempt to have influence in the policy process. The attempts may take the form of military threats, summit meetings, subversive activities, and more conventional means of communication between countries. The discussion that follows deals briefly with these more conventional means of communication.

A notion that clarifies this communication process is *protocol.* Protocol refers to an arcane set of customs and courtesies for communications between countries. According to proper protocol, nations communicate through official representatives. In the American system, foreign relations are conducted by the chief executive: he recognizes countries, receives and sends ambassadors, makes treaties with the advice and consent of the Senate, and negotiates executive agreements. The implications of protocol include the fact that Congress and its committees do not hear directly from officials of foreign nations. Committees hear testimony from a great range of people, but official representatives of foreign nations are not among them. Except for rare ceremonial occasions,# the American constitutional principle of separation of powers precludes such direct interaction.[43]

The major formal channel for representing the interests of foreign systems, particularly before Congress, is the State Department. The State Department is organized into eight functional bureaus (for example, the Bureau of Economic Affairs, the Bureau of Intelligence and Research) and five regional bureaus (Bureaus of African Affairs, European Affairs, and so on).[44] Under the regional bureaus are country directors. Much of the communication between the United States and a given country is through the country directors and the respective ambassadors. Country directors are involved in affecting policy made in foreign countries. In return they are concerned about policies made in the United States that bear upon "their" countries. Within the State Department such considerations affect the formation of policy proposals which eventually get congressional consideration, and also prompt the kinds of testimony given before Congress on policy proposals initiated elsewhere. When Congress wants information on international issues, its primary source is usually the State Department.

In a related fashion, officials in bureaus of other departments likewise speak in behalf of the interests of foreign nations. For example, in the Food for Peace program, which Congress enacted in 1966, the State Department and the Agriculture Department act in concert to supply commodities, particularly to developing nations. As noted earlier in this chapter, bureaus become advocates for their own functions, and, in foreign relations issues, may be the prime source of information available to congressmen who take part in making the policy.

There are informal and more personalized channels to congressional personnel. A substantial number of social affairs such as receptions, luncheons, and cocktail parties are sponsored by foreign embassies. These polite functions typically include members and staff from Congress. Washington social life plays an extralegal, but not insignificant, part in the communication network that undergirds the policy process. Distinguishing the formal and informal communications between diplomats and congressmen, former Senator Fulbright, chairman of the Senate's Foreign Relations Committee, observed that: "We have never, to my knowledge, invited diplomatic agents, except to lunch. We never invited them to testify about a

---

#Foreign heads of state sometimes address a joint session of Congress. Courtesy requires the speaker to talk about "common goals of our countries" and other such high-level abstractions. It would be extremely bad form for such a guest to argue for some policy which the president opposes or is a matter of controversy in the American society.

bill or a piece of legislation that I have ever heard of."[45] But it is well known that congressmen and their staffs find it educational and often entertaining to travel to foreign countries for policy-related information. While abroad, they are accorded deference and hospitality as "very important people," and may develop a heightened appreciation for the policy perspectives of their hosts. There is no empirically defensible way to estimate how weighty these informal communications are in affecting policy, but a good deal of time and effort is expended on them.

A device not widely known to the public is that in which a foreign nation employs what one practitioner has called "nondiplomatic representatives."[46] It is but one form of what Lewis Dexter refers to as "Washington representation." Specialists are for hire who are "ready to act in regard to policy implications of specific cases and situations; . . . they are Washington representatives in our sense."[47] Klein, the practitioner, says that, "Nondiplomatic representatives are unfettered by protocol. They can represent their client or interest to all segments and levels of the society in which they operate. They are not limited to presenting their client's position to their counterpart."[48] By the last sentence Klein means that a diplomatic representative is limited to communicating with one or a few specific officials. The nondiplomatic representative can function just like any American lobbyist in the regular policy process. One example of an issue that made the "nondiplomatic representatives" of other political systems visible in 1971 was the extension of the Sugar Act of 1948, as amended. Just to recap the issue, in 1934 Congress passed the first Sugar Act to stabilize the price and supply of sugar to American consumers while protecting domestic producers from foreign competition and allowing limited imports from favored nations. The act had been revised and extended several times. In 1971 it was extended until the end of 1974 (at which time the law was allowed to expire). A crucial characteristic of the act was that it set quotas for production: by law about two-thirds of the production was domestic; additionally, Congress determined quotas for production by other nations. Arguments for raising or lowering quotas for any particular country were highly variable. In 1971 Chairman Poage of the House Agriculture Committee, which developed the bill, said that the committee would consider past friendliness of quota countries, their dependability as suppliers, whether or not they bought American goods, their need for economic assistance, and whether the farmers and workers got benefits as well as large landowners and industrialists. Peru's quota was cut. It had recently expropriated American property. South Africa's was slightly cut, and several congressmen, including black members, sought to eliminate it entirely because of its policy of apartheid.

Table 5.2 shows the registered agents, their sponsoring countries, and their fees. Table 5.3 reports previous and 1971 quotas. Liberia, trying to break into the quota list, failed despite having a well-paid former congress-

Table 5.2 Nondiplomatic Representatives, Countries Represented, and Fees

Agent	Country[a]	Fee[b]
William R. Joyce, Jr.	Argentina	$1000 per month
Alejandro Orfila		$12,000 per year
Robert C. Barnard	Australia	Bills for services
Cleary, Gottlieb, Steen, & Hamilton		
Hugh C. Laughlin	Bahamas	No amount listed[c]
Blake Franklin	Bolivia	$10,000 per year
Coudert Brothers		
Albert S. Nemir	Brazil	$180,000 per year
A. S. Nemir Associates		
Arthur L. Quinn	British Honduras	$10,000 per year[b]
Arthur Lee Quinn		
Thomas H. Boggs, Jr.	Central America	$36,000 to $50,000
Patton, Blow, Verrill, Brand, & Boggs		per year
Tom Kuchel	Colombia	$200 per hour (in last six-month period reported $13,156)
Dina Dellale	Costa Rica	$15,000 per year
James N. Juliana	Dominican Republic	$3000 per month
James N. Juliana Associates, Inc.		
Arthur L. Quinn	Ecuador	$25,000 per year
Arthur Lee Quinn		
Daniels & Houlihan	England	$18,000 per year
Charles H. Brown	Fiji	$2000 per month
Walter S. Surrey	Guadeloupe, Martinique	$12,500 per year
Surrey, Karasik, Greene, & Hill		
Philip F. King	Haiti	Expenses only
Michael P. Daniels	India	$25,000 per year
Daniels & Houlihan		
George W. Bronz	Ireland	Bills for expenses
Harold D. Cooley	Liberia	$10,000 fee plus $1000 per month
Walter S. Surrey	Malagasy Republic	$25,000 per year

Table 5.2 cont'd.

Agent	Country[a]	Fee[b]
Surrey, Karasik, Greene, & Hill		
Jerry Collier Trippe	Malawi	$15,000 per year
W. DeVier Pierson Sharon, Pierson, & Semmes	Mauritius	$25,000 per year
Dennis O'Rourke Sutton & O'Rourke	Mexico	$4000 per month
Arthur L. Quinn Arthur Lee Quinn	Panama	$18,000 per year[b]
Sheldon Z. Kaplan	Paraguay	$500 per month
Prather, Levenberg, Seeger, Doolittle, Farmer & Ewing	Peru	$15,000 per year[d]
John A. O'Donnell	Philippines	$3750 per month (does not include bonuses in recognition of services. Last reported bonus was $6000)
George C. Pendleton Culbertson, Pendleton, & Pendleton	Republic of China	$600 per month
John Mahoney Casey, Lane, & Mittendorf	South Africa	$20–$65 per hour (reported $38,573 receipts for past year)
Justice M. Chambers	Swaziland	$20,000 per year
Harold D. Cooley	Thailand	$15,000 per year
Andreas F. Lowenfeld Fox, Flynn, & Melamed	Uganda	$16,000 per year
Edward L. Merrigan Smathers & Merrigan	Venezuela	$50,000 per year[b]
Arthur L. Quinn Arthur Lee Quinn	West Indies	$35,000 per year[b]

[a]Includes private and government interests.

[b]Fee includes expenses.

[c]Laughlin is not listed as a foreign agent because he represents a U.S.-owned firm. No amount was listed under his lobby registration with the House Clerk.

[d]From lobby registration filed with House Clerk.

SOURCE: *Congressional Quarterly Weekly Report*, May 21, 1971, p. 1133.

Table 5.3   Foreign Sugar Quotas: Existing, Proposed, and New[a]

Producing Area	Existing Quota (tons)	House Proposal (tons)	Senate Proposal (tons)	Final New Quota (tons)
Argentina	67,102	76,050	67,062	76,050
Australia	203,785	206,025	196,162	203,785
Bahamas	10,000	33,537	10,000	27,000
Bolivia	6,494	17,005	6,193	6,193
Brazil	545,581	525,737	577,904	547,905
British Honduras	13,752	33,537	14,874	33,537
Colombia	57,723	73,688	61,047	67,368
Costa Rica	64,217	65,185	71,110	68,610
Dominican Republic	545,481	525,737	659,874	634,874
Ecuador	79,370	80,774	79,084	80,774
El Salvador	39,682	40,151	43,964	42,693
Fiji	44,719	44,806	43,034	44,719
French West Indies	59,384	0	63,868	0
Guatemala	54,115	55,265	59,835	58,350
Haiti	30,305	30,704	30,305	30,704
Honduras	6,494	17,005	6,494	11,750
India	81,514	82,494	77,973	81,514
Ireland	5,351	5,351	5,351	5,351
Malagasy Republic	9,623	15,075	9,223	12,149
Malawi	0	0	0	0[b]
Mauritius	18,681	30,150	17,761	30,150
Mexico	557,748	537,545	590,894	561,581
Nicaragua	64,217	65,185	64,217	64,217
Panama	40,406	41,567	40,406	41,567
Paraguay	0	15,116	0	6,193
Peru	435,087	418,982	391,839	391,839
Philippines	1,362,120	1,314,020	1,300,264	1,314,020
Republic of China	84,910	85,844	81,734	84,910
South Africa	60,003	60,300	57,745	57,745
Swaziland	7,359	30,150	7,084	30,150
Thailand	18,681	18,844	14,152	18,681
Uganda	0	15,075	0	15,075
Venezuela	27,419	36,845	61,025	61,026
West Indies	188,777	192,251	204,520	204,520

[a]"New" refers to 1971.

[b]Granted a quota to take effect in 1973.

SOURCE: *Congressional Quarterly Almanac, 1971* (Congressional Quarterly Inc., 1972), p. 481.

man (who had previously been chairman of the House Agriculture Committee) for its agent. On the other hand, Mauritius did very well, nearly doubling its quota. Brazil paid most, but for only a trifling increase in its quota. There is no obvious relationship between fees paid and quota changes.

Nondiplomatic representatives of foreign countries or corporate interests within them behave similarly to lobbyists for domestic interests. Their public relations problems may be somewhat different—imagine representing Germany or Japan in the early 1950s or South Africa at present. In some instances their clients have difficulty understanding the complexity of the American political system. But the basic task of acting in the client's interest to enhance its image before various segments of society and to participate in the policy processes that have implications for the client is the same as for lobbyists of domestic interest groups. But that is a topic which will be discussed in more detail in Chapter 10.

CONCLUDING OBSERVATIONS

This is a book on the legislative process. But to understand this process one must have a good grasp of how authorities from parts of the governing system other than the legislature, and even officials from other political systems, are involved in what legislatures do. Some specific ways in which they are subject to the legislature have been outlined. Their dependency is a basis for their activity to affect what legislatures do. For example, bureaucrats are not merely servants who carry out policy determined elsewhere; frequently they are advocates for their agencies and for certain ways of dealing with specific societal problems. Courts have more discretion over some legislative decisions than others. Innovations developed slowly and painfully in one political system are sometimes picked up and quickly copied in others.

Interactions within and between political systems are especially numerous in American society with its federal structure of governments. In the vast complex of overlapping authorities, legislative bodies typically provide ready access to officials from other branches and from other levels. It is well to be aware of how penetrable the legislative process is to the large number of public officials who are not members of the legislative subsystem. They impinge upon that process in a special way because of their official status.

Of course, legislatures are not at their mercy. The legislative subsystem can both make substantial responses and generate its own initiatives. The next section of this book considers the legislative system in detail, beginning with a brief chapter that describes the range of options legislatures command in the process of policy making.

NOTES

1. For descriptions of organization and legal authority of the national bureaucratic subsystems, see the most recent annual *United States Government Organization Manual* (Washington, D.C.: General Services Administration), available from the superintendent of documents. Most states publish a biennial manual or bluebook that describes state structure and organization (the quality of description is uneven from state to state) and usually it is available from the office of the secretary of state.

2. For a readable and more thorough treatment of policies and their legal bases, see Don Allensworth's discussion of housing, urban planning, transportation, and environmental policies in *Public Administration: The Execution of Public Policy* (Philadelphia: J. B. Lippincott Co., 1973).

3. See, for example, Dean E. Mann, "The Selection of Federal Political Executives," *American Political Science Review* 58, no. 1 (March 1964): 81–99; John J. Carson and R. Shale Paul, *Men Near the Top: Filling Key Posts in the Federal Service* (Baltimore: Johns Hopkins Press, 1966); Ira Sharkansky, *Public Administration: Policy Making in Government Agencies*, 2d ed. (Chicago: Markham, 1972); and W. Lloyd Warner, Paul P. Van Riper, Norman H. Martin, and Orvis F. Collins, *The American Federal Executive: A Study of the Social and Personal Characteristics of the Civilian and Military Leaders of the United States Federal Government* (New Haven: Yale University Press, 1963).

4. Allensworth, *Public Administration*, p. 194.

5. See Norman H. Martin, "Personalities of Federal Executives" in *The American Federal Executive*, eds. W. Lloyd Warner et al. (New Haven: Yale University Press, 1963), pp. 193–205.

6. Wildavsky, *Politics of the Budgetary Process*, p. 19.

7. For a fascinating case study, see John C. Donovan, *The Politics of Poverty*, 2d ed. (Indianapolis: Pegasus, Bobbs-Merrill Company, Inc., 1973). See particularly Chapter 2, "The Executive Writes a Bill," pp. 27–38.

8. Charles E. Lindbloom, "The Science of Muddling Through," *Public Administration Review* 19, no. 2 (Spring 1959): 79–88; quotation is from p. 80.

9. Ira Sharkansky, *The Politics of Taxing and Spending* (Indianapolis: The Bobbs-Merrill Company, Inc., 1969), p. 200.

10. Louis C. Gawthrop, *Administrator Politics and Social Change* (New York: St. Martin's Press, 1971), p. 28.

11. *Daniel and Kyles* v. *Paul*, 395 U.S. 298 (1969).

12. See *The Supreme Court: Justice and the Law* (Washington, D.C.: Congressional Quarterly Inc., 1973), Appendix, pp. 113–18.

13. *Baker* v. *Carr*, 369 U.S. 186 (1962).

14. 347 U.S. 483 (1954) and 349 U.S. 294 (1955).

15. *Escobedo* v. *Illinois*, 378 U.S. 478 (1964) and *Miranda* v. *Arizona*, 384 U.S. 436 (1966).

16. *Engel* v. *Vitale*, 370 U.S. 421 (1962).

17. *Abington Township School District* v. *Schempp*, 374 U.S. 203 (1963) and *Murray* v. *Curlett*, 374 U.S. 203 (1963).

18. *Roe* v. *Wade*, 410 U.S. 113 (1973) and *Doe* v. *Bolton*, 410 U.S. 179 (1973).

19. 396 U.S. 295 (1970).

20. 398 U.S. 333 (1970).

21. Oliver P. Field, *Judicial Review of Legislation in Ten Selected States* (Bloomington, Ind.: Bureau of Government Research, Indiana University, 1943).

22. See William J. Keefe and Morris S. Ogul, *The American Legislative Process: Congress and the States*, 3d ed. (Englewood Cliffs, N.J.: Prentice-Hall, Inc., 1973), pp. 451–52.

23. Quoted from J. W. Peltason, *Corwin and Peltason's Understanding the Constitution*, 6th ed. (Hinsdale, Ill.: Dryden Press, 1973), p. 29, based upon Justice Brandeis's concurring opinion in *Ashwander* v. *TVA*, 297 U.S. 288 (1936).

24. Kenneth N. Vines and Herbert Jacob, "State Courts," Chapter 8 in *Politics in the American States: A Comparative Analysis*, 2d ed. (eds.) Herbert Jacob and Kenneth N. Vines. (Boston: Little, Brown and Company, 1971), pp. 272–311, especially pp. 298–301.

25. *Watkins* v. *U.S.*, 354 U.S. 178 (1956).

26. *Barenblatt* v. *U.S.*, 360 U.S. 109 (1959).

27. 385 U.S. 116 (1966).

28. 395 U.S. 486 (1969).

29. *Gravel* v. *U.S.*, 408 U.S. 606 (1972).

30. For a discussion of the powers of the Supreme Court in relation to other branches, see Stephen L. Wasby, *Continuity and Change: From the Warren Court to the Burger Court* (Pacific Palisades, Calif.: Goodyear Publishing Company, Inc., 1976), pp. 97–98.

31. Quoted by Peltason, *Corwin and Peltason's Understanding the Constitution*, p. 27.

32. Daniel J. Elazar, *American Federalism: A View from the States*, 2d ed. (New York: Thomas Y. Crowell Company, 1972), pp. 47–48.

33. Ibid., p. 168.

34. *New York Times*, April 3, 1970, pp. 1 and 12.

35. *Massachusetts* v. *Laird*, 400 U.S. 886 (1970). The motion for leave to file a bill of complaint denied. See also *New York Times*, November 10, 1970, pp. 1 and 40.

36. 327 *Federal Supplement* 378 (1971).

37. 451 *Federal Reporter*, 2d series, 26 (1971); quotation from p. 34.

38. See John N. Kolesar, "The States and Urban Planning and Development," in *The States and the Urban Crisis*, ed. Alan K. Campbell (Englewood Cliffs, N.J.: Prentice-Hall, Inc., 1970), pp. 114–38, especially pp. 125 and 126.

39. Jack L. Walker in *American Political Science Review* 63, no. 3 (September 1969): 880–99. A less technical discussion by the same author is entitled "Innovation in State Politics" in *Politics in the American States*, eds. Herbert Jacob and Kenneth N. Vines. pp. 354–87.

40. Walker, "Innovation in State Politics," pp. 358–59.

41. Duane Lockard, *Toward Equal Opportunity: A Study of State and Local Anti-Discrimination Laws* (New York: Macmillan Company, 1968), pp. 20–21.

42. It should be noted that data for these conclusions were drawn mostly from interview responses by state administrators in 10 states. See Walker, "Innovation in State Politics," especially pp. 379–85.

43. For comments on this, see the testimony of George W. Ball, then Undersecretary of State, in *Activities of Nondiplomatic Representatives of Foreign Principals in the United States* in Hearings before the Committee on Foreign Relations, Senate, 88th Cong., 1st sess., 1963, pp. 11 and 15.

44. For a brief and up-to-date description of organization, see the most recent *United States Government Organization Manual*, published annually by the Office of the Federal Register, National Archives and Records Service, General Services Administration (Washington, D.C.: Superintendent of Public Documents, U.S. Government Printing Office).

45. Hearings before the Committee on Foreign Relations, Senate, 88th Cong., 1st sess., 1963, p. 17.

46. Julius Klein, President of Julius Klein Public Relations, Inc., in his prepared statement for Hearings before the Committee on Foreign Relations, Senate, 88th Cong., 1st sess., 1963, p. 1795.

47. Lewis Anthony Dexter, *How Organizations Are Represented in Washington* (Indianapolis: The Bobbs-Merrill Company, Inc., 1969), p. 10; see also pp. 26–29.

48. Klein, Hearings, p. 1795.

Inside the
Legislative
Subsystem

Legislatures are not easily understood. They are structurally complex, having two houses, many committees and subcommittees, and usually two party organizations. Their procedures are complex. "Parliamentary procedure" means something threatening to most people. Besides, so many forms of legislative activity go on at the same time: legislators move from committee proceedings to floor activity and back again, sometimes as advocates but mostly to render judgment on the advocacy of others. Legislatures are decentralized, so that different members act as public spokesmen, announcing what is going on—pointing with pride or viewing with alarm. Yet their messages are inconsistent or, sometimes, downright contradictory. The legislature has no single individual to speak in its behalf. Understanding of the two-party system helps one to sort out things, but not all issues divide legislatures along party lines. Besides, some legislators can better achieve their policy goals in a complex, difficult-to-master subsystem than in one that is simple, so they labor to prevent organizational and procedural simplification. For one thing, delaying legislation is a means of defeating it. Complexity and delays discourage public attention to the process, so that members who can manipulate such delays can use them to defeat new proposals.

The next chapters are not encyclopedic. They analyze the options and procedures by means of which legislatures carry out policy adoption. In policy adoption, legislatures engage in a filtering process, with some legislatures more porous than others. Sometimes they get clogged up. But the process is more than a filtering one, because new ideas for policy take form in the process. Some become policy quickly, while others die and disappear, and still others are given repeated consideration over a period of years. Legislatures and the authorities in them have a broad range of options for handling policy proposals. Chapter 6 clearly spells out several of these options. Chapter 7 identifies the key structural characteristics of legislatures and explains the implications of those characteristics. Because committees are so significant in legislatures, they are carefully considered. The discussion goes beyond structural description to examine the norms legislators apply to one another and their leaders. Similarly, bill procedure is given a thorough review, not for the details of rules, but to see the various decision points in the policy process. With the procedural context in mind, the structure and patterns of leadership offered by the political parties can be understood both for their strengths and frailties.

These chapters do not offer sufficient detail for one to become a master of legislative complexity. They outline the dimensions of complexity and the main patterns of legislative activity. They do not incorporate direct criticism or praise as much as they identify functions and assess the extent of their occurrence in contemporary legislatures. There is great vitality in American legislatures. In considering the basic patterns, imagine how you would work for your policy objectives in the legislative arena. Such vicarious involvement will help you to overcome the barrier of legislative complexity and to appreciate just how exposed legislatures are to societal pressures.

6

The Legislative Subsystem: An Overview of Policy Adoption and the Range of Options

American political systems are legalistic systems. While procedures within institutions may reflect custom and informal rules, the policies of the political system are formalized into law. Institutions are created by law (including constitutions) and spending is appropriated by law. As a child I could not understand why Congress, which made the laws, was never finished with its job. Weren't there enough laws? When would the job be done? The questions were naïve. I simply did not understand the continuing responsibilities of the legislative system. This chapter considers some of these issues.

POLICY ADOPTION

The primary function of the legislative subsystem for the political system is policy adoption. A legislature renders policy proposals that arise from throughout the political system into the authoritative language of the law. A policy enacted as law remains to be refined by application and judicial interpretation, but it is authoritative. It is binding upon the society. It is to be enforced. By flouting it, a person makes himself vulnerable to a long and painful hassle. Enactment, or as I prefer to call it, policy adoption, is a central function for the whole political system, and the subsystem that majors in this function is the legislative subsystem.

155

A basic rule of the policy adoption process is that for a bill to become law majorities in each of the two houses must approve it in the same form. I will elaborate on structure and procedure in the next two chapters, but this rule bears on my characterization of the legislative subsystem as chiefly concerned with policy adoption. Adoption implies accepting something that one did not originate or create. Legislative bodies are made up of colleagues, relative equals. To enact policy, a majority must act in concert. It is very difficult for a majority—a substantial number of policy participants—to literally create, initiate, author, or originate policy together. In fact, they do not. Policy proposals are initiated throughout the political system; ideas come from citizens, groups, social critics, other political systems and subsystems, individual legislators, staff people, and the like. These ideas may be promoted by political leaders within or outside the legislative subsystem. Typically the chief executive majors in this function. But policy adoption, accomplished by the action of a majority of legislative colleagues, tends to be a responsive action. This is not to say that the legislative subsystem is simply passive. But policy adoption is a culminating activity.

Legislators, including those holding positions of leadership, often act as advocates of particular policies, but advocacy is definitely an individual mode of behavior. It stretches reality out of shape to argue that Congress or a state legislature is an advocate, an initiator, or a policy promoter. The legislative subsystem incorporates an arena to which initiators, including its own members, come to obtain policy adoption. It is probably accurate to say that most legislators, in their individual activities, spend more of their time and energy in policy adoption than in policy initiation or promotion. They are considering, listening, reviewing, evaluating, and criticizing proposals generated and promoted by others much more than they are creating proposals of their own and/or actively enlisting the support of others for some specific proposal to which they have committed themselves.

The legislative subsystem is best understood as a responding subsystem. There is opportunity within it for creativity and innovation, but these activities are secondary. The policy adoption process is complex and time consuming. Choices must be made about priorities. A variety of policy alternatives must be weighed in relation to particular problems that can and should be confronted. Constituents, groups, and policy participants in other political subsystems want particular policies made authoritative to meet their specific needs. The legislative subsystem is a crucial bottleneck in a political system that produces authoritative allocations of values. So there are continual pressures upon the legislative system to respond. And it does but, of course, not necessarily to the satisfaction of those in the society with wants, interests, and demands. More often than not, the response is a negative one—the legislature adopts some policies, but not nearly the number of policies nor the specific provisions demanded of it.

There is a scarcity value operating in the legislative subsystem. More policy is demanded than is adopted. Of course, a legislature could vastly increase its production by simply adopting all proposals coming before it. Obviously, however, this would produce chaos. Various proposals contradict one another. So selecting among alternative proposals is a significant part of the policy adoption process. But the relevance of scarcity extends further. Legislatures probably never deal with all the issues for which contradictory alternatives have been proposed. For reasons of time, pressure, priority, and intentional omission, many issues are ignored. In a hypothetical sense there is a limitless supply of policy, but in an actual sense the legislative system does limit the supply. It may expend vast time and effort on regulating sugar supplies while ignoring the problem of delivering health care services.

Understanding the policy adoption orientation of the legislative subsystem, along with the policy promotion orientation typical of the chief executive, helps us understand a good deal of the rhetoric about the "rise of the executive and the decline of the legislature." [1] The "rise-decline" phrase does sum up a marked change in the American policy-making process during the last century. It hides a good deal too. During this century the society changed fantastically in size, wealth, and international involvement. Demands for authoritative policy expanded enormously. New means of communication and forms of media significantly changed those who could, would, and should be visible in leadership and policy promotion. Chief executives, often with the encouragement of legislators if not always legislatures, expanded their activities in policy promotion. Their attention to policy application, the traditional executive task of taking "care that the laws be faithfully executed . . . ," [2] was left more and more to their subordinates. Increasingly the chief executives gave attention to public policy prior to legislative handling rather than waiting around to affect it in application. In the meantime the scope of legislative activity did not decline. Actually it has grown, as legislative enactments have expanded the range of governmental regulation and service. The task of responding has itself grown so much that legislators have lessened their own activities in generating and promoting policy proposals.

It is true that legislatures have met the scarcity problem by trying to expand output. Sometimes enactments have given wide discretion to other agencies, including the chief executive, thus expanding their authority. For example, the president's discretion in wage and price controls is provided by law for a limited time period. This certainly does not diminish the function or powers of Congress. On the contrary, these facts testify to the significance of Congress. The situation in the states is essentially similar, except that disparity between the chief executive and the legislature is less apparent. State executives are subject to less flexible constitutions and they have no international relations responsibilities. The prerogatives of the president, in contrast to the other branches, are clear in foreign policy even though the limits on those prerogatives are not.

The policy process is complex, with basic changes in policy priorities often taking a long time. The legislative subsystem has a significant function in the process, and its participants may frustrate, as well as be frustrated by, the activities of authorities in other subsystems. The authority of the legislative subsystem is broad and therefore the policy adoption in which it engages substantially shapes what the content of public policy is and will become.

THE RANGE OF OPTIONS IN THE LEGISLATIVE SUBSYSTEM

The legislative subsystem has a great range of options available to it in the policy adoption function. Some are specific accommodations to decisional options available to other subsystems. For example, the chief executive's veto power has its complement in the legislature's power to override a veto. The judicial subsystem can invalidate a law on constitutional grounds, but the legislature can propose constitutional revision. The bureaucracy may apply public policy in a way that distorts legislative intent, but the legislature can amend the original act to make its intent clear. There is no policy-making mechanism which is beyond the reach and recourse of the legislative subsystem. Certain decisions may be untouchable—the chief executive's decision to recognize a country or grant clemency to a convict, a court's decision in a particular case—but the chief executive and the courts can be checked, even chastised, by the legislature.

The remainder of this chapter will be devoted to some options available in the legislative subsystem. While the list is not exhaustive, not mutually exclusive, nor are all the options of equal significance, it will help us to appreciate the significance of the legislative subsystem in the policy process and the significance of certain decision points. All involve both the discretion of individual members and the collective judgment of majorities in two houses.

1. To Introduce a Bill or Not To Introduce One

Legislation has its beginning in the form of a bill. Since bills may only be proposed by members, there is the possibility of great discretion here. Proposals of substantial merit could be precluded from legislative adoption if they were not introduced. The legislature could ignore everyone from the chief executive on down if bills containing their proposals were not offered for adoption. In practice this is rarely a barrier to policy proposers who are not legislators. For a chief executive, getting a policy proposal introduced in bill form is the least of his problems. In many states it is an honor to be the sponsor of one or more of the governor's bills. A governor may carefully distribute proposals to obtain "good sponsors" for his bills. Prestigious interest groups often have a similar problem—that is, choosing among willing legislators. Persistent constituents can usually get the legislator from their district to sponsor a bill. Except for residents of Nebraska, each constituent has at least two likely sponsors—his legislator in the upper house and the one in the lower. The existence of two channels probably helps to keep both open.

Bill sponsorship is an easy response. It requires little time or effort for the legislator to put in a bill. He needs only to rough out his ideas and the legislature's professional drafting bureau will render it into appropriate legal language and form. In the Ninety-third Congress (1973-74) 26,219 bills and resolutions were introduced. Introductions in the New York legislature exceeded 23,000 in 1971 and 1972. Even South Dakota had more than 1300 bills in 1971 and 1972.[3] Members may file as many bills as they wish. In addition, in Congress and in many states, a member may "sign on" as a cosponsor with other legislators. Practices vary in states, but often one member will sponsor a bill that is a duplicate of another member's. It is not uncommon for a member of the Senate to introduce a duplicate bill previously introduced in the House.

Most legislators occasionally (and some legislators often) introduce bills as a courtesy to some group or person, whether or not they really care for the particular policy solution implied in its content. Usually such decisions are not very noticeable to the general public. Perhaps unfortunately for Senator George McGovern, this courtesy may have hurt his presidential candidacy in 1972. Previously he had introduced a bill in behalf of the National Welfare Rights Organization which called for a minimum income for poor families of $6500 a year. During his own campaign, however, he advocated an annual $1000 per person income grant to all Americans as a substitute for the existing welfare program. His opponents, including Senator Hubert Humphrey in the California primary debates, suggested he was hypocritical, confused, or both. In fact, McGovern had never committed himself to the National Welfare Rights Organization plan, but out of courtesy to the group he had sponsored their bill to get it legislative consideration.

2. To Push a Bill or Not To Push It

The one who makes this decision varies with the origin of the bill and its scope. If the bill contains the chief executive's proposal for some significant change, the bill will be pushed by the executive's staff, administrative department spokesmen, and the executive's supporters in the legislature. The situation is similar for a major interest group's bill. However, if the bill is of modest scope and is not a proposal of the chief executive or a significant political interest group, then the choice is pretty much in the hands of the sponsor. Perhaps the legislator wants to get a state highway bridge built in his home district or he wants to change the length of the waiting period between the application for and receipt of a marriage license. A congressman may want to change federal regulations on libraries which are repositories for federal documents. He will have to decide whether or not the bill is important enough to him to spend time to get it passed. For a congressman especially, getting a relatively minor bill passed will take a great deal of effort—seeing that hearings are held, shepherding his bill through committees and subcommittees, winning passage in the first chamber, then going over to the second house for more of the same, and finally getting approval from the chief executive.

A legislator's political stature affects his potential for success. However, as a legislator's stature increases, so does the pressure from others, within and outside the legislature, for him to push for or against bills of larger scope and more controversial nature. The "pushing" decision is a significant one to a legislator, and his choices, his visibility, and his success affect the development of his stature in the legislative process. A point worth noting here, but to be enlarged on later, is that it is usually easier to defeat a bill than to get it passed. This is especially true in Congress, but it is also the case in many states. Thus the choice to push against a bill may be easier, less time-consuming, and likelier to succeed than the choice to push for one.

3. To Pass a Bill or Not To Pass It

This, of course, is a collective decision, comprised of the individual voting decisions of the members, made separately in each house of the legislature. Many bill decisions fit within a pattern of previous and later decisions in a substantive policy area. Some are unique to particular circumstances. For major bills the decision is usually the culmination of complex interactions and long consideration. Many bill decisions are routine and sometimes rapid. Bill passage patterns will be discussed in more detail later. The "to pass or not to pass" decision point is a crucial one in the legislative process; it comes up in a variety of forms—to spend or not to spend, to spend more or less, to consent or not to consent to an appointment, to include or not to include an amendment, to pass one policy instead of another, to legislate a policy or to legislate none.

4. To Make a Permanent Policy or
To Make a Temporary One

Some legislation is designed to be enduring, but much is not. In Congress, for example, the Legislative Reorganization Act of 1946 restructured the entire congressional committee system and expanded legislative staffing. The Taft-Hartley Act of 1947 set up new rules and procedures for regulating conflict between business and labor unions. These laws were written to be enduring, and most of their provisions remain in force today, but this does not mean they are exempt from change. Both have been changed in important ways by subsequent laws which amend the original provisions.

However, a great many policies are put into effect on a temporary basis. The Voting Rights Act of 1965 was a major, innovative piece of legislation, but its major provisions to encourage voting, particularly by blacks in the South, were only to remain in law for five years. The act was written to expire in 1970. During 1970 Congress considered the provisions of the 1965 act anew, made some amendments (including the 18-year-old provision), and extended the law to 1975. Revenue sharing, a significant departure from past policies of federal aid to states and localities, was passed in 1972 as a five-year program. It is renewable, but without the expenditure of a substantial amount of energy in the legislative process, that program will simply expire in 1977. The same is true of numerous other public policies, including the Sugar Act, mentioned in Chapter 5.

Appropriations for the budget last only a single year, so that appropriations must be made on an annual basis. Every year the spending units of the political system must stand scrutiny for the funds to be extended in the upcoming year. Long-term spending plans in American politics are highly tentative. Such plans are often written, but during the term of the plan new considerations may arise, such as competing appeals for money. The War on Poverty was such a plan. The "War" was lost, not because poverty put up such a fight, but because demands for massive military spending in Southeast Asia were granted higher priority and political approval.

On any given policy problem, the legislature can attempt to create an enduring policy or a temporary one. Even those passed as "enduring" can be modified with new legislation. But American policy making, particularly through its legislatures, tends to be oriented toward the near future—next year or the next few years. So the majority of policies, particularly at the national level, are enacted on a temporary basis and are subject to periodic reconsideration.

5. To Regard or Disregard
Parochial Interests

Legislators hold their positions at the pleasure of the constituency that elects them. Constituencies vary in the extent to which they are similar to the system constituency, whether that is a state or the entire country. Some public policies affect specific constituencies more than others; they satisfy or offend such constituencies more than those in the rest of the system. For example, the oil depletion allowance issue stirs more concern in oil production areas than in other areas. So do military spending and space exploration which affect people who work for contractors in the aerospace industry and at military installations. Legislators themselves are uniquely affected by some policies, for example, apportionment decisions. What consequences will boundary changes have? If new voters are incorporated into the constituency, will they defeat a "strange" incumbent? These kinds of considerations affect legislators in their decision making. Should they reflect the narrow and provincial interests close to their immediate constituency or their own career, or can they look to the broader needs and interests of the system as a whole? Is some compromise available? Obviously there are many occasions when choices of this sort must be made by the legislator.

6. To Enlarge or Not
To Enlarge the Conflict

In a stable organization, decision making becomes routinized and patterned. Most legislatures are stable in this sense. There may be alternative procedures for getting bills through, but certain ones are typical. Additionally there are extraordinary channels and procedures too. A particular issue or policy proposal may regularly be disposed of in the standard process, but a member who is exasperated with what typically happens may take the extraordinary channels. In the United States House, for example, most bills die in committee. However, a member may petition to get the bill out of committee and, with the help of a majority of all the members of the House, it can be pried out of the committee's control. Similar procedures are available in the states. The disgruntled member using such a tactic has *enlarged the scope of the conflict.* Unable to succeed with the committee, a small subsystem, he appeals to the whole house to decide the matter.

There are other ways of enlarging the scope of a conflict. Legislative committees having difficulty maintaining oversight of particular bureaus through their ordinary committee hearings may launch a special investigation. Armed with a resolution from its chamber and perhaps a special appropriation to pay for extra staff, the committee can hire investigators to do a much more thorough inquiry than would be typical. Such a device can be used in a rivalry with the chief executive. The significance of the Senate Select Committee on Presidential Campaign Activities, which held the dramatic and nationally televised hearing on Watergate, illustrates the point beautifully. Senator Ervin and the other senators, staff members, and witnesses discussed not only campaign improprieties, but the very functioning and decision-making processes within the White House and in top departmental offices. The committee's basic legal power was to recommend new legislation on presidential campaign practices. But its significance was really in publicizing evidence of corrupt practices by an incumbent president's campaign team (many of whom had been part of his administration) and hinting that only the tip of the iceberg had been revealed. The Select Committee hearings and events attendant to them made politically possible another enlargement of the scope of conflict—namely, the House Judiciary Committee impeachment hearings.

To me the significance of the McCarthy presidential campaign in 1968 lay in its enlargement of the scope of conflict concerning the Southeast Asia war. Eugene McCarthy was but one of a few vocal doves in the Senate. In 1967 and early 1968 the antiwar movement was getting nowhere in the policy process. However, with essentially a one-issue campaign and a cadre of youthful volunteers, McCarthy lost the New Hampshire primary against an incumbent president of his own party, but attracted the attention of a national electorate with his views concerning the war.* Shortly thereafter President Johnson withdrew from the contest. McCarthy went on to win some primaries, notably Wisconsin and Oregon, but his candidacy also stimulated Robert Kennedy to a candidacy of his own. The assassination of Kennedy, nomination of Humphrey, and election victory of Nixon are a matter of history. Yet the McCarthy challenge was a remarkable appeal concerning the president's war policy by a frustrated senator, over the heads of his colleagues in the Senate and his party's president in the White House, directly to the people. Its initial consequences were dramatic. An incumbent

---

*When students are asked about that primary, and reminded that McCarthy and Johnson were the major Democratic alternatives, most "remember" McCarthy winning. With his name on the ballot, he obtained about 42 percent of the vote, while Johnson obtained write-in votes to achieve about 48 percent. Subsequent analysis of the primary indicates that what became known as a McCarthy victory grew only partially from antiwar sentiments among the voters. McCarthy supporters were unhappy with Johnson, but more actually wanted a stronger war effort than those opposing the war. See Philip Converse, Warren Miller, Jerrold Rusk, and Arthur C. Wolfe, "Continuity and Change in American Politics: Parties and Issues in the 1968 Election," *American Political Science Review* 63, no. 4 (December 1969): 1083–1105, especially pp. 1092–95.

president withdrew as a candidate for reelection and new candidacies blossomed.†

A legislator occupies a formal position of limited power, but with the position goes access to the decision points in the policy process and sufficient political significance to attract attention. With skillful use of that access and significance, a member can attempt to broaden the scope of a particular conflict. Obviously, neither success nor failure is assured. The results are not inevitably good or bad. The McCarthy of an earlier era, Senator Joseph McCarthy, a young and ambitious politician, raised a tremendous public stir by his repeated "discoveries" of Communists in high places, particularly in the Departments of State and the Army. Broadening the scope of conflict is a tactic open to the ingenuity of the legislator who takes it up.

CONCLUDING OBSERVATIONS

The legislature is an arena of policy making that is rich with opportunities for its members. There is too much to do, too many bills to consider, a variety of opportunities to be aggressive or attempt to lead, but there are numerous colleagues pursuing their own careers with similar options. The options allow great discretion to the individual—selecting among initiatives from outside the legislature, introducing bills, advocating them, choosing between parochial and broader perspectives, fighting for policies within the conventional channels, or trying to enlarge the conflict. To adopt policy, the individual must work in concert with others to form working majorities that can win passage at the formal decision points in committees and on the floor of the legislature in an atmosphere of scarcity which requires priorities and harmonizing of policies with one another. The next two chapters will concentrate on the internal structure and norms of the legislative system.

NOTES

1. James MacGregor Burns makes the case for a strong presidential government. See his *Presidential Government: The Crucible of Leadership* (Boston: Houghton Mifflin Company, 1965). See also his critique of Congress in *The Deadlock of Democracy: Four Party Politics in America* (Englewood Cliffs, N.J.: Prentice-Hall,

†Two Republican House members tried to emulate McCarthy by challenging Nixon in 1972—California Representative Paul McCloskey, an antiwar advocate, and Ohio conservative, Representative John Ashbrook. Neither achieved much public attention in the 1972 primaries. They too tried to enlarge the scope of the conflict, but neither could arouse a following.

Inc., 1963). In stark contrast, see Alfred de Grazia, *Republic in Crisis: Congress Against the Executive Force* (New York: Federal Legal Publications, 1965). See also Alfred de Grazia, *Congress: The First Branch of Government; Twelve Studies of the Organization of Congress* (Washington, D.C.: American Enterprise Institute for Public Policy Research, 1966).

    2. United States Constitution, Article 2, Section 3.

    3. For Congress, see the *Congressional Quarterly Almanac*, vol. 30 (Washington, D.C.: Congressional Quarterly Inc., 1975), p. 29; for the states, see *The Book of the States: 1974-75*, vol. 20 (Lexington, Ky.: The Council of State Governments, 1974), pp. 84-85.

7

The Legislative Subsystem: Internal Structure and Norms (1)

The political system's function is to make authoritative public policy. The legislative subsystem's part in that general task is in policy adoption. For a political system to persist, it must satisfy the needs in the society by setting goals, meeting them, resolving conflicts, and accommodating demands for change. If the process is democratic, members of the society will have regular opportunities to choose and replace authorities of the political system, as well as to make policy demands that receive serious consideration in the policy process. In American political systems, representativeness has been institutionalized, particularly in the legislative subsystems. A persisting system becomes institutionalized—its structure, form, rules, and procedures are standardized, formalized, and regular.

Legislatures differ in the extent to which they are institutionalized organizations. Polsby has identified three aspects of legislative organization for comparing legislatures in order to describe "how institutionalized" a particular legislature is.[1] A highly institutionalized legislature is, first of all, *distinct and well bounded*. There are clear and specific channels of recruitment. It is hard to become a member. The sorting process for potential recruits is rigorous. Second, *its organization is complex*. A highly institutionalized legislature is marked by specialization of labor among its members. The members have widely shared expectations, or norms, about how their colleagues should behave as members. Finally, *items of internal business are taken up or decided according to rules and precedents, and disagreements are settled on the merits of the issue at hand.* Decisions about procedures are not decided according to personal favoritism or a "buddy system." Rules are made to apply as automatically as possible.

There is variety in the degree to which American legislatures are institutionalized. In this and the following chapter I will describe the implications and extent of specialization as well as the procedural regularities in legislatures, particularly in the way committees function. In the Congress there are real contrasts between the House and Senate. There are also marked differences between Congress and the state legislatures. While comparisons will be largely qualitative, many of the implications of legislative institutionalization will become apparent from the descriptions.

STRUCTURAL ARRANGEMENTS

A full discussion of structural details in legislative subsystems is not necessary for students who want a general understanding of the legislative process, its major participants, inputs, and outputs.[2] However, there are some essentials that must be described and the present discussion will be limited to those.

Bicameralism

Except for Nebraska's, national and state legislatures in this country are bicameral, consisting of two nearly equal chambers, or houses. This is a remarkable arrangement. In contrast, local governments in this country have "one house" legislative bodies: city councils, county commissions, school boards, and the like. The parliamentary systems, though they may in fact have an upper house (for example, the British House of Lords), make most of the policy decisions in one house. In Britain the powers of the upper house have been taken away by the lower, and at most the upper house can delay, not prevent, policy adoption. The American states and nation have persisted in the use of two equal houses in policy adoption.*

The traditional reasoning for a legislature consisting of two houses is probably best explained by summarizing some of the events of the Constitutional Convention and the arguments in behalf of the Constitution offered

---

*Some of the early states experimented with unicameralism, but Vermont, the last to abandon it, did so in 1836. Nebraska adopted it in 1934 as a response to the Progressive movement, efficiency and economy reformism, and a depression economy. For a review of those circumstances and a discussion of its effectiveness, see Richard D. Marvel, "A Member Looks at the Nebraska Unicameral," *State Government* 42, no. 3 (Summer 1969): 147–55.

by Madison.[3] The unicameral Continental Congress under the Articles of Confederation was associated with failure. When discussion of a new government took place, there was never much dispute about whether or not there would be two houses. However, there was a good deal of disagreement about what each would represent and how members of the upper house would be chosen. The lower house was to be elected directly by the people. A compromise between the large and small states provided that states would be represented equally in a Senate and senators would be selected by state legislatures. For Madison this was balanced representation, and the Senate would be a check on the House. "The necessity of a senate is . . . indicated by the propensity of all single and numerous bodies [such as the House] to yield to the impulse of sudden and violent passions, and to be seduced by factious leaders into intemperate and pernicious resolutions."[4] The Senate, less directly responsible to the people and their passions, could slow or prevent impulsive decisions. The longer (six years) and staggered terms (maximum change of one-third of the members every two years) would provide stability and a more knowledgeable legislature. The Senate could take a longer view of policy implications and consequences and be more national in its outlook. Its members would likely be men of national or, at least, statewide reputation, and as such they would be able to achieve the respect of world leaders. Thus the Senate's special powers, distinct from those of the House, would be to advise and consent in treaties and executive appointments. The House, according to the Constitution, would have the authority to originate all bills that raised revenue.

Comparison of the United States House and Senate

The actual differences between the House and Senate of the U.S. Congress are substantial and important. They arise out of the differences in size (the House has 435 members, the Senate has 100) and constituency (senators are elected from states and representatives from nameless districts).

1. The House is more anonymous and impersonal. With 435 members, House members are not well acquainted with one another. Not all are familiar to the press and gallery observers. They do not have assigned seats. Many rarely speak on the floor, and when they do, speeches are short. Debate is dominated by senior members from the committees and party leaders. Senators are much more easily recognized, share speaking privileges with fewer than a hundred others, have their own seats on the floor, and are likely to say something and be referred to by name when they come on to the floor.

2. House rules expedite business better and are more rigorously enforced than is the case in the Senate. In the House a specific time period for debate is assigned a bill, time is divided between proponents and opponents, and when time expires debate is terminated. Rarely does debate on a specific bill extend for more than one afternoon. Members literally ask for "one more minute." In the Senate the pace is more leisurely. Party leaders try to schedule bills, but changes in scheduling occur often. A senator who wants to participate in debate on a particular bill, but who will be out of town for some reason on the scheduled day, can ask that debate be held over for his convenience. Usually his request will be honored. Amendment rules are looser in the Senate and, with the use of amendments, issues may swiftly change from one substantive concern to quite another. Conventional wisdom suggests that "the House can function because of its rules and the Senate functions in spite of its rules."

3. House session business is handled faster. Business in the House is conducted with regimen and regularity. There are fewer roll call votes, less time spent on the floor, and fewer days in session, as Table 7.1 indicates.

4. Expertise and influence is more concentrated in the House. In all aspects of its functioning, the more extended division of labor in the House means greater specialization and differentiation of activity. Members serve on one or two standing committees. Senators often serve on three, each of which has fewer members than in the House, thus increasing the senator's responsibilities to each. In the House, a member rarely achieves a position of leadership in subcommittees, committees, or party with less than 10 years of seniority. Rank and titles come much more quickly in the Senate. The primary spokesmen on issues in the House are specialists from affected committees. Ordinarily formal leaders and members with substantial seniority dominate discussion in committees and on the floor. In the Senate where there is less specialization, looser rules, and an overabundance of work for

Table 7.1   Résumé of Congressional Activity in the 93d Congress

	First Session (Jan. 3–Dec. 22, 1973)		Second Session (Jan. 21–Dec. 20, 1974)	
	Senate	House	Senate	House
Days in session	184	175	168	159
Hours in session	1084	790	1068	813
Record roll calls (including House record teller votes)	594	541	544	537

SOURCES: *Congressional Record,* Daily Digest, December 26, 1973, D 1485, and *Congressional Record,* Daily Digest, December 20, 1974, D 1425.

all members, anyone who wants to pitch in on an issue may readily have his say and as much involvement as he cares to give it.

5. Senators have much more prestige. The Senate is the "upper house." Its members, being fewer in number and more visible, have higher status than House members. To Washington hostesses, two senators outrank 10 representatives every time. Senators represent an entire state, entitling them to "point with pride" or "view with alarm" any event or issue of some significance to their state. Representatives come from numbered districts which have no particular dignity or community identity. Because the office of senator is higher than that of representative, ordinarily its members have had more noteworthy presenatorial careers; in fact a normal pattern of upward mobility to the Senate is to have served previously as a representative or to have held statewide elective office such as governor, lieutenant governor, attorney general, or the like.[5] Members of the House, by contrast, are more likely to have served previously in other than statewide elected positions, particularly the state legislature or some local office such as mayor of a small town, county prosecutor, judge, or the like. Senators have more titles. As Table 7.2 indicates, in the majority party at least, almost all senators are chairmen of some committee or subcommittee, while a few are chairmen of several. In the House, on the other hand, nearly half the majority party members chair neither a committee nor a subcommittee, and of those who do, none has more than two titles.

6. Senate elections are more competitive than those for members of the House. Recent data for this was previously illustrated in Chapter 2. However, Table 7.3 reports a longitudinal study of comparative turnover in

Table 7.2 Distribution of Committee and Subcommittee Chairmanships Among Democrats in the Senate and House, 93rd Congress, 1st Session (1973)

No. of Chairmanships for Each Member	Senate	% of Democratic Senators	House	% of Democratic Representatives
5 or more	6	11	0	0
4	5	9	0	0
3	15	27	0	0
2	22	39	27	12
1	7	13	100	43
0	1	2	105	46
TOTAL:	56	101	232	101

SOURCE: Assignment data are from *Congressional Quarterly Weekly Report,* April 28, 1973, pp. 960–88. My thanks go to Lowell Fentress for summarizing the data.

Table 7.3   Comparative Turnover of U.S. Representatives and Senators, 1914–1958

Office	No. of Offices	No. of Elections	No. of Personnel Changes	Turnover Rate
Senator	96	819	399[a]	.487
Representative	435	9507[b]	2228	.234

[a] Personnel changes among senators were determined for each seat of the pair from each state.

[b] Reapportionment makes perfect tracing of turnover impossible. Where districts were substantially redrawn, the count of electoral turnover started anew with the new apportionment. Therefore the figure stated does not include all changes of representatives for the period.

SOURCE: Adapted from Joseph A. Schlesinger, *Ambition and Politics: Political Careers in the United States* (Chicago: Rand McNally & Company, 1966), p. 40.

the House and Senate from 1914, when senators were first elected, through 1958. Senate constituencies, generally larger in population than those for House members, are more heterogeneous and diverse in the political interests they contain. House apportionments often intentionally concentrate particular kinds of people in specific districts in order to make the districts relatively homogeneous in population characteristics.

7. *The Senate tends to make more liberal policy adoptions than the House.* This tendency is not true in all policy areas, and may be a temporary phenomenon, but it seems to be warranted at least since the 1960s.[6] The statement is ambiguous without at least some specification of the key terms, liberal and conservative. In contemporary America liberals perceive the ills of society as curable, often by bringing the government's resources and policies to bear on them. They value change and new solutions to old problems. Where problems persist, liberals encourage governmental initiative to solve them. To the extent that this results in growing governmental power and centralizing of that power in the national government, they favor such growth and centralization. Conservatives value stability in the institutions and functions of government. The ills in society may appear less threatening to the conservative than the growth of government and its costs in attempting public policy approaches to these ills. Interhouse disagreements that fit the liberal-conservative description more often have the Senate position on the liberal side and the House position on the conservative side. This is noteworthy on appropriations bills. Typically the Senate is willing to spend more in policy solutions to problems than the House. In fact, in the Senate Appropriations Committee the working assumption of the members is to be more liberal than the House. Fenno quotes one senator as follows:

"They call us the 'upper body' because we 'up' appropriations, and it's true. We cut some, but usually we raise appropriations."[7] In domestic social welfare legislation Senate versions tend to enlarge the federal government's role more than those from the House. Some major policy innovations have been stymied in the House, despite passage in the Senate. Medicare legislation, for example, proposed in a variety of forms by presidents from Truman to Johnson, was not passed in the House until 1965. Once through the House, passage was easily obtained in the Senate. The one domestic policy area that has been a special exception to the general statement is civil rights legislation. The Senate, in which southern opponents have used the filibuster as a tool for opposition, has been difficult for liberals to break through. However the feat has been accomplished with bills passed in 1957, 1960, 1964, 1965, 1968, and 1970.[8]

Parallels and Differences in State Legislatures

In every state the upper house is smaller than the lower house. The proportional differences vary from state to state. On one extreme is New Mexico with a ratio of 1 to about 1.7 (42 in the state senate and 70 in the house) and on the other is New Hampshire with a ratio of 1 to 16.7 (24 in the senate and 400 in the house). In a majority of the states, the ratio is between 1 to 2 and 1 to 4. Some legislatures are relatively small: Delaware has only 21 in the senate and 41 in the house. New Hampshire's is the largest. In most states the total is between 100 and 200 members.[9]

Data to evaluate the differences between chambers in the states in relation to the differences between congressional chambers are sparse. It is highly likely that anonymity tends to be greater in lower houses, but this is not likely to be a meaningful difference where both houses are relatively small. Where chambers are fairly large and ratios between them exceed 1 to 3, difference probably is meaningful. It is, of course, affected by variations across states in the time they spend in session.

As size increases, the tendency toward specialization ordinarily increases, and typically expertise, as in Congress, is more concentrated in the lower houses. Clearly there is more prestige in being a state senator than in being a lower house member. The ambiguity of titles is noteworthy. While members of the upper house are called senators, convention is less clear for lower house members because U.S. representatives are usually called *congressmen* and this title is not transferable to states. *Representative* is probably the most widely used title for members of the state lower houses, but there are alternatives, such as *assemblyman* and *delegate* or the more nondescript *legislator*. In senates more members bear a prestige title such as committee chairman. It is not unheard of for legislatures, especially in the upper house, to reshuffle the number and jurisdictions of standing committees so that every member of the majority party can be chairman of some committee.

No studies I know of report data which help to answer whether or not senate seats are more competitive than house seats, whether or not senates are more liberal, slower in their conduct of business, or less rigid in their procedures. Some of these notions suggest hypotheses for testing. It is doubtful that state senates tend to be more liberal than the lower houses. Prior to the reapportionment revolution of the 1960s, senates were further from the "one man, one vote" standard of fairness than were the lower chambers.[10] Research on the implications of post reapportionment impact suggests that fairer apportionment has had liberalizing consequences. Probably change has been greater in upper houses than in lower,[11] but at present there is no clear pattern, and circumstances vary from state to state.

Bicameral or Unicameral Legislatures?

The arguments for bicameralism should receive some comment. For instance, does a two-house system prevent hasty legislation? The answer must be *not necessarily*. Many examples could be cited, but to mention one congressional action, consider the Gulf of Tonkin Resolution, passed by Congress in August 1964. On August 2 North Vietnamese PT boats reportedly made an unprovoked attack on an American destroyer in international waters. A similar attack reportedly came two days later. On August 4 President Johnson met with congressional leaders and requested passage of a resolution clearly asserting that Congress backed the president in Vietnam. On August 5 leaders of both parties introduced identical resolutions in each house, including the following key statement: "That the Congress approves and supports the determination of the President, as Commander-in-Chief, to take all necessary measures to repel any armed attack against the forces of the United States and to prevent further aggression." August 6 was a day of committee testimony. In the Senate, consideration was by a joint hearing of the Armed Services Committee and the Foreign Relations Committee. The resolution was reported out by a vote of 31 to 1. The House Foreign Affairs Committee also held one-day hearings, reporting out the identical resolution 29 to 0. On August 7 the House adopted its resolution by a 414 to 0 roll call. The Senate adopted the House version the same afternoon by a vote to 88 to 2 (Oregon's Senator Wayne Morse, the only opponent in the Senate committee consideration, voted against, along with Senator Gruening of Alaska). In the years following the resolution, consideration of the factual background of the early reports, as well as the merits, meaning, and implications of the resolution have been debated ad nauseam. The point is clear: *bicameralism is not by itself a deterrent to hasty action.*

Data drawn from the states support the point as well. In committee and floor consideration of bills, it is not uncommon to hear a legislator remark in response to an objection, "There are details in this bill that can be cleaned up in the other house." Some bills get double treatment: as noted previously, identical bills may be introduced in both houses. Sometimes both survive the legislative process. In Illinois, for example, in 1965 the governor vetoed 48 bills which duplicated bills he had already signed. In 1967 he vetoed another 70 for the same reason. They were simply superfluous. Two houses may mean confusion, not careful review.

On the other hand some proposed legislation attracts little public attention or concern during its first consideration. However, passage in one house can arouse heightened publicity, editorial attention, and critical concern. These may stimulate broader consideration of the implications of the legislation when it is processed by the second house. In such cases there is a check against hasty legislation.

Is the unicameral legislature more vulnerable to pressures by lobbyists than a bicameral legislature? Arguments on this question have generated more heat than light. It is sometimes alleged that the unicameral legislature is all too sensitive and responsive to lobbyists.[12] Respondents argue that the one-house organization is simple, membership is small, there are no complex and secret negotiations between two houses, and therefore the opportunity for unscrupulous manipulation by interest groups is less likely in the unicameral legislature.[13]

Let me make a few observations and evaluative comments about the issue: (1) Comparable data on the influence of interest groups on legislatures are very difficult to obtain, and methodological problems make interpretations of such findings difficult. (2) A two-house arrangement means more barriers to passage, probably enhancing the success of groups opposing legislation; if this is the case, proponent groups may be more successful in a unicameral setting. Each arrangement has a unique bias, but the influence of interest groups is not prevented in either. (3) Perhaps more relevant to the impact of interest groups and lobbyists on the Nebraska legislature is the fact that it is nonpartisan and there is relatively little in the way of pattern and predictability in voting on issues.[14] Such a context is ideal for interest groups. "Pressure groups are strongest when political parties and legislative cohesion are weakest and when the socioeconomic variables [that is, urban population, per capita income, and industrialization] are lowest."[15] Nebraska is such an environment, and was found to have a "strong" pressure group system affecting its political process. In short, the nonpartisanship and cultural context of Nebraska politics may well be more relevant to the success of its pressure group system than the unicameral structure of its legislature.

One compelling argument for the unicameral legislature in contrast to the bicameral is the clarity and simplicity of its procedures. Much of the complexity of bicameral legislatures arises from the fact that there are two chambers and both must pass the same bills, with both frequently exercising their respective rights to amend the other's bills. This necessitates conference committees and more procedure, which will be discussed in detail later in the chapter. Legislative politics is confusing and mystifying, even to close observers and members, because of the complexities of structure that stem in part from bicameralism. Democratic participation is enhanced by citizen understanding, and to the extent that the legislature is not very comprehensible, it discourages participation and community support.

One aspect of bicameralism may be of dubious value and have its remedy in unicameralism. In the era of executive leadership and preeminence, the legislature is the main rival and check on executive power. But the legislature, divided as it is, consumes much of its members' energy in the rivalry between the two houses. Besides, a bicameral legislature has no single legislative spokesman. In a unicameral legislature with a single chamber, the elected head (by whatever title: speaker, president, majority leader, or the like), the leader could speak with one voice in behalf of the legislature in competition with the chief executive. A unicameral legislature might well be a more effective competitor with its main rival, the chief executive.

To me the most significant characteristic of the legislature is its task of providing representation for and access to the political community. The paramount activity of legislators is the representation of their constituents. In a bicameral arrangement the constituent has "his senator" and "his representative." They should function as the citizen's points of access. Continuing citizen support for the political system depends in part upon the rapport between the legislators who adopt policies and the people who must live under those policies. As constituency size increases, the difficulty of a citizen to be heard will also increase. However, a senator, with the larger constituency, doubtless listens more closely to his constituents precisely because he has a rival listener, the representative, who competes for their attention as well.

In this context let me comment on one of the arguments for unicameralism. It is that a unicameral legislature is more "efficient and economical" than a bicameral structure. Surely the argument is true, and it focuses on direct dollars and cents cost of operating a legislature. It is true that Congress would be millions of dollars a year cheaper to maintain without the House of Representatives. Further millions could be saved with only one senator per state. Great duplication of effort would be eliminated. But the suggestion is ridiculous because the savings would be at the cost of the citizens' opportunities to be represented. Saving money, while losing representation of the essential interests of the public, is false economy. Reducing representation restricts channels by which the people express their demands to those who govern. The hidden cost in such "reform" is a loss in the capacity for representation.

It is sometimes argued that "one man, one vote" has eliminated the distinctiveness of the two chambers. While a distinctiveness may have been reduced, it has not been eliminated. Variations in constituencies because of size and different degrees of homogeneity and competitiveness will produce different coalitions of supporters on particular legislative issues. Access to the two houses will not be the same. For example, committee arrangements and jurisdictions will differ nearly everywhere because typically lower houses have more committees than upper ones. It should be noted too that legislative office opportunities are not important for their own sakes only. They are a major entry point for budding political leaders, some of whom will earn their political spurs there and move up to higher offices in the state and national political systems.

Perhaps the considerations argued above are "only academic" in the sense that there is little pressure for or likelihood of change in political structure toward unicameralism. It is true that tradition is a powerful argument for particular structural forms. When Alaska drafted its constitution prior to statehood, consideration of a unicameral legislature ended when its opponents argued that Congress might not grant statehood if a unicameral legislature were part of the proposal.[16] In state constitutional revision such proposals usually die in the face of the argument that incumbent legislators will campaign against such a proposal which, in nearly all states, must be passed in a public referendum. Nevertheless, public moods do change and the arguments in behalf of unicameralism are not insignificant. Probably they will be most appealing in the smaller population states which are relatively homogeneous in social/political characteristics and in which representational problems are not particularly salient.

COMMITTEES IN THE LEGISLATIVE SUBSYSTEM

While social critics are rarely satisfied that legislative committees "do as they ought," no legislature tries to function without them. Even the sharpest critics do not call for the abolition of committees, but there are constant appeals for reorganization and different rules for leadership selection, member participation, and bill consideration procedures.

Committees are best understood as *subsystems* of the chambers they serve. In the same sense that legislatures are subsystems of the larger political systems, committees assume a significant part of the legislature's job, but they cannot and do not do the whole job. A committee is a subset of a legislative body, and its members specialize in considering, preparing, evaluating, and recommending a specific subset of the policy proposals placed before the legislative body for policy adoption.

To understand legislative committees, it is crucial to realize that they are substantially influenced by the expectations of external groups.[17] Four are particularly prominent: those from the legislative system itself, especially the parent house; those from its client systems and subsystems (chief executive, bureaucratic subsystems, and the like); those from its constituents; and those from the political parties. The relative prominence of these four categories may vary from political system to political system, but the order given above is likely to be typical. This is a tentative generalization, however, and three reservations should be noted. First, in states with strongly organized parties (such as Massachusetts or New York), the expectations of the party leaders may take unusual significance. Secondly, there are variations in the prominence of the four categories for different committees within a given legislative house. The parent chamber may exercise much stronger effort to impose house expectations on one committee than on another. Third, each of these external groups consists of many people and the degree to which there are consensual expectations from each may vary from system to system or over time within a particular system. Even the chief executive may be much more concerned about the activity in an appropriations committee in one set of circumstances than in another.

My remarks thus far should make it clear that committees are certainly not all alike. They differ within a particular legislative house, and they certainly differ across political systems. On the other hand the variation is not ideosyncratic (totally unique to each committee in each legislature); rather it is patterned in relation to some specific variables.† Let me suggest some values associated with committees and the expectations various groups may have of them. These will help you understand both how legislative committees function and how they may vary from place to place.

---

†In this case the variables have not been carefully observed and measured in more than a couple of systems at specific times. The Fenno book is a significant work. However, it examines carefully only six committees of the U.S. House and briefly compares them to six counterpart committees in the Senate. The basic data of Fenno's study are from interviews conducted with numerous political participants in the time period of 1959–68. Really comparable studies of state legislative committees do not exist. Political scientists have only begun to scratch the surface in this area of research.

Values

1. Committees should be specialized. This is the most pervasive expectation for committees. Legislatures have such broad jurisdictions in policy adoption and the matters in question are certainly too complex for all members to know and wrestle with in detail, so some functional division of labor must be arranged. Subsets of members will be assigned to deal with specific policy jurisdiction. The degree to which committee specialization will occur varies across systems. Certainly it is constrained by the size of the membership. Ordinarily there are more committees in the lower house than there are in the upper. However, the differences in numbers of committees are usually small and are not comparable to the differences in the ratio of lower house members to upper house members. For example, in Congress the ratio of House members to senators is 4.35 to 1. The House has 21 standing committees and the Senate has 17, a ratio of less than 1.2 to 1. Circumstances are similar in the states, although in a few states the smaller upper house actually has as many or more standing committees than the lower house.‡

It is commonplace for committee jurisdictions to be made according to substantive contents of policy proposals. There is usually an appropriations committee which considers spending bills, an education committee for educational policy, a judiciary committee for court management and criminal procedures, a taxation or revenue committee for raising governmental revenue, and so on. In some legislatures specialization is more detailed. Education policy is but a part of the U.S. House Education and Labor committee's jurisdiction. In some states, however, there may be separate committees for primary, secondary, and higher education. Some states have committees with few or no parallels elsewhere: in 1971–72 the Michigan House had a standing committee entitled "Youth and Student Participation."

Some committees have a special functional task rather than a subject matter jurisdiction. In the U.S. House, the Rules Committee has a unique function. Bills that do not have special "privilege" (most appropriations and taxation bills *are* "privileged") must receive a "rule" from the Rules Committee that defines when the bill can come to the floor, how long it will be debated, and the circumstances by which it can be amended. Most House bills receive consideration in two committees—first in the substantive one (for example, the Judiciary Committee) and then in the Rules Committee—

‡In South Carolina, the balance was senate 26, house 8; in New York, senate 24, house 21; in Washington, senate 17, house 17; in West Virgina, senate 17, house 13. Data for 1973 from *The Book of the States: 1974–75,* vol. 20 (Lexington, Ky.: Council of State Governments, 1974), p. 74.

before they can be considered on the floor. The House Rules Committee is primarily a traffic manager for the whole membership, although from time to time it has used its discretion over the flow of business to affect the content of policy proposals.§ In the states it is not unusual for a chamber to have a committee with an ambiguous jurisdiction (sometimes titled "Executive Committee") to which bills of a highly partisan nature are referred. The majority party leadership may use it regularly to kill bills or sometimes to hold them there as "hostages" for trading with other legislators or external leaders, such as the chief executive. The specific function of such a committee is to give a particular group in the chamber, ordinarily the majority party leaders, resources for influence. The specialty of the committee is in drawing fine partisan political distinctions in the policy process.

An important variable affecting the degree of specialization in committees is the legislature's expectation of *reciprocity*. Reciprocity refers to the exchange of privileges, respect, or assistance on the part of two or more actors. In a legislature, reciprocity may take numerous forms. "You vote for my bill and I'll vote for yours" is a highly individualistic form. It may apply to committees: "You respect our committee reports and we will respect yours." Matthews, in his study of the U.S. Senate, noted that, "the

§For the most comprehensive study of this committee, see James A. Robinson, *The House Rules Committee* (Indianapolis: The Bobbs-Merrill Company, Inc., 1963). For a more recent assessment, see Douglas M. Fox and Charles H. Clapp, "The House Rules Committee's Agenda-Setting Function: 1961–1968," *Journal of Politics* 32, no. 2 (May 1970): 440–43; and, by the same authors, "The House Rules Committee and the Programs of the Kennedy and Johnson Administrations," *Midwest Journal of Political Science* 14, no. 4 (November 1970): 667–72. During Representative Howard W. Smith's tenure as chairman of the House Rules Committee (1955–66), he was well known for his skill in using the committee's discretion to obtain substantive changes in bills. See case studies such as those of the 1960 and 1964 civil rights acts, Daniel M. Berman, *A Bill Becomes a Law: Congress Enacts Civil Rights Legislation,* 2d ed. (New York: The Macmillan Company, 1966), and the Area Redevelopment Act of 1961, in John F. Bibby and Roger H. Davidson's "The Power of the Rules: The Tangled History of the Depressed Areas Question" in *On Capital Hill: Studies in the Legislative Process,* 2d ed. (Hinsdale, Ill.: The Dryden Press, Inc., 1972), especially pp. 214–17. By a series of events over time, the House has insisted that the Rules Committee return to the narrower function of managing traffic. See Robert L. Peabody, "The Decision To Enlarge the Committee on Rules: An Analysis of the 1961 Vote" in *New Perspectives on the House of Representatives,* Robert L. Peabody and Nelson W. Polsby eds. (Chicago: Rand McNally and Company, 1969), pp. 253–81. Fox and Clapp conclude that the committee's capacity to keep bills bottled up has been confined mostly to matters "of secondary importance," and even that capacity has declined noticeably since 1964.

In the Ninety-third Congress the Rules Committee suddenly seemed more liberal than the House as a whole, and in 1973 alone the House rejected rules 13 times (compared to 50 times in the preceding 44 years). Before the Ninety-third Congress expired, however, there was some evidence to suggest that the Rules Committee had not forgotten how to play an obstructionist role. See "Rules Committee Regains Obstructionist Stance," *CQ Guide to Current American Government, Fall 1974* (Washington, D.C.: Congressional Quarterly Inc., 1974), pp. 43–49.

committees are highly autonomous organizations; the spirit of reciprocity suggests that it is best to allow other committees to go their own way if one's own committees are to enjoy a similar freedom." [18] In some chambers, certainly in both houses of Congress, the expectation of reciprocity is high. In fact, Fenno observed reciprocity in the relationships of subcommittees in the U.S. House Appropriations Committee. Mutual trust between subcommittees "becomes a basis for preserving subcommittee autonomy." [19] The expectation of reciprocity should be understood as a variable, not as a constant; that is, in Congress it is high. But it may not be high in many legislatures. It may be that a few, perhaps the large and prestigious committees, reciprocate with one another, but not with several others. Such considerations are affected by another legislative variable, the degree of turnover and stability in membership generally, and on committees in particular. If turnover on committees is high, specialization tends to be hampered, and the likelihood of intercommittee reciprocation will be low.

2. *Committees should be centers of expertise.* This expectation is closely related to that of specialization. Reciprocity will be facilitated if the committees are indeed centers of specialization and expertise. For example, a member of the education committee may be expected to spend hours and days in attending hearings, considering bills, voting on amendments, dealing in policy details that are unlikely to get careful treatment at the floor stage when noncommittee members consider the legislation. In a four-state study of state legislatures, members were asked about their own areas of expertise and the reasons they could give for that expertise. A number of responses were offered, but the second largest category was "legislative assignment." The authors note that "the needs of the system play an important part in selection of a specialty. This category includes responses attributing expertise to information or interest acquired as a result of experience as a committee member or legislative investigator. This class of responses appears more frequently in Ohio and California, the two states [of the four studied, the others were New Jersey and Tennessee] where committees play an important part in the decisional process." [20] It is also the case that legislators tend to obtain assignments in relation to expertise that they bring to the legislature. The tendency is common to put educators on the education committee, lawyers on the judiciary committee, sheriffs on the county government committee, people with experience in the insurance industry on the insurance committee, and farmers and agri-businessmen on the agricultural committee. Thus it is noteworthy that the largest category of legislator's responses to explain their own expertise was their occupational experience.

The demand for expertise is not only a legislative pressure. It is expected by the bureaucracies, spokesmen from other systems such as local government officials, and interest group spokesmen. Spokesmen from these external groups want specialists and people who are knowledgeable. They expect that their arguments made in committee hearings will be more meaningful to experts than nonexperts, and if they can convince real experts, those experts will be effective proponents at other stages of the legislative process. Nonexperts, on the other hand, are more vulnerable to the "most recent advice" they have received. They change their minds and cannot be counted on to stay with a judgment that at one time they considered convincing.

The positive value placed on expertise offers the possibility of achievement to individual members. At the same time the potential for individual achievement makes the individuals defenders of the institution in which they serve. Speaking of the U.S. House, Polsby analyzes it this way:

> The increasing complexity of the division of labor presents an opportunity for individual Representatives to specialize and thereby enormously increase their influence upon a narrow range of policy outcomes in the political system at large. Considered separately, the phenomenon may strike the superficial observers as productive of narrow-minded drones. But the total impact of a cadre of specialists operating over the entire spectrum of public policies is a formidable asset for a political institution; and it has undoubtedly enabled the House to retain a measure of autonomy and influence that is quite exceptional for a 20th century legislature.[21]

The reward for expertise is getting one's legislation passed. In the California legislature, at least, experts authored significantly more successful bills that became law than did nonexperts.[22]

3. Committees should narrow the range of policy alternatives. Legislators and leaders of external interests agree that it is not good practice to try to rewrite legislation on the floor. A piece by piece amending process with all the members expected to vote item after item is broadly discouraged. Committees are expected to put forward well-constructed legislation and to discourage amendments. This is especially true in the U.S. House. Other legislatures vary; in many, committees will report out competing bills, two or three full-blown approaches to a particular policy problem, and let the whole house choose among the alternatives. Yet the committee has provided a valuable service by winnowing alternative approaches to a range of issues and putting together whole bills which are internally consistent and deal with a significant problem. Usually when there are major alternatives, spokesmen who present them on the floor are from the standing committee in which the bills were considered; thus the committee achieves for the house an orderly way of considering alternatives. In effect it manages a substantial amount of conflict by simplifying the whole house's choice. Again, such a procedure is often acceptable to clientele leaders. If the competition before the committee has been keen but not decisive, the spokesmen for the chief executive, bureaus, interest groups, and the like have the chance to consolidate support for their own preferences and/or opposition to the preferences of others.

One form of narrowing the range of alternatives, but seeing to it that the range is not too narrow, is for the committees to meet the expectations for essential policy. Bills from some committees are, at certain times, essential. For example, the Appropriations Committee has to produce annual appropriations bills. No matter how complex the matters or how intense the disagreement within the committee or with someone outside (typically the chief executive), the committee has to get bills out for the operation of the various agencies of the government. Budget bills are the most typical "must" bills, but there are others. Sometimes when "temporary" laws are about to expire, there is great pressure to renew or extend them. A frequent example in Congress has been the statutory debt limit. In the states new apportionment plans usually are "must" legislation.

4. *Committees should be a means of meeting the needs and goals of individual legislators.* Fenno argues that "Of all the goals espoused by members of the [U.S.] House, three are basic. They are: *re-election, influence within the House,* and *good public policy.* . . . All congressmen probably hold all three goals. But each congressman has his own mix of priorities and intensities—a mix which may, of course, change over time." [23] The mix of motives and the variation in constituencies of legislators make different committees appealing to different members. A legislator from a safe constituency may be able to seek a position that will give him influence in the legislature. He is likely to want a place that permits him to use his occupational experience, one in which he already has some expertise and may have particular policy goals. If he desires influence in his party, he may try for the Executive Committee. The legislator from a competitive district wants a committee that can enhance his chances for reelection. Perhaps the black voters in his district can provide a margin of victory. Service on the Civil Rights Committee may be desirable. If the constituency is rural and unemployment is high, perhaps the Public Works Committee is a way to get roads, bridges, and buildings into the district. Fenno found that differing member goals were significant to members' committee service. Studying six committees, he learned first that 81 percent of the members interviewed had deliberately worked to get the assignments they obtained. Secondly, assignments fit in with members' goal priorities. "Appropriations and Ways and Means are populated mostly by influence-oriented members; Interior and Post Office are populated mostly by re-election-oriented members; Education and Labor and Foreign Affairs are populated mostly by policy-oriented members." [24]

5. Committees should help in the advancement of political careers. Politics is a dynamic process with many forces for change. A significant kind of political pressure is ambition to attain political office. That objective achieved, political authorities seek to advance their careers. The advancement may be within the institution in which one has a position or it may be for some "higher" office. The latter politician has *progressive* ambitions.[25]

Committee arrangements are of obvious significance to progressively ambitious legislators. The committee is a place to make a reputation. In a state in which party organization counts, committee work is a way to show loyalty, vigor, and skill. Such effort may not be noticed by the news media, but it will be noted by political insiders—the party elders. It is worth mentioning that in a political system in which the parties are strong, it is not necessary for ambitious candidates to seek publicity. Organizational leaders are highly attentive to whether or not new legislators look promising. Upon choosing a legislator for advancement, the organization can provide public exposure to make election to a higher office possible.

Where the political environment is more fluid, the progressively ambitious legislator needs public exposure. This describes the situation in American national politics in relation to the presidency. The presidential nomination for the party that is out of power (the Republicans in 1968, the Democrats in 1972) is usually "up for grabs," with one or more senators likely to enter the fray. It is interesting to note that in 1973 one of the most visible Senate committees, the Foreign Relations Committee, had among its most recent five additions four men with conspicuous presidential ambitions: Senators Muskie, McGovern, Humphrey, and Percy. In state legislatures committee chairmanships and party leadership positions are prized for obtaining visibility and possible higher office.

There are external pressures upon committees in behalf of nonlegislators too. An ambitious chief executive can be helped or hindered by the makeup of key committees which will assume jurisdiction over major elements of his program. If a governor can, he will try to get committee appointees who will look favorably on his budget proposals. Such considerations can affect his public image, his potential for moving up toward the U.S. Senate or the presidency. These realities can be seen in the careers of governors such as Reagan (California), Askew (Florida), and Wallace (Alabama). It is also true of lower-level state executives, such as Adlai Stevenson III (Illinois), who moved from state treasurer to U.S. senator, and John D. (Jay) Rockefeller (West Virginia), secretary of state who failed in a bid for governor.

External groups, especially the political parties in strongly organized states, try in some cases to enhance opportunities for political careers, and in others to block them. Among New York and California legislators, it is a fact of life that the chief executive of their state is a perennial presidential prospect. In other states it is an occasional but significant fact, as it was in Michigan during Romney's tenure as governor, and legislators know they are within arm's length of affecting future national political directions.‖

Committees can make interest group leaders look good (or bad) to group members. The state highway builders' association may have relatively modest influence over state highway building policy, but if the Roads and Highways Committee appears to give the organization ready access or if the leaders can get the committee chairman to address the group at its annual convention, then the association's leaders probably look successful to the group's membership. These appearances may be crucial to the careers of interest group leaders.

6. *Committees should show responsiveness to public moods.* Political participants speak from time to time about legislation "whose time has come": legislation such as civil rights, Medicare, and others that were proposed and killed numerous times, but at some point a ground swell of support arose from somewhere. In 1964 the "time had come" for a strong civil rights bill, even though the congressional cast of characters had not changed substantially since the 1960 act, which Thurgood Marshall said "Isn't worth the paper it's written on." [26] In response to the public mood, stimulated as it was by the heroism of Martin Luther King, the March on Washington, and other civil rights events, committee consideration of the bill resulted in *strengthening* of the bill's legal requirements instead of watering them down, as in the past. The time had come for a substantial number of social welfare proposals in the Eighty-ninth Congress (1965–66), refreshed as the House was by the election of 48 northern Democrats and the loss of 10 southerners.

It is possible too for a legislature to respond to a mixture of public moods through its committees. As the Vietnam War took its course and there was a shifting polarity in opinion, the Senate Foreign Relations Committee heard and amplified the opinions of the doves, while the hawks received sympathetic hearing from the Senate Armed Services Committee.

7. *Committees should contribute to enhancing the image of the political system, the legislature, and important political authorities.* There is a concern in all political systems by those who have authority positions to make the political system and its conspicuous institutions and leaders seem praiseworthy before the public at large. Certainly this is more conspicuous at the national level than in the states, but it can be noted in the latter as well. In the aftermath of Spiro Agnew's resignation from the vice-presidency, President Nixon named a House leader, Gerald Ford, to be his vice-

---

‖ As a student in a political field work assignment, I served briefly in the office of Romney's legislative aide. Legislators were from time to time reminded that their behavior would affect the governor's future and, if destiny beckoned, they too might be remembered.

president. The committee hearings on the nomination, especially in the House, were very probing. Evaluative comments, even from Ford's opponents, emphasized Ford's honesty and candor in sharp contrast with that of Agnew and then President Nixon. Consider too the Senate Select Committee on Presidential Campaign Activities which conducted the Watergate hearings. Early on, it moved very circumspectly in relation to the president. Seeking to obtain the president's tape recordings of proceedings in his office, the committee moved slowly, first requesting the tapes, seeking various compromises, and finally voting to subpoena them. Chairman Ervin then said:

> I deeply regret this action of the committee. . . . I was in hopes that the President would accede to the request of this committee for these tapes and these papers. I love my country. I venerate the office of the President, and I have the best wishes for the success of the . . . present incumbent of that office, because he is the only President this country has at this time. [27]

My assessment of the long Watergate hearings is that the committee tended to reflect the view that there was corruption and malpractice during the campaign and in the president's administration, but it was by bad people, not a bad political system. The hearings themselves were evidence that the political system works even in the face of serious maladies. Instead of being the committee's target, the president was given repeated opportunities to provide information and witnesses favorable to his position. The committee would have given public exposure to real evidence that the president was not directly responsible for the pattern of campaign immorality. The president did not provide such evidence. The appearance of contrary evidence, in the courts as well as in Congress, led to the impeachment hearings and Nixon's ultimate resignation.

It is instructive to look back at an earlier example of Senate investigations. Senator Joseph McCarthy, Republican from Wisconsin, made his career exposing real or imagined Communists in the Department of State and the United States Army. After the senator conducted numerous muckraking hearings, in December 1954, the Senate voted to censure him for his conduct. The censure resolution is noteworthy because it did not seek to punish McCarthy for hurting innocent citizens, soldiers, or State Department officials. It condemned the senator for having "affected the honor of the Senate," "obstructing the constitutional processes of the Senate," for conduct "contrary to Senatorial traditions," for having "acted contrary to Senatorial ethics and tended to bring the Senate into dishonor and disrepute, to obstruct the constitutional process of the Senate, and to impair its dignity." [28]

The committees have their part in contributing to the maintenance of the political system at large as well as the success of the legislature. While they are arenas of conflict, the committees are also agents of the legislature to make the whole system work and to publicize the views of those who believe the system does work. In return, good committees, good chairmen, and good committee members obtain recognition, opportunities to shape policy, and political advancement.

CONCLUDING OBSERVATIONS

The seven values suggested here do not comprise an exhaustive list, but they provide some insight into the legislative system. Some are regarded more highly within the legislature than in the larger political system. The importance, placed on these values varies according to time, place, and group, and more empirical data are needed to validate their existence and significance. I have stated them here to emphasize that committees are more than merely mechanisms for dividing the legislative work: they are institutional forms that give expression to underlying values. If the values change, procedures will also change, and gradually the institutions themselves will change. Note too that state legislatures are quite different from Congress. Legislatures reflect the priorities, values, and expectations of the constituencies and clients they serve. Chapter 8 considers legislative committees and bill consideration procedures in more detail.

NOTES

1. From Nelson W. Polsby, "The Institutionalization of the U.S. House of Representatives," *American Political Science Review* 62, no. 1 (March 1968): 144-68. Polsby examines the U.S. House over time. However, one could use these characteristics to compare several legislatures at a particular time. For an initial attempt, with reports on the Montana and Wisconsin legislatures, see Douglas C. Chaffey, "The Institutionalization of State Legislatures: A Comparative Study," *Western Political Quarterly* 23, no. 1 (March 1970): 180-96.

2. For a more detailed but extremely readable description, see Lewis A. Froman, Jr., *The Congressional Process: Strategies, Rules, and Procedures* (Boston: Little, Brown and Company, 1967). Another excellent source is *Congressional Quarterly's Guide to the Congress of the United States* (Washington, D.C.: Congressional Quarterly, Inc., 1971).

3. On the House, see Nos. 52-58, pp. 325-61; on the Senate, Nos. 62-66, pp. 376-407; on bicameralism as such, see especially Nos. 62 and 63, pp. 376-90 in Alexander Hamilton, James Madison, and John Jay, *The Federalist Papers*, with an introduction by Clinton Rossiter (New York: The New American Library of World Literature, Inc., 1961).

4. No. 62 in Hamilton et al., *The Federalist Papers*, p. 379.

5. See Joseph A. Schlesinger, *Ambition and Politics: Political Careers in the United States* (Chicago: Rand McNally & Company, 1966), p. 99.

6. For an extended discussion, see Sam Kernell, "Is the Senate More Liberal than the House?" *The Journal of Politics* 35, no. 2 (May 1973): 332–66.

7. Richard F. Fenno, Jr., *Congressmen in Committees* (Boston: Little, Brown and Company, 1973), pp. 160–61.

8. Froman offers more arguments and some data from the early 1960s. See Lewis A. Froman, Jr., *Congressmen and Their Constituencies* (Chicago: Rand McNally & Co., 1963), esp. pp. 69–84. Robert S. Erikson argues that the conservative bias of the House is partly explained by what he calls a "natural" Republican gerrymander of northern congressional districts. See his "Malapportionment, Gerrymandering, and Party Fortunes in Congressional Elections," *American Political Science Review* 66, no. 4 (December 1972): 1234–45.

9. These data are drawn from *The Book of the States: 1974–75*, vol. 20 (Lexington, Ky.: Council of State Governments, 1974), pp. 66–67. Nebraska's unicameral legislature is the country's smallest with 49 senators.

10. See Glendon Schubert and Charles Press, "Measuring Malapportionment," *American Political Science Review* 58, no. 2 (June 1964): 302–27; and corrections published in the same journal (December 1964): 966–70. For a good discussion of inequities in selected states, see Malcolm E. Jewell, ed., *The Politics of Reapportionment* (New York: Atherton Press, 1962).

11. For California, see Bruce W. Robeck, "Legislative Partisanship, Constituency and Malapportionment: The Case of California," *American Political Science Review* 66, no. 4 (December 1972): 1246–55. Erikson notes comparisons of both chambers in 10 states, but the data do not confirm the point. However, the comparison in 10 fortuitously selected states may not be typical of all. See Robert S. Erikson, "The Partisan Impact of State Legislative Reapportionment," *Midwest Journal of Political Science* 15, no. 1 (February 1971): 55–71; see also note 11 and Appendix.

12. This was the key argument in the Rhode Island Constitutional Convention. See Elmer E. Cornwell, Jr., and Jay S. Goodman, *The Politics of the Rhode Island Constitutional Convention* (New York: National Municipal League, 1969), pp. 56 ff.

13. See Patricia Schumate Wirt, "The Legislature," Chap. 5 in *Salient Issues of Constitutional Revision*, ed. John P. Wheeler, Jr. (New York: National Municipal League, 1961), especially pp. 70–73.

14. Susan Welch and Eric H. Carlson, "The Impact of Party on Voting Behavior in a Nonpartisan Legislature," *American Political Science Review*, 67, no. 3 (September 1973): 854–67.

15. See L. Harmon Zeigler and Hendrik van Dalen, "Interest Groups in the States," in *Politics in the American States: A Comparative Analysis*, 2d ed. (eds.) Herbert Jacob and Kenneth N. Vines (Boston: Little, Brown and Company, 1971), pp. 122–60; quotation from pp. 126–27.

16. See John Bebout, "Charter for the Last Frontier," *National Civic Review* 45 (April 1956): 158–63.

17. This theme is drawn from Fenno, *Congressmen in Committees*, p. xv; see particularly Chap. 2, "Environmental Constraints," pp. 15–45.

18. Donald R. Matthews, *U.S. Senators and Their World* (New York: Vintage Books, Random House, 1960), p. 147.

19. Richard F. Fenno, Jr., *The Power of the Purse: Appropriations Politics in Congress* (Boston: Little, Brown and Company, 1966), p. 163.

20. John C. Wahlke, Heinz Eulau, William Buchanan, and LeRoy C. Ferguson, *The Legislative System: Explorations in Legislative Behavior* (New York: John Wiley & Sons, Inc., 1962), pp. 193–215; quotation is from p. 206.

21. Polsby, "Institutionalization of the U.S. House," pp. 144–68; quotation is from p. 166.

22. Wahlke et al., *The Legislative System*, pp. 212–13.

23. Fenno, *Congressmen in Committees*, p. 1; emphasis in original. (Some of the remaining discussion draws on Fenno's material.)

24. Ibid., pp. 13–14.

25. The distinction is from Schlesinger, *Ambition and Politics*, p. 10.

26. Quoted from Berman, *A Bill Becomes a Law*, p. 135.

27. Quoted from a transcript published in *Watergate: Chronology of a Crisis*, vol. 1 (Washington, D.C.: Congressional Quarterly Inc., 1973), p. 211.

28. The resolution adopted by the Senate on December 2, 1954 is reprinted in *Congressional Quarterly's Guide to the Congress of the United States* (Washington, D.C.: Congressional Quarterly, Inc., 1971), p. 312.

8

The Legislative Subsystem: Internal Structure and Norms (2)

Legislatures are policy-adopting subsystems. This chapter suggests the complexity of legislative institutions, the diffusion of authority within them, and the potential for policy problems to become entangled in procedural hassles. The complexity, diffusion, and procedure characteristics partly explain why legislators are not more conspicuous in policy initiation and promotion. The complexity of legislatures means that legislative leaders devote much of their time and effort to just processing demands from outside, managing their consideration in the legislative subsystem, and maintaining the institutional continuity of the legislature.

COMMITTEE ORGANIZATION

In Congress

Because committee arrangements are so important to the work of Congress and the careers of congressmen, there is a great deal of detail which is significant to their behavior. Formal rules and informal etiquette are detailed. However, because many of these details are not relevant to the student who wants only a basic understanding of committee organization and process, I will dispense with them and outline only the most significant characteristics.

1. Kinds of committees. Congressional committees fall into three categories: joint, select, and standing, with the last the most important. *Joint committees* are single committees consisting of both senators and representatives. In the first session of the Ninety-third Congress (1973), there were nine such committees. With the exception of one, Atomic Energy, none of these report bills for legislative passage. Their major function is to generate studies in policy areas associated with their names, such as Congressional Operations, Defense Production, and Internal Revenue Taxation. The Joint Economic Committee studies the recommendations in the annual economic report of the president to the Congress. Each reports its findings to the Congress, and such reports are often useful to relevant standing committees which do report legislation. Ordinarily the joint committees contain an equal number of senators and representatives, and senators, who typically have heavier committee assignments than representatives, tend to avoid deep involvement in joint committee work. In the absence of aggressive effort and easy cooperation, the joint committees have only occasionally functioned as vital contributors to the legislative policy process.

Select committees are special purpose investigative committees of a particular house. Usually the word "select" is part of such a committee's name, as in the case of the Senate Select Standards and Conduct Committee, which investigates behavior of Senate members and employees. Sometimes the word "special" is a part of the name, such as the House Special Committee to Investigate Campaign Expenditures. At the beginning of the Ninety-third Congress, there were four select committees in the House and seven in the Senate, including the recent and well-known Senate Select Committee on Presidential Campaign Activities, chaired by Senator Sam Ervin.* Select committees, created to deal with a special problem, are supposed to be temporary. However, this rule, like many others in legislatures, is not rigorously followed. Select committees on small business have existed in the Senate, with one brief interruption (1949–50), since 1940, and continuously in the House between 1941 and 1975. These, like all select committees, must be continued for each Congress by the enactment of a resolution of the house in which they exist.[1]

Standing committees are the major, enduring committees of Congress. In 1946 Congress reorganized itself under the Legislative Reorganization Act, the major consequence of which was to reduce standing committees from 48 to 19 in the House and from 33 to 15 in the Senate. Since then each chamber

---

*Created by a Senate resolution, passed unanimously, February 7, 1973. The committee expired in 1974.

has made a few additions.† Standing committees are, for all practical purposes, permanent bodies with specified policy jurisdiction. Nearly without exception, bills must be given substantive consideration in one such standing committee in each house before being considered on the respective floors. (See Table 8.1.)

Most standing committees have subcommittees. Until very recently subcommittees had been thought of strictly as creatures of the standing committees. As Froman notes, the chairman of the standing committee, working within the seniority system, but not strictly bound by it, "decides whether there will be subcommittees, how many members will be on each, who the majority party members will be, and who will be the [subcommittee] chairman."[2] Additionally, the chairman determines which subcommittees will consider which bills. The distinctiveness of subcommittees varies from standing committee to standing committee and chairman to chairman. In some committees the subcommittee structure has long been stable and institutionalized. This is especially true, for example, in the House Appropriations Committee.[3] It has been much less the case in the House Armed Services Committee, most of whose subcommittees had numbers, not names, and were reshuffled from Congress to Congress.

Subcommittees are becoming more institutionalized.[4] The rules for the Ninety-fourth Congress require that all House committees of more than 20 members have four subcommittees. The object of that change was really the Ways and Means Committee, which for the first time now has subcommittees. In 1975, for the first time, the House Democratic caucus took upon itself the task of naming subcommittee chairmen in the Appropriations Committee. House Democrats also have rules requiring that caucuses of Democrats within the committees select subcommittee chairmen as well as determine the number and jurisdiction of the subcommittees. Even the Armed Services Committee now has named subcommittees with fixed jurisdictions.

†Standing committees can be created within either house simply by adoption of a resolution. In 1958 parallel committees were added: Science and Astronautics in the House and Aeronautical and Space Sciences in the Senate. The House Standards of Official Conduct Committee was added in 1967. The Senate created a Veterans Affairs Committee in 1970. Additionally, in 1969, the House Un-American Activities Committee was retitled the Internal Security Committee. Changes adopted in 1974 and 1975 established new committees on the budget in the House and Senate. The former Select Committee on Small Business became a standing committee in the House. The Internal Security Committee was disbanded and most of its jurisdiction assigned to the Judiciary Committee. Name changes also occurred: Banking and Currency became Banking, Currency, and Housing; Public Works became Public Works and Transportation; Science and Aeronautics became Science and Technology; and Foreign Affairs became International Relations.

Table 8.1   Committees of the House and Senate, 94th Congress, and the Party Ratios

House		Senate	
Agriculture	29D–14R	Aeronautical and	
Appropriations	37D–18R	Space Sciences	6D–4R
Armed Services	27D–13R	Agriculture and Forestry	9D–5R
Banking, Currency,		Appropriations	16D–10R
and Housing	29D–14R	Armed Services	10D–6R
Budget	17D–8R	Banking, Housing, and	
District of Columbia	17D–8R	Urban Affairs	8D–5R
Education and Labor	27D–13R	Budget	10D–6R
Government Operations	29D–14R	Commerce	12D–6R
House Administration	17D–8R	District of Columbia	4D–3R
Interior and Insular		Finance	11D–7R
Affairs	29D–14R	Foreign Relations	10D–7R
International Relations	25D–12R	Government Operations	9D–5R
Interstate and Foreign		Interior and Insular	
Commerce	29D–14R	Affairs	9D–5R
Judiciary	23D–11R	Judiciary	9D–6R
Merchant Marine and		Labor and Public	
Fisheries	27D–13R	Affairs	9D–6R
Post Office and		Post Office and	
Civil Service	19D–9R	Civil Service	5D–4R
Public Works and		Public Works	9D–5R
Transportation	27D–13R	Rules and Administration	5D–3R
Rules	11D–5R	Veterans Affairs	5D–4R
Science and Technology	25D–12R		
Small Business	25D–12R		
Standards of Official			
Conduct	6D–6R		
Veterans Affairs	19D–9R		
Ways and Means	25D–12R		

SOURCE: *Congressional Quarterly Almanac, 1975* (Washington, D.C.: Congressional Quarterly Inc., 1976), pp. 52–62 and 66–83.

2. Stature of committees. Standing committees may, in a sense, all be created equal, but they are not equal in practice. By House convention, three committees—Rules, Ways and Means, and Appropriations—are exclusive committees. Presumably their tasks are so demanding that their members have only one committee assignment. There are 10 "semiexclusive committees"—Agriculture; Armed Services; Banking, Currency, and Housing; Education and Labor; International Relations; Judiciary; Public Works and Transportation; Interstate and Foreign Commerce; Science and Technology; and Post Office and Civil Service. With occasional exceptions, members may serve on one of these and on one of the remaining "nonexclusive" committees. In the Senate the distinctions are not as fine. The "major" committees are Appropriations, Agriculture, Armed Services, Banking, Finance, Labor, Foreign Relations, Commerce, Judiciary, and Public Works. With few exceptions, all senators have at least one assignment to a major committee.

In practice members of Congress have defined a "pecking order" of committees, although as previously suggested, there is individual variation in the value of particular assignments. As Goodwin has shown, "A more systematic way to measure the desirability of committees is to find the relation between the number of members who transfer to, and the number who transfer from, each committee over a period of time. If the numbers are weighted according to the number of members on each committee a fairly accurate indication of the committee caste system can be made."[5] Studying movement in the committees that existed throughout the period 1949-68, Goodwin produced the rankings shown in Table 8.2. Notice that parallel committees have about the same rank in both houses: Finance and Appropriations in the Senate go with Ways and Means and Appropriations in the House; so do the committees of Commerce, Armed Services, Agriculture, Post Office, and Labor. There are a few variations. There is no parallel to the House Rules Committee in the Senate (despite a similarly titled Rules and Administration Committee, which actually parallels the House Administration Committee). In the Senate, Foreign Relations is at the top, while the House Foreign Affairs Committee (now named the House International Relations Committee) is of lower rank. The prerogatives of the Senate in acting on treaties and ambassadorial nominations are significant to that observed difference. Similarly the Senate Judiciary Committee is relatively more prestigious than the House Judiciary, perhaps because it alone considers the nominees of the president for positions in the federal courts.

3. *Committee assignment considerations.* Technically and legally, assignments are made by enactment in each house. In practice, however, each party in each chamber has its own machinery, a "committee on committees," and although there are variations in the way the four committees are organized, they have the same task—that of placing members on the various committees. The size of that task varies according to turnover from Congress to Congress because once a congressman has an assignment, he is entitled to keep it as long as he wishes (assuming he continues to win reelection). When Congress convenes following an election, there are a number of freshmen waiting for assignments as well as some veterans who want their assignments changed. The party committees that make the assignments are similar in the sense that their members are nearly all veterans of long standing in their house and party, as well as men in middle- or high-level positions in the committees and/or party leadership them-

Table 8.2   Preference Ranking of Congressional Committees, 81st Through 90th Congresses[a]

	(A) To	(B) From	(C) Net Shifts (A–B)	(D) No. of Committee Members	(E) Net Transfers per Unit of Membership (C ÷ D)
HOUSE COMMITTEES					
1. Rules	32	8	24	132	0.182
2. Ways and Means	44	5	39	250	0.157
3. Appropriations	72	13	59	496	0.119
4. Foreign Affairs	43	9	34	316	0.108
5. Armed Services	38	9	29	368	0.079
6. Un-American Activities	12	5	7	90	0.078
7. Interstate & Foreign Commerce	37	23	14	314	0.045
8. Judiciary	28	16	12	323	0.037
9. Agriculture	30	22	8	331	0.024
10. District of Columbia	27	26	1	249	0.004
11. Public Works	33	35	−2	321	−0.006
12. Education & Labor	17	23	−6	293	−0.020
13. House Administration	38	43	−5	250	−0.020
14. Govt. Operations	42	52	−10	302	−0.033
15. Interior & Insular Affairs	28	43	−15	302	−0.050
16. Banking & Currency	26	41	−15	301	−0.050
17. Merchant Marine & Fisheries	28	48	−20	299	−0.067
18. Post Office and Civil Service	26	48	−22	250	−0.088
19. Veterans Affairs	16	53	−37	253	−0.146
SENATE COMMITTEES					
1. Foreign Relations	30	2	28	160	0.175
2. Finance	25	3	22	156	0.141
3. Appropriations	37	6	31	245	0.141
4. Judiciary	23	5	18	148	0.122
5. Armed Services	20	5	15	157	0.096
6. Commerce	25	10	15	158	0.095
7. Agriculture and Forestry	15	15	0	152	0.000
8. Interior and Insular Affairs	8	9	−1	155	−0.006
9. Labor & Public Welfare	9	15	−6	142	−0.042

Table 8.2 cont'd.

	(A) To	(B) From	(C) Net Shifts (A–B)	(D) No. of Committee Members	(E) Net Transfers per Unit of Membership (C ÷ D)
10. Banking & Currency	9	19	–10	144	–0.069
11. Public Works	10	27	–17	145	–0.117
12. Rules and Administration	15	29	–14	98	–0.143
13. Government Operations	9	29	–20	127	–0.157
14. Post Office and Civil Service	8	29	–21	114	–0.184
15. District of Columbia	6	38	–32	89	–0.360

[a]Information in this table was gathered from appropriate volumes of the *Congressional Directory*. Column A gives the number of members who transferred to each committee during the 81st through the 90th Congresses. (Initial 80th Congress appointments, when the new committee system went into effect, and freshmen appointments are excluded.) Column B lists the number of members who transferred off each committee during the same period. Column C gives the number who transferred on to the committee less the number who transferred off. Column D lists the total number on each committee for the period under study. Column E, which gives the net transfers per unit of membership, was arrived at by dividing column C by column D.

SOURCE: George Goodwin, Jr., *The Little Legislatures: Committees of Congress* (Amherst, Mass.: The University of Massachusetts Press, 1970), pp. 114–15.

selves. Their choices reflect consideration for not only the wishes of those seeking assignments, but the personnel needs in the committees and the wishes of committee and party leaders.

A recent commentator has argued that "Six factors are of primary influence upon the committee assignment process: interpersonal relations, geography, reelection needs, seniority, ideology and expertise."[6] While all these elements are present, they are not evident in equal proportion in every assignment. Also the significance of assignments is probably greater for veteran congressmen asking for new assignments than for freshmen being assigned for the first time.

By the time a committee on committees convenes, it is broadly known which committee vacancies are available for assignment. Typically veterans looking for reassignment seek one specific vacancy, and ordinarily they must give up one of their current assignments. Veterans are a known quantity to the committee on committees. Their seniority does not guarantee them anything except careful consideration. Being known quantities may work to their disadvantage. Consider the following quote from a senior member on the House Republican Committee on Committees: "I don't want to kid you. Names come up and the question of whether he is a maverick comes up. I couldn't say that a McCloskey or a Riegle would be turned down because of it, but it certainly would be an element."[7] Both representatives mentioned are liberal Republicans who have often opposed their own party leaders and the Republican president.‡

Geographical balance is important in some committees, especially the large ones that deal in broad national policies such as taxation and appropriation. If the vacancy to be filled was created by the death or resignation of a midwestern Republican, a midwestern Republican with some expertise would have a good chance of getting the position, even as a freshman. On the other hand interior and agriculture committees are regularly dominated by westerners and congressmen from agricultural constituencies.

Politically alert members seeking new assignments make the rounds of calling on members of the committee on committees, the party leaders, the chairman of a desired committee, and, if they come from large states, the senior member of their party's state delegation. The latter, the "dean" of his state party delegation, is expected to look out for the future prospects of his own state and, because he has seniority, to be well regarded by the members of the committee on committees (if, indeed, he is not already a member). The *Congressional Quarterly* reports the experience of freshman Patricia Schroeder (D., Colo.) this way:

> . . . Schroeder emerged in January [1973] with a prized position on the Armed Services Committee. She worked hard for the position she got. First she discussed the matter with Frank E. Evans (D., Colo.), dean of her delegation. Then she visited Speaker Albert, Majority Leader O'Neill, and assignment committee members such as Al Ullman (D., Ore.) and James A. Burke (D., Mass.)
>
> "Ullman was very helpful," Schroeder said. "He told me, 'What you must do immediately is to see every member on [the committee on committees]. Talk to them and try to get their support.' I talked to Chairman Hebert [then chairman of the Armed Services Committee], but he wasn't terribly receptive. That's why I did all these other things, because I didn't [t]hink he'd be too receptive." She met with Hebert again later and resolved some of their initial differences.[8]

Less aggressive members simply put in a request to the committee on committees, listing their preferences for known vacancies, and let the committee decide. Some members think that pushing for positions on major

‡Riegle has since switched to the Democratic party.

committees is not a good idea. A senior Republican says: "I keep telling freshmen that they are better off in their first term or two to get on a minor committee, one that doesn't get all the controversial bills. You get involved in controversy, and often you are around here on Friday and can't go back to your district and take care of your constituent needs." He also counsels freshmen not to aim too high by requesting key committee assignments because they may receive none of their requests.[9]

Data on the satisfaction among members for their assignments are sparse, but Fishel's study of assignments for the Eighty-ninth Congress (1965–66), as reported in Table 8.3, is suggestive. Notice that frustration was greater in the minority party, which actually lost many positions because of a change in the party balance. However, Fishel reports that reactions were generally low key and offers three explanations:

(1) despite misgivings about other aspects of seniority, most freshmen accept it as fair in the distribution of new assignments;
(2) a considerable minority (43 percent) of the Democrats were in fact able to obtain their first preference;
(3) among those disappointed, all believed they would be able to initiate a successful move and/or that committee assignments were simply not that critical during the first two years of a representative's career.[10]

Finally, it should be noted that the assignment process is one which takes seriously the preferences of the members seeking assignment. Where two likely and qualified members are seeking the same position, all other considerations being about equal, the member with greater seniority usually wins the assignment. This is especially true for prestigious committees. But

Table 8.3   Evaluations by Freshmen of Their Original Committee Assignment in the House of Representatives, 89th Congress

Rankings	Democrats		Republicans	
	%	N[a]	%	N[a]
First choice within realistic limits	43	24	16	2
First choice within context of delegation caucus	12	7	—	—
Second choice	33	17	42	6
Lower than second choice	12	7	42	6
TOTAL:	100	55	100	14

[a]N = number of Freshmen Democrats and Republicans polled.
SOURCE: Jeff Fishel, *Party and Opposition: Congressional Challengers in American Politics* (New York: David McKay Company, Inc., 1973), p. 133.

seniority is rarely the decisive factor. In fact, a recent study of House Democrats concluded that about three-fourths of the freshmen got a committee they requested. Veterans, who are more precise in their requests, usually seeking a specific transfer, are much more often disappointed.[11] The several committees on committees have a significant task in maintaining a system of specialization and harmony in the standing committees.

4. Committee ratios. Each chamber sets the size of its committees. While they vary slightly over time, size is fairly stable. The tendency since the 1947 reorganization has been to gradually enlarge the committees, which means enlarging the number of positions that can be assigned.[12] But a significant characteristic is the partisan balance in the membership. A basic rule of the legislative system is that the majority party will have a majority on every one of the standing committees. Even within committees, the subcommittees are regularly made up of more majority party members than minority party members. This means that if either party makes an issue a partisan one, the majority party can win at every decision point in the legislative process, as long as its members are loyal in voting.

In practice, committee ratios are worked out by majority and minority leaderships of both houses and adopted when the chambers adopt their rules at the beginning of each new Congress. Occasionally these are matters of intra- or interparty bickering,[13] but the leaders ordinarily can come to an amicable agreement. The usual rule of thumb for deciding ratios is that partisan balance in the committees approximate the partisan balance in the whole chamber. (The House Rules Committee is an exception: the ratio favors the majority party 2 to 1.) For example, in the Ninety-third Congress Democrats made up 56 percent of the membership and the Appropriations Committee had 33 Democrats and 22 Republicans. In the Ninety-fourth Congress the percentage of Democrats was 67 and the seats on the Appropriations Committee went to 37 Democrats and 18 Republicans. The ratios in the committees usually vary somewhat, but they approximate the ratio for the total house. Imbalance is strongest when the chamber balance is close to 50 percent for each party. Then, with all committees favoring the majority party, ratios in the committees tend to be more favorable to the majority than the whole house ratio.

5. Seniority. Seniority is an often maligned principle by which members of Congress obtain advancement. Clearly, however, it is not the only criterion for many forms of advancement. There are two kinds of seniority to be kept in mind. One is within a member's party, and this seniority is of lesser significance. Members are given a rank in their party as they enter, and with a large group of freshmen, there are many ties for last. This seniority ranking is considered in committee assignments, as noted above. It has more importance when choices are made about the amenities of office holding — choosing office suites, parking places, and, for Senators, the desk they will have on the floor. Seniority in the party mainly has to do with perquisites and honorific titles.

The seniority of real consequence in Congress is committee seniority. Until very recently the "seniority rule" could be summed up in a single sentence—the majority party committee member with the longest continuous service on the committee automatically becomes its chairman. When committee memberships are listed, Democrats are listed on the left in descending seniority order and Republicans are listed similarly on the right. In 1970 both parties revised their rules to scrap seniority as the sole criterion. No chairman was successfully challenged until the election of the Ninety-fourth Congress. Wilbur Mills, ill and disgraced by his alcoholism and public involvement with a stripper, resigned the chairmanship of the House Ways and Means Committee, but remained on the committee as the second-ranked Democrat, and the previously second-ranked member, Al Ullman, became chairman. Three other incumbent chairmen were defeated in the House Democratic caucus and were succeeded by men of lower rank on the committees. The point is, the absoluteness of seniority has been broken, but in no case was serious consideration given to naming as chairman any person lacking long-time seniority on the committee to be chaired.

This "seniority system" has many implications. Although there is leeway in legislative parties to designate as chairmen members not qualified by seniority, it has and will happen only rarely. The nearly automatic character of the system means that at any given time only a few of the most senior members of the majority have any realistic chance to displace a current chairman. Thus, there is deference to senior members, from junior members as well as from other senior members. Fenno summarizes the point this way:

> Seniority signifies experience, and experience brings that combination of subject matter knowledge and political wisdom which alone is held to qualify a man for leadership in the House. Before a member can be certified as an experienced senior member, he must first be an apprentice and a protégé. Each new member of the House is expected to observe an apprenticeship—to work hard, attend to his constituency, learn his committee work, specialize in an area of public policy, appear often but speak very seldom on the floor, and cooperate with the leaders of his committee and of his party.[14]

Another consequence is that members will not achieve rank by hopping from committee to committee; thus, after a few terms in office, most congressmen settle down to serious pursuit of specialization within the committee assignments they have.

The road to the top rank of a committee is often a long one, depending as it does on continuous service. Clearly the advantage goes to those who come from constituencies that will repeatedly reelect them. Incumbent legislators stress such considerations in their electoral campaigns, and House members emphasize them to state legislators at reapportionment time. The seniority game and its implications probably have a depressing effect on the competitiveness of congressional elections.

6. *Chairmen.* While it is misleading to suggest that committee chairmen have life-and-death control over their committees, their authority is substantial, and skillful chairmen are legislators of major influence. Traditionally, chairmen have managed committee procedures, set agendas, called hearings, organized subcommittees, assigned subcommittee members and subcommittee chairmen, determined subcommittee jurisdictions, assigned bills to subcommittees, hired and overseen the work of most committee staff members, determined who will manage bills that go to the floor, and negotiated committee matters with party leaders and with members of the other house when competing versions of the same legislation had to be reconciled. This is a broad range of responsibilities. All suggest some sanctions over others, both within and outside the committee. But all likewise imply the need for the chairman to be responsive to those with whom he works. For a chairman to attain his own policy ends—whether to adopt new policy or prevent adoption—he will need the help of others, especially members of his own committee, but also congressmen outside his committee. It takes good committee work to refine legislation. It takes majority agreement to report a bill out, or to prevent reporting it out. A chairman with substantial committee support can usually win floor contests, but when opposition from his own committee is strong, chances increase that he will lose on the floor. Such losses are more than simply policy defeats; they are conspicuous evidence that Chairman So-and-So cannot handle his committee.

Since 1970 constraints upon chairmen have been increasingly formalized. In some committees the jurisdictions of subcommittees are specified in writing. By 1973 committees had adopted formal rules of procedure.[15] In the same year both the Senate and House adopted rules to open more of their sessions to the public. In 1972, before the new rules, 44 percent of House committee sessions were closed to the public as were 37 percent in the Senate. In 1973 the overall percentage for both chambers was 16, and in 1974 it was 15, a substantial change.[16] Before the beginning of the Ninety-fourth Congress, the Democratic caucus in the House assigned the party's Steering and Policy Committee (now the party's committee on committees) the job of nominating chairmen of the subcommittees of the House Appropriations Committee.

Despite these changes, chairmen still have significant powers, but to be effective they must obtain cooperation and support both within their committees and on the floor. It is important that they encourage thorough work, accommodate different points of view, labor in the house in behalf of their own committees and committeemen, help others to fulfill their ambitions, and have a reputation for knowledge, fairness, and integrity. This is a tall order, of course, and some men are more successful than others. Until his recent denouement, Wilbur Mills was usually regarded as the most influential man in the House of Representatives. His influence was based partly on his authority as chairman of the Ways and Means Committee, but mostly it came from the fact that he was tremendously knowledgeable, fair, and accommodating.§

The senior member of the *minority* party on a committee is called the "ranking minority member." He is a shadow chairman. If partisan control of the chamber moves from the Democrats to the Republicans, the ranking minority member assumes the chairmanship and the former chairman becomes the ranking minority member. The ranking minority member has some authority over his party members in the committee. He designates members of his party on subcommittees, manages the minority staff members, negotiates committee matters with the minority party leadership, organizes opposition in the committee and on the floor to the majority, and chooses minority conferees for conference committee (discussed below). Relations between chairmen and ranking minority members vary, but typically they are cordial and often cooperative. The two may lead rival interests, but usually they have worked together on the committee for a number of years and can manage to disagree without being disagreeable.

Finally, it is worth noting how long it does take to win top rank in a committee. Hinckley reports that:

... The number of years it takes a congressman to gain top committee rank from his first entry into the House or Senate varies from one party and chamber to the other. The median years required to gain top rank for the chairman and

§One close student of Mills and the Ways and Means Committee puts it this way:

... the influence of Mills in the legislative process is not based on the sanctions that he, as the Committee Chairman, could use. Sanctions are defined as actions designed to bring about results through nonphysical coercion or force and hence, in contrast to rewards, generate negative effect on the part of other members of a group.

The mark of Mills' leadership is that in doing the job as he defines it he relies on rewards, favors, expertise, persuasion, negotiation, and bargaining, not on coercing the members by using the sanctions that are available to him.

John F. Manley, "Wilbur D. Mills: A Study in Congressional Influence," *American Political Science Review* 63, no. 2 (June 1969): 442–64; quotation is from p. 460.

the ranking minority members of 1947 through 1966 are as follows:

Senate Democrats	10
House Democrats	16
Senate Republicans	7
House Republicans	12 [17]

As noted earlier, achieving in the Senate happens faster than in the House. Higher turnover rates among Republicans than Democrats are evident in both chambers.

Committee Organization in State Legislatures

State legislative committees are much less institutionalized than is the case in Congress. My remarks here are more impressionistic than those made about Congress because comparative research on the states is in relatively short supply. What follows is a rough generalization about 50 state legislatures on the basis of the few comparative reports and sources on particular states.

1. Kinds of committees. The three types of committees, joint, select (or special), and standing, are used in the states. Several states, particularly the New England states of Connecticut, Massachusetts, and Maine, have made joint committees the forum in which nearly all committee work on bills is done. In several states parallel committees of the two houses meet jointly for the purpose of hearing witnesses, but they separate to deliberate and report legislation to their own houses. States often create select committees for special purposes, although there is no consistency in the use of the word "select" in the committee titles. Because state legislatures are not in session for as long a period as Congress, there are often interim committees and commissions studying particular policy problems. Sometimes these interim committees are joint committees in that they include members of both houses. Except for Connecticut, all legislatures have standing committees for each chamber. Increasingly the standing committees function not only during sessions, but continue to work and study problems in their areas of jurisdiction during the time that the legislature is in recess; in short, they continue their activity much in the vein of interim committees.

Except in the three New England states mentioned above, the standing committees are the major, enduring work subsystems of the legislative chambers. While legislatures are still criticized for their numerous committees, there has been a real decline since 1946,[18] when the median number of committees in state senates was 31. By 1973 it was 13. In the lower houses the median changed from 39 to 16. There are still extremes. In 1973, the Missouri House had 41 standing committees and North Carolina had 38.

The Mississippi Senate had 32 and Oklahoma had 29. Numerous committees are not necessarily bad, but traditionally two patterns have occurred when there were many committees. One is numerous assignments for members. A multiplicity of assignments for a member (as many as 10) means little real specialization or full involvement in each assignment. Secondly, some become paper committees, doing little business while others carry most of the legislative load. Jurisdictions are blurred and both member and bill assignments can be capricious. In short, there is no real institutionalization; specialization of labor and clearly defined roles do not develop, and internal business is not conducted according to rules, precedents, and merit. Instead the conduct of business is fractionated, communication about "what's happening?" is uneven, and decisions may be the product of fast shuffles and surreptitious deals.

Subcommittees are not common in state legislative standing committees, with the one probable exception being the appropriations committees. Some committees have informal or temporary subcommittees, but the degree of specialization that occurs in Congress is atypical in the states' legislative committees.

2. *Stature of committees.* There are pecking orders in states as in Congress: typically, taxation, appropriations, education, banking, judiciary, state government, and commerce committees are among the more important ones. Commonly, "executive" committees, noted previously, may have unique status, handling what legislators consider "important" bills, without real substantive similarity. Doubtless there is some variation in committee pecking order within legislatures from session to session. Sometimes a major policy issue emerges—such as "no fault insurance"—and for a time the insurance committee is of major significance. When apportionment comes up, the apportionment committees assume great importance. In a recent study of the Michigan Senate, a point system was developed from interview data. Senators were asked to rank the four most important of the chamber's 15 committees. Table 8.4 summarizes the results. Appropriations was far and away the most important. Four others have substantial significance. Half a dozen more get a smattering of recognition, while more than one-fourth were totally disregarded even, apparently, by those who served on them.

3. *Committee assignment considerations.* Formal rules on assignments are more consistent in lower houses than in upper houses. In all but three states the speaker of the house (elected by and from among the house membership) appoints committee members. Generally, this includes the power to name the chairmen as well. Such authority is a tremendous asset to the speaker's potential for leadership. In the states where there are substantial numbers of members in both political parties, the competition for the post occurs mostly within the majority party. After the majority party

Table 8.4   Preference Ranking of State Senate Committees: Michigan, 1967

Committee	Point[a]
Appropriations	121
State Affairs	54
Judiciary	51
Taxation	39
Senate Business	18
Education	6
Labor	5
Commerce	4
Highways	3
Municipalities	3
Conservation & Tourism	2
(Four others)	0

[a] Each of 32 senators interviewed was asked to name in rank order the four most important committees in the Michigan Senate. First choices were assigned 4 points, second choices were assigned 3 points, and so on. Committees are ranked in the table according to points ascribed by the responding senators.

SOURCE: Adapted from Table 6 in Richard Balkema, "Legislative Service, Selection of Committee Chairmen and Committee Assignments in the Michigan Senate: 1937–1967," *Public Affairs Bulletin* 4, no. 3 (May–June 1971): 6.

resolves the matter in private, the decision is made on the floor with all majority members supporting the party's candidate, and minority party members opposing. The vote is pro forma along party lines. Occasionally, however, party bonds are insignificant and candidates bid for support wherever they can get it. In most real contests for the speakership, the promise of committee assignments and chairmanships is part of the bartering to obtain support from a winning coalition in the party (or occasionally the whole house). The winner's supporters are rewarded with choice assignments, while the opponents receive the leftovers.

Standard procedure is for members to communicate their committee preferences to the speaker. In two-party houses, minority members usually convey them to their own party's minority leader. The leaders work out their assignments separately. Either or both may consult willingly with a coterie of friends and veterans. Sometimes the chief executive is consulted, and sometimes even party or group leaders outside the legislature voice their opinions. Discretion for such consultation is in the hands of the speaker or minority leader. The strength of informal norms varies. The preferences of veteran legislators are usually given great regard, except for those who may have fought on the losing side in a previous leadership contest. Seniority distinctions are not as fine as in Congress. Chamber seniority may count more than continuous service on a particular committee. A veteran of several terms in the house may be made chairman of, say, the judiciary committee, even though he was not a member of that committee in the previous term. On the other hand, seniority and past committee experience and expertise are not ignored and tend to obtain regard for members who have previously served on committees high on the chamber's pecking order. Usually, the speaker respects the minority party leader's wishes about assignments for minority party members.

In upper houses the pattern is similar except that there is a greater tendency (evident in roughly one-third of the states) to have a formal committee on committees. Usually these are bipartisan and each party chooses its own members. Sometimes the majority leader has powers similar to those of the speaker of the house. In several the presiding officer (usually the statewide elected lieutenant governor) has nominal power, but usually he works with the chamber's party leaders. It is safe to say that in all these arrangements party leaders assume a prominent role in making assignments to legislators of their own party.

4. Committee ratios. Ratios are more volatile in states than in Congress. They may be defined in the rules, but of course the rules are subject to easy change, especially if a united majority party cares to change them. The rule of thumb that the partisan ratio for the chamber be applied to the committees is given some heed, but if the party balance is close, the majority party regularly pads its margin particularly in the important committees. Correspondingly the majority may permit the minority party overrepresentation in the less significant committees.

5. Seniority. As previously noted the relevance of seniority, particularly committee seniority, is a good deal less in the states than in Congress. In the states members cannot automatically move up to chairmanships by right of survival, term after term. Committee chairmen owe their positions and, in a large way, their loyalty, to party leaders. It is possible, however, that as state legislatures tend more to be full-time jobs with attractive pay and perquisites, they will attract more career-oriented legislators.[19] Seniority, as an automatic device for settling assignment problems without intra- and interparty infighting, may become more significant in state legislatures.

It is possible that seniority may seem less important than it really is. A careful study of Michigan Senate committees illustrates the point. Balkema's study of chairmanships from 1937 to 1967 reports that:

> Of the three hundred and two possible occasions on which a less senior committee member could have been designated chairman, there were one hundred and thirty-two occasions on which it occurred. In the same period of time there were seventy "ties . . . ." [H]owever, the data reveal that all but eight

occasions on which the less senior majority party committee member was designated chairman, the more senior member was serving as chairman of another standing committee.[20]

6. Chairmen. In state legislatures committees and their chairmen are more subject to management by party leaders than is the case in Congress. Ambiguity about committee jurisdictions, floor leaders' control in referring bills, frequent changes in the number of committees and their importance, changing committee memberships and chairmen—all these considerations mean that ordinarily state legislative committees are not strongly institutionalized. Therefore, they are not a solid base for power by chairmen. The tenure of chairmen depends upon their skill and responsiveness to the house leadership. Typically, therefore, state committee chairmen are not independently influential in the political process to the extent that congressional chairmen are.

Within their committees, chairmen are usually the dominant figures: they manage committee proceedings, set agendas, call hearings, and hire staff. But internal proceedings tend to be more loosely conducted than in Congress. Stakes are not as high largely because state legislative committees do not defeat as high a proportion of bills as is the case in Congress. Indeed, in some bodies an intense sponsor can get a bill reported almost as a matter of personal privilege. This is still the case in Illinois. Steiner and Gove write:

> . . . committees tend to be unwilling to assume responsibility for formally killing a bill . . . . Time and again a member will explain an affirmative committee vote by saying that he believes the bill 'to be important enough to merit consideration by the whole house' although he may vote 'No' on the floor. The sponsor of a bill cannot be certain, but he can feel confident that, even in the face of organized opposition, his bill will be reported out favorably. Committee members tend to be anxious to share with the whole house the responsibility for negative action just as they must share the responsibility for positive action.[21]

Because in practice there is no real committee control exercised over the flow of bills, committee chairmen lack important resources for bargaining with legislators in the political process outside the committee. Also, committee members rely relatively little on the chairman. The lack of member dependence on the committee and its chairman to get along in the legislative process means committee consideration is seldom expected to be the most significant hurdle in the passage of legislation. Typically, therefore, a chairman's voice is only of modest significance when he speaks in behalf of or in opposition to specific bills.

Circumstances do vary, however. If the chairman is a recognized expert, or he heads a strong committee—a committee made strong by the legislature itself—his influence may be substantial. Also some influential chairmen were, in fact, previously influential members who were then appointed to chairmanships. Thus, the fact that a man is made chairman may simply be evidence of his influence rather than the source of the influence. Finally, in most legislatures the appropriations committees are real centers of discretionary action. If any chairmen are influential, the chairmen of the appropriations committees are likely to be.

Summing Up

In external appearance state legislative committee arrangements resemble their congressional counterparts. However, congressional committees are much more firmly institutionalized. The jurisdictions of committees are more clearly defined, specialization within the committees is often reflected in subcommittee arrangements, the expectation that members specialize is stronger, the discretion of committees over legislation is sharper, the position of chairmen is much more important, and the patterns of accession to committees and upward mobility within them are by clearer standards and precedents. Within and across states, there is a great degree of variation and, unfortunately, most of that variation is as yet uncharted by empirical studies.[22]

HOW A BILL IS PASSED—CONGRESS

This is a brief overview of mechanics. The rules of procedure, debate, and parliamentary propriety are complex and detailed. But, as important as these details may be to the life or death of a specific bill, I will not attempt to give a detailed exposition of those rules. What follows is an outline of the major decision points in the process.

1. Introduction of bills. As noted in Chapter 6, introducing a bill is not difficult, and any congressman may do so. A congressman may not be prevented from introducing a bill, even, for example, one that is obviously unconstitutional. Such a bill, say, to dismiss the president and replace him with a four-person executive committee (one from each major party of the Senate and House), would probably not get serious consideration, but it may not be prevented at the introduction stage.

Bills are introduced by members in their own houses, and are not considered by the other house until passed by the house of origin. This technical requirement is in fact short-circuited when a House member and a Senate member agree to each introduce identical proposals in their own chambers. All bills are received and assigned a number (that is, HR 316 in the House of Representatives, S 14706 in the Senate). At the beginning of a Congress, each house starts at HR 1 and S 1 and numbers consecutively until the end of the Congress nearly two years later. The member who introduces a bill is called its sponsor. Bills may be cosponsored (in the House by no more than 25 members, while in the Senate there is no limit), but only by members in the same house. All bills, printed with their numbers and sponsor's names on them, are referred to standing committees by the presiding officer. Usually referrals are routine, but occasionally differences of opinion occur about which committee should receive a particular bill. The presiding officer's opinion can be appealed to the whole chamber. This happens rarely, and even more rarely is the decision of the presiding officer overturned.

2. *Committee considerations.* This is the stage where bills get their closest scrutiny, sometimes line-by-line scrutiny. Bills may, by the way, be brief (only a few lines) or very long (more than 100 pages). Copies of bills are often sent to government agencies affected by them for written comments. Agencies may want to send staff members to testify on such bills. The committee chairman may assign the bill to a subcommittee or decide to consider it in the whole committee. Failure to act on a bill is equivalent to killing it. If a bill is to be considered seriously, hearings are scheduled; they may be "open" to the public and press or "closed" to all but members and staff. Witnesses are invited and occasionally compelled (by subpoena) to testify before the committee. Interested citizens, group spokesmen, bureau members, and the like may request such an invitation and the chairman or subcommittee chairman exercises discretion on these invitations. Typically the sponsor of the bill is a witness and frequently congressmen not on the committee ask to testify. After hearings, the committee, or subcommittee, analyzes the bill, often "marking it up" or making amendments. Sometimes parts of competing proposals are combined. If "marking up" is extensive, the committee may order a "clean bill" introduced with its own number. If a subcommittee has done the work, it votes on the marked up bill and may recommend it to the whole committee, which then considers the bill anew and, depending on the members' judgment of the subcommittee's treatment, may begin from scratch or accept/reject the subcommittee's recommendations. The full committee then votes on its recommendation to the House or Senate. This is called "ordering a bill reported." If committee action is favorable, the bill is accompanied by a written report, often a detailed analysis. Sometimes included is a "minority report" expressing the views of committee members opposed to the bill. The original bill may be reported along with committee proposed amendments. When that is the case, the chamber must approve, change, or reject the committee's amendments before taking final action on the bill itself.

3. Getting to the floor in the House. Patterns differ in the House and Senate. The House, with its larger membership and greater number of original bills, has a heavier workload. In response to this load, the House has several calendars, with more specialized procedures. The calendars are, in effect, a list of bills in the order they came from committees.‖ The main ones are the Union Calendar (tax and appropriations bills, nonprivate bills directly appropriating property or indirectly appropriating money or property) and the House Calendar (all other public bills). According to the rules, some committees are privileged to obtain floor consideration of their bills simply by their own initiative.# All other bills not privileged by the rules must receive a "rule" from the Rules Committee. In fact, for parliamentary and strategic reasons, rules are sometimes obtained for privileged bills. The Rules Committee is, in effect, the traffic manager of the bill consideration process. For a bill to get to the floor, it must have a rule specifying how long

‖The *Private Calendar* consists of bills which compensate or give a particular benefit to a specific person. For example, if a mailman killed a citizen's dog, and the citizen did not receive the settlement he wanted from the Postal Service, he might be able to get a "private bill" passed to compensate for his loss. Citizenship can sometimes be obtained by aliens in this fashion. Private bills are typically the "last resort" of a person who tried to get favorable action by some other agency of the national government. Several hundred such bills pass each Congress. The *Consent Calendar* is another calendar to expedite noncontroversial issues. In effect, bills put on it are passed in the absence of objection. In practice when a bill on this calendar is called, it passes only if no one objects. If there is an objection, the bill goes back on the calendar to be called another time. On the second call it passes unless there are three objections. Three objections result in the bill being stricken from the Consent Calendar. To be passed it must go through the normal bill process. As Froman puts it:

Because virtual unanimous consent is required to pass bills on the Consent Calendar, bills placed on this Calendar with any chance of passing must be noncontroversial. Normally such bills involve relatively small requests for the benefit of particular constituencies, such as in the disposal of public lands, or requests by executive agencies for authorization to make small changes in existing laws.

To watch the Consent Calendar carefully, each party informally designates three members to act as "objectors" to be sure that the other side does not "put one over on them." However, any member may object on his own initiative. See Lewis A. Froman, Jr., *The Congressional Process: Strategies, Rules and Procedures* (Boston: Little, Brown and Company, 1967), pp. 46–48; quotation is from p. 46.

#Committees whose reports are privileged and the legislation on which such reports are privileged are:

1. Appropriations (on general appropriations bills);
2. Rules (resolutions involving rules and the order of business);
3. House Administration (on contested elections, enrolled bills, printing, and expenditures from the contingent fund of the House);
4. Standards of Official Conduct (on recommendations pertaining to any member, officer, or employee of the House);
5. Budget Committee (on matters pertaining to Title III and IV of the Budget and Impoundment Control Act of 1974).

it will be debated, whether or not amendments from the floor will be allowed (an open rule allows amendments, a closed, or "gag," rule does not), and whether it may "waive" points of order.** This power to specify the rules for floor consideration is significant. As noted in Chapter 7, this power has been abused, but not often. In most instances the Rules Committee routinely supplies needed rules. In general it tends to favor the requests of standing committees concerning points of order waivers, length of debate (usually one or two hours), and whether or not the bill gets a closed rule (most closed rules go to tax measures which are usually highly complex and which the Ways and Means Committee does not' want undone by amendments). However, Rules Committee discretion can be significant and in notable instances obstructive tactics by the Rules Committee and/or its chairman have disrupted or delayed floor consideration of major bills.[23]

4. Consideration on the floor of the House. A bill accompanied by a rule comes to debate when the Speaker of the House recognizes a Rules Committee member who calls for consideration of the rule setting the procedures for debate on the bill. The rule itself is debatable, but ordinarily it is approved pro forma. It calls for general debate in the "Committee of the Whole House," with debate led by the chairman of the committee from which the bill came, and opposition by the ranking minority member of that committee. The "Committee of the Whole House," a mechanism for facilitating business, can conduct business with a smaller quorum (100) than can the House in regular session (218, more than half the membership), and no regular roll call votes are used in its proceedings. All members may participate, but most usually do not. The committee chairman and ranking minority member mentioned in the bill are, respectively, manager of the bill and manager of the opposition. Members who want to speak on the issues in the debate are given time by one or the other. Members speak briefly, usually pointing out good or bad features of the bill. Typically participants in the debate are members from the standing committee that reported out the bill, but any and all others may join in or ask questions. After debate, amendments are taken up. Ordinarily those amendments that accompanied the bill from the committee reporting it are adopted. Amendments may be offered from the floor by either proponents or opponents of the bill. Ordinarily the manager of the bill wants to get it through without such amendments; in fact, it is rather a mark of achievement for a manager to fight off such

---

**In effect, a rule from the Rules Committee may set aside, for the bill in hand, the regular rules of debate. For instance, a program must be authorized by law before an appropriation is "in order." But the authorization bill could be stuck in the Senate after action in the House, while the House is ready to vote the appropriation. The appropriation could be defeated by any House member raising a "point of order" against the appropriation. A Rules Committee rule may "waive," or temporarily rescind, that point of order problem.

amendments. However, proponents of a bill must weigh the decision to oppose or not to oppose amendments in terms of the likelihood of passage of the whole bill. To allow a particular amendment may be to pick up more supporters for the bill as amended. A member who offers an amendment has it read and then has five minutes for explanation. Often the amendment is familiar to many of the participants, it having been offered previously in the standing committee and considered at length or discussed moments before in the general debate.

After the explanation of the amendment and a response by the bill's manager, the amendment is voted. Until 1971 there were three voting procedures in the Committee of the Whole House: voice vote (shouted yeas and nays), division vote, (members stand to be counted yea or nay) and teller vote (members walk past counters in the center aisle and individually report their vote). All these ways of voting are much quicker than a roll call, but all are relatively anonymous. None leave an official record of how individual representatives voted on a particular amendment. Because amendments are so significant to the content of legislation, anonymous voting keeps constituents and others from holding representatives responsible for their decisions. The Legislative Reorganization Act of 1970 required the added possibility of a recorded teller vote: on the request of one-fifth of a quorum (20 members) in the Committee of the Whole House, members' votes are individually recorded and become part of the public record.

A floor manager's success in handling debate and winning the votes on amendments varies a good deal. The solidarity of his supporters may vary with whether or not the issue is clearly partisan, his reputation and the reputation of opponents and supporters, his skills and the number of technical details in the bill and his mastery over those details. (A detailed bill which the manager really understands is difficult to amend; a detailed bill which arouses questions the manager cannot handle is in trouble.) Ordinarily amendments are attempts to weaken or water down the effect of the bill, and they are usually voted up or down in rather rapid order. When debate and amendments are completed, the Committee of the Whole House "rises" and, technically, reports the bill as amended to the full chamber. The Committee of the Whole, in effect, recommends its product to the House of Representatives.

The House is now ready to vote on the amendments previously adopted in the Committee of the Whole. Usually these are voted on "en bloc," or all at once. This may be done by a roll call, but ordinarily is not. Often after handling the amendments, opponents move to "recommit the bill," or send it back to the standing committee that originally considered it. A motion of recommital *without instructions* to the standing committee is actually a motion to kill the bill, and if it prevails the bill is sent back to committee and buried. A recommital motion *with instructions* requires the committee to reconsider the bill and make specific amendments to it. Sometimes the vote on such a recommital motion is the crucial decision point. On the demand of 20 percent of the members, this vote is by roll call,†† but otherwise may be by voice, division, or teller vote. If the recommital motion passes, business on the bill is ended until it comes back from committee. If it fails, the next order of business is a vote on final passage. If a recommital roll call lost, it may simply be voted through by a voice vote. Again, a roll call can be demanded by one-fifth of those present. If the bill is fairly important, a roll call is usually requested so that members will be "on the record." After the vote on passage, there is a pro forma motion to reconsider the bill and that is quickly defeated by a voice vote.

5. *Getting to the floor in the Senate.* Introduction and committee handling are essentially similar in both houses, but there are differences between House and Senate in getting a bill to the floor and consideration once on the floor. Senate procedures for getting a bill on the floor are much simpler than those of the House. There are only two calendars: the Executive Calendar is for the president's proposed treaties and nominations for appointments to executive branch positions (no bills) and the Calendar of Business is for all bills and other business. By convention noncontroversial bills are passed "without objection," usually at Monday afternoon sessions.

There is no Rules Committee procedure as in the House. The majority party has a Policy Committee, usually dominated by the majority leader, which schedules bills. Conventionally the majority leader cooperates with the minority leader to schedule debate at an agreed-upon time. There is great courtesy, cooperation, and reciprocity in these arrangements, with strategic delays very rare. Actually any member can have a say in scheduling because the leadership tries to accommodate requests from the senators if at all possible. It is not exceptional for the Senate to fit its schedule to the wishes of a senator who wants to participate on a particular bill, but who has a commitment to be somewhere else the day the bill is to come up. The Senate, contrary to the House, may juggle the debate of two or more bills on the floor at the same time, moving from one to the other by unanimous consent—again illustrating the informal rule of reciprocity.

6. *Consideration on the floor of the Senate.* According to the leaders' schedules, a bill is taken from the calendar for consideration. The manager for the bill, often a committee or subcommittee chairman, will lead in arguing the bill's merits. There may be an opposition manager, but not necessarily. Proponents and opponents in the Senate are not under time

††With the installation of electronic voting in the House in 1973, roll call voting has become speedier (about 15 minutes) and is more frequently used.

limitations, as is the case in the House. Senators may drift in and out, speaking by informally agreed-to turns or by asking the senator speaking at the moment to "yield" for a time. Debate goes on until no one cares to speak further. Because the leadership tries to schedule upcoming legislation, estimates of time to be expended on a particular bill will be made. To expedite matters, a leader, usually the majority leader, may ask unanimous consent to bring debate on a particular bill to a close at a specific time so that senators know when the vote will be taken. This is for the convenience of all, and is not intended to cut off discussion of serious issues. If it were, only a single objector could prevent this means of ending debate.

Votes are taken first on amendments and then on final passage of the bill as amended. Many of the votes are by voice, with some by division (the Senate does not use teller votes), but one-fifth of those present can demand a roll call. Often significant amendments are voted by roll call. In the Senate, opponents of a bill often offer major amendments, even complete substitutes, so that votes on amendments are sometimes the most significant decision points. When amendments are disposed of, the Senate usually proceeds to vote on final passage. Recommital motions are not typical in the Senate largely because the amendment process is more open than is the case in the House. If the bill passes, someone moves for reconsideration, and someone else moves that reconsideration be tabled, and action on passage of the bill is completed.

7. Action in the second house and conference committees. A bill may be introduced in either house, and each considers the bill in its own way. Significant legislation is usually amended, and it is not uncommon for the second chamber to revise the bill after it comes out of the first. According to the Constitution, a bill must pass both houses in precisely the same language before it can be sent to the president for his signature. If the second house's version is not very different, or the differences are not controversial, the second house may simply request concurrence with its version from the first. If granted, the bill goes to the president. If neither house will give way, a conference committee must be formed.

The presiding officer of each chamber appoints conferees, usually three to nine members from each house, with most but not all from the majority party. Ordinarily conferees are actually named by the standing committee chairmen and ranking minority members of the committees that considered the bill. Typically those active in the various consideration stages (subcommittee, committee, and floor) are named. The conference committee, strictly temporary, deals only with the single bill in question. Conferees are expected to fight for their own house's version, but to accommodate competing views. Committees meet in private to hammer out disagreements. Sometimes members go back to their own chamber for advice. Votes in the conference committee are decided by concurrent majorities of each house delegation. In short, a majority of both the House conferees and the Senate conferees is required before an agreement is reached. The conference committee writes a report of its agreement, embodying the new language of the bill. If both houses accept the report, the bill is passed. If either does not, the bill is dead, or the conferees can try again. The bill is not passed until both houses agree to a single version.

Formal rules require that conference committees compromise without introducing substantively new language into the bill. The spirit of this rule is usually maintained, but it is not unknown for conference committees to modify a topic beyond the scope of the earlier two versions. Reciprocity calls for accommodation, but nonconferees of both houses do not want conferees to go too far in changing the original bills. The political check on this is simply that both houses must adopt the conference version. Adoptions obtained, the bill goes to the president.[24]

8. *Final action.* If the president approves the bill, he signs it and it becomes law. If he prefers not to sign it within 10 days (Sundays excepted), Congress still being in session, it automatically becomes law. If Congress adjourns before the 10 days expire and the bill remains unsigned, the bill is "pocket vetoed." Typically, however, Congress is in session, so to veto a bill the president refuses to sign it and sends it back to the house of origin with his reasons for the veto. It can be returned to committee, amended, and passed again. If Congress prefers to insist on the bill as passed, the veto can be overridden by a two-thirds vote on a roll call in each house, in which case the bill becomes law. If the bill fails to get two-thirds support in either house, it is dead. To be revived, it must be reintroduced and go through the entire process again.

Passed bills are either public laws or private laws (the latter began as "private bills") and are assigned a number associated with the Congress that passed the bill. For instance, the congressional action on revenue sharing was completed in October 1972 by the Ninety-second Congress. The president signed what originated as a House bill, HR 14370, which is now Public Law 512, 92d Congress, abbreviated PL 92–512.

Summing Up Congressional Procedures

Congressional procedure is complex and I have tried to be brief without losing the flavor of how things "really" happen. Although I have omitted discussion of numerous examples of how specific bills have been handled, as well as the many "exceptional" strategies available under the rules,[25] it is evident that congressional procedures, being complex, are far from neutral in their political effects. New legislation is difficult to achieve in Congress. It may be killed at any one of numerous decision points. To be enacted, it must survive all of them. The numerous check points mean that typically legislation is compromised *down* not *up*. In a later chapter the coalitions that struggle to pass or defeat legislation at these various decision points will be discussed.

The preceding pattern is "normal," but one pattern, uniquely provided by the Senate, is that involving "extended debate," better known as filibustering. There is no limit on debate in the Senate except by unanimous consent or by cloture. The first can be prevented by any member, although such is discouraged by ordinary courtesy. Yet one or a few members can delay voting on a bill or amendments by simply talking and talking. When the number of obstructors is only a handful, the delay is simply a nuisance, yet it is one that can upset the capacity of the Senate to take action. Especially near the end of a Congress when many matters need final consideration for passage, such delay may threaten measures. Taking time out for extended debate as well as the time necessary to end the filibusters may be "too expensive," and compromise may be sought on the matter at issue to expedite business.

More significant are the occasional full-blown filibusters which have occurred most often when the legislation at issue was to enlarge civil rights. Traditionally this has worked on intense opposition by a minority from the South, but a substantial sized minority. The Civil Rights Bill finally enacted in 1964 was on the floor of the Senate for 83 days. The point of the strategy is that delay is so intolerable that the proposal causing it will be left to die. Until 1975 it took one-third of the senators to bring this about because the only mechanism for ending debate by less than unanimity is by cloture. A motion for cloture, requiring that debate be limited to one hour on the pending issue, can apply to any debatable issue before the Senate. (Even after cloture, Senators enjoy more debate time than is ever the luxury of a representative.) The point is that the end of debate is made certain. For a cloture motion to be introduced, 16 senators must sign it. It is put to a vote on the second day following the introduction of the motion. To pass, it must obtain support from 60, or three-fifths of the elected membership. Before 1975 the rule was two-thirds of those present and voting.‡‡

Table 8.5 shows that the motion is only used occasionally, and that it rarely carries. What the table does not show directly is that in many instances of "extended debate," cloture had not even been attempted because the opponents of the filibusters knew that they could not win. The long

‡‡The two-thirds majority is still necessary to efforts to cut off debate on rules changes of the Senate.

Table 8.5   Cloture Votes Taken Since Adoption of Rule 22 (1917)

Period	Votes	No. Passed	% Passed
1917–1946	19	4	21.1
1947–1956	3	0	0
1957–1966	15	3	20.0
1967–1975	86	25	29.1
TOTAL:	123	32	26.0

SOURCE: *Congressional Quarterly Almanac, 1975* (Washington, D.C.: Congressional Quarterly, Inc., 1976), p. 37.

drought of civil rights legislation attests to this fact. So too does the credit assigned the cloture rule by Senator Richard Russell of Georgia in 1957:

> . . . the fact that we were able to confine the Federal activities to the field of voting and keep the withering hand of the Federal Government out of our schools and social order is to me, as I look back over the years, the sweetest victory of my 25 years as a Senator from the State of Georgia.[26]

Russell was around to taste later defeats, particularly the one on June 10, 1964, when cloture ended debate on the Civil Rights Bill of 1964 by a vote of 71 to 29. On June 19 the bill passed the Senate 73 to 27. The intensity of the conflict was indicated by the fact that all senators were present and voting on both roll calls.

The filibuster is an occasional but powerful tool of conflict in the Senate. Cloture is difficult to impose—and impossible against more than two-fifths of the membership who are willing to fight an all-out contest against some policy proposal. Unquestionably the filibuster is a possibility that favors conservative interests, interests that want to prevent change in existing policy. Occasionally it can be used by liberals, but ordinarily to prevent change in policy victories previously won—including those won in other political arenas. An example of the latter was a filibuster by northern Senate liberals against an attempt to delay the Supreme Court's decision to require that both houses of state legislatures be reapportioned according to population.

HOW A BILL IS PASSED—
STATE LEGISLATURES

The general pattern of bill handling—introduction in one house, committee consideration, reporting to the floor, floor consideration, sending bills to the second house for committee and floor consideration, conference committee treatment if necessary, and action by the chief executive and legislative treatment of vetoed bills—is similar in all legislatures to that followed by Congress. There are, however, some variations that should be noted just briefly.

1. Committee consideration is more casual. Legislative committees do not, as Congress does, publish the testimony received in hearings on bills. Hearings tend to be briefer and less formal. The survival of a bill in committee depends more significantly on the activities in its behalf by the bill's sponsor. The sponsor usually must get an agreement by the committee chairman concerning when the bill will be heard; without such a sponsor's demand, a committee chairman will probably assume that the sponsor simply introduced the bill without expecting it to be seriously considered or passed. If there are to be witnesses in the bill's behalf, the sponsor usually must arrange for their testimony. Many bills receive no testimony beyond that offered by the sponsor. In the majority of instances in which the sponsor works earnestly for his bill, the committee will report it out. In some legislatures bills are reported out even though the committee sends along a recommendation that the bill should not pass. In short, committees and committee chairmen take less responsibility for the bills that emerge from the committee. Primary responsibility is that of the sponsor.

2. On the floor—second and third reading. As in Congress, committee reported bills are put on a calendar. In state legislatures every bill receives three "readings" in each house. In earlier years entire bills had to be read aloud three times in each chamber—no doubt, for the benefit of illiterate legislators. This word use continues, although actual reading is usually dispensed with. Technically a bill is "read" the first time when it is introduced. After consideration in committee, a bill is called up for consideration on "second reading." This is the crucial floor consideration stage in many state legislatures.§§ For most bills the sponsor is the chief spokesman; he presents the bill to the whole house, speaking in its behalf and answering questions. Then if there are amendments to be considered, these are taken up—one by one. Committee amendments, if any, are considered first. Debate is usually rapid and debaters rarely present formal speeches. While delaying tactics may be used (usually by posing amendment after amendment), debate can be easily cut off by a majority vote in support of a motion for the previous question. (The question actually is, "Shall the main question be now put?" Majority support of this motion ends debate on the amendment at hand. Then the amendment itself must be voted on.) In state legislatures, even senates, there is no unlimited debate as in the U.S. Senate.

---

§§In some legislatures this is done in a "committee of the whole" as in the U.S. House. Most do it in regular session.

When amendments have been voted—by voice vote, division, or roll call— the bill is advanced to "third reading."

The requirement of three readings, besides the reason of communication, includes the rule that each reading must take place on a separate legislative day. Introduction, amendment, and final passage are intended to take not less than three separate days so that opponents of a bill may have time to develop their opposition. Ordinarily, of course, the three readings take much more than three days. After amendments on second reading, the bill must "lie over" at least a day before final passage. On third reading the bill is presented as already amended. No further amendments are in order, and final passage of the bill is voted. (If new amendments are desired, the rules usually allow that a bill may be returned to second reading for further amendments. Final passage is, of course, delayed.) In most legislatures a record roll call vote is required at this final passage stage, and the votes of the members must be noted in the written record of the legislature. It is worth mentioning that legislatures do not keep *verbatim* records of debate as the Congress does. All record roll calls do appear, however, because typically this is a legal or constitutional requirement to document the actual passage of new legislation. In most legislatures the vote on final passage requires an elected majority; that is, in a chamber of, say, 59 members, 30 or more yea votes are required to pass a bill. A few states require, as Congress does, only a majority of those present and voting to pass a bill.

3. Handling in the second house. Procedures in the second house usually closely parallel those of the first. Because the activities of a bill's sponsor are typically so significant in legislatures (in contrast with Congress), often the sponsor in the first house will have the task of finding someone in the second house to advance the bill there. This can be a significant choice, for sometimes bills that pass the first house with relative ease die in the second chamber because the sponsor there was not as aggressive as the original. The original sponsor, then, must try to find someone in the second house who will see the matter through.

Sometimes handling in the second house is more casual than in the first. It is not as uncommon in state legislatures, as it is in Congress, for the second house to simply advance a bill from first reading to second reading "without reference to committee." This is particularly the case at the end of a legislative session when bills are piling up. If the majority party leader requests such advance to second reading, this can speed up the process a good deal. A majority leader, who "has the votes," can shepherd a bill past the committee consideration stage to final passage with much more ease than is the case in Congress.

4. The importance of legislative party leaders. The floor leaders of the two parties are significant managers in the bill-passing process. In state legislatures they have substantial eminence over regular members in a number of ways: regular members are ordinarily highly interested in the handling and passage possibilities of a relatively small number of bills— those vitally affecting interests in their own districts, bills in subject areas in which they have special expertise, and some of the major controversial bills of statewide significance. Most legislators are relatively indifferent to the majority of bills on which they will be required to vote. Leaders, especially majority party leaders, are expected by members to keep together a coalition of support among the indifferents to help those with intense interests to win on the floor. The leaders are at the center of the legislature's communication network. In return for the few tasks most individual legislators want to accomplish, they provide the leaders with support on a range of issues about which they are relatively indifferent.

The significance of party leaders is substantial also because most legislative committees are not strongly institutionalized and do not exercise sharp discretion over bills. Bills are not severely sorted out, as is the case in Congress, so floor decisions usually are the critical ones. So much more of a legislature's time and effort is expended on the floor in precisely the environment in which floor leaders are the major figures in organizing support and opposition to bills that the relative significance of floor leaders in legislatures is much greater than for leaders of similar title in Congress.

5. *Legislative caucuses.* Usually a caucus is a private meeting of all the members of one party in a particular chamber; for example, all house Democrats. In some of the one-party states, there are occasional caucuses of particular factions of members. Typically caucuses are informal party meetings, and there is great variety across states in the frequency and regularity with which they are held.

The significant characteristic of the caucus is that it is for "members only." It is sometimes used by leaders or members to try to rally the group to take a particular position on a controversial issue. Often it is a situation in which leaders try to find out the degree of unity among members on upcoming issues. Sometimes the crucial question is, "Should this party make issue X a party matter, or not?" In some party caucuses there are explicit rules that call for a matter to be decided by a vote, and after the vote all members are expected to follow the "party line" on the floor of the legislature. The privacy of the meeting—no press, opposition members, or public—means that discussion in the caucus can often be more candid than on the floor. A party leader's discussion may go something like the following:

> Several issues are coming up this week that I want you to be prepared for. First, the governor's education budget bill will come up. We have to support him on that even though I know several of you don't think schools in your district are

getting enough money. I told the governor I wouldn't help you on that, but if you want to try to amend the bill, you are on your own. Whatever happens though, we have to stick together on that one for final passage. Second is the gun registration control bill. We're pretty divided on that and, although I personally support the bill, I know that many of you have strong opposition in your constituencies. We won't make a party stand on that one. Third, the public works bill will be controversial. Bill Jones from our party has worked very hard on that and one of the items in the bill authorizes a big project in his district. He needs that for reelection next time. The other party is going to "grandstand" in opposition to that, but I don't want anyone on our side away from the floor when that is debated. We will fight off all the amendments and get that through intact. The fourth item. . . .

The caucus is not necessarily a one-man show, nor is it necessarily peaceful. But conflicts are usually brief, and "horse trading" is often evident. The norm of reciprocity is frequently invoked. Practice varies from state to state, but sometimes the caucus will decide, by a majority vote, that all members will support the party position. Disloyalty after such a decision is dealt with severely. Such required loyalty is only occasional, and in many circumstances it is understood by all that some members will, for good and acceptable reasons, be voting against their fellow partisans.

6. *Conference committees.* As in Congress, for a bill to become law, both the upper and lower chambers must pass it in exactly the same form. Because of amendments the versions may differ, and conference committees are created to resolve these differences. In form, procedures are not unlike those in Congress. In practice, however, state legislative conference committees usually have an easier time than congressional ones. Usually the legislation at stake is much briefer and the issues for compromise are clearer. Typically the compromise is reached quickly or, if conflict between the two houses is not easily resolved, the bill is allowed to die. This pattern is typical because of the usual flow of legislative business. Conference committees are needed most near the end of the legislative session when the log jam of bills for consideration means many, sometimes more than 100 floor votes each day. So, except on major bills, the conference committee quickly determines whether or not a bargain can be struck, and then the members hasten back to their respective chambers for the floor business at hand there. It should be noted too that conferees of the committee are usually selected by the respective party leaders in each house, so that the leaders' views are well represented in the proceedings, and afterwards the outcome is quickly communicated to them. The leaders' knowledge of the circumstances and the conference outcome, as well as their control of the floor, gives them substantial influence over whether or not the conference committee report will be accepted or rejected.

7. *Final action.* Bills passed in the same form by both houses go to the governor for signature or veto. As noted previously in Chapter 4, the veto power is greater for most state governors than for the president. In all states except North Carolina, the governor can veto bills. In all but a half dozen states he can veto items, or specific parts, of appropriations bills. Because state legislative enactments are usually more numerous and narrower in scope than those that come before the president, the governor can be more specific than the president in killing legislation that he opposes. Finally, legislative overrides are not common. In many states the override requirement is two-thirds of the *elected* members of both houses. With a few absences at the time of the vote, perhaps three-fourths of those present to vote are necessary to defeat the governor—not an easy task. Finally, vetoes often come after the legislative session is over and the legislators have gone home. Reconvening for a "veto session" is problematic, for often the circumstances which assisted in the original passage of a vetoed bill have dissolved—the log jam at the end of a session, the reciprocity ("Well, I did vote for your bill before because you voted for mine. But now that yours has been vetoed, I'm not going to vote against the governor"), or the timeliness of the legislation. Of course, there are occasions when a governor's veto so offends members of a legislature that they unite in common cause to defeat him, but such occasions are rare. Ordinarily a bill controversial enough to be vetoed by a governor arouses sufficient division of opinion in a legislature to prevent the achievement of the extraordinary majorities in both houses necessary to override the veto.

Summing Up State Legislative Procedures

The focal point of activity in the states is on the legislative floor; it is there that crucial amendments are voted up or down and final action must be completed with a roll call vote. This contrasts with Congress and its highly institutionalized committees. In Congress floor consideration is a stage at which committee decisions are usually ratified and legitimated. In the states it is the major decision point, although anticipation of the decision may stimulate one or both parties to resolve internal conflicts in their party caucuses before floor consideration actually occurs.

The significance of floor consideration in legislatures explains the fact that the floor leaders, especially those from the majority party, wield substantial influence in nearly all controversies. The members in each party have slight influence alone. Each legislator, intensely interested in a few bills, moderately interested in several, but indifferent to most, finds the party leaders ready brokers. These brokers can combine the voting support of many indifferent legislators for the benefit of intensely interested legislators. By trading on and distributing benefits carefully, the leaders can depend upon followers for support when they need it. Dependable support, "having the votes," means the ability to control the floor and the central processing phase in the state legislative process. The party leaders, with their knowledge about who is interested in achieving what, are in the best position to exercise this control on a continuing basis. In contrast to Congress, where so many crucial decisions are made in the committees and under the discretion of committee chairmen, floor leaders in the legislature are the major participants in nearly all controversial decisions. The leadership is much more centralized in state legislatures than is the case in Congress.

CONCLUDING OBSERVATIONS

The institutional life of a legislative subsystem is complex. The rules do not determine what policies will be adopted, but they do constitute a significant bias. The rules and norms of Congress emphasize discretion in committees, with floor action usually a matter of ratification; thus, committee organization and procedure are a major concern of all congressmen. The action on the floor is the way in which a chamber insures that a committee is true to and fair with the wishes and expectations of most of the members most of the time. If a committee and/or its chairman achieve some other sort of reputation, the committee is likely to have difficulty getting its bills passed without amendments or controlling its internal affairs without external pressure. Roger Davidson pointed out that, in the Ninety-second Congress, committees varied from the average of "liberalism" rankings for all members (see Table 8.6).

The committees that differ most from the mean have had significant difficulty with the House and the parties. Notice the committees most deviant from the average. Education and Labor has had conspicuous difficulties getting its bills passed. Note, too, that the three veteran committee chairmen who were upset in the Democratic caucus in 1975 were from committees distant from the mean: Patman of Banking, Poage of Agriculture, and Hebert of Armed Services. The one committee that was disbanded was Internal Security.

Changes in structure and rules tend to follow or be affected by the way the legislature has adopted substantive policies and the responses of the public and other political actors to those policies. Disagreements about rules are often surrogate disagreements on issues. The fight to liberalize the cloture rule in the Senate is viewed by most participants as a fight about civil rights and liberties for minorities. The reforms in the House to open committees

Table 8.6 "Liberalism" Rankings of House Committee Members, 92d Congress, 1971 to 1972[a]

Committee	All Members (%)	Democrats (%)	Republicans (%)	No. of House Committee Members
Education and Labor	56	79	25	38
Judiciary	55	76	27	37
Government Operations	52	65	35	39
Foreign Affairs	51	67	31	38
Banking and Currency	49	63	27	37
House Administration	46	62	22	25
Science and Astronautics	45	56	28	29
Merchant Marine and Fisheries	44	50	34	36
Rules	44	59	14	15
Interior and Insular Affairs	43	60	17	38
Av. for Entire House	43	58[b]	21	432
Public Works	41	56	15	37
Interstate and Foreign Commerce	41	63	11	43
District of Columbia	40	51	25	24
Ways and Means	40	58	12	25
Post Office and Civil Service	39	57	14	26
Veterans Affairs	39	50	22	26
Appropriations	38	50	19	55
Internal Security	32	57	7	8
Agriculture	30	42	12	36
Armed Services	29	36	18	41
Standards of Official Conduct	21	31	12	12

[a]"Liberalism" rankings for individual members are drawn from Congressional Quarterly's "Opposition to Conservative Coalition" scores, with the figures recomputed to eliminate the effect of absences from the House floor. *Congressional Quarterly Weekly Report,* November 18, 1972, pp. 3022–27.

[b]For the 168 northern Democrats, the "liberalism" score was 76; for the 87 southern Democrats, the score was 25.

SOURCE: Roger H. Davidson, "Representation and Congressional Committees," *Annals of the American Academy of Political and Social Science* 411 (January 1974): 52.

and make public the votes of individual members on the Committee of the Whole are to enhance the passage, rather than the defeat, of legislation.

In the states, committees are not institutionalized to scrutinize and refine legislation. That burden falls to the whole membership, and to the leaders in particular. It is likely that as legislatures become more full-time operations, decision making will be decentralized and tasks more evenly distributed.

Having fewer committees is a step in that direction. As the business of state legislatures grows, committees will have increasing significance, and the patterns of member assignment, committee prestige, and discretion over bills will change in a related way. Norms and rules are part of the systemic nature of legislatures.

NOTES

1. See Dale Vinyard, "Congressional Committees on Small Business," *Midwest Journal of Political Science* 10, no. 3 (August 1966): 364–77. In 1975 the House converted this select committee into a standing committee.

2. Lewis A. Froman, Jr., *The Congressional Process: Strategies, Rules and Procedures* (Boston: Little, Brown and Company, 1967), p. 38.

3. See Richard F. Fenno, Jr., *The Power of the Purse: Appropriations Politics in Congress* (Boston: Little, Brown and Company, 1966), especially pp. 167–82.

4. For a preliminary analysis of reform and its consequences, see David W. Rohde, "Committee Reform in the House of Representatives and the Subcommittee Bill of Rights," *The Annals of the American Academy of Political and Social Sciences* 400 (January 1974): 29–47.

5. George Goodwin, Jr., *The Little Legislatures: Committees of Congress* (Amherst, Mass.: The University of Massachusetts Press, 1970), p. 116.

6. Robert Healy, "Committees and the Politics of Assignments," in *To Be a Congressman: The Promise and the Power,* eds. Sven Groennings and Jonathan P. Hawley (Washington, D.C.: Acropolis Books Ltd., 1973), pp. 99–120; quotation is from p. 109.

7. Quoted in *Congressional Quarterly Weekly Report,* February 10, 1973, p. 282.

8. *Congressional Quarterly Weekly Report,* February 10, 1973, p. 282.

9. *Congressional Quarterly Weekly Report,* February 10, 1973, p. 283.

10. Jeff Fishel, *Party and Opposition: Congressional Challengers in American Politics* (New York: David McKay Company, Inc., 1973), pp. 134–35.

11. David W. Rohde and Kenneth A. Shepsle, "Democratic Committee Assignments in the House of Representatives: Strategic Aspects of a Social Choice Process," *American Political Science Review* 67, no. 3 (September 1973): 889–905.

12. Goodwin, *The Little Legislatures*: on the House, pp. 66–69; on the Senate, pp. 80–83.

13. See, for example, "The Democratic Eighty-ninth Organizes for Business," in John Bibby and Roger Davidson, *On Capitol Hill: Studies in the Legislative Process* (New York: Holt, Rinehart & Winston, Inc., 1967), pp. 144–69.

14. Richard F. Fenno, Jr., "The Internal Distribution of Influence: The House," in *The Congress and America's Future,* ed. David B. Truman (Englewood Cliffs, N.J.: Prentice-Hall, Inc., 1965), pp. 52–76; quotation is from p. 71.

15. See U.S. Congress, *Rules Adopted by the Committees of Congress,* compiled by the Joint Committee on Congressional Operations, 93d Cong., 1st sess., October 11, 1973.

16. *Congressional Quarterly Weekly Report*, January 11, 1975, p. 81.

17. Barbara Hinckley, *The Seniority System in Congress* (Bloomington, Ind.: Indiana University Press, 1971), p. 20.

18. *The Book of the States: 1974–75* (Lexington, Ky.: Council of State Governments, 1974), p. 74.

19. So far there are few longitudinal studies of legislative membership, but one study strongly suggests that careerism in state legislatures is increasing. See David Ray, "Membership Stability in Three State Legislatures: 1893–1969," *American Political Science Review* 68, no. 1 (March 1974): 106–12.

20. Richard Balkema, "Legislative Service, Selection of Committee Chairmen and Committee Assignments in the Michigan Senate: 1937–1967," *Public Affairs Bulletin* 4, No. 3 (May–June 1971): 2.

21. Gilbert Y. Steiner and Samuel K. Gove, *Legislative Politics in Illinois* (Urbana: University of Illinois Press, 1960), p. 62.

22. For a good beginning, see Alan Rosenthal, "Legislative Committee Systems: An Exploratory Analysis," *Western Political Quarterly* 26, no. 2 (June 1973): 252–62.

23. See Froman, *The Congressional Process*, pp. 52–60.

24. For a careful and extended study of conference committees and their work, see David J. Vogler, *The Third House: Conference Committees in the United States Congress* (Evanston, Ill.: Northwestern University Press, 1971).

25. This discussion has drawn heavily upon Froman's *The Congressional Process: Strategies, Rules and Procedures*. This excellent book should be read by students interested in factual and procedural details. For readable accounts of action on all significant bills, see *Congressional Quarterly Weekly Reports* and annual *Congressional Quarterly Almanacs*.

26. *Congressional Record*, 85th Congress, August 30, 1957, p. 151–72 (daily edition).

9

Legislative Parties and Party Leaders

The participation of party leaders has been mentioned several times in the preceding discussion of committee organization and floor procedures in legislatures. This chapter will examine parties and party leadership in some detail.

In Chapter 4, I defined leadershp as *the ability and willingness to exercise interpersonal influence in a situation through communication to fulfill certain goals,* and noted that every person engages in leadership from time to time. A political system includes a structure of authority positions to which are attached specific resources and powers to enhance the position incumbent's capacity to influence others to fulfill goals. For some positions, the resources are great. These are intended to be leadership positions and are made attractive in various ways—with authority, salary, assistance, and other emoluments—in order to stir the ambitions of those who will be able and willing to choose goals and work at the task of moving others to achieve them.

All legislators have but one vote. In terms of that basic consideration, they are all equal. But in the course of legislative work, the division of labor and the unequal abilities of nominal equals produce patterns of leadership and followership. Nevertheless, distinctions are sometimes kept subtle for two reasons. First, legislators come to the legislature as men of substantial achievement. A senior staff aide for the Democratic leadership of the U.S.

House is quoted this way:

> The typical member comes to Congress, his ego inflated, ready to take on the world. He's just won out over all other competition in a district with over 400,000 people—so why shouldn't his ego be inflated?
>
> As far as the leadership is concerned he figures he could do the job as well as anybody else. But everybody can't be Speaker, so he's willing to let McCormack or Albert or somebody else do it. You have to give up a little bit of power to get the House organized. He's willing to concede that as long as it's the bare minimum.[1]

In the second place, "leader" and "follower" are pejorative terms. In American society it is good to be thought of as a leader, but less honorable to be considered a follower. Besides being egotists, legislators are public men and women who have reputations to maintain in their constituencies. Matters of honor and recognition are not to be ignored by persons in the public eye. Those who follow may not admit the leadership of others. Leaders may be cautious in their claims lest they embarrass current and, potentially, future followers. So an ethos of equality in the legislature is sometimes preserved by putting into leadership positions individuals who will not aggressively seek to lead. This trait was described as a qualifying asset by supporters of Senator Mansfield before his reelection as Senate majority leader:

> In nominating his senior colleague from Montana for his fourth term as majority leader, Lee Metcalf said of Mike Mansfield: "We have a majority leader who regards every senator as an equal in a peerage he respects. He enjoys the profound respect of all who have served—not under him, the majority leader— but with him as a coequal." This word, "coequal," sums up Mike Mansfield's view of his role as leader of the majority Democrats in the Senate: his principal duty was to maintain a system which permitted individual, coequal senators the opportunity to conduct their affairs in whatever ways they deemed appropriate. A more distinct departure from the approach of his immediate predecessor, Lyndon Johnson, would be difficult to conceive.[2]

Leading and following are enmeshed with one another. The resources for leadership are not as concrete and countable as money in the economic system, but they are based upon specific authority in positions and processes set forth in the regime of the political system.[3]

THE STRUCTURE OF LEGISLATIVE LEADERSHIP

The Constitution briefly anticipates three specific congressional offices, but adds that each house may choose more. For the House, only the speaker is mentioned. Interestingly, the speaker need not be a member of the House, but in unbroken tradition all speakers have been members. The Constitution asserts that the vice-president of the United States shall be the president of the Senate, and, although not regularly allowed to vote on issues before the Senate, he may cast the deciding vote when the membership has reached a tie. John Adams, the first vice-president, still holds the record, having cast a deciding vote 20 times. The Constitution made provision for a "temporary" president of the Senate with the office of president pro tempore. He is the presiding officer when the president of the Senate is absent. In contemporary practice, the vice-president has other responsibilities than presiding in the Senate, so he rarely appears except when there is likelihood that the Senate will come to a tie vote on some matter of significance to the administration or the vice-president's party.

Conventional practice has made the place of the president pro tempore honorific. Since 1949 the Senate has elected to this position the senator in the majority party with the longest continuous service. In practice the elected president pro tempore presides occasionally, particularly on ceremonial occasions. Ordinarily assignments for presiding over the Senate are made from day to day among junior senators. As this indicates, little power is actually exercised in this position, in sharp contrast with the speakership in the House.

Most state constitutions provide that each house shall choose its own officers. Ordinarily the lower house has a speaker as presiding officer. Some constitutions provide more detail, specifying the positions of majority leader, minority leader, and the like. In 42 states the lieutenant governor is a constitutional officer, and in 35 states he presides over the state senate.* Constitutions vary in the titles used and detail of description, but most specify that state senates may choose such other officers as they deem necessary. In short, there is a constitutional basis for a structure of legislative leadership, but the actual structure usually goes beyond constitutional language. More legal detail is contained in the rules that each chamber makes for itself. At least as important, however, are the informal practices developed in each chamber and the way the members respond to and deal with the manners and practices employed by their leaders.

American legislative leaders are primarily party leaders. Conventional practice in Congress and the states is for the newly elected legislators of each party and each chamber to meet in a caucus or conference to thrash out privately who their leaders will be. Those issues decided, the legislatures convene and each party puts forward nominees for speaker, president, or

---

*In recent years the legislative duties of lieutenant governors have been declining and the National Conference of Lieutenant Governors has urged that lieutenant governors serve mainly as executives, not legislative functionaries. See *The Lieutenant Governor: The Office and Its Powers* (Lexington, Ky.: Council of State Governments, 1973), pp. ix–32.

leader, whatever the title. All the majority party members vote for the caucus choice, and majority party nominees take over formal control of the chamber. Deviations from this pattern are rare in partisanly competitive chambers, but leadership contests in one-party and nonpartisan legislatures are sometimes free-for-alls of individual enterprise and competition.

In short, then, there is a constitutional basis for leadership positions, but these have been enlarged upon and converted into a structure of party leadership with a specific division of labor in which there are whips, floor leaders, and presiding officers. All hold their positions at the pleasure of the party membership, or caucus. Each of these will be dealt with in the pages that follow.

Whips and Floor Leaders

Each party in each legislative chamber has an elected floor leader. He usually appoints one or more assistants. In Congress and in most legislatures, the primary assistant is known as the party whip. Because the U.S. House is so large, the whip actually has a substantial operation under his direction. In 1973 House Democrats elected Thomas O'Neill (Massachusetts) their floor leader. He appointed John McFall (California) as his whip. O'Neill and McFall organized a team of 3 deputy whips and 19 assistant whips. At the same time the House Republicans retained Gerald Ford as floor leader and Leslie Arends as whip. The Republicans had 3 regional division whips, each of whom had 3 to 6 assistants, for a total of 13 assistant whips. These numbers and selection procedures vary according to changes in party rules and practice. In the Senate the organizations are much smaller.[4] Democratic whip Robert Byrd (West Virginia) had 4 assistant whips in the Ninety-third Congress, while Republican whip Robert Griffin (Michigan) had 7. In state legislatures the floor leader and whip organizations are usually more modest. There may be no titled assistants to the floor leader, and rarely are there more than 3 or 4.

The responsibilities of the assistants to the floor leader vary in relation to the degree of partisan interest and activity that marks the legislative body and the issues at stake there. A study of the Democratic whip organization of 1962 and 1963 in the U.S. House revealed that four particular functions were served.[5] First, the whip organization would try to get maximum attendance by party members for key votes. Second, the whips would inform members of the party about upcoming issues, when particular business would be considered, and even explanations of the contents of certain proposals. Third, they would try to ascertain how members of the party intended to vote on pending issues. Sometimes the members were specifically polled. These whip polls aided the leaders in planning strategy. A fourth function for the whips is to apply pressure to get members to follow the preferences of the leadership.

Some of these functions are less relevant in the state legislatures. For instance, most legislators are on the floor most of the time in the states. Getting members to vote is less of a problem. Keeping them in line certainly is, however. In highly partisan states the floor leader and his aides sometimes even take attendance and line up votes for committee actions. Floor leaders have been known to hurry into committee meetings, making their presence and interest known, and thereby encouraging "right voting" on the part of their fellow partisans. It is apparent, however, that most state legislatures do not have elaborate whip organizations like the one in the U.S. House.

Normally, both the minority and majority parties of each house have a floor leader who organizes, and often personally engages in, the debate on bills that occurs on the chamber floor. Floor consideration is a significant decision point in the legislative process since all bills must survive it to become law. Floor consideration is potentially a wide-open debate stage which any member can use to be heard on a bill or to propose amendments. However, if every member had to be heard from or all floor amendments were to be considered seriously, not many bills would be adopted. The legislative process would be overloaded. A significant portion of the floor leaders' efforts is devoted to expediting business at the time of floor consideration. As bills are taken off the calendar, the floor leaders stand ready with proper motions to begin consideration, quash involved new proposals offered as amendments, fulfill earlier promises made to members for speaking time or consideration of anticipated amendments, and bring the legislation to final consideration.

Why do the members submit to such "generalship" by the floor leaders? All have stakes in specific bills, but all are responsible for acting on all bills. All are aware that full floor consideration of everything is impossible. To be able to achieve expeditious handling of the things they want, they must concede the same to others. The gatekeepers and signal callers in this process are the floor leaders. According to regular practice, the floor leaders are always recognized when they wish to speak or make a motion. They are regularly supported by a majority of their own party members when they make a motion. In the heat of a contest, their fellow partisans faithfully line up behind them. If, over time, a leader proves to be inept, foolish, or vain, or uses this leadership resource to personal advantage at the expense of his followers, he will be replaced. In short, the floor leader exercises leadership in a context of trust.

The floor leaders are partisans, and often the majority floor leader and the minority floor leader engage as rivals—one for the Republicans and one for the Democrats. Where discipline is strong, the majority leader regularly wins and the minority leader loses. But most issues are not "straight party" matters, so either leader may win with a coalition of supporters from both parties. Some matters are "strictly partisan." The leaders choose, sometimes, to attach a partisan flag to substantive issues in order to achieve the benefit of party loyalty. So the floor stage of bill consideration is a point where many options can be exercised, but these options are subject to selection and counterselection by the floor leaders, who in turn are guided by intelligence on substantive issues from party specialists from the relevant standing committees, as well as by tactical intelligence on voting support in the party and in the opposition from the party whips.

The Presiding Officer and His Tasks

The speaker of the House and, in some states, the elected president of the Senate act as top leaders in the chambers of their responsibility. The presiding officer is, first of all, a party man. He owes his position to his party majority. Of course, he is the presiding officer of the *whole* house, so the informal norms require that he deal fairly with members as individuals, and give the minority members their chances to have a say in debate and to offer alternatives in policy consideration. However, with careful husbanding, he controls the resources to win as long as he keeps his fellow partisans' support. He is the top partisan, and the majority floor leader and whips are his assistants. The minority floor leader is, alternatively, his ally and chief antagonist. To expedite chamber business, set up committees, including conference committees, and promote relations with the other chamber or the chief executive, the presiding officer and the minority leader jointly speak for "both sides of the aisle."†

On partisan matters the minority leader contests the majority leader's intentions and seeks to defeat them. In the press conferences before and after specific policy contests, each acts as spokesman for the rival perspectives. Interestingly, the minority leader, as top minority spokesman, is in some ways the second-ranking leader in the legislature, paralleling the presiding officer. If, in the next election, the party balance in the chamber switches, the minority leader becomes presiding officer and the former presiding officer becomes minority leader. These exchanges took place in Congress back in the late 1940s and early 1950s. Sam Rayburn (Democrat) was speaker in the Seventy-ninth Congress (elected in 1944) and Joseph Martin (Republican)

† In Congress and in most states, Republicans sit on the right and Democrats on the left of the center aisle of the chamber.

was minority leader. In the 1946 election the majority shifted, Martin became speaker and Rayburn the minority leader. In 1948 the majority shifted back to the Democrats, and Rayburn and Martin exchanged positions again, this time for four years. In 1952 the Republicans regained the majority, Martin was speaker and Rayburn the minority leader. In the 1954 election the Democrats resumed control, and the exchange was made once more. The Democrats have retained control ever since.

Strictly considered, the speaker has autocratic control over very little. He recognizes members for debate. He assigns bills to committees and rules on parliamentary questions, but even these matters can be appealed to the whole membership. In fact, however, the speaker is almost never overruled. With control of the floor, the party apparatus (floor leader, whips, and party staff), and the votes of his party colleagues who constitute a majority, the speaker is the preeminent member of the House.

Two major resources of recent speakers in the U.S. House are personal prestige and respect. Speaker Rayburn became a living legend. John McCormack was accorded less regard, but Carl Albert was widely admired. All recent speakers have worked their way up the leadership ranks and have come to the office with support and sensitivity to the prerogatives of the position accumulated over a substantial career.

In most states the speaker's resources in the formal rules are greater than in the U.S. House. According to George Blair, the authority of the speaker in the California Assembly extends to:

    1. appointing the chairmen, vice-chairmen, and members of all assembly standing and special committees;
    2. referring all bills to committees;
    3. recognizing members who wish to speak;
    4. chairing the committee of the whole;
    5. serving as an ex officio member of all assembly committees and joint legislative committees;
    6. voting on all questions and participating in debate if he chooses; and
    7. exercising various other powers as presiding officer, such as keeping order, putting questions to a vote, interpreting the rules and deciding points of order, and signing all acts, resolutions, warrants, and other documents ordered by the assembly.[6]

Authority under the rules is a resource for leadership. Party leaders have been characterized as "bosses" and "czars," and occasionally they act forcefully and arbitrarily. But the power to recognize does not mean many members may be ignored time and again. Discretion with recognition may "steer" debate, "shape" it, "color" it, but not distinctively determine its outcome. The committee assignments must accommodate traditional rights of members, as well as the larger system needs for specific policy outputs.[7] In the long run party leaders will be hurt by a tactic such as loading loyal but weak-minded members onto a key committee.

The leaders also obtain resources from and accumulate obligations to the chief executive. These are at any given time a great enhancement or a liability. The point is dramatically illustrated by the flight from Nixon by Republican House and Senate party leaders as the probability of impeachment increased in the summer of 1974. But the direction reversed when Ford, a former House party leader himself, assumed the presidency.

Party Conferences,
Caucuses, and Committees

In most legislative chambers there are party bodies, usually referred to as the party caucus or conference; that is, a private meeting of all the members of a party in a particular chamber. In Congress relatively little use of the party conference has been made since the mid-1930s until recently. Use varies in the states, with little use made in the predominantly one-party states, but where parties are closely balanced, conferences may be frequent—weekly or even more often. Since 1969, Democrats in the U.S. House have increasingly used the caucus as an instrument for hammering out organizational reforms.[8] The caucus is, of course, a two-edged sword—a leader may dominate it or be dominated by it.

Similarly party committees—variously named steering committees, executive committees, policy committees—may be mechanisms of the leader or impose limits on the leader. Consider Lyndon Johnson as Senate majority leader in contrast to Mike Mansfield:

> One of the most important instruments available to Johnson in his attempts to control the Senate was the Democratic Steering Committee. As leader, Johnson appointed members of the Steering Committee, and then dominated its deliberations. . . . Senators who went along with Johnson would receive assignments to the committees they coveted, and those who didn't go along wouldn't. And everyone knew that it was Lyndon Johnson who controlled the outcomes. . . .
>
> As with other facets of his leadership, Mansfield has approached the Steering Committee differently. He has not attempted to control its decisions, but has permitted it to work its will.[9]

In Congress, at least, party committees do not have clearly defined or predictable powers. For example, during the Ninety-third Congress, a proposal to reorganize House standing committees was developed by a bipartisan House Select Committee on Committees. Its chairman, Democrat Richard Bolling, sought support for the proposal in the House Democratic caucus. The caucus voted to refer the matter to a special party committee, the Democratic Committee on Organization, Study, and Review. That party committee, contrary to the publicly expressed views of the speaker and majority leader, but to the satisfaction of a majority of the caucus, effectively delayed the Bolling reform proposal from receiving consideration on the House floor, and saw to it that its own substitute was scheduled on the floor at the same time. The substance of the substitute was eventually adopted.[10] In short, party committees are not highly institutionalized and their significance from issue to issue is variable and difficult to predict.

LEADERSHIP ROLE BEHAVIOR

In Chapter 3 *role* was defined as *a position-related pattern of expected behavior*. Party leaders expect and are expected to behave in certain ways. The expectations of the members are particularly important in congressional politics because, as noted previously, the authority of the leadership is very modest. It is by meeting the needs of the members with their authority and by fulfilling member expectations with their demeanor that the leaders establish a working capital of respect and indebtedness to obtain members' cooperation. Most of the process takes place within each party, but some of it extends across party lines as well.

Leadership Roles in Congress

Members' expectations are strong constraints upon the behavior of party leaders in Congress. Six particular expectations are noteworthy.

1. Members expect fairness. More than anything, the leaders command control of the floor. Whether it is to get someone's pet bill through or to provide a member with a chance to speak on a major, controversial issue of the day, these are privileges that leaders can confer or deny. Members want their share of these privileges. They want political information—does the bill the leaders desire contain any booby traps that a rival candidate might identify later saying, "The incumbent voted for that law which hurts the people of this district." Candor and openness with the members is part of being fair.

2. Members expect help. There are so many intricacies that make a difference to the individual member, especially the House member without much seniority. While a leader cannot go to bat for members on every little point, still he must show that he cares: help a member to get a good committee assignment, pave the way for a member's amendment to an administration bill, lend a party staff person for a particular project, make a campaign speech for a member in a competitive district, help pry a bill out of committee, and so on. As Congressman Clem Miller (D., Cal.) wrote to his constituents:

> . . . [A]uthority to refer bills, to side track them or pigeon-hole them . . . is one of the principal power levers of the Speaker. Particularly for lesser legislation (which may be the lifeblood of individual congressmen) the chasm between the standing committee and the House Floor is bridged with the unchallenged power of the Speaker. He has many combinations of courses available to him through this complex labyrinth.[11]

3. Senior members expect the leaders to support the standing committees. As indicated previously, policy is shaped in committee. Most members' careers are specialized and wrapped up in their committee work. Senior members, chairmen, subcommittee chairmen, and ranking counterparts of the minority see the floor as a place of appellate decision making. Committee leaders of the majority party expect their leaders

> . . . to take a committee bill as given and shepherd it through, protecting it from amendments from either side of the aisle. Conversely, many ranking [minority] committee members would seem to see the job of their leadership either to help them substitute their own version of a bill, modify unwise legislation, or indeed, subvert it altogether with a motion to recommit.[12]

4. Junior members expect the leaders to provide a good rationale for the party's position on controversial issues. Members are most vulnerable to defeat early in their careers; they are not specialists, not influential, not well known in their districts, and not on top of all the issues. They are not in a position to win plaudits, but they feel vulnerable for the role call votes they have cast and apologetic for the ones they have missed. However, if they can go back to their districts and respond to questions on the issues with a reasonable rationale, a partisan point of view, they can seem competent and on top of things. It is the leaders' job to help junior members look good. Leaders appear at press conferences and "Meet the Press" sessions to explain the party's position on matters. In these activities the leaders can interpret and shape the issues of the day, but the leaders tend scrupulously to speak for the center of their party, reflecting existing agreement, not staking out new positions in the hope that the members will support those positions. Thus the leaders "read the mood" of their respective chambers and interpret the issues. For junior members this is solid political intelligence which helps them sort out and explain their particular actions to constituents and interest groups back home.

5. Leaders of the president's party are expected to push his program and enjoy his confidence. Leaders have modest authority. Presidents have much more, but presidents need legislative adoption for the programs they promote. Legislative leaders can draw upon a president, particularly one of their own party, for resources to influence members. David Truman offers this description:

> A key leader in the House, who has been Majority Leader both when the President was of his party and when he was not, described his efforts under the latter circumstances to negotiate with the standing committee chairmen, individually, in order to develop an agreed on program for a Congressional session. When asked whether the President's being of his party made any difference in the performance of his task, the immediate reply was, "Much easier, much easier." A respected and experienced member of the Senate's staff, commenting on his own observation of the relations of Floor Leader and President, noted their tendency toward collaboration and emphasized particularly the inclination of Senate elective leaders not only to acquiesce in but to encourage presidential initiatives. He cited the case of a Floor Leader, not publicly known for his dependence on his party's President, who increasingly during his tenure solicited White House intervention with wavering senators in aid of agreed legislative projects.[13]

Obviously, legislative leaders and presidents must work out the extent of their intimacy and mutual loyalty. President Nixon did not cultivate close ties with Republican congressional leaders. However, President Ford moved quickly to establish lines of mutual assistance with leaders of his own party in both houses much as Presidents Johnson and Kennedy had before him.

6. *Party leaders are supposed to be process managers.* The leaders are expected to make workable the floor consideration stage of policy adoption. Their job is scheduling, getting the sponsors to the floor for debate, providing information, granting opportunities to debate and amend to members, and bringing matters to a decision point so they can be disposed of and new business can be considered. This is what leaders do and what they are expected to do. Interestingly, they are not expected to promote their own set of legislative proposals; it is not their job to put together a package of bills and amendments known as a legislative leader's "program." This is even true when the majority leaders face a minority accompanied by a president. We do not hear of "Mansfield's program" or "Albert's program," much less a program from minority leaders such as Scott or Rhodes. To the contrary, Peabody says, "Mansfield, in particular, tends to emphasize his ministerial role: 'Individual Senators have more power. All you have as majority leader is a title, but you are the servant of the other Senators.'"[14] Harry McPherson, an insider who served as staff assistant to Mansfield, says that in 1961 President Kennedy "needed a leader in the Senate who would serve as a conduit for his programs—not an independent source of power who wished to write on his own."[15] It has not been uncommon to find a lack of clear

leadership frustrating or disappointing to freshmen. Two freshmen Democrats are quoted as follows:

> I am dismayed by the lack of leadership on the Democratic side of the aisle, especially in view of the tight Republican discipline. I have never been pressured to vote in any particular way.
>
> I expected stricter discipline on the part of the leadership and thought they would probably invoke penalties if their suggestions were not followed. I haven't found it that way.[16]

Policy promotional leadership comes largely from outside the Congress. Policy leadership within derives almost entirely from the standing committee leaders in the House. In the Senate there is more possibility for individualistic behavior, and conspicuous policy promotional activity has come from senators vying for opportunities to seek the presidency. It is left to party leaders to facilitate, assist, and urge policies to final adoption, but not to select them, make substantive changes in them, or attach their names to them.‡

Leadership Roles in State Legislatures

Partisanship in the states varies. It is very high in New Jersey, New York, and, in recent years, California. It is much lower in Missouri, Idaho, and Georgia. Where partisanship is high, the likelihood of leader significance in policy making is also high. However, in some of the one-party states, for example, Georgia and Alabama, legislators report that decision making in their legislatures is highly centralized; that is, the most significant decisions of the legislature were actually made in a policy committee. Ordinarily the elected leaders of the legislative bodies are members of the policy committee membership.

The members' expectations of leaders vary somewhat from those noted in Congress. The mutual help relationship is commonplace, but notice that the legislator earns help from the leaders through loyalty.

> You're a member of the club, which you won't be if you don't go along with the party leaders. The non-conformists are given some consideration, but their

‡There are occasional exceptions to this generalization, particularly in the Senate. But the exceptions tend to be in matters in which the party leader has a "specialist's credentials" as a senior committee member. For instance, Senate Majority Leader Mansfield sponsored several amendments to military spending and foreign aid bills to achieve military withdrawal from Vietnam. At the time Mansfield was the third highest-ranking Democratic member of the Senate Foreign Relations Committee, and his action was viewed as that of a committee man rather than as the policy leader of his party in the Senate.

bills don't get anywhere. If you're in good standing with the Speaker and others, they can influence the members and put in a good word for you. They can do a lot toward seeing whether your bill will get on the calendar and pushing the hearings along. Since most members are simple followers, it helps a bill along tremendously if the leaders are for it.[17]

Supporting remarks come from Ohio legislators in particular, tying the party in the legislature with the electoral party outside:

If you stick with the party, they'll take care of you. Get you a job after defeat. If you look for security, better be a good boy and do what [you are] told.

Politically, if you fail to line up with the party, in all probability that failure will be brought to the attention of your county chairman. He, in turn, could make it rough on you if you wanted to run again. Your local party wants to know if you can be counted on to support party principles.[18]

An area of help that members like from party leaders is in staff work. State legislatures lack much professional staff, particularly staff that goes beyond factual analysis into political interpretation. If anyone has such staff, it will be the party leadership. Thus from time to time, when the legislator wants a report describing what effect a proposed bill will have on his district and the neighboring ones, or a speech for a special occasion, the party leader may be able to assign one of his staff people to such a task.

The "fairness" expectation is less well established in state legislatures. In highly partisan legislatures, the leadership of the majority may deal capriciously with members of the minority from time to time: a supposedly "dead" bill suddenly comes to the floor as an amendment to another bill, or an anticipated bill is "passed over" or referred back to committee. Occasionally such actions are shouted through over the impassioned appeals by minority opponents. Arbitrary handling is especially common as a legislative session comes to an end and there is a backlog of official actions to be taken. On such occasions the leaders, with their control of the floor and the rules, pretty much determine what will happen. The pressures of time are such that individual legislators do not dare object because their impatient colleagues want to conclude the session. Often it is not until several days after the session is over and the final copies of bills, journals, and roll call votes are printed that some of the members can review events sufficiently to determine what official actions actually took place in the last days of a session. In such an environment, it is not uncommon to find that advantages and disadvantages were far from fairly shared.

The expectations by senior committee members of party leaders do not have the relevance in states that they have in Congress. Party leaders control committee memberships through appointive powers, and the floor stage of bill consideration is so much more significant in the states than in Congress.

With few exceptions, committee chairmen are the party leaders' supporters. Thus it is the committee leaders who are expected to serve and support the party leaders in most states. In states where partisanship is low, committee leaders often have their positions because of factional alignments.

Because legislators, even legislative leaders, have relatively low visibility to the public there is less of an expectation by members that the party leaders provide a rationale for policy choices than is the case in Congress. Also, in the competitive states the party caucus is used sufficiently so that the legislators do have a chance to hear their leaders' views about why certain issues should be regarded as party matters, and what the rationales for such party matters are.

The political infighting in state legislatures is much more frequent and changeable than in Congress. Party leaders come and go much more quickly than in Congress, so new members are put on the spot soon after election about whom they will support in contests for leadership. Helping to pick a winner for party leader enhances a newcomer's career, but to be with the losers probably will result in appointments to minor committees and little help from the leaders.

The possibility that the party leaders in the legislature will take their roles beyond *process management* and into *policy promotion* does exist in some legislatures. Ordinarily, however, such policy promotion is offered by the legislative leader of the party opposing the governor. An apt example is offered by the activities of Jesse Unruh, long-time Democratic leader in the California Assembly (lower house). After Ronald Reagan, Republican, won the California governorship in 1966, the major spokesman for alternative programs was Unruh, speaker and leader of a majority opposition in the assembly. After losing some seats in 1968, he continued to lead the opposition as minority leader and ultimately became the Democratic candidate for governor in 1970.

Nevertheless, process management is the primary task of state legislative leaders. Referring to Unruh again, it is interesting to note that for most of his years as speaker there was a Democratic governor, Edmund G. (Pat) Brown. During that period Unruh obtained a national reputation as a legislative reformer when he gave leadership and impetus to changes in procedure and organization. A recent description of Unruh's accomplishments in the assembly states:

> The net result of his work was a marked strengthening and modernizing of that body. Committees were reduced in size, the number of committee assignments per member was cut to make workloads manageable, staffs were recruited to aid committees and the assembly, and legislative salaries were increased. Speaker Unruh did much to restore the assembly to a position of power in state policy-making matching that acquired by the chief executive, the governor.[19]

Improvements for process management are a consistent theme in the writings of legislative leaders. Almost without exception, they emphasize organization, procedure, staffing, and facilities as requiring change in the future. *None put into focus a felt need for legislative leaders to equip themselves for or engage in policy promotion.*§

Ordinarily legislative leaders of the chief executive's party accommodate themselves to serving as inside leaders for the governor's program while he is expected to play the public role—speaking for his program and legislative objectives before the news media and public audiences. Typically this is true in the partisanly competitive states, but it also occurs in states where factional strife is found. McClesky points out that in Texas the selection of two recent speakers in the house was undoubtedly affected by the governor's support,[20] and because of that support, they owed allegiance to the governor. Unruh observes that in Louisiana the governor dominates the legislature, using tools ordinarily reserved to legislative leaders; namely, the power to appoint chairmen and members of both the senate and house appropriations committees.[21]

THE MAKING OF LEGISLATIVE LEADERS

In Congress

There is substantial stability in the top party leadership positions. In the House the era of stability dates back to the accession of Democrat Sam Rayburn to the speakership in 1940. With interruptions caused by his party's minority status (1947–48, 1953–54), during which he served as minority leader, his tenure as speaker extended to his death in 1961. Rayburn chose lieutenants who have since succeeded him in the speakership: McCormack, speaker from 1962 to 1971, was majority leader under Rayburn; and Albert, speaker from 1971 to 1977, was Rayburn's whip. What has developed in the

§See, for example, essays by Charles F. Kurfess, speaker of the Ohio House of Representatives, Jesse Unruh, former speaker of the California Assembly, and Robert P. Knowles, majority leader and president pro tempore in the Wisconsin State Senate. Only Kurfess speaks about policy promotion, and then in general terms: "Leadership should be strong enough not only to guide the legislative body itself, but to forcefully represent its viewpoint to the administrative branch of government and to represent effectively the legislative branch of government to the news media and the public as well." The essays appear in Donald G. Herzberg and Alan Rosenthal, eds., *Strengthening the States: Essays on Legislative Reform* (Garden City, N.Y.: Doubleday and Company, Inc., 1971), especially pp. 140–71; quotation is from p. 145.

House among Democrats is a pattern of routine advancement to top leadership positions from lower ones.[22]

There have been several serious attempts to challenge the advancement of lower party leaders as they moved to higher positions; however, the challenges did not come close to success. In 1962 Congressman Richard Bolling mounted a challenge to Albert's succession from whip to floor leader. When the time arrived to make the effort in the House Democratic caucus, it was apparent to Bolling that he did not have the votes, so he chose not to formally contest the matter.[23] In 1968 when Morris Udall challenged the reelection of Speaker McCormack, he was defeated in the caucus by a 178–58 vote. But by 1970, McCormack had decided to retire. Automatic succession by Albert seemed assured,‖ but a fight ensued for the position of majority leader which was a challenge of automatic succession by the whip, Hale Boggs. The contest went two ballots. On the first ballot there were five contestants, and Boggs got the most votes with 95 of 248. A majority was necessary to win. After the withdrawal of the two candidates who obtained the least number of votes on the first ballot, a second ballot decided the matter: Boggs 140, Udall 88, and a third candidate with 17. Albert and Boggs then chose Thomas O'Neill as their whip.[24] In 1973, after Boggs died in an airplane accident, O'Neill was elevated to majority leader without opposition, and he and the speaker retained the right, on a closely contested set of caucus votes, to appoint their own whip. Subsequently, John McFall was appointed.

In short, challenge has been commonplace among House Democrats, but turnovers have not taken place. Case studies indicate that the selections and leadership behavior of those chosen for lower positions attract broad support from the party at large. It may well be that the challenges have sensitized the leaders to member concerns. After confirmation in their leadership positions, Albert and O'Neill agreed to reform and encourage the activity of the Steering and Policy Committee of the party to recommend party policy and legislative priorities.[25]

Top Democratic leaders in the Senate have enjoyed position security. There have been but two majority leaders since 1953: Lyndon Johnson, until 1961, and Mike Mansfield until 1977. However, consecutive contests occurred for election as majority whip in the late 1960s and early 1970s. Both Johnson and Mansfield moved to floor leader from whip. When Mansfield advanced, Hubert Humphrey became whip, remaining until he became vice-president in 1965. Russell Long won the position in a three-way contest in 1965. He retained the position until 1969, when Edward Kennedy challenged and defeated him. Both Long and Kennedy were erratic in the whip's job.

‖ Actually a challenge was made by John Conyers, black representative from Detroit, but Albert won 220–20.

Robert Byrd informally served as an assistant to his party leaders from 1967 on. In 1971, when Kennedy's interest in Senate affairs seemed to have flagged, Byrd challenged and defeated Kennedy in the Democratic conference, 31 votes to 24.[26]

Republicans have maintained less stability in their top leadership than the Democrats. In the House, stability among Republicans seemed the equal of the Democrats until 1959. Joseph Martin achieved the position of minority leader in 1939. He remained leader, and twice was speaker when the Republicans held a majority in the House, with no serious challenges until a bitter conflict in 1959. In the 1958 elections the Republicans lost 47 seats in the House. After 20 years as leader and nearly 35 in the House, Martin was thought by many Republicans to be losing his grip. His challenger was Charles Halleck, who had served Martin as majority leader in the two terms when Republicans were a majority. On a second secret ballot in caucus, Halleck won 74 to 70. Six years later, Halleck was challenged by Gerald Ford, who won on a 73 to 67 vote, in which two-thirds of his votes came from Republicans who had been in the House five terms or less. Ford remained leader until 1973 when he became the first appointed vice-president. John Rhodes emerged as a consensus choice and was elected without opposition.

Republican whips have enjoyed long tenure. The whip under Martin served 11 years and died in office. Leslie Arends won the position in 1943, and except for a challenge in 1965 which he survived 70 to 59, he served continuously until he retired in 1975. He was replaced by the election of Robert Michel, from Illinois, who easily defeated two other rivals.

Republican membership in the House is more volatile than is the Democratic membership. Only a few current Republican members have served in Congress when the party enjoyed majority status. Leadership turnover has been irregular and unpredictable. Several combatants in the 1959 and 1965 conflicts have moved to higher office and out of the House—including Ford, of course, but also Laird, Goodell, and Griffin. There is no particular reason to expect that stability and consensus of the present time to persist.

In the Senate, Republican conflict has occurred rather frequently. From 1947 to 1968, there were four contested elections for floor leader. Three were won by relative conservatives. Dirksen brought a decade of stability, serving from 1959 to 1969, with Thomas Kuchel, a moderate, as whip. A vacancy for whip in 1969 brought open competition, won by Hugh Scott against Roman Hruska, 23 to 20. Upon Dirksen's death, only months later, Scott defeated Howard Baker for floor leader. Griffin and Baker then ran for the whip vacancy, with Griffin winning a close contest, 23 to 20. Scott and Griffin remained the Republican leaders until Scott retired in 1977.

In Legislatures

Stability is not the hallmark of state legislative leadership. Turnover is relatively common. In fact, in several legislatures tradition requires that there be alternation of leaders from term to term. McClesky points out that Texas has had a tradition of one term for speakers of the house. From 1877 to 1959, only two speakers served a second term. Since then there have been three two-term speakers.[27] On the other hand a sharp contrast is offered by South Carolina. Sol Blatt resigned from the South Carolina House on July 31, 1973, after 33 years as its speaker.[28]

There are two significant reasons for rapid turnover among state legislative leaders. The first is the fact of high turnover among legislators generally; it is, therefore, difficult for leadership to become established. Secondly, top leaders in legislatures are often ambitious for higher political career opportunities. Some are content to be "big frogs in a little pond," but many are not. Speakers and floor leaders frequently try to win higher office—statewide elective office, Congress, and the like. The career position of a state legislative leader is quite different from that of a congressional leader. For the latter, there is little room at the top. To become a U.S. House leader in particular, one must have spent the best years of his career in the House. Occasionally Senate leaders try for the presidency. In contrast, a state legislative leader is lower in the career ladder, there are numerous higher opportunities, and the future perquisites of staying in a leadership position in the legislature are likely to be both modest and risky.

An interesting comparative analysis of state legislative party leaders indicates that leadership selection and tenure patterns do become evident in the more professionalized legislatures.[29] Considering legislative salaries, length of session, staffing, and measures of services available to legislatures, eight legislatures with two-party competition were ranked from high to low on professionalism. In order, the states were New York, Pennsylvania, Illinois, Wisconsin, Connecticut, Rhode Island, Iowa, and Montana. Then the legislative leaders were studied in terms of their number, experience, and turnover during the 1945–1970 period. The authors of the research conclude that:

> More professional legislatures tend to have: (1) less turnover of leadership, and (2) longer periods of apprenticeship for leaders. Evidence exists of (3) an established pattern of succession, and (4) fewer contests for leadership posts in some of the more professional legislatures, but the effects of professionalism on these aspects of leadership are very uncertain. Professionalism appears to be a necessary but not a sufficient condition for development of continuity and stability in leadership positions.[30]

ALTERNATIVE LEGISLATIVE LEADERSHIP

Are there alternative leaders to the formal floor leaders in legislative bodies? Data to answer the question are both spotty and ambiguous, but some partial responses can be made.

The Democratic Study Group

Until recently there has been a factional rival to the Democratic party leadership in the U.S. House. It is referred to as the DSG, for its title, Democratic Study Group. The very organization of the DSG, formed in September 1959, suggests some preexisting informal leadership patterns in the House of Representatives.

The Democratic party has, for a century, been a divided party, and in the years since Franklin D. Roosevelt, a party divided on social services, civil rights, and defense policies. The northern Democrats favor greater governmental social services, broader civil rights, particularly for blacks, and less emphasis on military and defense spending than the southern Democrats. These differences sharpened after World War II, in an era when Democrats regularly dominated Congress (except for 1947–48 and 1953–54). This period was also one in which the standing committee system rigidified and extended the prerogatives associated with seniority. For the House of Representatives noteworthy elections occurred in 1946 to 1952, and 1958 on the party mixture. In 1946 the Republicans obtained a majority by gaining 56 seats, nearly all of which were won at the expense of Democrats in the North. Control tipped back in 1948 when 75 seats were gained by Democrats, mostly in the North. In 1950 Republicans picked up 28 seats and in 1952, 22 more, gaining a slight majority. In 1954 Democrats reclaimed control of the House by gaining 19 seats. Control meant control of the party leadership and, more importantly, the committees. Election turnovers of recent years were in the North. The stable Democratic districts were in the southern and border states and within party-dominated large cities. Most of the senior Democrats on committees were southerners. In 1956 there were few turnovers and almost no net change in the party balance of the House, but in 1958 the Democrats made a dramatic gain of 48 seats, all outside the South.

What the new northern Democrats found, and the pattern that continued through most of the 1960s, was that there were about 100 Democrats from former Confederacy states, constituting something more than one-third of the Democratic House membership, but that these were the districts undisturbed by the election tides of the 1940s and 1950s. The members from these southern districts dominated the committee leadership in the party because chairmanships go to the member of the majority party with the longest continuous service on the committee. Table 9.1 shows the imbalance as it was in 1964.

To oversimplify, a substantial number of young liberal northern Democrats joined a majority party in the House to find that policy leadership was not offered by the party leaders, who managed the process of bill consideration *after* the committee work was done. If these liberals were to affect policy content, it had to be done in the committees and subcommittees. But a lion's share of these arenas were dominated by southerners who did not hold their liberal views and who knew how to use the legislative machinery to delay, amend, compromise, and water down the proposals of the junior hotbloods. The southerners by themselves did not have the votes to dominate the policy processes, but in combination with most of the Republicans they did. Liberals perceived a "conservative coalition" of southern Democrats with Republicans that frustrated their efforts at liberal legislation.#

Congressional Quarterly Almanac reports conservative coalition roll call voting. By its definition, a conservative coalition roll call vote is a House or Senate vote on which a majority of voting Republicans and a majority of voting southern Democrats oppose the stand taken by a majority of northern Democrats. The following table reports the percentage of recorded votes for both houses on which the coalition appeared and the percentage of times the coalition won.

Year	Appearances (%)	Wins (%)
1961	28	55
1962	14	62
1963	17	50
1964	15	51
1965	24	33
1966	25	45
1967	20	63
1968	24	73
1969	27	68
1970	22	66
1971	30	83
1972	27	69
1973	23	61
1974	24	59

SOURCE: *Congressional Quarterly Almanac, 1974* (Congressional Quarterly Service, 1975), p. 992.

Table 9.1   Southern Share of Influential House Committee Positions January 1964 (%)

All Democratic congressmen	38
Membership on top three committees	36
(Rules, Ways and Means, Appropriations)	
Major committee chairmanships	53
Subcommittee chairmanships	53
Holding first three positions on committees	49

SOURCE: Raymond E. Wolfinger and Joan Heifetz Hollinger, "Safe Seats, Seniority, and Power in Congress," in *American Political Science Review*, 59, no. 2 (June 1975): 339.

The response by northern liberals was to put together an organization, first to affect policy but also to reform the structure and rules of the Congress.[31] Membership has varied from session to session between 115 and 170 members, and dues are $100 per year. But staff salaries come in part from members' personal staff payroll. The DSG is essentially an organization of congressmen, but it has a staff of about 12 people, of whom 4 do research on legislation. The purposes of the organization are several. The first and most important one is to provide information on major legislation. Members and staff put out fact sheets on major proposals coming out of committees. They are a readable 5 to 10 pages of summarizing and analyzing the bill, possible amendments, and arguments for and against. There is a weekly legislative report indicating those matters that are coming up. The DSG also develops research reports for campaigns and sends them to Democratic challengers, who, if they win, may join the group.

Secondly, the DSG has operated a whip system independent of the regular leadership. In the past it was used particularly to get liberals to the floor for participation in teller votes before recorded teller votes were allowed. In recent years, however, this activity has been discontinued. Thirdly, the DSG coordinates its members for strategic bargaining with committee chairmen, the party leaders, and lobbying groups outside of Congress.

Measuring the effectiveness of the DSG is difficult. Stevens, Miller, and Mann conclude that:

> DSG cohesion has increased relative to that of other groups [Republicans, southern Democrats, non-DSG–non-southern Democrats] and . . . the positions taken on the issues by DSG members usually are easily distinguishable from those of nonmembers. More important, however, the evidence is unmistakable that the Democratic Study Group members are, on most issues, quite united and that they constitute a formidable bloc.[32]

The DSG has been active in obtaining procedural reforms both within the Democratic party and in Congress. The recorded teller reform adopted for the Ninety-second Congress was a DSG accomplishment. Another reform makes secret sessions of committees harder to obtain. In the Democratic party, a new rule requires that each standing committee chairman be subject to Democratic caucus approval. At DSG urging, a Steering and Policy Committee of the Caucus has been activated. Actual challenges to party leaders have not succeeded, but relations with the regular leaders are closer. *Congressional Quarterly* reports:

> Relations between the DSG and the Democratic House leadership have fluctuated through the years. During most of the Rayburn and McCormack periods, the DSG provided an alternative to regular leadership channels. But contact has increased somewhat under Albert, and somewhat more this year under O'Neill, the first DSG member ever to become a majority leader. . . . O'Neill is the first member of the House leadership who has generally been sympathetic to the peace-and-new-priorities position of most DSG leaders.[33]

There is no organized conservative group. The term "conservative coalition" is an analytical label for distinguishing likenesses in roll call voting, but does not have any organization. For awhile, attention was paid to some 30 to 35 southern Democrats who gathered from time to time to map strategy during the 1960s. The press dubbed them the Boll Weevils, but most of the leading members have since retired from office.[34]

State Delegations and Regional Groups

One other form of organization should be noted. For many states, delegations of the same party meet together. Ordinarily, the delegation considers the member with the most seniority its "dean," and in some groups he leads the meeting. Some state delegations are more active than others. Most do not deal with issues concerning which divisions of opinion are likely. A helpful quote comes from a big city northern Democrat:

> On the big stuff we meet in our dean's office. We usually meet only when there is some dissatisfaction with the leadership position. When they see us meeting, they worry about it.[35]

Ordinarily the state delegations use their numbers to increase their bargaining power. A united delegation can bargain with party leaders or the administration. One of the institutionalized patterns relating to deans and state delegations is in the assignment of members to standing committees.

The delegations can use their group strength to get good assignments for delegation members.

State delegation meetings tend to be casual; some might be characterized as "rap" sessions. Kingdon quotes a congressman this way:

> We happened to be meeting on another matter, and the guys started asking each other how they'd vote [on an emergency college loan proposal]. I said I'd vote for it, and _____ said he'd be against it. Then most of us, as we talked around the room, said we'd vote for it. When we came back, _____ had voted for it. There is some tendency to stick together. (Question: Why?) Look what happened to _____ last time. His opponent put ads all over the district, saying, "Look at education: All [the state's] congressmen voted aye; _____ voted no. Stand up for education." Education is kind of a sacred cow. You look funny if you're not with the rest of the guys on it.[36]

There are some parallels in state legislatures. It is not uncommon for certain geographic units to act with unity, particularly within one political party. In Illinois, for example, the Chicago Democrats make up a substantial voting bloc in the Illinois General Assembly. On a great many issues, those elected by the "Daley Organization" vote with near unanimity on issues relevant to the city of Chicago and the future strength of their party organization.[37] In the Pennsylvania House the urban axis dominates the Democratic party, and in 1968 when a Democratic majority was elected, a combination of the urban delegations from Philadelphia and Pittsburgh took over the party's leadership—the speaker was from Philadelphia and the majority leader was from Pittsburgh. In Texas, on the other hand, despite factional electoral politics among the Democrats, McClesky indicates that "legislative factions are poorly institutionalized, with a conspicuous lack of continuity and defined leadership. . . . The result, then is that factional feeling appears to have only limited impact on the legislative process."[38] The effects of factionalism in state legislatures are highly variable.

Informal Groups

Another level of leadership, that of informal groups, exists in legislative bodies. Legislators are, of course, socially involved with one another. These associations take the form of informal groups and, given the legislative interests of the members, their legislative work is affected by their associations. Samuel Patterson found friendship cliques of from six to eight members in the Wisconsin legislature and reported that they tended to vote together on the floor.[39] A similar tendency was noted in the California Assembly.[40] Monsma distinguished between *primary* groups, those associated because of affection, and *secondary* groups, those associated as members who discuss legislation together frequently. He found that in legislative voting, members of friendship groups and secondary groups voted similarly, but that secondary group affiliations seemed to have stronger influence on voting similarity than did the friendship groups.[41]

CONCLUDING OBSERVATIONS

The most significant observation about American legislative leaders is that they act as process managers. They are specialists in procedure, concerning themselves with the flow of bills through the committees and floor consideration. The substance of policy is usually a secondary concern. Policy leadership is expected from the chief executive. Even when the executive is of the opposite party, the majority leader waits for the chief executive's program. His party's policy specialists—committee leaders or potential candidates for the chief executive's office, perhaps—will dissect the chief executive's proposals. Perhaps they will sponsor alternative bills. But legislative leaders rarely view the development and promotion of an "alternative program" as their task.

For the task of process management, leaders have modest powers over procedures. But leaders have their positions because members of their party chose them. Skill, fairness, and political sensitivity can accumulate obligations from members. In state legislatures party leaders usually control committee leadership. These resources support the leader's efforts in process management. Most important, the legislature is a complicated subsystem processing tremendous amounts of information. Leaders are at the center of the information network. Using that information by selectively sharing it with some members and denying it to others, they manage the bill process.

There are competing leaders. The Democratic Study Group leaders in the U.S. House constitute the strongest institutionalized example of leadership rivaling the party leaders. The DSG has attempted to engage in both policy promotion and process management. In recent years it has lost its distinctiveness because its members have achieved significant positions in the regular organization of the Democratic party. They have, however, brought an increased emphasis on policy promotion to that party. In other bodies, however, clear alternative leaders other than those in party positions are uncommon.

The effectiveness of party leaders is difficult to evaluate. A recent study of decision making by members in the U.S. House, for example, reports that "the leadership of neither party is particularly important" in affecting the voting decisions of the members.[42] But the effects of leaders' process management have less than direct consequences on the legislators' actual voting; it is, rather, in structuring the choices that the legislators get to vote on. Consider the account written by Neil MacNeil of "How Ford Put the Lid on Cooper-Church," as it appeared in *Time* Magazine, July 20, 1970:

How Ford Put the Lid on Cooper-Church

Two weeks ago, the Senate administered a mild rebuke to President Nixon when it passed the Cooper-Church Amendment cutting off funds for U.S. Operations in Cambodia. The lengthy Senate debate embarrassed the Administration, and when the matter came before the House last week Republican Minority Leader Gerald Ford was determined that the embarrassment would not be repeated. *Time* Congressional Correspondent Neil MacNeil explains how he did it:

The parliamentary situation was this: the military sales bill that the House had passed some months back had been amended by the Senate and returned to the House in the form containing the Cooper-Church Amendment. The bill was destined for a House-Senate conference, but the rules provide for the House conferees to be "instructed" on their stance by the House itself. It was in this area that the game was played.

Under the rules, the minority party has the right to make the first motion to instruct. This option gave Jerry Ford a weapon that he used with devastating effect on the doves. He decided on a maneuver that would force the doves to lead from weakness. "I'm going to get the weakest guy on our side of the aisle to offer the motion," he told a fellow Republican. He picked Donald Riegle, Jr., of Michigan, 32, a dove who Ford accurately figured would provoke maximum opposition to the doves' own cause. Riegle is a brash young second-term Republican who has offended members of the House by open criticism of his seniors. "They really had it wired," one dove said when he heard of Ford's choice. "They got this potato head to make the motion."

Some of the dovish Republicans tried to talk Riegle out of it, but he would not be denied his moment on center stage. Riegle offered his motion for the House to join the Senate in approving Cooper-Church. Wayne Hays of Ohio, a Democratic hawk, instantly asked House Speaker John McCormack who would assign the speaking time during the debate on Riegle's motion. Riegle, replied McCormack. The prospect of Riegle cavorting, however briefly, in even a minor leadership role was too much for Hays, a veteran of 22 years in the House. He moved to table Riegle's motion, which, under House rules, automatically cut off all debate.

Hays had taken Ford's bait. His own hawkishness and enmity toward Riegle overwhelmed any reluctance he may have felt as a Democrat to abet the Administration strategy. The House approved Hays' motion, 237 to 153. The House's doves, who had little hope of winning on Cooper-Church but yearned for a floor debate on the war issue, had been outmaneuvered, outplayed, and outvoted. Ford knew the rules, he knew his colleagues, and he knew how to use both to get what he wanted.[43]

Robert Peabody posed the question, "What difference does the congressional party leadership make?" and concluded a lengthy discussion by saying the answer depends upon how broadly one looks at the context of their activity.[44] Direct measures, such as those by Kingdon, suggest little effectiveness. Case studies indicate timely acts when a leader tipped things one way or another. The circumstances in which interpersonal influence occurs are difficult to systematically observe. Subjective judgment suggests that, viewed as process managers, party leaders are significant forces in the legislative subsystem. To look for their influence in policy promotion is to look where their influence is only occasionally exercised. This is not to argue that party leaders should not or cannot affect policy, but that they consider policy of secondary importance. Managing legislative procedures is their prime task.

NOTES

1. Quoted by Robert L. Peabody in *Leadership in Congress: Stability, Succession, and Change* (Boston: Little, Brown and Company, 1976), p. 50.

2. John G. Stewart, "Two Strategies of Leadership: Johnson and Mansfield," in *Congressional Behavior*, ed. Nelson W. Polsby (New York: Random House, 1971), pp. 61–92; quote is from p. 69.

3. See James S. Coleman, "Political Money," *American Political Science Review* 64, no. 4 (December 1970): 1074–88.

4. Walter J. Oleszek, "Party Whips in the United States Senate," *Journal of Politics* 33, no. 4 (November 1971): 955–79.

5. Randall B. Ripley, "The Party Whip Organizations in the United States House of Representatives," *American Political Science Review* 58, no. 3 (September 1964): 561–76.

6. George S. Blair, *American Legislatures: Structure and Process* (New York: Harper & Row, Publishers, 1967), p. 156.

7. Compare to John C. Wahlke, "Organization and Procedure," in *The State Legislatures in American Politics*, ed. Alexander Heard (Englewood Cliffs, N.J.: Prentice-Hall, Inc., 1966), pp. 126–53, especially p. 140.

8. See "House Democrats: Dispute Over Caucus Role," in *Congressional Quarterly Guide to Current American Government: Fall 1975* (Washington, D.C.: Congressional Quarterly, Inc., 1975), pp. 26–30; and David W. Rohde, "Committee Reform in the House of Representatives and the Subcommittee Bill of Rights," *The Annals of the American Academy of Political and Social Science* 411 (January 1974): 39–47.

9. David W. Rohde, Norman J. Ornstein, and Robert L. Peabody, "Political Change and Legislative Norms in the Senate" (Paper presented to the Annual Meeting of the American Political Science Association, Chicago, Ill., August 29–September 2, 1974), p. 21.

10. See *Congressional Quarterly Guide to Current American Government, Fall 1974* (Washington, D.C.: Congressional Quarterly, Inc., 1974), pp. 50–51; Roger H. Davidson, "The Struggle for Congressional Committee Reform" (Paper presented to the Annual Meeting of the American Political Science Association, Chicago, Ill., August 29–September 2, 1974); and *Congressional Quarterly Weekly Report,* October 12, 1974, pp. 2896–98.

11. Clem Miller, *Member of the House: Letters of a Congressman,* ed. John W. Baker (New York: Charles Scribner's Sons, 1962), p. 44.

12. Peabody, *Leadership in Congress,* p. 56.

13. David B. Truman, *The Congressional Party: A Case Study* (New York: John Wiley & Sons, Inc., 1959), p. 295.

14. Robert L. Peabody, "Congressional Leadership: What Difference Does It Make?" (Paper presented to the 1973 Annual Meeting of the American Political Science Association, New Orleans, La., September 4–8, 1973). Copyright © 1973, American Political Science Association, p. 18.

15. Harry McPherson, *A Political Education* (Boston: Little, Brown and Company, 1972), p. 183.

16. Charles L. Clapp, *The Congressman: His Work as He Sees It* (Washington, D.C.: The Brookings Institution, 1962), p. 314.

17. John C. Wahlke, Heinz Eulau, William Buchanan, LeRoy C. Ferguson, *The Legislative System: Explorations in Legislative Behavior* (New York: John Wiley & Sons, Inc., 1962), p. 366.

18. Ibid., p. 367.

19. Winston W. Crouch, John C. Bollens, and Stanley Scott, *California Government and Politics,* 5th ed. (Englewood Cliffs, N.J.: Prentice-Hall, Inc., 1972), p. 125.

20. Clifton McClesky, with the assistance of T. C. Sinclair, *The Government and Politics of Texas,* 4th ed. (Boston: Little, Brown and Company, 1972), p. 134.

21. Jesse Unruh, in *Strengthening the States,* eds. Donald G. Herzberg and Alan Rosenthal (Garden City, N.Y.: Doubleday and Company, Inc., 1971), p. 157.

22. This section draws heavily upon Robert L. Peabody, "Party Leadership Change in the United States House of Representatives," *American Political Science Review* 61, no. 3 (September 1967): 675–93; reprinted in *New Perspectives on the House of Representatives,* 2d ed. (eds.) Robert L. Peabody and Nelson W. Polsby (Chicago: Rand McNally & Company, 1969), pp. 359–94; and Peabody, *Leadership in Congress,* especially pp. 3–22, 266–357, and 442–508.

23. See Nelson W. Polsby, "Two Strategies of Influence: Choosing a Majority Leader, 1962," in *New Perspectives,* eds. Polsby and Peabody, pp. 325–58.

24. See "Democrats: Changing the Guard," in *On Capitol Hill: Studies in the Legislative Process,* 2d ed. (eds.) John F. Bibby and Roger H. Davidson (Hinsdale, Ill.: The Dryden Press Inc., 1972), pp. 124–48.

25. Robert L. Peabody, "Committees from a Leadership Perspective," *The Annals of the American Academy of Political and Social Science* 411 (January 1974): 133–46.

26. "Democrats: Changing the Guard" in *On Capitol Hill,* eds. Bibby and Davidson, especially pp. 146–48.

27. McClesky, *Government and Politics of Texas,* p. 135.

28. *The American Legislator* 3, no. 3 (July 1973): 12.

29. Douglas Camp Chaffey and Malcolm E. Jewell, "Selection and Tenure of State Legislative Party Leaders: A Comparative Analysis," *Journal of Politics* 34, no. 4 (November 1974): 1278–86.

30. Ibid., p. 1286.

31. This discussion draws from *Congressional Quarterly Guide to Current American Government, Spring 1974* (Washington, D.C.: Congressional Quarterly, Inc., 1974), pp. 88–93; and Arthur G. Stevens, Jr., Arthur H. Miller, and Thomas E. Mann, "Mobilization of Liberal Strength in the House, 1955–1970: The Democratic Study Group," *American Political Science Review* 68, no. 2 (June 1974): 667–81.

32. "Mobilization of Liberal Strength," p. 681.

33. *Congressional Quarterly Guide . . . Spring 1974,* p. 93.

34. See Randall B. Ripley, *Party Leaders in the House of Representatives* (Washington, D.C.: The Brookings Institution, 1967), pp. 177–78.

35. Ibid., p. 173.

36. Quoted in John W. Kingdon, *Congressmen's Voting Decisions* (New York: Harper & Row, 1973), p. 87.

37. See David Kenney, *Basic Illinois Government: A Systematic Explanation,* Rev. ed. (Carbondale, Ill.: Southern Illinois University Press, 1974), pp. 116–19 *passim.*

38. McClesky, *Government and Politics of Texas,* p. 153.

39. Samuel C. Patterson, "Patterns of Interpersonal Relations in a State Group: The Wisconsin Assembly," *Public Opinion Quarterly* 23 (1959): 101–9.

40. Wahlke et al., *The Legislative System,* pp. 229–35.

41. Stephen V. Monsma, "Integration and Goal Attainment as Functions of Informal Legislative Groups," *Western Political Quarterly* 22 (March 1969): 19–28.

42. Kingdon, *Congressmen's Voting Decisions,* p. 135.

43. *Time* Magazine, July 20, 1970, pp. 12–13. Comments on this account from some of the participants play down Ford's subtlety: see *Congressional Quarterly Almanac, 1970* (Congressional Quarterly Service, 1971), p. 948.

44. Peabody, "Congressional Leadership," pp. 27–30.

Legislative
Subsystems:
Accessible and
Responsive

The internal complexity of legislative subsystems is not an end in itself. The end is to adopt authoritative policies in order to resolve conflict in the larger society. For the political system to persist, policy adoption must be both responsive to the pressures of society and responsible in allocating present resources for future prosperity. This is a balancing process in which there are a great many participants. Chapter 10 looks with some care at the way demands are raised and attended to in legislatures. Demands energize political systems. The notion of responsiveness is meaningless without them. But legislatures need resources to make policy, and at bottom resources are not available without support.

Since our concern is mostly with the processes and influences that account for legislative actions, I shall only briefly outline the compass of policy content. I will also list some reasons why policy analysis (which is beyond the scope of this text) should be regarded by both policy makers and students of the policy process.

Finally, I will consider the view that legislatures and legislators are unable to assume leadership in the American political system. Recent authorities in leadership positions of American legislatures have not exhibited conspicuous policy leadership, a fact that has been noted at several points in this book, and will be returned to later. American legislatures have great vitality, and I do not expect that vitality to decline. I believe they will be the source of increasing policy leadership.

10

Inputs to the Legislative Subsystem: Demands and Support

In Chapter 1, I presented an outline of the political system and its compelling task of authoritatively allocating values for the whole society. In subsequent chapters I described in some detail the part that the legislative subsystem assumes—namely, policy adoption. That part is shaped by expectations rooted in the political culture. It is molded further by the impingement of other subsystems and systems, especially that of the chief executive. Its procedures, or regime rules, some fixed in the Constitution (bicameral arrangement), others by its own self-imposed formal rules (unlimited debate in the Senate), and still others by tradition (seniority), define how the policy processing game is played. Finally there are the policy makers themselves who are products of the culture and aspire to participate in the policy process to meet system needs while satisfying their own ambitions and personal needs. All this constitutes a description of the context of the political system generally and the legislative subsystem in particular. What activates the system and what sustains that action? In a capsule statement—inputs of demand and support.

DEMANDS UPON LEGISLATIVE PROCESS

A *demand* is an expression of opinion that an authoritative allocation of some kind should or should not be made by the responsible authorities. I am using the word *demand* here in a general and value-neutral sense. That is, the word describes any assertion, whether it is accompanied by a clenched fist salute or is put forward in a meek and docile manner. On the other hand, demands should be understood as something different from wants, interests, or public opinion.

A *want* is simply some desired or desirable condition. Many parents want their children to achieve a college education. This want describes what for most would be a desirable state of affairs. But the notion of a want does not express a willingness to do anything to bring about that desired state of affairs.

The notion of an *interest* is similar to a want. An interest refers to a means by which a person or group seeks to fulfill some fundamental value or goal. Recall the eight values suggested by Lasswell which were noted in Chapter 1. If wealth is one's prime value, the paint store business through which Jones is seeking to achieve wealth is his interest. But that business does not speak for itself in the policy process. An interest is not a demand.

What about *public opinion*? An opinion is a verbal expression, or "answer," that a person gives in response to a stimulus, or "question." In short, opinions are verbal behavior. These are, of course, significant to a behavioral political scientist. Such opinions constitute meaningful data because they are observable, verifiable, and measurable. *Public opinion* is understood as the verbal behavior of a substantial mass of people in relation to some specific stimulus. The mass may be broad (all adults in the United States) or more focused (all students at Rockingham State University). Convinced of the validity of scientific sampling by probability theorists, we will accept the careful pollster's report of what opinions are held in a specific mass public on the basis of those reported by a small sample of that mass.

These opinions are not regarded as demands, however. Pollsters can elicit responses (verbal behavior) from people with all sorts of stimuli. For example, Gallup has repeatedly asked a national sample "Do you approve or disapprove of the way Ford is handling his job as president?" The poll might reveal that 34 percent approve, 56 percent disapprove, and 10 percent express no opinion. Certainly this is interesting political information, but it is highly ambiguous to one who wants to know what sort of authoritative allocation should or should not be made by responsible authorities.

Wants, interests, and public opinion are not irrelevant to demands. Those who articulate and promote demands—"The president should be impeached"—may take encouragement from the wanters, the individuals pursuing particular interests, and those who express certain opinions about specific stimuli. As the percentage of Nixon "disapprovers" grew, the proportion of those in Congress who were willing to take action to bring about his impeachment grew also. Thus demand specialists may obtain valuable clues from public opinion poll results about the likelihood that support for their demand can be mobilized into political action among portions of the public and the political authorities as well.

Demands grow out of needs and ideas, often linked together on the basis of the old nostrum, "Necessity is the mother of invention." A person or group may just intuitively feel its needs, or it may carefully assess achievements in relation to goals and thereby identify "what needs to be done" to achieve those goals. Once identified, needs are the stimulus for creative thought. Ideas are the creative response to problems and needs. The ideas may be moral and judgmental or they may be technical and operational. The great majority of ideas do not stimulate specific demands for authoritative action in the political system, but certainly a substantial number do.

The great technological advances of the twentieth century in this country and elsewhere have been a mixed blessing, bringing economic prosperity, cruel warfare, and new forms of both freedom and oppression. But certainly they have stimulated great creativity and vitality in producing ideas. Liberated from hunger and menial activity, people have the time and opportunity for education, thinking, collecting, and evaluating ideas. I think it is fair to say that in this country the First Amendment freedoms—of religion, speech, press, and assembly, accompanied by the right to petition the government for a redress of grievances—have never meant more than they do today. Many ideas will be faulty, confused, or even whimsical; certainly most will perish. But, written, studied, and argued, they are foils with which to sharpen one another. They are revised and interpreted into plans of action and some will be cast into public policy alternatives. They are the basis for demands—overt, often sophisticated, communications directed at authorities to create new or prevent change in old authoritative policies. "Close the loopholes in corporate income taxes." "Dismantle the program for an all-volunteer military, which is too expensive and is inadequate to the defense needs of the country." "Retain the electoral college for selecting presidents because alternative selection methods have undesirable consequences." "Impose wage and price controls to prevent inflation." The demands and the arguments about their policy implications are voluminous, but they are the stuff that energizes the political system. Demands are what the authorities deal with. Demands are the ultimate rationale for having a political regime with its procedures, division of labor, institutions, and formal and informal rules of the game. All of these constitute channels for dealing with demands.

Demands reflect stress in the lives of people and groups in the society and they constitute stress for the political system, particularly for the authorities called upon to fulfill the demands. What are the implications of a particular demand? Will fulfilling it have consequences on other current or pending policy determinations? Will it attract greater support for the political system from its demanders? Will it diminish support from those preferring the status quo? Are there distinct short-run and long-run consequences associated with meeting the demand? How do those relate to the political career ambitions of the authorities who must stand for election sooner or later? How numerous and diverse are the demands in competition with the one at hand? More questions could be posed, but these suggest the range of tensions implicit in policy making. They also suggest the difficulty of specifying an accounting system which can put all the pluses and minuses of fulfilling a particular demand into a general purpose measure. A profit-seeking corporation does have a significant yardstick of success—rate of return on investment. That measure may not summarize everything (for example, reputation for integrity), but for a broad range of decisions it is a compelling one. A political system may be able to render some parts of its policy evaluation into explicit measures of effectiveness—how much will a new freeway cost between points A and B; how much traffic currently travels between A and B on existing routes; how much will travel distance be cut by the new route; what are accident rates for existing routes compared to those on routes such as the projected one? Such questions have fairly estimable answers, but the questions that accompany many other policy alternatives are less estimable. What are the social implications of legalized abortion? What are the costs and gains of aggressive environmental protection legislation? What qualitative changes in the society's human resources would accompany a redistribution of wealth which took money from the rich to provide income to the poor? Implicit in each of these, especially the latter two, are immediate and calculable economic consequences. But what about the long-term economic consequences? Definitive predictions would be difficult. What about vague and abstract values such as improving the "quality of life," achieving a better standard of social justice, enlarging the life choices for many by reducing them for a few? Certainly it is difficult for anyone to specify all the measurable implications of such intangible abstractions, much less accurately measure them and draw valid conclusions about all the implications of alternative policies. Political authorities cannot avoid making responses to demands—in some fashion they decide to fulfill or reject them even though their behavior at times reflects a posture of ignoring or avoiding the issues implicit in the demands.

SOME VARIABLES AFFECTING THE WAY DEMANDS ARE EXPRESSED

Anyone may express a demand. He may give expression to his own idea which grows out of a unique need. He may give utterance, with a few or with many others, to a demand raised by someone else. The demand may be casual or intense, and it may be highly specific or very broad in compass. Several factors shape demands and the responses to them.

Cultural Constraints

As Easton says, "Although nominally each person may be able to cry out politically when the shoe pinches, in fact only certain kinds of persons or groups are likely to do so." [1] People define for themselves particular political roles. Verba and Nie, who intensively studied political participation in American society, observed four modes of participation: voting, campaign activity, cooperative activity, and citizen-initiated contacts. [2] The meaning of the first two modes is self evident, but in cooperative activity, the authors observed participation of individuals in groups, both formal and informal, to influence the actions of government in relation to social and political problems. "Citizen-initiated contacts" refers to acts by citizens to communicate directly and personally with selected political authorities.

Based upon data describing individual participation of a large national sample in the four modes noted, Verba and Nie were able to classify 93 percent of the respondents into six types of participants. [3] The *Inactives*, 22 percent of the sample, took almost no part in political life at any level. The *Voting Specialists*, 21 percent, regularly participated in elections, national to local, but rarely engaged in any other form of activity. A small cluster of respondents, 4 percent, were the *Parochial Participants*. They all reported making particularized contacts with political authorities, exercising initiative to affect public policy. But their efforts were to meet highly specific and personal kinds of needs. They engaged in neither cooperative nor campaign activity and were about average as voters. The *Communalists* constituted 20 percent of the sample. They all engaged in forms of cooperative activity, usually community problem-solving organizations. They were regular voters as well, but they avoided the conflict involved in campaigns. The *Campaigners* were both voters and combatants in political campaigns, but did not engage in cooperative group activity. Fifteen percent of the respondents fit this category. The final type, the *Complete Activists*, included 11 percent of the respondents. They engaged in all types of activity and even exceeded the participation of the Communalists and Campaigners in the mode of activity in which they specialized.

The participation activity that most nearly approximates what I have called demanding is what Verba and Nie characterize as citizen-initiated contacts. Verba and Nie's data distinguish contact activity engaged in as a member of a social/political group from that engaged in as a particular individual. They asked, "What about some representative or governmental official outside of the local community—on the (county, if local unit below county level) state or national level—have you ever contacted or written to such a person on some need or problem?" The data are in Table 10.1. The percentage of those making contact in the population is between 10.7 and 16.4 percent. Verba and Nie do not indicate how many of their respondents answered yes to both questions.

Verba and Nie nowhere specifically compared those who did and did not contact officials above the local level. However, they have concisely summarized their description of people and their participation:

> The overall pattern across the various types of actors is fairly clear. We can see from which groups the participation input comes. The following points emerge from the data:
>
> 1. Participants come disproportionately from upper-status groups. This is clearest if one compares the inactives with the complete activists.
>
> 2. Aside from the complete activists, the groups in which upper-status citizens are most overrepresented are the communalists and the partisan activists. Thus the more difficult activities are engaged in heavily by upper-status citizens.
>
> 3. Those who limit their activity to voting come disproportionately from lower-status groups.
>
> 4. Parochial participants come from all parts of the status hierarchy, though the upper-status citizens are somewhat less likely to limit themselves to this activity.
>
> 5. Men are somewhat overrepresented in the more activist groups, but not to a very great degree.
>
> 6. Blacks tend to be overrepresented in the inactivist category, and they are especially disadvantaged when it comes to communal activity and particularized contacting. On the other hand, they participate fairly proportionately in electoral politics, both as voting specialists and partisan activists. Though blacks are quite a bit more likely to be inactive, their degree of underrepresentation among the most active is not great. This asymmetry suggests that blacks are

---

Table 10.1   Have You Contacted the Political Authorities?[a]

	As a group member (%)	As a particular individual (%)
Yes	10.7	5.7
No	89.0	94.0
Missing data	0.3	0.3
TOTAL:	100.0	100.0

[a]Percentages are based upon the numbers of respondents reported as "Weighted N." The percentages reported on p. 353 are incorrect, but are corrected above.
SOURCE: Sidney Verba and Norman H. Nie, *Participation in America: Political Democracy and Social Equality* (New York: Harper & Row, 1972), pp. 353 and 355.

more likely to stay completely out of politics than are whites, but once they become involved they may participate at high levels.

7. Some interesting differences among the types of activists appear that are not linked to social status. Though both communalists and partisan activists come from similar status backgrounds, the former are much less likely to be Catholic, the latter much more likely. Catholics are also overrepresented among the voting specialists. In short, one sees a difference in political style between Protestants and Catholics, with the latter more likely to be involved in partisan activity.

8. Location plays a part, particularly *vis-à-vis* communal activists and those who work in electoral politics. The former are more likely to be found in rural areas and suburbs than in cities. In cities, on the other hand, electoral activists— both partisans and voting specialists—are more likely to be found.[4]

Demanding is a difficult form of political participation in which to engage. Few people choose to be demanders. Cultural variables (age, race, education, sex, religion, income, and location of home) sort people out, apparently affecting their ability and willingness to take the initiative in demanding.

Variations in Access

The opportunity to communicate demands to appropriate authorities defines the notion of access. Demands cannot energize the authorities except and unless the authorities sense those demands. Assuming that authorities in the political system want that system to persist—that is, they want the people in the society to be satisfied with the authorities and the binding policy decisions they make, and to keep supporting the political system—they will create and protect opportunities through which demands may be received. While demands induce tension, the tension is potentially of a creative nature. Demands raise challenges through which enlarged support for the political system may be attained in the present, or accumulated for the future. In the American political system, in which candidates seek opportunities to win office through elections, candidates may attract support by conspicuously giving people opportunities to see them, communicate with them, consider demands with them, and amplify the demands in campaigning as well as in office. Openness and responsiveness to demands by candidates are likely methods for them to achieve electoral support.

The legislature probably excels all the other major political institutions in providing access to demanders. Congressmen and legislators have come to be known as the servants of their constituents. A study of the Eighty-ninth Congress (1965–66) reports the following comments on the mail:

A typical congressional office with a small volume of mail receives one hundred to three hundred letters weekly, and one with a large volume receives five hundred to a thousand letters weekly. . . . About twenty-five percent of the letters received, on the average, contain constituent opinions or requests for the Congressman's view on legislation. About twenty percent contain requests for help in getting jobs, in dealing with Executive agencies, or in securing government publications and other information. In addition, the Congressman must meet with hometown delegations interested in various federal programs on legislation, and he is often asked to assist Washington visitors in other ways.[5]

Also enlightening are the analyses of how congressmen and their staff spend an "average work week."[6] Table 10.2 indicates that answering mail, handling constituent problems, visiting with constituents in Washington, and meeting with lobbyists and lobby groups consume, on the average, more than 30 percent of a congressman's time. Presumably some of the rest of his time is spent in trying to advance the demands that he has received.

But the effort in hearing and working in behalf of demands is not done by the congressman alone. Congressional staff members are active participants in receiving and making responses to demands. In Chapter 3 the reader will find a description of how staff time is spent. Refer to Table 3.11. The largest

Table 10.2   Average Work Week for a Congressman

Activity	Hours per Week (average)	% of Work Week
On the floor	15.3	26.0
In committee	7.7	13.1
Answering mail	7.0	11.9
On legislative research and reading	6.9	11.7
Handling constituent problems	5.1	8.6
Visiting with constituents in Washington	4.2	7.1
On committee work outside of committee	3.4	5.8
On writing speeches, articles	2.6	4.4
On leadership or party functions	2.4	4.1
Meeting with lobbyists and lobby groups	2.3	3.9
On press work, radio, & TV	2.0	3.4
TOTAL:	58.9	100.0

SOURCE: John S. Saloma III, *Congress and the New Politics* (Boston: Little, Brown and Company, 1969), p. 184.

percentage of time goes into casework, usually helping constituents solve a problem with some national governmental agency (internal revenue, immigration, social security, veterans administration, and so on). Added to the time spent with visiting constituents, with lobbyists, on pressure and opinion mail, on opinion ballots, and on requests for information, *activities directly related to receiving and responding to demands consume more than half the work time of congressional staffs.* Of course, some additional time is devoted to advancing the demands within the legislative process.

Although comparable data on how most other authorities spend their time and how much of it is devoted to hearing demands are not available, it is obvious that access to chief executives is extremely difficult to achieve. The president and even his high-ranking assistants are often unapproachable by significant authorities in other political subsystems, much less citizen demanders.* It is rarely possible for citizens to receive direct, personal attention from a state governor.† One study of a governor's schedule indicated no time spent with citizens except in ceremonial occasions. The governor did spend about 7 percent of his time in cabinet meetings and with department officials. Another 8 percent was spent in work sessions with legislators and legislative leaders. A substantial portion of his time (27 percent) was devoted to public relations—speechmaking, receptions, press conferences, and the like—but that did include meetings with local and civic leaders in communities away from the capitol.[7]

In the hierarchically organized bureaucracies, access is a problem too. Officials who deal directly with citizens (handling requests, approving forms, sending out checks, and answering calls for information) are typically very low in the hierarchy of the bureau. They handle these matters routinely hundreds or even thousands of times each year. As they perform their chores, they may receive citizens' demands for policy changes. However, other than on specific and minor matters, such bureaucrats have too little discretion or authority to act on the demands. They may "buck the demand up" to the next level of bureaucratic authority, but typically there are few

---

*This was a common complaint during the Nixon presidency from members and leaders of Congress and even from the president's own cabinet members. Dissenters such as Interior Secretary Walter Hickel, HUD Secretary George Romney, and Education Commissioner James E. Allen found they had almost no access to their superior, and their terms of service were quite short.

†When George Romney was governor, he initiated the practice of meeting with citizens on Thursday mornings. People would line up for a turn and be ushered before the governor for a carefully timed five-minute conference. The governor would listen to the plea and usually refer the citizen to a staff member for resolution of the request. An intern in the executive office at that time, I asked permission to gather data on these citizens. The request was turned down, but it seemed apparent that a great many cranks and special pleaders were, in effect, "wasting the governor's time," and the practice was discontinued.

rewards for such activity—the operative norm for low level bureaucrats is "don't make waves." It is easier to respond to the demander: "We don't make policy, we just do as we're told." If the citizen does not receive satisfaction from the office supervisor, it is unlikely that he will expend the time and energy to seek out and contact the district manager, the regional director, or some higher official. Middle-level bureaucrats may be willing to provide access, but the information costs to the demander in finding such access are probably more than he is willing to pay. So the citizen is likely to leave mumbling about "red tape" and "incompetent civil servants."

Courts constitute an access point too, but one that is costly in both time and money. Primarily they can be used to get an authoritative decision in relation to a specific grievance or injustice. One must feel the grievance or injustice very keenly to endure the hardship of getting it rectified in the courts. Even then, the case may result in a satisfactory settlement for the individual, but not rectify the general policy which brought about the grievance. For example, a person may fight state funding of abortion clinics by refusing to pay his state income tax as a way of demanding that abortion be declared illegal. When he is prosecuted, the probability is extremely high that the courts will resolve the matter on very specific grounds concerning the payment of income taxes without dealing authoritatively with the question concerning abortion policy. As noted in Chapter 5, the courts play a part in policy making, but the proportion of cases in which that part is a creative one in terms of general policy is extremely small. As a channel of access for demands, it is a difficult one to use effectively to change public policy.

There are opportunities open to individuals on their own as demanders in the political system, but it is difficult to evaluate their effectiveness. Legislators and bureaucrats seem to pay attention to casework demands, but demands of a broader sort, to make or change dimensions of public policy, tend to receive vague or ambiguous expressions of interest and concern rather than promises of action. A helpful but nondefinitive assessment comes from Congressman Clem Miller, whose letters to his friends concerning his experiences in Congress, were "an honest effort to depict the everyday life of Congress."[8] He offered the following observations to his constituents and friends about the meaningfulness of their expressions of opinion:

> During and after meetings in the district I was asked, "What influence do I have?" "What can I do to help?" "Do you read your correspondence?" Certainly, in the round, public opinion is decisive. How decisive varies with the congressman and the legislation, and the nature of the appeal. My counsel to everyone who asked was to write. One letter might spark an entirely new line of thought or endeavor. I can think of several issues last session upon which particular letters gave me a fresh or definitive focus.

Letters in aggregate may help to resolve congressional thinking. Every vote must be a consensus. Therefore, it must be a resolution of many stimuli. Sometimes a volume of mail seems to force an issue to a conclusion without seeming to have any particular effect on the actual result. The Labor Bill is a good case in point. The agitation for *a* labor bill pushed the House Committee on Education and Labor to take *some* sort of action. Our mail was not much help in deciding exactly *what* should be done. The congressional mail bore a doubtful relationship to the bill which actually resulted. Because of the parliamentary ins and outs, the complexities of the field, and the emotional involvement of the "experts" on both sides, most of the mail gave us little help. Most useful at such times are direct, first-person factual accounts of constituents' own personal experiences. This is the most difficult letter to write, because the humdrum of our lives cannot be seen as pulse and excitement for the nonparticipant.

On other types of legislation, heavy mail in aggregate seems to exert some influence. On the bill to permit self-employed persons to defer taxes on certain retirement funds, the sudden volume of mail, descending all at once, with no adverse mail, seemed to make passage a certainty. It tended to resolve any doubts one might have. And, indeed, the bill did pass with a thumping majority.[9]

ACCESS IS NOT EQUALLY AVAILABLE TO ALL DEMANDERS

While the point is difficult to demonstrate empirically, it is easy to understand. All authorities exercise discretion as to whom and what they will hear. Some have a forbidding array of staff and secretaries maintain a "gatekeeping" function.[10] The staff members manage the flow of traffic and inputs to the authorities. Some demanders are intimidated by the gatekeepers, while others intimidate the gatekeepers. The person with halting speech and wearing workman's clothes may find it difficult to get through the gates. The one with a business card who calls for an appointment and has a professional title may find it easy to get past the door.

One of the recurring themes in the literature of campaign finance is the observation that campaign contributions, particularly large ones, assure contributors access when they want it. A leading authority, Alexander Heard, puts it this way:

Access is the concept most frequently used by practical politicians to describe the objectives of large contributors. . . . In the pluralistic struggle of American politics, the degree of access commanded by an individual or group affects directly or indirectly the advantage or disadvantage he enjoys. Politicians argue that regardless of the motive behind a large political gift, the donor can later, if he insists, command access to at least some phase of the decision-making process of interest to him.[11]

Access is a valuable resource and is substantially within the discretion of authorities. One may hypothesize that the broader the policy responsibility of authorities, the greater the discrimination they exercise in making access available to demanders. They may exchange it for past or anticipated support. Those with significant resources to render that support are certainly more likely to obtain access than those without such resources.

An interesting contrast is suggested by noting the frequent resort by relatively powerless individuals in American society to protest activity. Marches, demonstrations, sit-ins, and other activities marked by showmanship and unconventional appearance are methods of creating bargaining resources. Michael Lipsky explains the dynamics in this example:

> It is intuitively unconvincing to suggest that fifteen people sitting uninvited in the Mayor's office have the power to move City Hall. A better formulation would suggest that the people sitting in may be able to appeal to a wider public to which the city administration is sensitive. Thus in successful protest activity the *reference publics* of protest *targets* may be conceived as explicitly or implicitly reacting to protest in such a way that target groups or individuals respond in ways favorable to the protesters.[12]

A significant initial favorable response is access. The incidence of protest activity is one meaningful indicator as to whether or not keepers have restricted access too narrowly.

Decision-making authority in the American political system is functionally specialized. In legislatures, particularly Congress, the emphasis on specialization is evident in the committee structure and in the informal norms of how members are expected to perform in the subsystem's work. This means that access is specialized too. Specialization goes hand in hand with expertise. Those with demands accompanied by demonstrable expertise find access easier to obtain than those who do not have this resource. Expertise is a resource that impresses the gatekeepers and opens the way to authorities for demands.

Finally, the policy process is both slow and complex. The development of policies for and within the legislative subsystem takes a great deal of time. Case studies of specific legislation—revenue sharing and medicare, for example—stretch over years. Thus, demanding is unlikely to be effective unless it is done persistently, patiently, and skillfully. To get new and innovative changes rendered into policy, there is the need for a "working majority." As noted previously, legislative proposals can be killed at numerous decision points. To become policy, they must survive them all. A bare majority in a legislature may at some particular point in consideration be outmanned in committee, in the committee of the whole, in the conference committee. It is this environment which encourages bargains, compromises, and amendments to broaden support for a proposal even at the cost of some of its content. This environment also explains in part why the policy process is so long and complex. The biases of complexity and slowness give advantages to those demanders who have a strong future orientation, who have the resources to stay involved in the policy process, and who can keep contributing support and expertise to policy makers.

Incrementalism Is the Rule, Innovation Is the Exception

Typically demands in the American political system are not programmatic, comprehensive, and unified. Innovations tend to occur when many demanders persist in requesting the same thing. This happens only occasionally, and the instances in which it occurs are most often precipitated by crisis or pseudo-crisis. The recent innovations in environmental protection, energy conservation, and inflation controls have occurred in crisis atmospheres.

Most policy decisions, certainly those adopted in legislatures, are incremental—building upon the past. A program is enlarged here, a loophole closed there, a budget is expanded a bit in one place and reduced somewhere else. The achievements and changes are usually modest by comparison with the large scope of government's spending or activities. What is worthy of note is that specialized interests benefit or lose from these marginal changes in a very direct fashion. A state's usury law may limit financial institutions to interest rates of, say, 8 percent. To raise that limit to 9 percent is hardly a major policy innovation, yet its consequence upon the profits of lending institutions may be very substantial.

Specialized Spokesmen Articulate Demands

The culture, specialized structure of the political system, unequal access, and norm of incrementalism explain the existence of specialized spokesmen for articulating demands. The discussion that follows suggests some categories of societal positions which are relevant, though certainly not exhaustive.

Journalists and Editors Increasingly American media are enlarging their activity in interpretive reporting of the news. There are the columnists—Reston, Wicker, Alsop, Anderson, and the like—who combine their interpretations of the news with continuing demands about what public policy ought to be. Televised views of Severeid, Smith, and Brinkley do as well. Investigative reporters, such as Robert Woodward and Carl Bernstein, who covered the Watergate investigations for almost a year for the *Washington Post*, have won a growing role as demand specialists.

Academics and Social Critics   Academics receive and use the rewards of tenure, research time, and scholarly publications to develop and articulate demands for public policy. Examples include Galbraith, Heller (revenue sharing), Erlich (population), Commoner (environment), Brzezinski (Soviet relations). Some, including recent cabinet members Kissinger and Butz, take stints in government policy-making positions. Nonacademics develop their own base of support by writing and lecturing (Halberstam)[13] and creating organizations (Nader and Gardner). Part of their task is in relating demands to the wants, needs, and opinions of the broader public. It is also to render demands into specific policy proposals, assessing alternatives and speculating about the implications of possible governmental actions.

Bureaucrats   The often maligned bureaucrats, busy in the doing end of government, are policy experts. They too make concrete demands about changing or retaining particular policies. Frequently they are called upon to assert their own as well as to evaluate and comment upon the demands of others. Often they speak in relation to the political system in which they have positions, but frequently enough local administrators make demands upon state political systems, and together with state administrators, upon political authorities at the national level. Administrators (certainly *former* administrators) play a significant part in making demands upon policy makers, especially legislators.

Ambitious Candidates and Officeholders   Elected authorities are more than simply authorities, receiving demands and making policy decisions in relation to them. They are also candidates. Many, especially members of Congress, are candidates with static ambitions, who want to win and keep winning election to their current offices. They articulate and demand policies which they perceive to be relevant to their constituents. They may simply amplify the demands they have received. They may create demands according to their perceptions of wants, interests, opinions, and needs among their constituents.

Authorities in office who are seeking election to higher office are commonplace in the American political system. Examples are the state legislator who wants to become governor and the U.S. senator who is ambitious for the presidency. By reaching out to a broader constituency for electoral support, these ambitious candidates assemble specific demands into broad and realistic policy alternatives. They challenge the incumbent chief executive (who has the resources to be chief "policy promoter") and his proposals.

Perhaps increasingly we will see alternatives to the chief executive's policy proposals coming from ambitious rivals who want to win the presidency. Looking to the recent past, among the leading Vietnam War opponents were Senators McGovern and McCarthy. Senator Edward Kennedy led the opposition to President Nixon on several policies, but in particular he promoted the major alternative to the president's proposed health insurance plan. Senator Muskie promoted alternative proposals for environmental protection. Senator Jackson has been sponsoring a variety of policies, particularly in relation to future energy needs in the nation. Ronald Reagan rivaled President Ford by advocating stringent social service policies and expanded military spending.

As explained in Chapter 9, the congressional party leaders usually do not take an aggressive policy promotion role; instead they have rather consistently acted as managers of the bill process. Most of their work occurs at the floor stage—rounding up members, arranging compromises, getting together enough votes.

The office of U.S. senator has become a stepping-stone to nomination for the presidency. For that reason the Senate has become a more significant institution than when presidential nominees came mostly from governorships. The Senate and its ambitious senators receive increasing public attention. It is likely that the Senate will be the institutional base for the development and promotion of public policy alternatives in competition to that of the chief executive. Therefore, the president's proposals will tend to come under sharper scrutiny in the Senate than in the House because his rivals are participants in the policy adoption process and because these rivals are putting forward their own proposals.[14]

Lobbyists Lobbyists are agents of organized groups who attempt, on a continuing basis, to affect the authorities in the policy process. People in groups of all kinds are affected by public policy. The effects, favorable or unfavorable, are a basis for trying to influence what those policies will be. A group with sufficient resources and interest may sponsor its own agent to communicate with relevant authorities. Perhaps the distinguishing notion about what a lobbyist does is that he gets close enough to the policy process so that he can communicate with the authorities in a face-to-face manner, and will do so again and again.

A common view of lobbyists is that they corrupt the policy process. However, the authorities are hardly at the mercy of lobbyists. In fact, the relationships between legislators and lobbyists have been found to be complex. According to Zeigler and Baer, "Whatever their image of lobbyists, legislators are more likely to look on them as service agents than as opinion manipulators."[15] Legislators call upon lobbyists for several services, including influencing other legislators, mobilizing public opinion, and working on strategy to pass legislation. In the view of legislators, lobbyists are primarily seen as "providers of information." This view is shared by lobbyists too. Zeigler and Baer quote an insurance lobbyist as follows:

> Last session there were eleven people on the House Financial Affairs Committee. Five of them were freshmen. My job was to introduce myself to them and let them know that I would be around, be at the Committee meetings, and that I am the fountain of all information with respect to the insurance industry, and if they have any questions they should call on me. Certainly I try to persuade them. But I try to persuade them with information.[16]

Lobbyists are information brokers. Besides representing their groups to the authorities, they carry the views of the authorities to their groups. Often lobbyists are themselves officers in the organizations which they represent. Zeigler and Baer's study of lobbyists in four states revealed that about 64 percent were officeholders of the association they represented.[17] Lewis Dexter argues further about the position of lobbyists:

> *The most important service of Washington representatives* [lobbyists] *to clients and employers* [interest group leaders] *is teaching the latter to live with the government and in the society. That is, Washington representatives instruct a good many clients how to adapt, accommodate, and adjust.*
> They do this in three ways:
> 1. by showing the client and employer that there are paths around, out, and through, if one is willing to settle for "half-a-loaf," and to settle for incremental gains or for avoiding substantial losses, even though one does not get what (one thinks) one is justly entitled to;
> 2. by convincing clients and employers that there has, indeed, been an all-out effort, that the government has handled the case fairly and that there is nothing further to be done; and
> 3. by interpreting for clients and employers in terms which they can appreciate the positions of (a) the government and of (b) other interests which the government has to take into account.[18]

The lobbyist finds himself between the group and the authorities. To be influential with the authorities, he must have realistic and practical objectives. The interest group members may know full well what demands they want fulfilled, but they may not know the feasibility of complete fulfillment of the goals. Realistic estimates by the lobbyist can guide them.

Commentary on the Way
Demands Are Expressed

A great many demands upon political authorities go unsatisfied. No doubt a great many are foolish and/or trivial. A great many are not heard by the authorities, or, if they are heard, leave no apparent impression. Others are negated by competing demands—either canceled out or defeated by an alternative. Some are modified and/or assimilated into broader proposals, while still others are rendered into the language of policy, adopted, and put into effect.

Obtaining satisfaction through the political process for one's demands is difficult at best. Processes are complex, long, and slow. Specialization and gatekeepers mean that John Doe, average citizen, has only a small and easily ignored place in the demanding process. To have an effect, he will probably have to exert himself a great deal, becoming something of a specialist in promoting his own particular demand. If he is not willing to expend that much effort, he may join with those who have access to authorities and expertise in the problem areas that affect him. He may start his own interest group, or, more likely, join one that already exists. The demands of the individual in problems of "casework" are rather readily met in the American political system, but for policy demands the individual has an exceedingly small voice.

INTEREST GROUPS AND THEIR ACTIVITY IN THE POLICY PROCESS

Interest groups are a major source of inputs to the political system and deserve some specific attention. The term *interest group* has a very broad meaning. David Truman's definition is still a good one. *Interest group* refers to a set of people that, "on the basis of one or more shared attitudes, makes certain claims upon other groups in the society for the establishment, maintenance, or enhancement of forms of behavior that are implied by the shared attitudes."[19] This definition includes as interest groups companies, churches, baseball teams, universities, units of government, unions, professional associations, and even families. Within each there are shared attitudes, and their members make claims, or demands, upon other groups for their own enhancement. Obviously society is made up of a fantastic array of interest groups, from small and intimate primary ones whose activities are immediate, to those that are large, dispersed, and whose members keep in touch through mass communication media.

In most groups the members spend the bulk of their energy pursuing shared interests in processes other than the political one. Corporations, business associations, labor organizations, and farmers' groups primarily pursue profits in the economic process. But there may well be more major objectives—in churches, the members seek spiritual enrichment; in photography clubs, the members seek skill with their cameras and derive satisfaction from their artistry.

A group may make claims upon, or demands of, the political authorities. Such a group is a *political* interest group. The great majority of groups in society make few, if any, claims upon the political system. Even those that come to mind as frequently involved in political demanding—the U.S. Chamber of Commerce, the AFL–CIO, the NAACP—spend most of their time, energy, and resources on activities that are not directly political. In short, for most groups political activity is a secondary, not primary, function of the group.

Nevertheless, numerous organizations spend substantial amounts of money, as well as time and energy, to affect public policy. No one knows how high the spending at all levels really goes. Under the Federal Regulation of Lobbying Act of 1946, organizations file their own reports of their spending on congressional lobbying. During 1972 the total reported was $6.1 million, slightly less than in 1971 ($6.5 million). However, the ambiguity of the law and its enforcement makes these figures only suggestive. Careful observers of the reports say that, "Figures reported under the Federal Regulation of Lobbying Act of 1946 probably represent only a fraction of the actual spending by groups for the purpose of influencing Congress. Differing views on the need to file spending reports and on just what to report lead to a wide variety of reporting practices. Consequently, the figures are often misleading." [20]

Why So Much Lobbying Activity?

It is difficult to explain fully why there is so much lobbying activity; but let us consider some reasons.

1. The proliferation theory of group activity. The many interest groups are simply evidence of a complex society. The development of technology, professionalization, and specialization have multiplied the number of real and potential groups. The media and rates of communication have increased, as has interdependency in the society. Both the actual and potential scope for governmental regulation has increased. All these have heightened the demands for new and often complex forms of authoritative regulation. As governmental regulation has grown, access points have been augmented somewhat as well, but the number of demands have multiplied more rapidly. The increase in specialization means more specialists (for example, lobbyists, information, staff work, and so on). As the demand "noise level" increases, there is the tendency of particular groups to increase their vocal power.

2. The disequilibrium theory of group activity. David Truman pointed out that groups tend to form in waves. [21] The formation of a union by bricklayers may give them advantages in dealing with other groups in the society, thus affecting and perhaps upsetting building contractors, plumbers, loan institutions, and others. These form groups, causing disequilibrium for others, stimulating more groups. Groups relate and affect one another both cooperatively and competitively. Changes in technology, disasters, new ideas, and leaders may raise new waves.

3. An exchange theory of interest groups. Salisbury, dissatisfied with the proliferation and disequilibrium theories, suggests that interest groups are "benefit exchanges." "[O]rganizers invest capital to create a set of benefits which they offer to a market of potential customers at a price. If, and as long as, enough customers buy, i.e., join, to make a viable organization, the group is in business. If the benefits fail, or are inadequate to warrant the cost of membership, or the leaders get inadequate return, the group collapses." [22] Groups get off the ground because an organizer—Martin Luther King, Jr., Ralph Nader, or Samuel Gompers—attracts people for some benefits. The benefits are often economic—more pay, better jobs—but they might simply be a sense of belonging or a feeling of satisfaction in fighting for a just principle ("Oppose this immoral war!"). Lobbying activity is a way of providing and enlarging benefits. A union may be able to get better safety protection for workers through legislation than by direct negotiation with the employer. Meanwhile, the lobbying activity itself may be perceived with satisfaction by the group members—in short, they derive satisfaction from knowing their union has its own men in Washington.

4. The marginal legality theory of group activity. [23] The boundaries of governmental regulation are related to broadly held conceptions of morality and virtue. Folk philosophy asserts that "you can't legislate morality." This statement is usually intended to convey the idea that the political system cannot convert a practice, adhered to by a substantial portion of the society as right and proper, into an immoral act simply by legislation making it illegal. For example, if many people enjoy smoking, but it is found to be harmful to health, and on that basis a law is passed to make smoking illegal (thus protecting people from harming themselves), few smokers will be convinced that this suddenly illegal smoking is really immoral.

On the other hand, the law does reflect conventional morality in many matters. It is interesting that nearly all of the Ten Commandments having to do with relations between men are reflected in legislation—killing, adultery, stealing, and several forms of lying are illegal as well as immoral. There are three zones of morality and three related zones of legality and law enforcement. There is the clearly moral and legal zone: the morals of doing business for profit, pursuing a profession, protecting one's property, raising a family, and so on. The law and enforcement concerning these activities are easy and clear. Similarly the law and enforcement are clear and straightforward about what is immoral and wrong. Those who cheat, steal, lie under oath, kill, and harm others are to be punished. Note that there is little interest group activity in relation to these activities or the prescriptions of the law concerning them; there is no Association of American Jewel Thieves seeking to reduce jail terms for jewel theft.

There are a great many activities that are ambiguous in terms of popular morality. Some practices are deemed immoral by some and moral by others. Others may simply seem amoral to many people. Definitions of legality are likely to be ambiguous and subject to change. Even where the law is clear, enforcement levels may vary by time and place. The morality of liquor use is ambiguous in American society. The law is ambiguous and changing, too. Should a community have the option to be "wet" or "dry"? At what age should drinking be legal? How many liquor licenses should be granted per 10,000 in population? There is great societal ambiguity about gambling, smoking, abortion, sexual relations between consenting adults, and other issues. Groups which share values and have definite views concerning the morality of specific positions tend to be active in trying to affect the legal definitions and levels of law enforcement. In general we may expect that *"the political activity of a group is proportional to its stake in the marginal definition of legality and of law-enforcement levels."* [24]

What about the high level of lobbying activity of many economic and social interest groups that have a morally and legally approved function; for example, auto makers, airlines, professional associations, consumer protection groups, and the like? Producing and marketing Fords is certainly appropriate and legal. But Ford Motor Company nevertheless spends time, effort, and money on lobbying. Why? Ford and the other auto makers are not lobbying just to sell cars; they are concerned about regulation of air pollution, safety devices, and price increase limits—matters that are not sharply moral or immoral. Other ambiguous matters affect the company too—tax "write-offs," profit accounting methods, excise taxes, franchise agreements with dealers, labor regulations. There is a mixture of private and governmental forces in the American economy. With complex regulations and tax laws, multimillion dollar corporations, unions, and voluntary organizations are constantly operating close to the limits of legality. Slight changes in the law or its administration may sharply change profits to losses or vice versa. Lobby activity to make a small policy change or to prevent a small change in policy may be very worthwhile. Meanwhile, lobbying just to make friends and "keep the channels of communication open" constitutes a hedge against the future. Substantial portions of lobbying activity are not directly associated with specific demands, but are simply done to preserve good will, prevent sudden changes, and be ready with friends and contacts in positions of authority in case "something comes up."

How Much Influence Do Interest Groups Have in the American Legislative Process?

There is no empirically persuasive answer to this question. Political scientists have not yet been able to measure influence in complex situations with any precision. If influence is the result of a relationship between two or more actors (lobbyists and legislators, for example), in which one leads another to act differently than the latter had intended to act, then the analyst must know how all the actors intended to act, and how, in fact, they did act. But the political analyst can rarely know these intentions. Sometimes even the actors are uncertain about whether or not they have influenced others or been influenced themselves. It is as easy to attribute influence where none is present as it is for it to go undetected. Groups want to be influential. Lobbyists want their interest group members to believe that the group has influence. If the authorities decide an issue to the advantage of the group, influence may be inferred whether there was any or not. Disavowals by lobbyists and decision makers alike may serve to convince no one.

Another problem concerns the comparison of influence in one situation to that in another. Is the prevention of a gun registration law by the National Rifle Association evidence of greater, lesser, or equal influence than the oil industry's success in clearing the way for an Alaskan oil pipeline? How does one rate the influence of a group whose interests seem to go unchallenged, as is the case with the Army Corps of Engineers? We are left with subjective judgments of these questions because no objective measure of influence has been established.

Some of these subjective judgments have been more carefully formed than others. Scott and Hunt studied a sample of U.S. representatives in the Eighty-seventh Congress (1961–62).[25] They found that freshmen representatives tended to view interest groups as powerful agents in the legislative process, and that there is a general impression that groups are significant. However, when the researchers looked at congressmen as specialists, they tried to determine whether they were well acquainted with and in regular contact with interest groups whose policy concerns fitted the legislators' specialization. They found that the visibility of the groups with specializing congressmen was generally low. The representatives perceived very little in the way of pressure; in fact, some seemed disappointed not to be pressured. The capacity of groups to coerce them on an issue was perceived by congressmen as very rare, in fact, they considered heavy pressure from lobbyists to be a violation of legislative norms. Scott and Hunt quote one congressman as saying, "When a man comes in here, pounds on my desk, and tries to exact a commitment from me, I'm just liable to tell him to go to hell."[26]

A major study of foreign trade legislation in the 1950s and early 1960s came to firm conclusions about the significance of interest groups, especially business groups, on trade policy.

> . . . our study of the reciprocal trade controversy led us to reservations about the extent of influence that has characteristically been attributed to pressure groups. . . .
>
> The stereotype notion of omnipotent pressure groups becomes completely untenable once the groups are aligned on both sides. The result of opposing equipotent forces is stalemate. But, even taken by themselves, the groups did not appear to have the raw material of great power. We noted shortages of money, men, information, and time. It was a particular surprise to us to find how dilute vast sums could become when divided among dozens of pressure groups.
>
> We were further unprepared for the fact that most activities of pressure groups involved interaction with people on the same side. It resembled modern warfare, in which only a small proportion of the troops ever make contact with the enemy and the vast majority are involved in servicing the front-line soldiers—in this case mainly the senators and representatives who were waging the battle within Congress. Direct lobbying was a very minor activity. The major efforts of the pressure groups went into persuading businessmen to write or talk to congressmen and to testify at hearings; into working with sympathetic members of Congress; and into public relations and education, with a special emphasis on the business community.[27]

A more recent study of Congress focused on how 60 congressmen made their voting decisions on 15 significant policy issues during 1969. Altogether the study analyzed 222 individual decisions. From his interviews with congressmen, Kingdon learned that in 1 percent of the decisions interest groups were of "determinative" importance; in 25 percent, of major importance; in 40 percent, of minor importance; and not important in about 35 percent of the decisions.[28] Interestingly, the importance of interest groups in decisions was reportedly greater on the "big issues" than on those of lesser salience. Kingdon says that, "In fact, it seems entirely plausible that congressmen and other participants even define issue *salience* partly in terms of interest group activity."[29] However, when Kingdon accounted for the impact of other variables (constituency, fellow congressmen, party leadership, administration, and staff), there was almost no relationship between the decisions of congressmen and the positions of interest groups. The relevance of groups to congressmen was in their constituencies. Quoting Kingdon and his respondents again:

> Congressmen repeatedly said during the course of the interviews that, unless an interest group had some connection with their constituencies, the group would have little or no influence on their decisions. Said one, "It doesn't make any difference to me unless it is from the district." Another said, "We get stuff in

here all the time from the Washington office of organizations and I often don't even read it." Another said that his mail from the national organizations went right in the wastebasket.[30]

The picture of interest group influence varies in the states. Indeed, when Milbrath studied Washington lobbyists, he was told that at the state level lobbyists handed out money and favors freely and that pressure was more obvious, more intense, and more freewheeling than at the national level.[31] When Zeigler and Baer asked lobbyists and legislators in four states about various modes of communication and which ones were most effective, they discovered several interesting things. Table 10.3 reports their findings in detail. First, the ratings for the various techniques are rather similar to findings obtained earlier concerning Congress; on all sides it is agreed that personal contact is the best method of communication. Second, lobbyists tend to rate almost all methods more highly than do legislators. Third, generally there is a low opinion concerning all the methods of "keeping communication channels open." Finally, no one concedes a very important place to bribery in the influence process. It may be, of course, that respondents want to offer a "socially acceptable" answer. However, interviews were confidential and the respondents were in a position to know whether or not bribery actually occurs.

The general strength of interest groups in state political systems appears to be clearly related to political and economic variables of the systems themselves. Zeigler and van Dalen used a rating of interest groups strength in 45 of the states, in which strength was related to party competition in state elections, party cohesion in state legislatures, and socioeconomic variables of urbanism, income, and industrialization. The findings are reported in Table 10.4. As Zeigler and van Dalen summarize:

> Pressure groups are strongest when political parties and legislative cohesion are weakest and when socioeconomic variables are lowest. Two patterns emerge from the table. The first consists of strong pressure groups, weak parties (both electorally and legislatively), low urban population, low per capita income and a larger proportion of the population engaged in nonindustrial occupations. The second consists of moderate or weak pressure groups, competitive parties and an urban, industrial economy. *In short, pressure politics, party politics and socio-economic structure are related.*[32]

Demands: Some
Summarizing Observations

There is no clear formula for American political systems generally, or legislative subsystems particularly, that we can use to accurately predict whether or not demands will be transformed into policy decisions. Demands

Table 10.3 Ratings of Methods of Communication

	Massachusetts		North Carolina		Oregon		Utah	
	Legis-lators	Lobby-ists	Legis-lators	Lobby-ists	Legis-lators	Lobby-ists	Legis-lators	Lobby-ists
Direct, personal communication								
Personal presentation of arguments	5.8*	6.6	4.7	6.7	6.7	6.9	5.3	6.4
Presenting research results	6.0	5.8	5.4	5.4	6.8	6.0	6.3	5.5
Testifying at hearings	5.2	5.6	4.8	5.3	6.1	5.7	5.1	5.0
Communication through an intermediary								
Contact by constituent	2.5	3.2	3.0	5.4	2.7	4.3	3.6	5.0
Contact by friend	2.0	2.5	3.0	4.2	2.4	3.7	3.4	4.0
Contact by other lobbyists	2.4	4.3	2.5	4.2	3.2	4.5	3.0	4.8
Indirect, impersonal communication								
Letter writing campaign	2.0	3.4	1.7	4.0	1.6	4.0	2.8	4.0
Publication of voting records	2.0	2.2	1.3	1.4	1.5	2.0	2.0	2.4
Public relations campaign	3.5	3.7	3.5	4.6	3.5	4.0	4.1	4.6
Keeping communication channels open								
Entertaining legislators	1.0	1.3	2.0	2.5	1.7	2.2	2.8	3.0
Giving a party	1.0	1.0	2.0	1.8	1.4	1.6	2.4	2.3
Campaign contributions	1.0	2.0	1.6	2.4	1.5	2.5	2.1	3.3
Withholding campaign contributions	0.3	0.1	0.3	0.4	0.1	0.1	1.0	1.0
Bribery	0.2	0.1	0.1	1.2	0.03	0.2	0.2	0.3
Mean for all techniques	2.5	3.0	2.6	3.5	2.8	3.5	3.2	3.7

KEY: *Ratings of effectiveness on a scale from 0 (ineffective) to 8 (effective).

SOURCE: L. Harmon Zeigler and Michael L. Baer, *Lobbying: Interaction and Influence in American State Legislatures* (Belmont, Calif.: Wadsworth Publishing Company, 1969), p. 176.

Table 10.4   The Strength of Pressure Groups in Varying Political and Economic Situations

Social Conditions	Types of Pressure Systems [a]		
	Strong[b] (%)	Moderate[c] (%)	Weak[d] (%)
Party competition			
One-party	33.3	0	0
Modified one-party	37.5	42.8	0
Two-party	29.1	57.1	100.0
Cohesion of parties in legislature			
Weak cohesion	75.0	14.2	0
Moderate cohesion	12.5	35.7	14.2
Strong cohesion	12.5	50.0	85.7
Socioeconomic variables			
Urban population	58.6	65.1	73.3
Per capita income	$1900	$2335	$2450
Industrialization index	88.8	92.8	94.0

[a]Alaska, Hawaii, Idaho, New Hampshire, and North Dakota are not classified or included.

[b]Twenty-four states have a strong pressure system; they are Alabama, Arizona, Arkansas, California, Florida, Georgia, Iowa, Kentucky, Louisiana, Maine, Michigan, Minnesota, Mississippi, Montana, Nebraska, New Mexico, North Carolina, Oklahoma, Oregon, South Carolina, Tennessee, Texas, Washington, Wisconsin.

[c]Fourteen states have a moderate pressure system; they are Delaware, Illinois, Kansas, Maryland, Massachusetts, Nevada, New York, Ohio, Pennsylvania, South Dakota, Utah, Vermont, Virginia, West Virginia.

[d]Seven states have a weak pressure system; they are Colorado, Connecticut, Indiana, Missouri, New Jersey, Rhode Island, Wyoming.

SOURCE: Herbert Jacob and Kenneth N. Vines, eds., *Politics in the American States: A Comparative Analysis*, 2d ed. (Boston: Little, Brown and Company, 1971), p. 127.

vary from those that are barely heard and easily ignored to those that literally cannot be refused. Success and failure do not simply grow out of head counts of the members of society for and against the substance of the demand.

From Verba and Nie's data, roughly 11 to 16 percent of the population directly contact state and national authorities about their needs or problems. But many more are involved in groups, engage in some campaign activity, work in a governmental agency, or know someone who does. The communication network through which demands can flow is vast.

To be seriously considered, demands must be heard by the authorities in a plausible form. Thus those who are skilled in organizing and communicating ideas have a disproportionate role in articulating demands—the journalists, editors, commentators, academics, social critics, bureaucrats, candidates, officeholders ambitious for higher political positions, and interest group leaders. It is appropriate to be suspicious of the motives and interests of these highly advantaged members of the society. Perhaps they should be scrutinized more carefully as a ruling elite.[33] Demanding, as characterized here, is an information communication process. Skilled communicators with substantial resources have obvious advantages over the poor and culturally deprived. As Parenti has observed, "Those who are most needful of substantive reallocations are, by that very fact, usually farthest removed from the resources necessary to command such reallocations and least able to make effective use of whatever limited resources they possess."[34]

It is obvious to say that advantages in demanding go to individuals who speak from an organizational base. That base is itself affected by numerous variables—prestige, size, financial resources, ideology, leadership skills, and cohesion—just to note a few. But a great deal more needs to be learned, and relationships must be measured with substantially greater precision, to explain the formulation, articulation, and selective fulfillment of demands in public policy than is presently the case. In particular, demand specialists do not function in a vacuum; they make exchanges with a broader, less articulate public—the potential media consumers, organization supporters, taxpayers, and public policy recipients. It may be that this level of interaction is the one that needs careful scrutiny if we are to understand how and why the political system succeeds and/or fails to fulfill demands.

Interest groups help to form and articulate the context of ideas within which public policy must be made. Lobbying is a conspicuous but late step in the process. Lobbying does not always translate bills into laws directly; for example, farm groups, labor unions, and trade associations have established cores of advocates for their views in legislatures. Senator Birch Bayh is no captive of organized labor, but he is often a willing advocate of the same views that labor leaders assert because he has grown up with value orientations similar to theirs and has attracted labor support throughout his political career. Senator Goldwater's relationships with business and military interests are parallel to those of Bayh's with labor. Consumer rights organizations and women's liberation activists have not built support as long and as well as farm, business, and labor interests, but they are taking steps to do so. As yet there is no consumers' "Bill of Rights" on the law books, and the Equal Rights Amendment to the Constitution has not passed, but convinced consumer advocates in and outside of legislatures regularly participate in new trade regulation proceedings, and discrimination based on sexual distinctions is everywhere subject to challenge. In the latter example, the "pressure," not always organized, is manifest in demands that women be appointed to the Supreme Court, cabinet, regulatory commissions, and advisory bodies. It is evident in more women candidates for public office, including legislatures, and pressures within the legislatures to assign such women to "important" committees.

Although it is difficult to demonstrate a direct relationship between the existence and interests of particular interest groups and the legislative adoption of policies sought by such groups, it is evident that they shape the context of policy making and thereby bias the policy process, its output, and the way policy is put into effect. There are, in effect, "policy subgovernments" that have achieved partial hegemony over particular policy areas; for example, the triangle of agriculture interests manifest not only in interest groups, but also the Department of Agriculture and the agriculture committees in Congress. When vacancies occur among the political administrators of the department, the groups and congressional committee people can expect to be consulted about who will be appointed to fill them. When congressional committee vacancies occur, agricultural groups and political executives in the department can expect they will be filled by congressmen from farm constituencies. When vacancies occur in districts where agricultural interests are strong, activists for those interests will be involved in the recruitment of candidates. All this is not secretive elite manipulation. Interests and issues attract adherents who participate over time and accumulate resources and influence policy making to their advantage. The legislator is often a willing participant, serving constituents and clienteles with whom he holds common values, and to whom he feels responsibility. A legislator can identify the prime support groups in his constituency—those who recruited him, worked for his election, made campaign contributions, created campaign events, and expect his loyalty when relevant issues come up in policy making. Cause and effect in such interest-related issues are difficult to sort out, but interest interaction leavens the policy process. The legislators are themselves the lobbyists—not directly in the hire of formal groups, but in sympathy and as advocates of values they hold, constituency concerns, and especially of their primary supporters.

SUPPORT FOR LEGISLATIVE SUBSYSTEMS

Support is a social relationship; it connects individuals with others—individuals, members of groups, and authorities in institutions such as legislatures. Expressed abstractly, "A supports B either when A acts on behalf of B or when he orients himself favorably toward B."[35] Ordinarily one thinks of support only in the positive sense, as Easton's definition does by including the word "favorably." But it is theoretically useful to consider

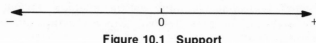

Figure 10.1 Support

support as a characteristic that varies from positive to neutral and from neutral to negative, as Figure 10.1 indicates. To illustrate support as a variable: Assume four individuals: A, B, C, and K. If A's support for K is high, A will help wash K's car, help K write his term paper, and may even cosign K's lease contract on an apartment. B could care less about K and his needs or problems. B feels neutral; not favorable toward K nor against him. C, on the other hand, dislikes K. Upon learning that K is getting help from A on a term paper, C just might make it a point to inform K's professor of the fact. A, B, and C illustrate differing degrees of support for K; positive, neutral, and negative.

Support can be manifested in two ways. One is in overt actions, such as A's helpful actions or C's harmful ones. Support may also be inferred from the attitudes A, B, and C have toward K. An attitude is a predisposition or readiness to act, a basis for anticipating possible further actions.

It is difficult to assess the degree of support in a political system for a specific subsystem such as the legislative subsystem. It would be helpful to know the extent of support in the society for the cultural basis of the legislative subsystem. No poll data are specifically addressed to this question. Prothro and Grigg sampled opinion in two American cities concerning whether or not Americans would agree to the following statements:

Democracy is the best form of government.
Public officials should be chosen by majority vote.
Every citizen should have an equal chance to influence government policy.
The minority should be free to criticize majority decisions.
People in the minority should be free to try to win majority support for their opinions.[36]

Agreement with these statements ranged between 95 and 98 percent. However, when these general statements were recast into specific applications—for example, "If a Communist were legally elected mayor of this city, the people should not allow him to take office"—54 percent of the respondents agreed. The democratic creed has high acceptance in the form of general principles, but when it was cast into specifics, especially politically offensive specifics, support for those principles fell off substantially. It is likely that if citizens were asked whether or not the president should be allowed to "declare Congress disbanded," most would support the continued existence of Congress. On the other hand, Congress is often criticized sharply for some of its specific actions, and in public opinion polls it gets low marks for its general performance.

To understand and use the notion of support, two further distinctions are helpful. First, support may be *specific* or *diffuse*. Easton says that specific support "flows from favorable attitudes and predispositions stimulated by outputs that are perceived by members to meet their demands as they arise or in anticipation."[37] Specific support is a direct response to policies and political actions. An interest group leader may support a particular action of Congress because the action helped his group. It is, in effect, an "I'll scratch your back because you scratched mine" pattern. Diffuse support is different. It is a general inclination to be for or against a person or group. It may well be that an individual feels this inclination but cannot really account for the basis of the feeling. The feeling perhaps is best explained by the person's socialization. In the process of maturing, individuals learn certain attitudes and values about citizenship. They may have no conscious memory of learning to like (dislike) or respect (disrespect) the person or group, yet these orientations continue to shape their perceptions and evaluations. Dawson and Prewitt put it this way:

> We suggest that the development of orientations is cumulative. Early orientations greatly influence later acquisitions. The range of beliefs, information, and attitudes one adopts in later life are limited by early political learning. The development of strong attachments to a particular political or social grouping will tend to prescribe one set of political choices and experiences, and to delimit others.[38]

The second distinction is between *overt* and *covert* support. Overt support is manifest in actions—making campaign contributions, voting, writing letters, testifying before committees, backing incumbents or challengers, paying taxes, rioting and demonstrating—the whole array of actions for preserving or changing the political system. Often the actions are more than simply observable; in many instances, they are purposely conspicuous. The "demonstrator" is politically relevant to the extent that his actions, as an expression of his support, intrude upon the awareness of others.

The accounting of support is incomplete without attention to covert support, what Easton calls "a supportive frame of mind."[39] This is an internal form of support, composed of attitudes, predispositions, and readiness for action. While these are not actions, they are likely to guide actions when events evoke an active response. To know attitudes is to have a basis for predicting and perhaps even controlling behavior by bringing about situations in which individuals of known attitudes have a narrow range of action opportunities. Dr. Martin Luther King's nonviolent demonstrators intentionally provoked those who believed in privileges for whites only, so that the latter would be discredited for the vulgarity of their actions in demonstration situations.

Attitudes must be inferred. As internal predispositions alone, they cannot be observed, measured, and compared across sets of individuals. They can be inferred from various forms of overt behavior. One simple form of behavior, a minimally overt one, is the response to a pollster's question.

Such an overt act is usually made anonymously and is in response to a specific question. A series of related questions and answers for a sample of people can provide the careful observer with a well-focused picture of popular attitudes.

A PARADIGM FOR
ANALYZING SUPPORT

With these ideas in mind, Figure 10.2 establishes a format for examining support for legislative subsystems. There are more data available for some cells of this paradigm than others, but no particular legislative subsystem has been studied with all aspects of this paradigm in mind. However, particular findings in a few states and for Congress illustrate the meaning of this model.

Overt Support for the Legislative
Regime and Authorities

Recall that *regime* refers to the norms, rules, procedures, and authority positions of the legislative system. *Authorities* are those in the positions, particularly the legislators, but also the staff. What is perhaps remarkable about American legislative subsystems is how rarely they are the object of *overt* actions either to change or preserve them in order to obtain specific policies or related political actions. Actions to change rarely come from outside; rather, changes are usually wrought by the efforts of those who have experienced the existing rules, and then feel moved to change them. Two recent and significant congressional rule changes concerning selection of committee chairmen and the Senate's cloture rule have already been noted. These had been the objects of criticism by social commentators for a long time, but little more than that. I know of no candidate who has won or lost election to Congress primarily on an issue to change/preserve any particular congressional rules, or any election in which the rules were broadly debated, much less a key issue, in any particular election year. If one considers the amendments to the Constitution, several have changed the presidency, but only one, the Seventeenth Amendment providing for direct election of senators, significantly altered Congress.‡

Over the years the constitutional powers of state legislatures have changed. In the early years of the republic, legislatures were relatively strong, and the powers of executives were circumscribed. After the Civil

‡ Others have affected Congress, of course. The Bill of Rights amendments limit the powers of the federal government, including Congress. Other amendments, such as the Fourteenth and Sixteenth, enlarged its authority. The Twenty-fifth Amendment gave Congress a major role in filling vacancies in the vice-presidency and in deciding whether or not a president has the ability to serve in his office.

Support	Regime	Authorities
OVERT		
Specific	Actions to preserve/change the institution in response to policies and political actions. *Example*: Petition drive to change the Senate's cloture rule.	Actions to preserve/change authorities in response to policies and political actions. *Example*: Election campaign activity to elect/defeat a particular incumbent.
Diffuse	Actions of allegiance to or renunciation of the legislative regime. *Example*: A demonstration around the Capitol building to close the legislature down.	Actions of allegiance to or renunciation of legislative authorities. *Example*: Hold a mock hanging in effigy of a dummy labeled "legislator."
COVERT		
Specific	Opinions about institutional change for policies and political actions.	Opinions about changing authorities for policies and political actions.
Diffuse	Opinions of allegiance to or renunciation of the legislative regime.	Opinions of allegiance to or renunciation of legislative authorities.

Figure 10.2   Support for a Legislative Subsystem

War, excesses of corruption in many states brought a trend of constitutional revision in which legislatures' powers were reduced. There were tax rate limitations, ceilings on state debts, limits on the number of days legislatures could meet,§ requirements that bills be passed by record roll call votes and an absolute majority of the membership, private bill prohibitions, limits on bills to a single topic, and the like. Since that era, however, especially since World War II, states have gradually enlarged the powers of legislatures and relaxed many of the strictures. Typically change has been generated within the institutions and, in the case of constitutional amendments, ratification was subsequently won from the public. A substantial regime change occurred in the reapportionment revolution, discussed in Chapter 2, with those changes sought by people who expected policy consequences. On the other hand, the bicameral structure of legislatures discussed in Chapter 7 has been the object of little popular concern and almost no change.

Note that the regular participants in the legislative process are mostly "system supporters." Presidents and department heads frequently question the wisdom of legislators, but they rarely attack the legislative subsystem's

§The obvious assumption was that the more the legislature was in session, the more mischief it would make. A New York court decision records this dictum: "No man's life, liberty or property are safe while the legislature is in session." 1 Tucker 248 (N.Y. Surr. 1866).

form or legitimacy. Nixon tried to subvert congressional policy actions by impounding funds, but he was attempting to enlarge a presidential power rather than change the Congress. The courts, as previously indicated, only modestly limit legislatures in policy matters and, with few exceptions, leave internal structural affairs to legislators themselves. Interest groups too rarely make direct attempts to change the structure or rules of legislative bodies, although they may take sides when polarization occurs within the legislature itself.‖ On the other hand, Common Cause, with its leader, John Gardner, has been an intense opponent of Congress's seniority system. Ralph Nader has also been a critical, ardent investigator of Congress and a proponent of internal change.[40] Nevertheless, it must be said that political activity to change legislative structures is not conspicuous.

From time to time there are public displays of pressure and displeasure. Martin Luther King's March on Washington in late 1963 brought 200,000 peaceful demonstrators to the Capitol grounds in search of a real civil rights bill. The Poor People's March of early summer 1968 was to obtain direct assistance for the poor from the Departments of Agriculture, Labor, Justice, and HEW. There were as many as 3000 campers in Resurrection City and 50,000 demonstrators on Solidarity Day, June 19. Some specific appeals were made to Congress, but the major impression was of a diffuse sort, a threatening presence of thousands of poor who wanted relief in some form— emergency housing, food, and jobs. State legislatures similarly witness occasional demonstrations, which constitute expressions of both demands and negative support for the subsystem and its policies, should the demands go unmet.

In the absence of conspicuous negative support, there are few actions of positive support for legislatures. It could be pointed out, perhaps, that the state constitutional revisions which occurred during this century were usually actions indicating positive support. In none of the recent state constitutional conventions or amendments to state legislative articles have there been serious and significant attempts to substantially weaken the structure or authority of state legislatures.[41] With regard to both specific and diffuse support, one must infer that it is at least mildly positive in that there is an absence of actions to change the status quo.

The opportunity to preserve/change legislative authorities is institutional-ized in the electoral processes of the American system. Again what is remarkable is the extent to which incumbent legislative authorities are able to renew their lease on public office. As Chapter 2 has indicated, there is no fact of greater significance in legislative elections than the one of incumbency. Incumbents who want reelection obtain it with great regularity.

‖ For instance, the AFL-CIO has favored changing Senate Rule 22, on limiting debate; but that has been more a matter of supporting its friends in the Senate who wanted the change, than of asserting a strongly felt AFL-CIO position.

While specific issues do make a difference in certain instances, reelection seems primarily an evidence of diffuse support. The voting of most constituents seems to express the assumption that the man already in office must not be doing too many things wrong, so it is safer to return him to office than to risk the unknown implications of electing a newcomer.

Occasionally certain events occur in elections which can be interpreted as negative support for congressional authorities. In 1967 the House of Representatives excluded one of its members, Adam Clayton Powell, Jr., for alleged financial misconduct. In 1968 Powell's constituents sent a message of negative support to Congress by reelecting Powell. Also, the U.S. Supreme Court, in *Powell* v. *McCormack*[42] chastised Congress for excluding Powell in the first place.

It is increasingly recognized that electoral swings in congressional elections are variations in response to national election factors. Katz has shown that variations in the voting in congressional districts are mostly explained by electorally relevant factors—unemployment, crime, foreign affairs—that are national in scope, rather than state or local ones.[43] Such national trends in congressional elections or statewide trends in legislatures could be interpreted, indeed they often are in the news media, as diffuse support. Democratic or Republican sweeps in a given election are affirmations that "things are going well," or renunciations of the "ins" and "throwing the rascals out." During 1973 and 1974 several special congressional elections occurred in which Republican candidates in normally Republican districts were defeated, apparently as a rebuff to and renunciation of President Nixon. Nevertheless, individual legislators will work to establish that special identity, that "home folks" reputation, that unique identification, all cognates for *support*, which can counter larger issues and voter responses in order to renew the option on political authority. Of course, the mechanism can also work in the other direction.#

In state legislative contests, outside the limelight of larger campaigns and press attention, the picture is much more fluid. A study of 46 state senate campaigns in Massachusetts during 1968 revealed that candidates rarely knew what they could do to win votes. Instead, "Experienced candidates know what they have done in the past (neophytes know what they have seen and heard), and the tendency is for all to reenact these performances."[44]

Perhaps what is most remarkable about the legislative subsystems in this

---

#As Mayhew points out, Congressman Chester Mize (R., Kans.) fell from 67.6 percent in 1968 to 45.0 percent in 1970, while the Republican share of the national vote dropped only 3.3 percent. David R. Mayhew, *Congress: The Electoral Connection* (New Haven: Yale University Press, 1974), p. 35. Mize lost more than 22.6 percent of his supporters; he lost his job. Notable losers in November 1974 were Republicans of the House Judiciary Committee who defended President Nixon in the impeachment hearings. The televised loyalty of David Dennis (Ind.), Wiley Mayne (Iowa), Joseph Maraziti, and Charles Sandman (both N.J.) cost them specific support.

country is that as subsystems they are rarely the objects of overt negative support. So often in the history of nations, sharp political shifts have been accompanied by the closing of legislatures and representative assemblies. American legislatures have suffered almost no such attacks and have not been closed down either by violence or political processes. If overt, positive support is not conspicuous, it is because negative support has been mild and uncommon. On the other hand, the expression of overt positive or negative support for the legislative authorities is institutionalized in the electoral process: the rascals can be thrown out—and sometimes they are. Perhaps the viability of that process taps off the discontent which might otherwise build up into more disruptive acts of negative support.

A set of political actors whose support behavioral political scientists have to study more thoroughly are those Seligman et al. refer to as the "sponsors" of legislative candidates. They are regularly involved in recruiting nominees for legislatures and Congress. In the absence of broad public involvement in recruitment, other than voting, a persisting set of political activists manage the incentives to recruit/discourage potential legislative candidates. In a cultural context in which as few as 5 percent of the adults have ever participated in a congressional campaign, the views and support of the few who do, loom large in the calculations of the legislative aspirants. The activists exercise highly specific overt support, and in doing so are significant gatekeepers in the recruitment process. As long as office aspirants lament the absence of readily mobilized public support—Fishel quotes one candidate this way: "Blessed are those [candidates] who do not expect very much, for they shall not be disappointed"—then sponsors will be very important.[45]

Covert Support for the Legislative Regime and Authorities

Assessments by citizens of legislatures and legislative systems are based upon relatively little specific information about the individual performances of members or the policy considerations under current scrutiny. Surveys typically indicate that citizens do not have a great deal of specific information about their own representatives or what bills are being acted on.[46] This is not surprising and ought not be thought shocking. Congress and legislatures are complex. Many things are happening all the time. Congressman Smith says what happened was good and Senator Jones says it was bad. The complexity of legislative information and the multiplicity of voices make legislatures, in contrast to executives, easy for citizens to ignore. As a consequence, covert support takes the form of diffuse more than specific support. Specific support, both overt and covert, requires a level of information and involvement which is only obtained by the investment of a good deal of time and effort to learn what legislatures and legislators are doing. Typically only specialists who have immediate stakes in legislative outputs—interested parties, journalists, political activists, and a few academics—care enough to make such investments. Evaluations tend, therefore, to be general inclinations rather than highly differentiated perceptions.

Diffuse Regime Support   Measures of general inclinations toward Congress and legislatures are rarely reported. It is interesting to note that in the mid-1960s a national sample of university students expressed substantial confidence in Congress as an institution.** On the other hand, Davidson, using responses from a national sample of respondents to four items[47] in 1968 found that favorable evaluations of Congress on three items or more came from only 12 percent of the population. (See Table 10.5.) One-quarter of the respondents gave no favorable response on any of the items. Muller obtained evaluations of Congress from beginning college political science students and some student protestors. He found that about one-third had no opinion. Fifteen percent felt that Congress did represent their interests, while 25 percent felt the opposite was true. Between those extremes, 19 percent expressed positive but rather apathetic support, and 7 percent expressed negative but apathetic support.[48]

The best research on diffuse regime support is that done on state legislatures, particularly Iowa. Diffuse support was examined using questions to ascertain attitudes toward complying with legislative enactments and other questions inquiring about commitment to the legislature itself. The researchers obtained opinions for the same questions from a mass public sample, political party leaders, attentive constituents (persons named by legislators as politically knowledgeable), a sample of lobbyists, and members of the Iowa legislature during 1966 and 1967. (See Table 10.6.) The authors note specifically that

> . . . legislative support in the mass public probably is quite high. The public rates low in support compared to political elite groups, but this should not imply in any sense that the mass of citizens does not support the legislature and political

---

**Students were asked, "How much confidence do you have in these institutions?" Of 20 institutions, Congress placed tenth. Responses were: Great Deal (39 percent), Only Some (52 percent), Hardly Any (8 percent), and Not Sure (1 percent). In order, according to confidence, the institutions were: (1) Scientific community, (2) Medical profession, (3) Banks and financial institutions, (4) U.S. Supreme Court, (5) Higher education, (6) Big corporations, (7) Executive branch of federal government, (8) the Arts, (9) Psychiatric field, (10) Congress, (11) the Military, (12) the United Nations, (13) Organized religion, (14) Civil rights movement, (15) the Democratic party, (16) the Press, (17) Advertising, (18) Organized labor, (19) Television, (20) the Republican party. See "Campus 1965," *Newsweek* Magazine, March 22, 1965, p. 45, from the Harris Survey.

elites do. In fact, we would expect analyses in other political systems to demonstrate that, relative to their mass publics, support for the legislature in Iowa is quite high. But legislative support grows very dramatically as one goes from the mass public to county party leaders to attentive constituents to lobbyists to legislators.[49]

While all the respondents were combined and analyzed according to education, occupation, income, political knowledge, and political participation, support varied regularly with stratification. The higher the social/political characteristics, the higher the support. These results are shown in Figure 10.3.

Table 10.5   Positive Support for Congress: 1968

Positive Support	%
High (3–4)	12
(2)	30
(1)	33
Low (0)	25
TOTAL:	100

NOTE: Positive support is inferred from the italicized responses to the following:

How would you rate the job Congress did in 1968—*excellent*, *pretty good*, only fair, or poor?

How would you rate the service your representative gave in looking after your district in Washington—*excellent*, *pretty good*, only fair, or poor?

Compared with what we have produced in the past, do you feel our present [1968] leadership in Congress—both the House of Representatives and the Senate—is now *better*, worse, or about the same as we have produced in the past?

How would you rate the honesty of members of the Senate and House of Representatives? Would you say that, generally speaking, they are *more honest*, less honest, or about the same as people in other professions?

SOURCE: Roger H. Davidson and Glenn R. Parker, "Positive Support for Political Institutions: The Case of Congress," *Western Political Quarterly* 25, no. 4 (December 1972): 603–4.

Table 10.6   Diffuse Legislative Support in the Mass Public and Among Political Elites

Diffuse Legislative Support	Mass Public (%)	Party Leaders (%)	Attentive Constituents (%)	Lobbyists (%)	Legislators (%)
High	15.2	39.6	49.8	45.5	63.5
Medium	32.0	31.9	29.8	38.4	23.8
Low	52.8	28.6	20.5	16.2	12.7
TOTAL	100.0	100.1	100.1	100.1	100.0

SOURCE: Samuel C. Patterson, John C. Wahlke, and G. Robert Boynton, "Dimensions of Support in Legislative Systems," in *Legislatures in Comparative Perspective*, ed. Allan Kornberg (New York: David McKay Company, Inc., 1973), p. 297.

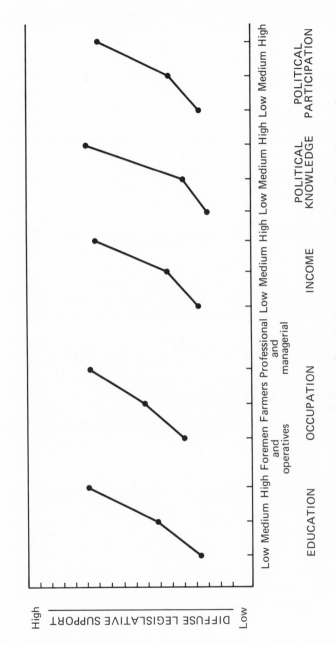

Figure 10.3 Mean Diffuse Legislative Support Scores by Education, Occupation, Income, and Political Knowledge and Participation (All Groups)

SOURCE: Samuel C. Patterson, John C. Wahlke, and G. Robert Boynton, "Dimensions of Support in Legislative Systems," in *Legislatures in Comparative Perspective*, ed. Allan Kornberg (New York: David McKay Company, Inc., 1973), p. 300.

To extend their research, Patterson and his colleagues interviewed in another 13 states and compared support for the legislatures with that found in Iowa. The results are in Table 10.7, with support highest in California and the midwestern states, middling support in the industrial east, and the lowest support among people in the southern states. When the order of states on support was compared to other social/political variables, the two that were most related were political party competitiveness and legislative conflict. These findings suggest that (1) the highest legislative support occurs where, at the state level, there is relatively hot and even two-party competition, and (2) legislative support occurs in states in which the legislators report sharp conflict within the legislative process. It is possible that legislative conflict enhances visibility and respect for the legislature as an arena of real decision making.

Specific Regime Support   Most of the data that pollsters have gathered indicating attitudes of support for Congress are of specific support. Results of Harris Surveys are reported in Table 10.8. The question Harris asks is, "How would you rate the job Congress is doing this year—excellent, pretty good, only fair, or poor?" The answers "excellent" and "good" are pooled as positive, while "fair" and "poor" are counted as negative. Clearly Congress rarely gets high marks for its work, at least not when "fair" is taken to be a negative assessment.

Specific support for Congress is evidently fragile, it being highest in the halcyon years of 1964 and 1965, when President Johnson and Congress were

Table 10.7   Rank Order of Diffuse Legislative Support in 14 American States

State	Rank
California	1
Iowa	2
Minnesota	3
Ohio	4
Texas	5
Massachusetts	6
Pennsylvania	7
Illinois	8
Florida	9
North Carolina	10
New York	11
Louisiana	12
South Dakota	13
Alabama	14

SOURCE: Samuel C. Patterson, John C. Wahlke, and G. Robert Boynton, "Dimensions of Support in Legislative Systems," in *Legislatures in Comparative Perspective*, ed. Allan Kornberg (New York: David McKay Company, Inc., 1973), p. 303.

Table 10.8   Support for Congress: 1963–1975

Date	Positive	Negative	Not Sure
1963	33	60	7
1964	59	33	8
1965	64	26	10
1966	49	42	9
1967	38	55	7
1968	46	46	8
1969	34	54	12
1970	26	63	11
1973	38	45	17
1974 January	21	69	10
1974 July	29	64	7
1974 September	38	54	8
1975 March	26	67	7

SOURCE: Louis Harris, "Harris Survey," *Chicago Tribune*, September 23, 1974, sec. 2, p. 4, and *Southern Illinoisan*, March 31, 1975.

in high accord, the economy was growing, and the war in Vietnam had taken little toll. From there, support slipped. Tentative optimism followed the 1972 election and again, in late 1974, after Congress functioned effectively in the impeachment proceedings, but since that time malaise in the society concerning a variety of matters means that, when asked by a pollster how good a job Congress was doing of "handling taxes and spending," the response was sharply negative.††

Specific Support for Legislative Authorities There are not many studies of specific support concerning individual legislators. Pollsters rarely report data for subnational samples, and scientific sampling in congressional districts is almost never done except for legislators as candidates. The modest visibility of legislators means that citizens are not very knowledgeable about how well or how badly a legislator is doing his job. Nevertheless, at election time voters are willing to express support in terms of broader political orientations, particularly party identification.

One such campaign study was conducted in 1974 in the southernmost congressional district of Illinois. The respondents were *not* a random sample of the population; they were, rather, a group of registered voters from randomly selected households who reported their intention to vote in the 1974 primary election. At the time the incumbent U.S. senator, Adlai Stevenson, was up for reelection. The incumbent congressman, Kenneth Gray, was about to retire after 20 years of service. An incumbent state

††In March 1974, 80 percent felt Congress had not done a good job, only 12 percent felt it had, and 8 percent were undecided. Louis Harris, "Harris Survey," *Southern Illinoisan*, March 31, 1975.

Table 10.9 Job Ratings for Legislative Incumbents by Respondents Intending to Vote in a Party Primary

Job Rating	U.S. Senator Stevenson (%)	U.S. Representative Gray (%)	State Senator Buzbee (%)
Very good	13	42	3
Good	24	25	17
Average	31	14	27
Poor	8	3	2
Very poor	2	1	0
Don't know	23	15	50
TOTAL:	101	100	99

SOURCE: Southern Illinois Research Associates, Inc., prepared for Paul Simon, *The Climate of Opinion Among the Primary Electorate, 24th Congressional District of Illinois, as of February 1, 1974.* Mimeo, February 16, 1974, pp. 11–13. By permission.

senator, Kenneth Buzbee, was serving his second year in office and was running for reelection to the state legislature. All three incumbents were Democrats. The primary voters were asked to evaluate jobs being done by each. Table 10.9 reports the results.

It is interesting to note that at the same time that Congress was being rapped with low approval nationally, a set of respondents intending to vote in a primary election viewed their legislators, particularly their U.S. representative, as doing a good job. It is arguable, at least, that specific support for individual legislators generally exceeds the support people will express for the job Congress as a whole is doing.

Diffuse Support for Legislative Authorities What are popular opinions of allegiance to or renunciation of legislative authorities? Are the impressions people hold about legislators favorable or unfavorable? What are the stereotypes, the pictures in people's minds, about the authorities of the legislative subsystems? Again, hard data are rather sparse. I have already noted what legislators think of themselves; most view themselves as trustees—elected to make wise choices and decisions in good conscience for the future best interests of their constituents. Some view themselves as delegates—to do their constituents' bidding. Others are politicos— accommodating wisdom to popular pressure. It is interesting that citizens do not feel the same way. Davidson reports that in 1967 an Indiana congressman asked his constituents how he should vote on various issues. Of 7474 responses, 69 percent preferred that he vote according to his interpretation of the majority wishes, in contrast to 31 percent who wanted him to vote according to his "conscience and judgment." [50]

Popular stereotypes of legislators are not very positive. "Senator Claghorn" is more fool than father figure. "Senator Snort" is a cartoon character full of windy rhetoric but afraid to make decisions. Popular literature and cinema rarely lionize American legislators; most are presented as being obviously flawed by ambition, venality, or naïveté.

Studies of children's views of government reveal that from the fifth grade on most children recognize that Congress is the chief lawmaker.[51] Most have positive sentiments about government but, interestingly, compared to other authority objects in the American political system, "the average United States senator" had far less salience. The senator received far less regard than *government, president, policeman,* and *Supreme Court.* Easton and Dennis observed that, "As a mechanism of attachment to the structure of authority, the senator operates as a considerably less influential point of contact with the child."[52]

One other glimpse of diffuse support can be gleaned from the terms in which people describe U.S. congressmen. As part of a larger study, Jennings and others gathered information by personal interviews on the images of congressmen and high federal appointees.[53] Respondents were asked, "If you were to describe your general idea of a United States congressman, what sort of person would that be?" A similar question was asked about high federal appointees. The views of 10 categories of respondents were compared. Responses were separated into *clearly* favorable, unfavorable, and ambiguous categories. Results indicated generally favorable images, both for congressmen and high-level federal appointees, as Table 10.10 indicates.

Table 10.10 Clearly Favorable Descriptions of Congressmen and High-Level Federal Appointees

Respondents	Congressmen (%)	Federal Appointees (%)
General employed public	64	62
General federal employees	71	77
High school juniors and seniors	81	85
Nongraduates of high school	61	50
College seniors	67	85
College graduates	65	75
Graduate students	58	78
College teachers	54	76
Business executives	48	71
Federal executives	72	82

SOURCE: Adapted from M. Kent Jennings, Milton C. Cummings, Jr., and Franklin P. Kilpatrick, "Trusted Leaders: Perceptions of Appointed Federal Officials," *Public Opinion Quarterly* 30, no. 3 (Fall 1966): 368–84.

Interestingly, however, federal appointees tended to receive favorable evaluations from more respondents, particularly from the higher achievement groups. In fact, it was the graduate students, college teachers, and business executives who distinguished most sharply between the two sets of officials, and in every case more were favorable toward the appointees. Those of modest achievement, the general employed public and those with less than a high school education, were slightly more favorable toward congressmen than federal appointees, but the percentages of those clearly favorable were relatively modest.

Findings are sketchy, but there does seem to be a reservoir of positive diffuse support for legislators. The importance of such support is not fully known, of course, but it is likely to be substantial. If the future of the American society is difficult because of population growth, resource shortages, international rivalry, and other pressures, then political authorities will have to make hard and, often, unpopular choices. The legitimacy accorded those decisions may depend more upon diffuse support for the regime and authorities than upon approval for specific policies and actions of individual members.

ASSESSING SUPPORT FOR LEGISLATIVE SUBSYSTEMS: CONCLUDING OBSERVATIONS

Data on support are too scattered, casual, and recent to interpret them with great confidence. The data of recent years were collected during a period of stress for the whole American system, a period in which national studies reveal a decline in the trust that Americans have in their political system.

Figure 10.4 plots the responses to three questions about government:

1. How much do you feel that political parties help to make the government pay attention to what the people think: a good deal, some, or not much?

2. And how much do you feel that having elections makes the government pay attention to what people think: a good deal, some, or not much?

3. How much attention do you think most congressmen pay to the people who elect them when they decide what to do in Congress: a good deal, some, or not much?

A percentage difference index was computed for each of the three questions by subtracting the percentage responding "not much" from the percentage answering "a good deal." Positive values of the PDI therefore specify the degree of confidence, whereas negative values denote a lack of confidence. These PDI values are plotted in Figure 10.4 for whites and blacks.

It should be noted that these items indicate the respondent's confidence in elections, parties, and congressmen to make government responsive and not the respondent's confidence, *per se*, in the institutions and leaders referred to by the questions.[53a]

Although Figure 10.4 indicates a drop in the confidence that Americans have in leaders, parties, and elections, it has been argued that many

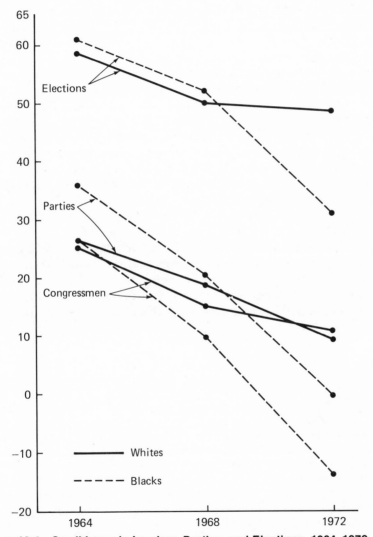

Figure 10.4   Confidence in Leaders, Parties, and Elections, 1964–1972
SOURCE: Arthur H. Miller, "Rejoinder to 'Comment' by Jack Citrin," *American Political Science Review* 68, no. 3 (September 1974): 990.

Americans are expressing cynicism born of "bad times" rather than repudiating the entire political system, root and branch.[54] In the context of the larger change and the ambiguity of its meaning, it is well to be cautious in interpreting levels of support for legislators and legislative subsystems. Certainly specific support is likely to be more volatile than diffuse support. If and when American society enjoys peace, prosperity, and relative calm, approval for presidents and Congress will grow. It appears, however, that representatives, legislative institutions, and basic rules for representation are not being challenged, and are not likely to be. It may well be that most of the data gathered here are the least significant sort to know about legislative subsystems. Approval or disapproval of the job Congress is doing is less relevant to the future of the system than the kinds of attitudes reported about Iowans: they expressed a strong commitment to the legislative institution and a willingness to comply with properly authorized legislative enactments.

My view of the data is that support for legislative systems is positive and rather high, despite real dissatisfaction with political system outputs and outcomes. There will always be a lag between events and evaluations. Note too that opinions about outputs are subject to change as they accomplish, or fail to accomplish, desired outcomes.

Finally, verbal grumbling about legislative bodies and ludicrous cartoons about Senator Snort are in relation to an abstract ideal. The real world rarely compares well with an ideal one. Americans take their institutions for granted. On the other hand, perhaps scholars need to inquire whether or not Americans would be willing to have policy made without the benefit of representative assemblies. American legislatures may be less than ideal, but they are strong, viable, and accessible. Without them, citizen distrust would likely be much greater than it is.

NOTES

1. David Easton, *A Systems Analysis of Political Life* (New York: John Wiley & Sons, Inc., 1965), p. 93.

2. Sidney Verba and Norman H. Nie, *Participation in America: Political Democracy and Social Equality* (New York: Harper & Row, 1972), pp. 52–53.

3. Ibid., pp. 77–80. Seven percent were unclassifiable.

4. Ibid., pp. 100–101.

5. Donald G. Tacheron and Morris K. Udall, *The Job of the Congressman: An Introduction to Service in the U.S. House of Representatives* (Indianapolis: The Bobbs-Merrill Company, Inc., 1966), p. 62.

6. Based upon responses of 150 congressmen and the reports of 60 congressional offices concerning staff during the Eighty-ninth Congress. See John S. Saloma III,

Congress and the New Politics (Boston: Little, Brown and Company, 1969), pp. 183–84.

7. Data are drawn from Ronald D. Michaelson, "An Analysis of the Chief Executive: How a Governor Uses His Time," *Public Affairs Bulletin* 4, no. 4 (September/October 1971). The report is on the June 1971 schedule of Governor Richard B. Ogilvie, then governor of Illinois.

8. Clem Miller, *Member of the House: Letters of a Congressman*, ed. John W. Baker (New York: Charles Scribner's Sons, 1962), p. v.

9. Ibid., pp. 71–72.

10. See Easton, *Systems Analysis of Political Life*, pp. 87–96.

11. Alexander Heard, *The Costs of Democracy* (Chapel Hill, N.C.:, The University of North Carolina Press, 1960), p. 88.

12. Michael Lipsky, "Protest as a Political Resource," *American Political Science Review* 62, no. 4 (December 1968): 1144–58; quotation is from pp. 1145–46.

13. David Halberstam, *The Best and the Brightest* (New York: Random House, Inc., 1972); a critical account of brilliant advisers caught up in their own ambitions and self-righteousness in the escalation of the Vietnam War.

14. See also Nelson W. Polsby, "Strengthening Congress in National Policy Making," *The Yale Review* 59, no. 4 (June 1970): 481–97, especially pp. 485–90.

15. L. Harmon Zeigler and Michael L. Baer, *Lobbying: Interaction and Influence in American State Legislatures* (Belmont, Calif.: Wadsworth Publishing Company, 1969), p. 102.

16. Ibid., p. 65.

17. Ibid.

18. Lewis Anthony Dexter, *How Organizations Are Represented in Washington* (Indianapolis: The Bobbs-Merrill Company, Inc., 1969), pp. 103–4; italics in original.

19. David B. Truman, *The Governmental Process: Political Interests and Public Opinion* (New York: Alfred A. Knopf, 1951), p. 33.

20. *Congressional Quarterly Weekly Report*, June 9, 1973, p. 1424.

21. Truman, *The Governmental Process*, p. 59.

22. Robert H. Salisbury, "An Exchange Theory of Interest Groups," *Midwest Journal of Political Science* 13, no. 1 (February 1969): 1–32; quotation is from p. 11.

23. This discussion owes a great deal to Richard H. McCleary, Charles R. Adrian, and Charles Press. See Adrian and Press, *The American Political Process*, 2d ed. (New York: McGraw-Hill Book Company, 1969), pp. 219–21.

24. Ibid., p. 220; emphasis in the original.

25. Andrew M. Scott and Margaret A. Hunt, *Congress and Lobbies: Image and Reality* (Chapel Hill, N.C.: University of North Carolina Press, 1966).

26. Ibid., p. 59.

27. Raymond A. Bauer, Ithiel de Sola Pool, and Lewis Anthony Dexter, *American Business and Public Policy: The Politics of Foreign Trade* (New York: Atherton Press, 1963), pp. 396–98.

28. John W. Kingdon, *Congressional Voting Decisions* (New York: Harper & Row, 1973), p. 19.

29. Ibid., p. 140, emphasis added.

30. Ibid., p. 143.

31. Lester Milbrath, *The Washington Lobbyists* (Chicago: Rand McNally & Company, 1963), especially pp. 302–3.

32. L. Harmon Zeigler and Hendrik van Dalen, "Interest Groups in the States," in *Politics in the American States: A Comparative Analysis*, 2d ed. (eds.) Herbert Jacob and Kenneth N. Vines (Boston: Little, Brown and Company, 1971), pp. 126–27; emphasis added.

33. One of the more recent books in this genre of social criticism is that of G. William Domhoff, *The Higher Circles: The Governing Class in America* (New York: Vintage Books, Random House, 1970).

34. Michael Parenti, "Power and Pluralism: A View from the Bottom," *Journal of Politics* 32, no. 3 (August 1970): 501–30; quotation is from p. 530.

35. Easton, *Systems Analysis of Political Life,* pp. 159 ff. are the starting point for some of the distinctions which shall be made.

36. James W. Prothro and Charles M. Grigg, "Fundamental Principles of Democracy: Bases of Agreement and Disagreement," *Journal of Politics* 22 (Spring 1960): 281.

37. Easton, *Systems Analysis of Political Life*, p. 273.

38. Richard E. Dawson and Kenneth Prewitt, *Political Socialization* (Boston: Little, Brown and Company, 1969), p. 24.

39. Easton, *Systems Analysis of Political Life*, p. 160.

40. For a massive study, see *Ralph Nader Congress Project: Citizens Look at Congress* (New York: Grossman Publishers, 1972–73). This is an encyclopedic study of individual members during the Ninety-second Congress, 1971–72. See also Mark J. Green, James M. Fallows, and David Swick, *Who Runs Congress?* (New York: Bantam Books, 1972).

41. The most convenient and authoritative source on state constitutional changes is *Book of the States*, published biennially by the Council of State Governments, Lexington, Kentucky.

42. 395 U.S. 486 (1969).

43. See Richard S. Katz, "The Attribution of Variance in Electoral Returns: An Alternative Measurement Technique," *American Political Science Review* 67, no. 3 (September 1973): 817–28. Of the variance explained, 54.6 percent is explained by national level forces, while 19.2 is accorded to state level forces and 26.2 to local. The data analyzed were for the congressional contests between 1952 and 1960.

44. Jerome M. Mileur and George T. Sulzner, *Campaigning for the Massachusetts Senate: Electioneering Outside the Political Limelight* (Amherst: University of Massachusetts Press, 1974), p. 161.

45. See Lester G. Seligman, Michael R. King, Chong Lim Kim, and Roland E. Smith, *Patterns of Recruitment: A State Chooses Its Lawmakers* (Chicago: Rand McNally College Publishing Company, 1974), pp. 28–29 and *passim*; Jeff Fishel, *Party and Opposition: Congressional Challengers in American Politics* (New York: David McKay Company, Inc., 1973), quotation is from p. 99; David A. Leuthold, *Electioneering in a Democracy: Campaigns for Congress* (New York: John Wiley & Sons, Inc., 1968); and Mileur and Sulzner, *Campaigning for the Massachusetts Senate*, for some starting points. For a slightly different slant, see the "recruitment capability of attentive constituents" in G. R. Boynton, Samuel C. Patterson, and

Ronald D. Hedlund, "The Missing Links in Legislative Politics: Attentive Constituents," *Journal of Politics* 31, no. 3 (August 1969): 700–21, especially pp. 713–15.

46. See, for instance, George Gallup's American Institute of Public Opinion Survey, September 20, 1970, reported in *The Gallup Poll: Public Opinion 1935–1971*, vol. 3 (New York: Random House, 1972), p. 2264. About three-fourths of the respondents said they did not know how their congressman voted on any major bill that year, and 81 percent did not know of anything the congressman had done for the district.

47. Davidson and Parker created an index which mixes responses to "Congress," "your representative," "present leadership in Congress," and the honesty of congressional members—support of specific and diffuse kinds for both authorities and regime. See Roger H. Davidson and Glenn R. Parker, "Positive Support for Political Institutions: The Case of Congress," *Western Political Quarterly* 25, no. 4 (December 1972): 600–12.

48. Edward N. Muller, "The Representation of Citizens by Political Authorities: Consequences for Regime Support," *American Political Science Review* 64, no. 4 (December 1970): 1149–66.

49. Samuel C. Patterson, John C. Wahlke, and G. Robert Boynton, "Dimensions of Support in Legislative Systems," in *Legislatures in Comparative Perspective*, ed. Allen Kornberg (New York: David McKay Company, Inc., 1973), p. 297.

50. Roger H. Davidson, *The Role of the Congressman* (New York: Pegasus, 1969), p. 115.

51. David Easton and Jack Dennis, *Children in the Political System: Origins of Political Legitimacy* (New York: McGraw-Hill Book Company, 1969), p. 119.

52. Ibid., p. 282.

53. M. Kent Jennings, Milton C. Cummings, Jr., and Franklin P. Kilpatrick, "Trusted Leaders: Perceptions of Appointed Federal Officials," *Public Opinion Quarterly* 30, no. 3 (Fall 1966): 368–84.

53a. The interpretation of the items as indicators of "diffuse public support" was suggested by Jack Dennis in "Support for the Institution of Elections by the Mass Public," *American Political Science Review* 64, no. 3 (September 1970): 819–35.

54. For a significant discussion, see Arthur H. Miller, "Political Issues and Trust in Government: 1964–1970"; Jack Citrin, "Comment: The Political Relevance of Trust in Government"; and Arthur H. Miller, "Rejoinder to 'Comment' by Jack Citrin: Political Discontent or Ritualism?" *American Political Science Review* 68, no. 3 (September 1974): 951–1001.

11

Outputs of the Legislative Subsystem: Policies and Responses to Influence

Each Congress expresses millions of words, expends billions of dollars, enacts hundreds of public laws, refuses to enact thousands more, listens to tens of thousands of witnesses, handles hundreds of thousands of letters and telegrams, calls for hundreds of staff reports, and publishes millions of pages of printed material. Each consumes vast amounts of energy, emits large quantities of hot air, arouses some anger, evokes some praise, but more than anything, its outputs are received with tolerant indifference by most people, most of the time. In the states the indicators of legislative output are similar, but smaller in scale and salience.

The most interesting outputs are those that specify public policy. David Easton defined policy as "a web of decisions and actions that allocates values,"[1] and, of course, the essential function of a political system is to authoritatively allocate values. Legislatures do not make policy alone, nor are legislative enactments the last word on policy enunciation, but "the law" is significantly what the legislatures have enacted.

CLASSIFICATION OF POLICY

Policies may be classified in a number of ways that point out differences in their significance. For instance, policies can be differentiated according to their *durability*, *scope*, and *type*.

Durability of Policy

It is easy to assume that all public policy is intended to be enduring. It is not; in fact, a good deal of policy is temporary and some is unmade (policy in the absence of explicit policy to the contrary). Each type will be discussed briefly in turn.

Short-Term Policy Most legislative enactments are for a specified period. With few exceptions, all the budget actions of legislatures are for a single year.* Even within a year, budgetary alterations occur and agencies initiate and/or legislators impose supplemental appropriations. An interesting irony of such policy making is the fact that when a governmental unit is appropriated an amount for a specific time period (ordinarily a fiscal year), thus controlling, even restraining, future spending, it means that agencies cannot save money from year to year. In the parlance of administrators, such monies that are left at the end of the fiscal year will *revert* back to the Treasury. The bureaucrat will not benefit from saving money; instead, he is likely to be considered rather dull or naïve for not spending every dollar he had while he controlled it.

Short-term policy includes more than budget bills since a great many other bills have expiration dates. Two very significant pieces of domestic legislation are examples of temporary laws. The Voting Rights Act of 1965 was enacted for only five years. Its provisions were of major significance: it took the registration of voters out of the hands of local officials in counties or states in which fewer than 50 percent of the voting age public was registered or had voted in the 1964 presidential election. In 1970, prior to the expiration of the Voting Rights Act, the law was renewed for another five years, along with a controversial addition allowing 18-year-olds to vote. That portion of the act was later declared unconstitutional and then reestablished by the Twenty-sixth Amendment in 1971. In 1975 the act was extended again, this time for seven years. Similarly revenue sharing was enacted for five years in 1971 and came up for renewal again in 1976. Expiring legislation tends to favor the interests of those who opposed it when it was originally proposed; instead of having to generate an enactment to strike or amend the existing legislation, they only have to wait for it to expire. Those who seek its continuation must win its renewal through all the regular legislative channels. Similarly temporary legislation functions as a

---

*Almost all states draw up an annual budget. In 1974 North Dakota, Oregon, Washington, and Wyoming used biennial budgets, but even in those states some functions are budgeted annually. See *The Book of the States: 1974-75* (Lexington, Ky.: Council of State Governments, 1974), pp. 158–61.

particularly sharp check on the chief executive and bureaucrats. A short-term program usually requires new personnel and sometimes new agencies. When the program expires, the positions do too. For a chief executive this may mean proposing and working for a renewal of the program. Sometimes that is a constraint, but other times, given an intervening change in chief executives, it may fit the new chief executive's desires, and he simply allows legislation to expire, leaving continuation up to the legislature. For the bureaucrats, of course, the stakes are often much higher: they may lose their jobs entirely. To the extent that they can, therefore, it is normal for bureau personnel to seek the continuation of their agencies. They become significant advocates for preserving or enlarging government functions and staff, and they strenuously resist cutbacks.

A postwar innovation in short-term policy making is the device of annual authorizations for agencies and their programs. Since 1837 the House has had a rule requiring that no appropriation be reported to the House for action for any expenditure "not previously authorized by law. . . ." Congressional procedure on spending consists of two distinct steps. The legislative committees establish programs and agencies and "authorize" what they can do and spend. Once the authorization has been enacted, funds for it are budgeted and appropriated by action of the Appropriations Committees and both chambers. Typically the authorization sets a spending ceiling, with actual appropriations lower than amounts authorized. Members of the substantive committees in the House have felt that the Appropriations Committee used its fiscal control to specify policy, thus invading their policy discretion. Committees such as Education and Labor began to insist that programs under their jurisdiction be authorized for short periods, often only one year at a time. What were formerly permanent or multi-year authorizations became short-term ones—in matters such as foreign aid, space and military construction, and agricultural subsidies. This pattern has increased the policy activity and discretion of the legislative committees and has given them, and Congress as a whole, the means for tightening control of the executive branch and the bureaucracies.[2]

Enduring Policy A small portion of policy is enacted with the intention that it endure; for example, the laws establishing basic cabinet departments, such as the Department of the Treasury, originated early in American history. From term to term of Congress, new legislation intended to be enduring is passed. In 1965 Congress enacted the Elementary and Secondary Education Act, the basic features of which remain more than a decade later. In 1973 Congress enacted, over the president's veto, the War Powers Act, a new set of constraints upon the president in the use of troops in foreign lands. These laws were enacted to endure. This does not put them beyond change. Indeed, the Elementary and Secondary Education Act has been amended numerous times. Yet these policies remain in effect until positive action is taken either to rewrite or repeal them. The point to retain here is that some congressional enactments are *intended* to endure. In the states, the pattern is reversed; most state legislative bills, particularly when appropriations bills have been excluded, are enacted to be permanent.

Policy by Nondecision   Sometimes it is hard to specify clearly what policy is, from an enacted and documented perspective at least, simply because not all policy is so enacted and documented. Other times the law states what a policy is not rather than what it is. In other contexts legislatures simply leave a void in the law where formal policy could exist. Bachrach and Baratz say that:

> When the dominant values, the accepted rules of the game, the existing power relation among groups, and the instruments of force, singly or in combination, effectively prevent certain grievances from developing into full-fledged issues which call for decisions, it can be said that a nondecision-making situation exists.[3]

To put the statement in more casual language, sometimes even the policy makers do not know what they are missing. The biases of the society simply preclude some matters from coming to policy enactment.

There are policies implicit in deciding not to act—for example, the American steel industry is privately owned by its stockholders, not publicly owned or nationalized, because Congress has not acted to nationalize the industry. There are also policies implicit in decisions not to decide. In the 1950s and 1960s, Congress decided not to decide on many foreign affairs matters, leaving discretion primarily in the hands of the president and his civilian and military subordinates. The War Powers Act of 1973 is a policy requiring Congress to decide on the propriety of presidential military intervention in other nations.

Scope of Policy

Although it is a rough division, it is meaningful to distinguish between foreign and domestic public policy. It is, of course, true that outputs in one may have consequences upon outcomes in the other. Vietnam policy certainly affected the context of domestic policy and public debate thereon. Nevertheless, despite some overlapping, domestic and foreign policies are fairly distinct.

Foreign Policy All of a political system's policies directed primarily toward safeguarding a nation's security from the challenge of other political systems may be summed up as its foreign policy. Implicit in foreign policy making is the understanding that in this scope matters are highly delicate, complex, and remote to the experience of most Americans and, indeed, most political authorities. What the nation does in Food for Peace or counterintelligence has little tangible impact on most Americans most of the time. Of course, years of news coverage and disappointing policy outcomes in Vietnam finally made the American war effort there salient and embarrassing to many Americans, but that aspect of American foreign policy long ago outgrew the "little tangible impact" description typical to foreign policy. The environment of foreign policy making has also condoned and, frequently, encouraged secrecy. There is a legitimate need for secrecy, of course, but it must not become a cover for mistaken judgments by an elite few among the political authorities. Given the existence of nuclear weapons and intercontinental missiles, foreign policy has been made in a context in which many Americans have wanted to entrust decision making into the hands of their leaders, rather than consider alternatives on their merits. As Gabriel Almond observed a quarter century ago:

> In the degree to which issues and decisions are remote, the incapacity of the public to grasp the issues and its consequent indifference accords a special importance to the initiatives and pressures of interested elite and minority groups. Under circumstances of peace or of only moderate international tension, most of the daily decisions of diplomacy and foreign policy are "remote."[4]

From the end of World War II until the late 1960s, the making of foreign policy was a highly insulated process. The forms of democracy were periodically respected. Some international agreements were formalized as treaties and were consented to by the Senate. Appropriations for military spending were enacted, assistance to other nations was periodically debated, but Congress's part in policy making was essentially as legitimizer of the president's policy pronouncements.

Nevertheless, Congress did function as a fiscal check on the president. Table 11.1 indicates that Congress regularly appropriated less than presidents requested in foreign economic and military assistance. Assistance was very high during the Truman administration. Requests fell off during the Eisenhower years, but Congress cut the requests by about 20 percent. Assistance requests increased under Kennedy and congressional cuts were smaller. Johnson pared his requests and got greater percentages appropriated until Congress cut his proposals very sharply during his last two years in office. Assistance levels rose somewhat in the Nixon years, but congressional reductions were sharp in three of the five years.

Table 11.1 History of Foreign Aid[a]

Fiscal Year	President's Request (Billions of $)	Appropriation (Billions of $)	% Cut
1948–49	7.37	6.45	12.5
1950	5.68	4.94	13.0
1951	8.17	7.49	8.3
1952	8.50	7.28	14.4
1953	7.92	6.00	24.2
1954	5.83	4.53	22.3
1955	3.48	2.78	20.1
1956	3.27	2.70	17.2
1957	4.86	3.77	22.5
1958	3.39	2.77	18.3
1959	3.95	3.30	16.5
1960	4.43	3.23	27.2
1961	4.28	3.72	13.1
1962	4.78	3.91	18.0
1963	4.96	3.93	20.8
1964	4.53	3.00	33.7
1965	3.52	3.25	7.6
1966	3.46	3.22	7.0
1967	3.39	2.94	13.3
1968	3.25	2.30	29.4
1969	2.92	1.76	39.9
1970	2.71	1.81	33.1
1971	2.20	1.94	11.8
1972	3.09	2.23	27.7
1973	3.12	2.23	28.6
1974	2.50	1.92	23.4
1975	4.19	2.53	39.6

[a]The chart shows the percentage cuts (enacted appropriation below request) for total foreign aid spending from fiscal year 1948–49 through fiscal year 1955. From fiscal year 1956 on, the percent cut reflects the change in Title I spending only, which includes most economic and military assistance, but not foreign military credit sales, various international financial institutions, the Export-Import Bank, the Peace Corps and emergency and refugee programs.

SOURCE: *Congressional Quarterly Almanac, 1975* (Washington, D.C.: Congressional Quarterly Inc., 1976), p. 857.

Perhaps more revealing is congressional accommodation of presidents in defense spending. Table 11.2 details the data. Typically, congressional cuts have been very small, at least in percentage terms. As recently as fiscal year 1967, Congress appropriated a greater amount than the president's budget called for. Of course, budget proposing is itself a political process. The

Table 11.2   History of Defense Budget

Fiscal Year	President's Request[a] (Billions of $)	Appropriation (Billions of $)	% Cut
1950	13.25	12.95	2.2
1951	13.08	13.29	*1.6[b]*
1952	57.68	56.94	1.3
1953	51.39	46.61	9.3
1954	40.72	34.37	15.6
1955	29.89	28.80	3.6
1956	32.23	31.88	1.1
1957	34.15	34.66	*1.5[b]*
1958	36.13	33.76	6.6
1959	38.20	39.60	*3.7[b]*
1960	39.25	39.23	0.1
1961	39.34	40.00	*1.7[b]*
1962	42.94	46.66	*8.7[b]*
1963	47.91	48.14	*0.5[b]*
1964	49.01	47.22	3.7
1965	47.47	46.75	1.5
1966	45.25	46.89	*3.6[b]*
1967	57.66	58.07	*0.7[b]*
1968	71.58	69.94	2.3
1969	77.07	71.87	6.7
1970	75.28[c]	69.64	7.5
1971	68.75	66.60	3.1
1972	73.54	70.52	4.1
1973	79.59	74.37	6.6
1974	77.25	73.71	4.6
1975	87.06	82.58	5.2
1976	97.86	90.47	7.6

[a]This does not include supplemental estimates or appropriations.

[b]Italicized numbers show the percent increased by Congress.

[c]President Johnson's original proposal, reduced a few months later by Nixon, was $2.5 billion higher.

SOURCE: *Congress and the Nation*, vol. 3, (Washington, D.C.: Congressional Quarterly Inc., 1973), p. 198; *Congressional Quarterly Almanac, 1973* (Congressional Quarterly Service, 1974), p. 168; *Congressional Quarterly Almanac, 1974* (Washington, D.C.: Congressional Quarterly Inc., 1975), p. 41; *Congressional Quarterly Almanac, 1975* (Washington, D.C.: Congressional Quarterly Inc., 1976), p. 873.

accommodation indicated in the table showing that in 1970 Nixon anticipated congressional opposition to the previously announced Johnson proposal and reduced the request $2.5 billion probably headed off congressional cuts, but had little effect upon the appropriation level. One should not draw sweeping conclusions from the figures. Meanwhile, political infighting was heavy on some specific issues (TFX fighters, B70 bombers, antiballistic missiles). A closer scrutiny of the 1960–70 budgets shows that although the average of change over the 11 years was only 2.3 percent, when the budget was broken down into its component parts, changes (in percentage terms) were about four times as high in "research, development, testing and evaluation" and "procurement" as they were in "personnel" and "operations and maintenance."[5]

Besides exercising significant policy discretion over foreign affairs through budgetary control, Congress has substantially imposed its will upon war policy generally and American involvement in Southeast Asia specifically since 1968. Interestingly, Senator J. William Fulbright, for many years the chairman of the prestigious Senate Foreign Relations Committee, observed in 1971 that

> The gradual take over by the executive of the war and treaty powers of the Congress is part of a broader process of expanding presidential authority in the conduct of foreign relations and in those broad areas of domestic life which are closely related to foreign policy, especially in its military aspects. It may not be too much to say that, as far as foreign policy is concerned, our governmental system is no longer one of separated powers, but rather one of elected, executive dictatorship.[6]

In my view the rejoinder offered by Senator Stennis, chairman of the Senate Armed Services Committee, is really more to the point:

> As I understand it, the principal complaint the Senator [Fulbright] has raised so far is not that the Senate has failed to vote or exercise its power, but that the votes just haven't come out the way he thought they should.[7]

In fact, during 1966–72 a total of 94 roll call votes were cast on the war. More than 80 were taken during Nixon's first term. Only a few of those votes occurred in the House and, when Senate amendments were dealt with in conference committees, the House regularly deleted antiwar amendments from the legislation. On the other hand, defense appropriations bills to finance the war were approved annually by large voting margins. It was not until after U.S. military forces were withdrawn from Vietnam in 1973 that Congress specifically ruled out the use of defense appropriations for combat activity in Cambodia.[8] During the same year Congress legislated a stunning reduction in presidential foreign policy authority by enacting the War Powers Act—an enactment intended to be enduring—to limit presidents in their use of troops. Not only was the bill passed, but when President Nixon vetoed it, Congress overrode the veto 284–135 in the House and 75–18 in the Senate.[9]

Another dimension of Congressional authority is in oversight. Morris Ogul has offered a useful definition of that legislative output in these terms:

> Oversight is defined as the behavior of legislators, individually or collectively,
> formally or informally, which results in an impact on bureaucratic behavior in
> relation to the structure and process of policy implementation.[10]

With the decade of the 1970s has come a more aggressive attitude, particularly in the House of Representatives, toward exercising oversight of foreign
policy. Based on interviews conducted in 1955–57, Lewis Dexter captured an
all too colorful vignette when he quoted a member of the House Armed
Services Committee, who said, "Our committee is a real estate committee,"
meaning that the committee did not dig into the premises, assumptions, and
priorities in defense, but simply dealt with those congressional districts that
would have military bases and the transfer, purchase, and sale of such
properties.[11] The inference has been drawn that such oversight is no
oversight at all. In retrospect it is perhaps more accurate to realize that
oversight is not automatically conflictive or acute. Instead, "some oversight
might be collaborationist, designed to protect and defend a particular
program, policy, or administration unit. The denial of oversight is generally
thought to be the mechanism for defense; but supportive, circumscribed, and
formalized oversight activities might produce the same effect."[12] Kaiser's
study of the House Foreign Affairs Committee (renamed the Committee on
International Relations in 1975) revealed that by 1973 it was the third most
active of House committees in conducting oversight hearings and meetings,
that the number of hearings by the committee and its subcommittees had
been increasing (Ninetieth Congress, 318; Ninety-first Congress, 358; Ninety-
second Congress, 327; Ninety-third Congress, 495), that members had
increased their participation in field investigations (Ninety-second Congress,
9; Ninety-third Congress, 28), and that the number of reports to it by the
General Accounting Office (GAO) had grown in recent years (1971, 24; 1972,
36; 1973, 30; 1974, 43). Kaiser concluded that, "This review of oversight
activities of House Foreign Affairs reveals that the committee is one of the
most productive overseers in the chamber, based on cross-committee
comparisons, and that its activities in this realm have expanded in the recent
past, according to longitudinal data."[13]

As this brief review indicates, congressional authority in foreign policy is
actually substantial. Until the late 1960s, foreign policy decision making was
not divisive, with Congress playing a secondary but supportive part in policy
enactment and oversight. Increasingly, however, as presidents pressed for
policies that aroused public controversy, congressional opposition was
awakened, and Congress insisted upon its prerogatives to change policies
and reduce presidential authority in specifying those policies.

Governors, of course, do not exercise foreign policy authority. As chief
executives they lack the flexibility of presidents for that very reason. Prior to
the late 1960s, governors appeared weak when compared with presidents

because in no area of state policy making could they exercise the discretion and flexibility that presidents could in foreign affairs. On the other hand, recent presidents have lost domestic influence as their reputations have become tarnished in foreign affairs. As noted earlier, President Johnson's "box score" with Congress dropped when the nation's frustrations in the Vietnam quagmire increased.

The executive branch, in the name of the president, has played the preeminent part in foreign policy making. Interestingly, policy participants range "from those who seriously question the value of resisting others as a means toward helping ourselves and who prefer military strength over strong allies . . . , to those who feel that an active involvement in international affairs is an investment that serves the national interest."[14] Clausen's study covered the period of 1953–64 and 1968–69. Presidents and their policies differed, but all supported active international involvement, and all were able to influence congressmen, especially of their own party, to support their policies.

Domestic Policy   The American political system adopts an incredibly broad array of policies affecting domestic affairs. Instead of trying to differentiate them subjectively I shall draw upon some systematic findings by others which examine the distribution of benefits, particular policy dimensions, and some explanatory variables.

Policies Distinguished According to How Values Are Allocated

Theodore Lowi has suggested a classification of public policy that distinguishes how benefits and coercion are shared among members of the political system.[15] *Distributive* policies are those that dispense units of benefit to individuals and groups. Traditional examples include the tangible goods and services dispensed by old-time political machines: coal, Christmas baskets, jobs, and favors. In contemporary politics they are government contracts, military bases, and other forms of "pork barrel" legislation. *Regulative* policies are not as easily divisible. Regulations apply to categories of people, whereas distributive policies are more individualized. Examples of regulative policies are those specifying safety and antipollution devices on automobiles, rules governing rivalry between unions and corporations, regulations to obtain or preserve competition in various manufacturing and service industries, and laws to define, protect, and extend the civil rights of certain groups of people in the society. *Redistributive* policies are those that take benefits from large categories of people who have more (or less) than their share and conferring them upon others whose circumstances are different. Beneficiaries are broad categories of people—even social classes. Taxation policy in a political system is potentially redistributive; it can be set up to "soak the rich," as well as provide funds for direct payments (Job Corps, food stamps, welfare checks) or indirect ones (Head Start, Model Cities, public health programs) for the poor. "Soak the poor" policies fit here too. Regressive taxation prevents the poor from developing a sense of independence and efficacy, while leaving profits and privileges to the few who gain from capital investments.

Lowi has applied his classification scheme to congressional enactments and has been able to distinguish bills of the three types. A systematic review of major pieces of legislation revealed some interesting patterns. Distributive policies were pounded out in congressional committees through the conventional politics of horse trading and logrolling. Trading relationships persisted over time and, although lobbyists sometimes had creative impact and the chief executive also had to be taken into account, the battles were resolved in the committees and ratified on the floor. In regulative policies there was more competitive involvement of major interest groups, and relationships between policy participants were much less stable. Involvement and influence by the president varied but never controlled, and the legislative process was creative, both in committee and on the floor. In short, Congress dominated in the making of regulatory policies. Redistributive policies were decided on ideological bases, with the large conglomerate interest groups major contestants in behalf of social classes. The chief executive did not always win, but usually assumed a major role in the policy contest. The group and class interests are stable and enduring (essentially those who have against those who have less), and although more sound and fury occurred in Congress, it usually was not as creative in developing or amending the legislation. Lowi illustrated his findings with the data in Table 11.3. As column (3) clearly shows, on distributive bills after the pork has been cut up and the deals made in committee, changes are not made on the floor over the objections of the bill's sponsor (usually the chairman of the committee from which the bill came). Floor creativity by means of significant amendments passed over the bill sponsor's objections is most evident in regulative bills, those on which several interest groups are likely to be active. Such floor action occurs similarly in both chambers. On redistributive legislation some significant changes occur on the floor, but not a great many. The bills at stake are the policy promotions of the chief executive. Notice from column (4), however, that amending action is substantially greater in the Senate than in the House. This fits in with the earlier comparison of the House and Senate (see Chapter 7) which suggested greater creativity of Senate floor action compared to that of the House. It also fits in with Polsby's description

Table 11.3 Evidence of Floor Creativity in Congress: Actions on Amendments

	(1) Average No. of Amendments Offered per Bill	(2) % Passed of Amendments Offered	(3) % of Significant Amendments Passed Contrary to Wishes of Bill's Sponsor	(4) Weighted Means: Summary of 8 Levels of Amending Action[a]:	
				House	Senate
Distributive Bills (N[b] = 22)	5.8	41.8	0	0.05	0.16
Regulative Bills (N = 15)	12.8	48.9	67	0.46	0.50
Redistributive Bills (N = 25)	9.1	62.4	24	0.15	0.45

[a] Amending action includes (a) number of amendments offered, (b) % passed, (c) number of important amendments offered, (d) % passed, (e) number of amendments offered over objections of sponsor, (f) % passed, (g) number of important amendments offered over objections of sponsor, (h) % passed. These were weighted to reflect the degree of difficulty in getting amendments adopted. The higher the score, the easier it was for the chamber to change a bill as reported by one of its committees.

[b] N = number of bills.

SOURCE: Adapted from Theodore Lowi, "Four Systems of Policy, Politics and Choice," *Public Administration Review* 32, no. 4 (July/August 1972): 306; also see his "Decision Making vs. Policy Making: Toward an Antidote for Technocracy," *Public Administration Review* 30, no. 3 (May/June 1970): 321.

of the Senate's three central functions: "cultivating national constituencies; formulating questions for debate and discussion on a national scale (especially in opposition to the president); and incubating new policy proposals that may at some future time find their way into legislation."[16] Redistributive policy, though executive-centered arouses alternatives in the Senate, the office base for active presidential aspirants.

The important idea Lowi has raised with his policy categories and initial findings is that *"policies determine politics."*[17] This sharply contrasts with the usual logic for discussing politics and policy analysis. Ordinarily political scientists seek to explain how different political process variables affect policy outputs—an inquiry to be dealt with in the remainder of this chapter. But Lowi has offered an alternative view that deserves consideration; namely, that policy stakes activate different political processes. Predictions of legislative and executive behavior, interest group effectiveness, political party unity, bureaucratic processes,[17a] and the like need to be examined in light of theory concerning the types of policy at issue and the kinds of benefits being distributed and coerced by political systems.

Major Dimensions of Domestic Policy

Not all behavior of American legislators which is relevant to making public policy is visible. But proper legislative procedure does require reporting of particular decision points. One of those is voting on bills. Most significant policy decisions in Congress are finally decided by a record roll call. In many instances amendments are likewise by roll call vote. Typically state constitutions *require* that enactments occur only by record roll call. As a consequence, there is an abundance of documented evidence about how legislators vote. One approach to understanding and explaining public policy is to look for patterns of similarity in the hundreds of roll call votes.

At first blush it might seem reasonable to think that each policy choice made in a legislative body is unique. Certainly the contents of the bills differ. They differ in what they do, the effect they will have on constituents, their cost, and so on. However, it is already evident that bills have similarities— some are part of the chief executive's program, some are for urban districts, some arouse the wrath of southern Democrats, while others affect a particular set of interest groups, elicit a sense of party loyalty, or stir other attitudinally based responses. It is even possible that legislators mentally sort out the hundreds of voting decisions they must make on bills and motions into only a few categories—categories common to other legislators, the variety of other political activists in the bureaus, the chief executive's subsystem, the interest groups, the party organizations, and the other levels of government.[18] For example, imagine the existence of a policy dimension whose essential notion is *civil liberties*. The notion of dimension was illustrated in Chapter 10 with the concept of support and extends from the left (negative) to the right (positive). The dimension implies that civil liberties policies could vary on the one hand from being very broad to the other of being very narrow. If civil liberties consist of the rights and privileges guaranteed by the authority of the political system, policies defining them may be broad or narrow. Support for the Equal Rights Amendment to eliminate distinctions based upon sex would be an example of a policy to enlarge civil liberties. A variety of policy issues raise the opportunity to increase, maintain, or narrow citizens' rights. The "no knock" provision of the Comprehensive Drug Abuse Prevention and Control Act (Public Law 91–513) and the District of Columbia Court Reorganization and Criminal Procedure Act (Public Law 91–358) authorized search warrants under certain circumstances which allowed law enforcement officers to enter a place for search without first giving notice of their presence and intentions. This policy reduced the civil liberties of citizens.

It is reasonable to suggest that legislators do sort issues into policy categories, that they can arrange them along a dimension from left to right, that they have their own position on that dimension, and that, comparing the relation of policy proposals to their own positions, they can decide how to vote. Clausen describes a legislator's decision process this way:

> If the legislator's level of support for the policy concept is exceeded by the legislation, he will *reject* it, either by working against it or voting it down. The congressman will *accept* the legislation if the level of support granted by the legislation is equal to, or less than, his ideal level, providing that the only perceived alternative is weaker, or no legislation at all; in other words, half a loaf is better than none.[19]

The Clausen study reveals that, despite a great deal of complexity in the legislative process, there have been five distinct and enduring dimensions evident in the politics and voting in Congress during 1953–64 and 1969–70, and that these five account for approximately three-fourths of the votes taken in Congress.[20] These dimensions were at the center of the conflicts in committees, on the floor, in the news, and in the votes of the members. One of these was foreign policy, which was discussed earlier in this chapter. The others were civil liberties, agricultural assistance, social welfare, and government management of the economy and resources of the nation. Clausen found that repeatedly the same kinds of issues came up from Congress to Congress, and that members established patterns of voting which they repeated again and again. The analysis was done separately on the House and Senate with the finding that parallel forms of the dimensions occurred simultaneously in both houses. The same dimensions persisted over the 12-year period and all but one, agricultural assistance, also appeared in 1969–70. Clausen found an additional policy dimension associated with the Vietnam War. The persistence of the issue dimensions and the fact that congressmen take relatively stable positions on them indicate that there is substantial continuity in national policy making. On the other hand, the political context is not as simple as it is sometimes made out to be in a one-dimensional politics of "liberals," "moderates," and "conservatives," who respond to all issues from a fixed ideological point.

The meaning of the civil liberties dimension has already been described, but it is noteworthy that in Clausen's findings a significant portion of the roll call votes included were those concerned with attempts to enlarge the rights of blacks. The *agricultural assistance* dimension consisted primarily of roll calls on farm subsidies, with the contestants ranging from those who wanted a "free market" for commodities to those who wanted to guarantee farmers set commodity prices. In between were those who supported a variety of price support levels. *Social welfare* refers to a dimension of support for relatively direct aid by government to individuals—in policies of public housing, urban renewal, labor regulation, education, urban affairs, and employment. The *government management* dimension incorporates anti-trust policy, wage and price controls, public and private power conflicts, conserving natural resources versus allowing their consumption through private enterprise, regulation of private enterprise generally, taxation, and balancing the government's budget.

One of Clausen's significant findings is that legislators take a policy position on a dimension and hold to it. Observing legislators over time, he not only found those with fairly extreme positions remaining the same, but those with moderate positions did not change much either. The importance of this finding is, simply, that in order to change an existing policy output pattern, the voting public will likely have to accomplish that by changing their authorities, electing new ones with different policy positions than the former ones.[21]

Studies of policy making in the states suggest that, similar to Congress, there is a good deal of stability and continuity in voting patterns, but, of course, there is variety across the states concerning the conspicuous and enduring issues. One study of state legislators from all 50 states asked respondents to "name the most important matters of policy to come up before the most recent session of your legislature."[22] Of the nearly 300 issue mentions, the majority could be accommodated into 20 areas, with one-fifth being taxation and another 45 percent in apportionment, education, finance, and labor. As Table 11.4 indicates, particular issues are common to almost all the states.

An indication of the continuity of some issues over time in the Nebraska legislature is offered in Table 11.5. With techniques similar to those used by Clausen, Welch and Carlson examined voting in the Nebraska Senate.† They found that the proportion of roll calls that they could put in dimensions declined over time (1927 = 47 percent, 1937 = 48 percent, 1947 = 43 percent, 1959 = 35 percent, 1969 = 27 percent); nevertheless, two issue areas appeared in all five sessions and three occurred in four of the five sessions over a time span exceeding 40 years.

---

†Unicameral and nonpartisan since 1934, in 1927 this was the upper house of a partisan body. See Susan Welch and Eric H. Carlson, "The Impact of Party on Voting Behavior in a Nonpartisan Legislature," *American Political Science Review* 67, no. 3 (September 1973): 854–67.

Table 11.4   Issue Distribution into Policy Areas

Policy Areas	Number of Issue-Mentions	Number of States Represented by Respondents
1. Taxation	624	50
2. Apportionment	472	42
3. Education	447	50
4. Finance	206	47
5. Labor	206	42
6. Health	147	44
7. Business	124	34
8. Civil rights	109	28
9. Highways-transportation	103	29
10. Administration	89	35
11. Local government	55	17
12. Social welfare	53	22
13. Courts-penal-crime	51	25
14. Liquor	51	19
15. Gambling	48	8
16. Land	43	12
17. Elections-primaries-conventions	33	19
18. Constitutional revision	30	11
19. Water resources	23	11
20. Agriculture	18	9

SOURCE: Wayne L. Francis, *Legislative Issues in the Fifty States: A Comparative Analysis*, (Chicago: Rand McNally & Company, 1967), p. 11.

Despite the fragmentary nature of the findings, the studies of policy suggest enduring issues and enduring patterns of decision making. Interestingly, the data to extend and elaborate such findings in the states are accessible and could become the basis for a more comprehensive theory of policy making.

One genre of research which has tapped historical patterns is that focused on taxing and spending. Consistently researchers have concluded that spending is done incrementally. Sharkansky puts the point this way:

Of all the norms, of the claims of special interests, and of the environmental features that have potential relevance for taxing and spending, the one that dominates continuously is incrementalism. It is evident in the stability of relative spending positions from one budget to the next, in the practice of executives and legislators to cut most severely the requests of acquisitive agencies, and in the reluctance of tax officials to consider seriously the proposals that they overhaul the entire tax code.

Table 11.5   Categorizing Scales of Roll Call Voting According to Predominant Issue: Nebraska

Issue Areas of the Scales	1927	1937	1947	1959	1969	Total
Revenue, taxation, or appropriations	5[a]	1	2	2	2	12
Regulation	1	1	2	1	5	10
Local government	3	2	2	1	0	8
Social welfare	1	1	0	2	1	5
Salaries	1	0	2	1	1	5
Education	0	0	1	1	0	2
Civil liberties	0	0	0	0	2	2
State institutions	1	1	0	0	0	2
Highways and transportation	1	1	0	0	0	2
Agriculture	1	1	0	0	0	2
Elections	1	0	0	1	0	2
Judiciary	1	0	0	0	0	1
Private bills	0	1	0	0	0	1
Labor and employment	0	0	0	0	1	1

[a]The numbers indicate the number of scales in this area.

SOURCE: Susan Welch and Eric H. Carlson, "The Impact of Party on Voting Behavior in a Nonpartisan Legislature," *American Political Science Review* 67, no. 3 (September 1973): 867.

But why? Sharkansky explains:

> To inquire into the justifications of an agency's expenditure base, or most of the existing tax provisions, would reopen an infinite number of complex issues and settlements that had been negotiated in the past.[23]

In the continuing task of conflict management, the incremental approach in policy making dampens conflict, habituates compliance, and resists sharp shifts (as well as those who advocate them). The politics of redistribution, with all the potential for class conflict that Lowi suggests is present, is muted, if not avoided altogether in incrementalism.

PARADIGM OF INFLUENCES IN LEGISLATIVE POLICY MAKING

Probably there is no aspect of legislative politics to which more words have been directed than explaining legislators' votes. Political scientists offer numerous books and hundreds of articles; legislators have left memoirs and thousands of speeches.[24] In the Illinois legislature, for example, there is a tradition in both chambers allowing members, during or after a roll call, to rise to "explain" their vote. Explanations by political scientists tend to obscure their descriptions in complex statistical designs and qualified generalizations. Legislators offer highly personalized rationalizations. All this attention to how legislators vote is the result of votes being highly visible. They are reported in hometown newspapers, they are analyzed in political scientists's studies, and they are critically viewed by rival candidates seeking election to office. Although the point is hard to demonstrate, congressmen appear to vote consistently with how they act in committee and how they speak out on the issues.‡ Explanations of voting, therefore, should also help to explain how legislators behave in committee, introduce bills, engage in oversight, and pursue other activities that produce legislative outputs.

Explaining Legislative Voting Patterns

Having distinguished among policies, and suggested that different policies are subject to different mixtures of inputs and political pressures (or, as Lowi suggests, different policies produce different politics), one cannot account specifically for the variance in decisional behavior without a detailed analysis of policy variations. That goes beyond the scope of this book. Nevertheless, there is a need to discuss the segments of the paradigm to estimate or at least suggest the relevance each has in explaining legislators' policy decisions.

The preceding chapters have distinguished and described various elements, actors, and rules in the American policy process as they bear on the legislators who make policy. Figure 11.1 is an attempt to summarize and integrate those elements. Even without precise measurement of the relative impact of all the variables, it is evident that they combine differently over time and in relation to the substance of issues and the intensity of demands concerning them.

The complexity illustrated in Figure 11.1 is not intended to suggest that the mix of variables is so intricate that no patterns can be distinguished. It is

---

‡There may be a handful who act contrary in committee to how they vote on the floor or occasional issues that encourage several to do so, but the argument of close students of congressmen is that their policy positions taken in roll call votes transfer to committees, voice votes, and cloak room conversations. See Clausen, *How Congressmen Decide*, pp. 19–20. Fenno adds that when congressmen explain themselves to constituents, they are consistent whether the hearers are friendly or hostile. Richard F. Fenno, Jr., "Congressmen in Their Constituencies: An Exploration" (Paper delivered at the American Political Science Convention, San Francisco, Calif., Sept. 2–5, 1975), p. 42.

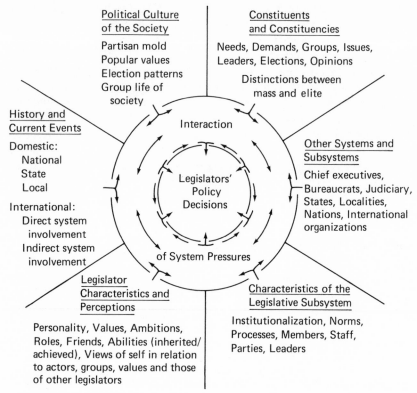

Figure 11.1   Paradigm of Influences Upon Legislators in Policy Making

a reminder that much must be taken into account when one tries to explain policy making and also suggests bases for criticizing some of the existing explanations of how public policies are adopted. The segments will be treated as they appear in Figure 11.1 in clockwise order.

History and Current Events   This book has consistently argued that the authoritative allocation of values occurs in a complex system lodged in an interdependent world. Various actors control pieces of the action. Few political authorities *control* anything beyond themselves, but they exercise resources and can influence events beyond themselves, (they get resources from others and receive influence). History and current events, then, are only partially under control. Significant events always have a variety of consequences, often far beyond what their movers could ever have imagined. Thus movers do not control the events they set in motion. For example, who would have imagined the degree to which policy differences between the North and the South would still be evident in Congress after nearly 120 years? Current history likewise is significant. Those who sought to prosecute the war in Vietnam had no particular intention of lowering the voting age to 18 years, but it is plausible to argue that the slogan, "If we're old enough to fight, we're old enough to vote," carried great weight. The appeal obtained support among policy makers who sympathized with young opponents of the war and from those who wanted to curry favor and continued system support from the young in order to continue the war effort. Such did not occur in 1917 or 1943 because the legitimacy of the conflict was almost unquestioned among those who bore the burden of fighting. But in 1970, that was not the case.

History and events require or, alternatively, prevent particular policies. They also significantly affect the policy agenda. The outcome of World War II left Europe vulnerable to advances by either the Soviet Union or the United States. The U.S. developed the Marshall Plan. That policy could have taken many forms, but the circumstances elicited a positive policy.

Political Culture of the Society   The divisiveness between Yankees and Rebels was passed on to succeeding generations, and the South is still distinctively different from other American states.[25] The South's political culture is different in its traditions, the attitudes of its people, and their patterns of political behavior. American political culture is not without its hypocrisies, but the value placed upon fair elections and electoral processes has been evidenced anew by the popular and legislative condemnation of President Nixon and his cohorts for their subversion of the governing process to manipulate the 1972 election. In the United States the process of impeachment became the preeminent concern in the Congress and, had it been drawn out, would have delayed indefinitely consideration of a great many other policy questions.

Aspects of political culture, the partisan mold upon candidates, issues and voting identities, the durability of election patterns and outcomes, the persistence of interest groups and group values—all these constrain and narrow the options in public policy making. It remains true, for instance, that party is the best single predictor of voting in the United States Congress[26] and in most state legislatures. One's party is first of all an identification: it gives a person, especially a political activist, orientations about issues, heroes, and friends to help and support. Members of Congress have accumulated debts and favors in their party identity. Party identity is occasionally a set of constraints, but most of the time it is a familiar harness which allows teamwork in achieving valued ends.

Constituents and Constituencies   Despite the decline of trust in government and widespread cynicism about political authorities, the needs, demands, and opinions of constituents—as individuals, in groups, and in mass expressions—are both important constraints upon and overarching goals to legislators. This is asserted by legislators in explaining their behavior:

> "Most of the time, the congressman and his constituency agree. That's why we're here."

> "If you have a conflict between you and your district very often, you don't belong here anyway."

> "I understand farm problems. I have one of the most heavily agricultural districts in the country. I grew up with these people and I guess I reflect their thinking."[27]

It is evidenced in correlations between constituents' opinions and legislative voting, and even more so between what legislators *think* their constituents want and how the legislators vote (legislators do not always interpret correctly).[28] It is certainly part and parcel of the partisan patterns in many electoral districts. There are characteristic differences between Republican-dominated districts and Democratic-dominated ones.[29] In short, legislators voting in behalf of party are frequently voting in behalf of their constituents. While party voting and constituency voting overlap, they are not the same thing. When Clausen attempted to disentangle these two sources of legislator influence, he concluded that partisan influence was distinctively sharper on agricultural assistance, social welfare, and government management policies, but constituency influence was at least as significant as party on civil liberties and international involvement voting. In fact, Clausen argues that, at least in matters of civil liberty, "the differences between the party regional groupings are more properly allocated to the differences in the constituencies represented by the congressmen from the various groupings, rather than to a divergence in partisan views."[30]

The legislator typically considers the constituents as a body to be respected and informed—but not unnecessarily disturbed. Clausen puts the analogy well by describing the constituency as a "somnolent giant" usually unaware of the representative's activity. But the giant has tender spots that the representative must protect and not irritate.[31] Meanwhile, when issues arouse diverse views among constituents, legislators are freer to respond to other sources of policy guidance.

Other Systems and Subsystems   Other sources include chief executives, bureaucrats, officials from other political systems and subsystems, and the like. Interestingly, roll call analyses at least give evidence of very little effect upon legislators by these actors. Kingdon found a persistent but small part of the variation in congressmen's decision making accountable to the "administration." [32] The clearest influence relationship he found was between the president and members of the president's party. Clausen reported that as presidential turnovers occur, those congressmen who are responsive to presidential leadership change. Even then, however, he reports that in domestic policy he can find little clear evidence of influence by the president on congressmen. The chief executive's power, both in the nation and in the states, is not in manipulating legislators' votes so much as it is in setting a specific policy agenda with his legislative proposals and budget. His visibility allows him to narrow the general terms in which the debate will take place. No one would suggest that President Ford, while completing Nixon's term of office, directed the Congress. But he did limit the majorities' preferences through his initiatives (for example, achieving a reduction in oil imports by increasing federal tax on oil), proposals (a $12 billion tax rebate proposal; Congress enacted a Democratic alternative returning $21.3 billion), budget, and vetoes (stopping Congress from enlarging regulation of strip mining, for example). The interaction of the chief executive and others in the executive branch with the legislature stimulates inputs of information and opinion which affect the content of policy.

Characteristics of the Legislative Subsystem   It is not easy to specify precisely the consequences of institutional characteristics upon policy adoption. The pride within Congress of its institutional independence from the presidency made possible the impeachment investigation and eventual resignation of President Nixon in a way that the Justice Department could not have accomplished. Its processes allowed the impeachment proceedings of the House Judiciary Committee to go forward in a thorough and fair manner. The norms of legislative behavior made House action deposing leader-turned-alcoholic Wilbur Mills as inconspicuous as possible. Staffing, reflecting the legislature's organization, is decentralized and uncoordinated. Comparing American legislatures, Congress included, the less professional the legislature, ordinarily the smaller and less professional its staff. [33] One study of congressional staff indicates that there is substantial correlation between the views of staff and the legislators they serve. However, instead of revealing that staff determines how legislators will decide, the analysis suggests that staff agrees with the policy decisions that legislators make for themselves. In effect, staff are influenced by the same factors that affect legislators, are affected by the views of those they serve, and express congruent policy choices with them. [34]

In keeping with the decentralized organization of legislatures, particularly Congress, party leaders are rarely policy leaders, rather they are process managers who typically permit their colleagues to develop the content of policy. Thus, to examine roll call voting for leader influence is probably to look in the wrong place for influence or leader effectiveness, particularly in Congress.[35] In the states, however, where information for evaluating policy proposals is scarcer, where committees are less institutionalized, and where floor action constitutes a much larger portion of the members' legislative activity, process management is far more likely to include manipulation of policy enactment. Thus, the policy influence of leaders in state legislatures is usually much stronger than is the case in Congress.

A recurring finding in legislative research is that legislative subunits often achieve unity in policy making and constitute significant blocs of votes on particular kinds of policy. This is true of committees, for example. Research indicates that committees whose members vote together have greater success in getting their bills accepted by Congress.[36] In the U.S. House, delegations from particular states, usually the larger states and according to party, try to achieve cohesion in order to enlarge their influence, to protect their political flanks with constituents ("Yes, I voted against that bill, along with all the other Republicans from our state"), and to rely on one another for information. The shared state identity is an institutional basis for a degree of cohesive behavior.[37] In state legislatures there may be metropolitan delegations that vote with cohesion produced by local party strength; the "Daley Democrats" constitute a cohesive group in the Illinois General Assembly. Interestingly, cohesion has declined in some of the metropolitan delegations following new districting plans requiring single-member districts rather than large multimember ones.[38] Institutional characteristics affect processes and outcomes. Winston Churchill strenuously argued the importance of retaining the size and seating arrangements in the British House of Commons. Research on the Iowa legislature suggests that voting cohesion in political parties is affected by the spatial proximity of the members.[39] Specifically sorting out the "variance in behavior accounted for" by all such subsystem characteristics may be difficult to accomplish, but the evidence of individual studies is that many do have behavioral consequences.

Legislator Characteristics and Perceptions   Public choices of political authorities reflect their own abilities, personalities, and how they relate to others. It is not always possible to trace a causal line from a particular characteristic to a decisional pattern. For instance, Barber identified four types of legislators—Spectators, Advertisers, Reluctants, and Law-makers[40]—whose approach to the legislative process differed substantially. Lawmakers were diligent activists, concerned with the substance of policy, conscious of who influences whom about what, and committed to getting on with the job. Lawmakers differed from Spectators in their activity and readiness to work, from Reluctants in their involvement with the

political process, and from Advertisers in their job satisfaction and willingness to pursue the legislative tasks. But there is no hint that at roll call
Advertisers were liberals, Spectators were moderates, and Lawmakers were
conservatives, or some such regularity with regard to policy content. But one
cannot read Barber without feeling that the community will be better served
by authoritative allocations if most of the legislators are Lawmakers rather
than the other types. Similarly, role orientations, such as Delegates, Trustees, and Politicos,[41] do affect the legislators' outlook on how they approach
and solve legislative problems, but role orientations show no relationship
with how well informed legislators are about their constituents' policy
preferences or how the legislators will vote on roll calls.[42] Similarly, there is
no evidence that all intellectually bright legislators vote one way and "slow
learners" vote another. Still it is reasonable to suggest that those who are
bright will discover, consider, and perhaps introduce more alternatives in the
policy process than will the others. Those who confidently relate to other
people probably get more input from staff, friends, constituents, and outside
experts than those who are private, inner-directed people.

On the other hand, there is strong evidence that legislators influence one
another and affect each other's roll call voting. Kingdon concluded that
congressmen search for consensus in their perceptual field, and that a
significant part of that search is conducted among the colleagues with whom
they usually agree and whom they respect for knowledge and experience. In
fact, holding the effects of several other variables constant, Kingdon found
that the correlation between congressmen's votes and the views of their
fellows was .71, the highest value among the variables he studied.[43] Other
studies report that many legislators ask advice from and consult with
colleagues they consider experts and whom they like. It should be noted, of
course, that the advice and opinions do not reach the legislator in a vacuum.
Friends and respected experts are that because of previous relationships not
unrelated to personality, shared values, similar constituency, party identity,
and the like. A legislator makes friends with those whom he expects to have
similar values and goals. Similarly a legislator's response to urgings from the
chief executive, lobbyists, bureaucrats, and others will be conditioned by his
views about them before they offer advice.

But the legislator is his own man as well. As Miller and Stokes have
shown, legislators not only vote their perceptions of constituents' attitudes,
they frequently vote their own.[44] They found this particularly the case for
congressmen voting on social welfare and foreign policy matters.

To sum up, it is necessary to say that there are numerous interrelated
predictors for legislative decision-making behavior. Researchers have defined their predictor variables in a variety of ways, frequently focusing them
upon measures of roll call voting. The strength of predictions (or correla-

tions) depends in part upon how narrowly "policy voting" has been defined. History, events, and culture set broad limits upon policy decisions, and party identifications, with their attendant implications in electoral patterns, are major influences upon legislators' decisions. Constituents and constituency-related facts overlap with cultural and especially partisan influences, but incorporate additional and independent influences. Other systems and subsystems help set the agenda for policy making, particularly the chief executive. Some policies and some individuals are markedly affected, but there is not much evidence to show that legislators are dominated by executives, bureaucrats, or authorities of other systems and subsystems outside the legislature itself.

Characteristics of the legislative subsystem limit and constrain legislators in their capacity to develop policy. In some, leaders have sufficient authority to dominate portions of the decisional process, thus limiting and directing legislators into decisions. But there are few "czars" in American legislatures, and Congress, long noted for strong committee leaders, has recently reduced their influence a good deal. Instead, legislators have refined their own norms and institutionalized decentralization to preserve the autonomy and policy discretion of the legislative subsystem. Polsby makes the point very well:

> The increasing complexity of the division of labor presents an opportunity for individual Representatives to specialize and thereby enormously increase their influence upon a narrow range of policy outcomes in the political system at large. . . . [T]he total impact of a cadre of specialists operating over the entire spectrum of public policies is a formidable asset for a political institution. . . .[45]

Within narrowed policy ranges, then, legislators still exercise discretion which expresses their individual personalities, values, ambitions, and views of how they should act in relation to friends and rivals, both within and outside the legislative subsystem.

POLICY IMPACT

Too little research by political scientists has been devoted to measuring and analyzing the impact of policies. Experience with policy suggests that two kinds of errors are commonly made by policy makers, and that these errors can be independent of one another.

Intended and Unintended Consequences

The federal highway program to build interstate freeways throughout the country had a number of intended consequences: to improve road travel between cities for citizen pleasure as well as for commerce; to provide jobs and benefits, as a public works program, throughout all the states; to facilitate civil defense especially by providing a road system to evacuate major cities and to allow easy truck movement of missiles.

It was not intended that the cities be evacuated each evening between 3 and 6 P.M. and reinvaded the following morning by an occupying army of suburban workers. Nevertheless, the interstate highway system intensified an existing pattern of suburbanization in metropolitan areas accompanied by ghettoization of all but the downtown commercial portion of the big cities. It was not intended that automobile travel increase as fast as it has, nor auto ownership, nor the foreign invasion of the automobile market, nor the auto-related air pollution problems. But these unintended consequences occurred partly because of the interstate highway system enacted and financed primarily by the federal government.

Predicted and Unpredicted Consequences

Prediction is always risky. But it is important that policy makers consider predictions of policy impact. Social scientists did predict that the federal highway program would change the nation's cities; however, even they underestimated the scope of changes that have since taken place in those cities. There were no accurate predictions of the tremendous increase in the use of petroleum fuels and the kinds of shortages that would thereby occur in the petrochemical industry—affecting not only the availability of gasoline, but also that of plastics, herbicides, fertilizers, and the like. Of course, society and its interrelations are complex. However, it is imperative that prediction and intention be developed as explicitly as possible by policy makers, including legislators, to cope with the needs and demands of society. Figure 11.2 brings together the ideas of predictability and purposiveness.[46]

Predictability of Impact

		Unpredicted	Predicted
	Unintended	1	2
Purposiveness of Impact			
	Intended	3	4

Figure 11.2   Predictability and Intention in Evaluating Policy Impact

Goal: Policies with Predicted and Intended Consequences

Policies will not have ideal consequences, perfectly solving all problems and fulfilling needs to everyone's satisfaction. But in order for policy makers to distinguish among policy proposals to obtain intended impact, there has to be analysis which predicts that impact. The goal, therefore, is that policy makers be in a position to select policies that have predicted and intended impact—those that fall into cell 4 of Figure 11.2. This is not to suggest that all predicted and intended results are going to be pleasantly received by everyone. But even if predicted consequences have certain social costs, as long as decision makers knowingly accept the costs in order to obtain other benefits, the decision-making procedure has been rational and proper.

Only policies that will produce an impact are worth putting into effect. Policy makers are accountable for both the intended and unintended consequences. Therefore, predictability is desirable in any political system. But it is particularly valuable in a democratic society whose preeminent values are to be selected by the people.

CONCLUDING OBSERVATIONS

My bias concerning the policy process is that it must be open to demands and inputs of information, including predictions about the consequences of policy. Any open policy-making process that will consider and evaluate a wide range of information is likely to function slowly and unevenly. Thorough prediction will not make hard choices unnecessary; it may make choices even more difficult. But it is necessary to obtain intended results. Prediction is a necessary (if not sufficient) condition for controlling the consequences of policy. This, by the way, suggests an important role for social scientists in the political process. It is desirable that more effort in teaching and research be applied to *policy analysis* so that political authorities can go about their jobs in an informed fashion. To put the point another way, as scholars we in the social sciences sometimes scoff at the choices made by politicians because we foresee unintended results in their decisions. The creative role for us in the social sciences is to predict policy impact so that authorities can make wise choices. Obtaining intended results through public policy is a job for more than those in positions of political authority.

NOTES

1. David Easton, *The Political System: An Inquiry Into the State of Political Science* (New York: Alfred A. Knopf, 1953), p. 130.

2. Neustadt identifies the annual authorizations as one form of Congress's effort to reach for control over its executive competitors. See Richard E. Neustadt, "Politicians and Bureaucrats" in *The Congress and America's Future*, ed. David B. Truman (Englewood Cliffs, N.J.: Prentice-Hall, 1965), p. 105.

3. Peter Bachrach and Morton S. Baratz, "Decisions and Nondecisions: An Analytical Framework," *American Political Science Review* 57, no. 2 (September 1963): 632–42; quotation is from p. 641.

4. Gabriel A. Almond, *The American People and Foreign Policy* (New York: Harcourt, Brace and Company, 1950; Frederick A. Praeger, Inc., 1960), p. 143. A more recent perspective, but one which also indicates a preeminent role by an attentive few among the public, is offered by James N. Rosenau, *Public Opinion and Foreign Policy* (New York: Random House, 1968).

5. Arnold Kanter, "Congress and the Defense Budget: 1960–1970," *American Political Science Review* 66, no. 1 (March 1972): 134.

6. In John C. Stennis and J. William Fulbright, *The Role of Congress in Foreign Policy* (Washington, D.C.: American Enterprise Institute for Public Policy Research, 1971), p. 62.

7. Ibid., p. 75.

8. For a concise review, see *Congress and the Nation*, vol. 3 (Washington, D.C.: Congressional Quarterly Inc., 1973), p. 900.

9. For a review of the politics and a thoughtful analysis of the implications, see Alton Frye, *A Responsible Congress: The Politics of National Security* (New York: McGraw-Hill Book Company, 1975), pp. 177–215.

10. Morris S. Ogul, "Legislative Oversight of Bureaucracy," U.S., Congress, House, *Committee Organization in the House*, Panel Discussion Before the Select Committee on Committees, vol. 2, pt. 3 (Washington, D.C.: U.S. Government Printing Office, 1973), p. 701.

11. Lewis Anthony Dexter, "Congressmen and the Making of Military Policy," in *New Perspectives on the House of Representatives*, eds. Robert L. Peabody and Nelson W. Polsby (Chicago: Rand McNally and Company, 1963), pp. 311–12.

12. Fred M. Kaiser, "The Changing Nature and Extent of Oversight: The House Committee on Foreign Affairs in the 1970's" (Paper presented at the Midwest Political Science Association, Chicago, Illinois, May 1–3, 1975), p. 12.

13. Ibid.; quotation is from p. 13; data drawn from pp. 4, 5, 9, and 11.

14. Aage R. Clausen, *How Congressmen Decide: A Policy Focus* (New York: St. Martin's Press, 1973), p. 209.

15. Theodore Lowi, "American Business, Public Policy, Case-Studies and Political Theory," *World Politics* 6 (July 1964): 677–715; "Decision Making vs. Policy Making: Toward an Antidote for Technocracy," *Public Administration Review* 30, no. 3 (May/June 1970): 314–25; and, "Four Systems of Policy, Politics and Choice," *Public Administration Review* 32, no. 4 (July/August 1972): 298–310.

16. Nelson W. Polsby, "Strengthening Congress in National Policy-Making," *The Yale Review* 59, no. 4 (June 1970): 487.

17. Lowi, "Four Systems of Policy, Politics and Choice," p. 299; emphasis in the original.

17a. For an analysis built upon and extending Lowi's theory, see Randall B. Ripley and Grace A. Franklin, *Congress, the Bureaucracy and Public Policy* (Homewood, Ill.: the Dorsey Press, 1976), especially pp. 71–142.

18. This and the following draw heavily upon the arguments by Clausen, *How Congressmen Decide*, pp. 15 ff.

19. Ibid., p. 17.

20. Ibid., p. 53.

21. Ibid., especially chap. 4, "Continuity and Stability: 1953–1970," pp. 52–85.

22. Wayne L. Francis, *Legislative Issues in the Fifty States: A Comparative Analysis* (Chicago: Rand McNally & Company, 1967), quoted from the questionnaire on p. 110.

23. Ira Sharkansky, *The Politics of Taxing and Spending* (Indianapolis: The Bobbs-Merrill Company, Inc., 1969), p. 201.

24. Significant books by political scientists include the following: Julius Turner and Edward V. Schneier, *Party and Constituency: Pressures on Congress*, rev. ed. (Baltimore: Johns Hopkins University Press, 1970); Duncan MacRae, Jr., *Dimensions of Congressional Voting* (Berkeley: University of California Press, 1958); David B. Truman, *The Congressional Party: A Case Study* (New York: John Wiley & Sons, Inc., 1959); Lewis A. Froman, Jr., *Congressmen and Their Constituencies* (Chicago: Rand McNally & Company, 1963); Leroy N. Rieselbach, *The Roots of Isolationism: Congressional Voting and Presidential Leadership in Foreign Policy* (Indianapolis: The Bobbs-Merrill Company, Inc., 1966); David R. Mayhew, *Party Loyalty Among Congressmen* (Cambridge, Mass.: Harvard University Press, 1966); Aage R. Clausen, *How Congressmen Decide: A Policy Focus* (New York: St. Martin's Press, 1973); John W. Kingdon, *Congressmen's Voting Decisions* (New York: Harper & Row, 1973); and Morris P. Fiorina, *Representatives, Roll Calls and Constituencies* (Lexington, Mass.: Lexington Books, D.C. Heath and Company, 1974). There are literally hundreds of related articles in political science journals.

Illuminating books by practitioners include Clem Miller, *Member of the House: Letters of a Congressman*, ed. John W. Baker (New York: Charles Scribner's Sons, 1962); Richard Bolling, *House Out of Order* (New York: E. P. Dutton, 1965); Donald Riegle, with Trevor Armbrister, *O Congress* (Garden City, N.Y.: Doubleday & Co., 1972); and Paul H. Douglas, *In the Fullness of Time: The Memoirs of Paul H. Douglas* (New York: Harcourt Brace Jovanovich, 1972).

25. See Norman R. Luttbeg, "Classifying the American States: An Empirical Attempt to Identify Internal Variations," *Midwest Journal of Political Science* 15, no. 4 (November 1971): 703–21.

26. Clausen, *How Congressmen Decide*, p. 91.

27. Quoted from Kingdon, *Congressmen's Voting Decisions*, p. 45.

28. Warren E. Miller and Donald E. Stokes, "Constituency Influence in Congress," *American Political Science Review* 57, no. 1 (March 1963): 45–57.

29. See Froman, *Congressmen and Their Constituencies*, especially chap. 7, "Constituency Differences Between Parties and Congressional Roll-Call Voting," pp. 95–97; and Mayhew, *Party Loyalty Among Congressmen*.

30. Clausen, *How Congressmen Decide*, pp. 141 ff.; quotation is from p. 222.

31. Ibid., p. 133.

32. See Kingdom, *Congressmen's Voting Decisions*, pp. 18–23 and 169–91.

33. John G. Grumm, "Structural Determinants of Legislative Outputs," in *Legislatures in Developmental Perspective*, eds. Allan Kornberg and Lloyd D. Musolf (Durham, N.C.: Duke University Press, 1970), pp. 429–59, especially pp. 447–51.

34. Kingdon, *Congressmen's Voting Decisions*, pp. 18–23 and 192–95.

35. Ibid., pp. 107–26.

36. See James W. Dyson and John W. Soule, "Congressional Committee Behavior on Roll Call Votes: The U.S. House of Representatives, 1955–64," *Midwest Journal of Political Science* 14, no. 4 (November 1970): 626–47. For "committees whose members vote together," committees were measured according to "the proportion of times each committee member agrees with every other committee member on proposals from their committee" (see Dyson and Soule, pp. 633–35). For a simpler procedure and similar kind of finding for the Senate, see Donald R. Matthews, *U.S. Senators and Their World* (New York: Vintage Books, Random House, 1960), pp. 169–70.

37. See Truman, *The Congressional Party*, pp. 247–69; Clausen, *How Congressmen Decide*, pp. 181–88; Alan Fiellin, "The Functions of Informal Groups: A State Delegation," in *New Perspectives on the House of Representatives*, eds. Robert L. Peabody and Nelson W. .Polsby (Chicago: Rand McNally & Company, 1963), pp. 59–78; and Barbara Deckard, "State Party Delegations in the U.S. House of Representatives—A Comparative Study of Group Cohesion," *Journal of Politics* 34, no. 1 (February 1972): 199–222.

38. See Malcolm E. Jewell, *Metropolitan Representation: State Legislative Districting in Urban Counties* (New York: National Municipal League, 1969).

39. Samuel C. Patterson, "Party Opposition in the Legislature: The Ecology of Legislative Institutionalization," *Polity* 4, no. 3 (Spring 1972): 344–66.

40. James David Barber, *The Lawmakers: Recruitment and Adaptation to Legislative Life* (New Haven: Yale University Press, 1965).

41. See John C. Wahlke, Heinz Eulau, William Buchanan, and LeRoy C. Ferguson, *The Legislative System: Explorations in Legislative Behavior* (New York: John Wiley & Sons, Inc., 1960); and Roger H. Davidson, *The Role of the Congressman* (New York: Pegasus, 1969).

42. See Ronald D. Hedlund and H. Paul Friesema, "Representatives' Perceptions of Constituency Opinion," *Journal of Politics* 34, no. 3 (August 1972): 730–52; H. Paul Friesema and Ronald D. Hedlund, "The Reality of Representational Roles," in *Public Opinion and Public Policy*, rev. ed. (ed.) Norman R. Luttbeg (Homewood, Ill.: Dorsey Press, 1974); and Jack R. Van Der Slik, "Role Theory and the Behavior of Representatives: Some Empirical Observations on the Theory of Heinz Eulau and His Friends," *Public Affairs Bulletin* 6, no. 2 (March/April 1973): 1–7.

43. Kingdon, *Congressmen's Voting Decisions*, pp. 16–23 and 69–104.

44. Miller and Stokes, "Constituency Influence in Congress," p. 56.

45. Nelson W. Polsby, "Institutionalization in the U.S. House of Representatives," *American Political Science Review* 62, no. 1 (March 1968), pp. 144–68; quotation from p. 166.

46. This figure is adapted from Robert L. Lineberry and Ira Sharkansky, *Urban Politics and Public Policy* (New York: Harper & Row, 1971), p. 199.

12

Legislative Subsystem: Stress, Adaptation, and Potential for Change

David Easton notes that "A system will finally succumb unless it adopts measures to cope with the stress."[1] Certainly this is a reasonable notion. It is not necessary to wait until the American political system disintegrates to take seriously the notion that stress must be dealt with. It is met with tangible policies and with procedures for policy making. The former includes acts ending the war in Vietnam, assisting New York City in avoiding bankruptcy, subsidizing the construction of highways, spending for an antimissile system, altering the level of price supports for agricultural commodities, increasing the per-pupil assistance of states to local school districts.

Sometimes a political system is slow to produce the policies that satisfy demands and handle stress. If stress persists and increases, authorities come under fire. The democratic rules of the game usually produce turnover. Remaining incumbents scramble for political survival by changing the institutions, reforming the structures, and adapting the norms of behavior. Typically this is called "reform." Because legislatures not only make policy, but also have the primary authority for making and changing the rules in legislatures and all other political institutions, they are repeatedly besieged by reform movements and reformers. Legislatures do enact reforms, but they are alive with controversy about what should take precedence—adopting new programs or reforming procedures. These are not mutually exclusive, and sometimes they occur together, but legislative subsystems have finite resources for dealing with stress so that sometimes reform is an alternative to programmatic policies.

While we may disagree on *how* successful American political systems have been in dealing with stress, it is my opinion that several important stress-relieving decisions and policies have recently been put into effect. Congress has been vitally involved in some of them. Certainly the Vietnam War, the draft, and military spending were significant sources of stress in the late 1960s and early 1970s. Military spending remains an issue, but stress associated with the draft has been dissipated. The War Powers Act of 1973 was an important piece of legislation because it delimits the President's war-making capacities unless he obtains a positive endorsement by members of Congress. It is difficult for students of the 1970s to appreciate the divisiveness of the apportionment issue and "one man, one vote" representation as it was fought out through the political process in the first half of the 1960s. The rule changes wrought were really extraordinary. The implication of changing the rules was that political power was to be redistributed. With the benefit of hindsight, it turns out that the policy consequences were not very dramatic. But the constitutional principle of citizen equality and rights to equal protection under the law were reaffirmed and broadened in a significant way. In so doing, the legitimacy of state legislative bodies was significantly shored up so that they could more effectively pursue and fulfill the task of conflict resolution.

LEGISLATURES AND CHANGING CULTURAL VALUES

Great stress has occurred in the political system concerning the rights of blacks, chicanos, and native Americans. These intense minorities have raised the fist. Dissident opposing whites have raised the gun. Harsh and unjust violence has occurred. Political authorities have protected antagonists from one another, and the opposing spokesmen have had access to decision-making bodies—legislative, administrative, judicial—with the result that ground rules defining rights, freedoms, and limits have been established and affirmed.

Some will object to say, "Your words are too facile. You put a good face on unjust solutions. Blacks and other minorities are still socially and economically deprived. The system does not provide justice. It only lengthens and lightens the chains a bit." The objection is an important one because it focuses attention on the possibility for social change through a democratic representational system. In the constitutions of the nation and states, there is a philosophy of equality of men in terms of their rights to participate in the political process. For half the nation's history, it has applied only to white men. In this century it has increasingly applied to women and has come to have reality for nonwhites. The formal and informal rules of the game, which some believe are so superficial but which are the objects of endless tinkering, are rules of procedure. Still imperfect, they provide a policy-making process. Decisions and decision makers are not equally accessible to all in the political community, a fact that is both the boon and bane of the system. Selective access allows policy makers to get on with their jobs. It also accommodates and allows adjustment for the views of intense minorities. But in operation it does not always make it possible for those with opposing views to receive equal consideration.

Legislation Lags Behind Cultural Changes

Legislative subsystems are not promising agents for changing cultural values, since they contain a hubbub of voices on many issues all at one time. The legislature is an arena in which votes are taken to reveal, endorse, and legitimate a shift that has taken place in the larger society. The changing of community values requires leadership and promotional activity. Group leaders, executives, and even social critics are likelier agents for change than legislators. Particular legislators can use the legislature as a forum for promoting change, but the chief executive is in a much more promising position to be an agent for change.

As representatives of the grass roots, legislators are typically reticent about endorsing changes in cultural values. Keynesian economics? Legalized abortion? Affirmative action on behalf of women? Decriminalization of soft drugs and sexual practices? Elimination of the death penalty? The legislature is typically the last bastion of momism, apple pie, and traditional morality (not necessarily for the members or their families, but in behalf of the constituents they represent). It is precisely those policy questions that imply new cultural values that legislators put off and about which they prefer to procrastinate. Meanwhile the members test the winds of change in their constituencies. Perhaps they edge toward the issue with a token policy, and if suddenly there is a broadly felt awareness that the people back home have changed their values, then the legislators will endorse a new cultural standard. Issues based upon new cultural values are not routine. Legislatures deal effectively and even efficiently with routine issues—annual budget requests, bills to close or open loopholes, proposals to increase or cut back existing programs, changes in agencies of government. These are the sorts of issues that fit the "major policy dimensions" that Clausen found recurring in congressional voting, but the issues related to cultural values seem more threatening. Not uncommonly these are the questions that get bogged down in the complex machinery of the legislature: they are the objects of delays and jurisdictional disputes by committees, and the questions for which hearings are opened, closed, and reopened. Such backing and filling is a sign that the legislature is trying to avoid the enactment of a positive policy. Instead members are waiting for cultural forces to wear themselves out. Recall, for example, how Congress was one of the last major institutions to affirm by a public enactment the rights of blacks. Significant legislation did not come until the mid-1960s. By that time not even major league baseball teams were holding the color line and major league baseball has certainly not been in the forefront of social movements. Congressional action lagged behind progressive change in industrial unions, major corporations, the military, many civilian government agencies, the presidency, the courts, and even the American Medical Association. Likewise, it is not surprising that legislatures were the last governmental bastion of "Red-baiting," that is, looking for Communists. At its zenith in the McCarthy era of the early 1950s, this policy did not emanate only from Congress. There were parallel investigating groups in several state legislatures. The U.S. House had an Un-American Activities Committee until 1969 when its name was changed to the Internal Security Committee. The committee was not broken up until 1975. All this is to say that legislatures are organized to preserve parochial interests, and are essentially conservative about cultural values. The status quo is policy until the legislature enacts a new one, but a proposal may fail through default at any of a dozen decision points. Thus the institutionalized procedure of legislatures reinforces the legislative bias against policies that reflect new cultural values.

Anticipating Future Stress

Legislatures handle routine stress due to structural, organizational, and even personnel problems in the governing system well enough. Stress of the latter type has been as heavy recently as at any time in American history. There was the forced resignation and replacement of the vice-president at a time when the president himself was subject to controversy. There were the turnovers in the cabinet and the creation of the Office of Special Prosecutor. Congress was actually to the point of adopting articles of impeachment against the president.

Legislatures handle reform in the institutions around them quite well. Interestingly, this is supported by cultural values both within and outside the legislatures. The rivalry of the legislature with the other branches and particularly with the chief executive is sanctified in the Constitution, in the views of scholars, in public opinion, and certainly in the minds of authorities in the separate subsystems. For instance, the War Powers Act of 1973 reformed procedures by which a president can continue the emergency use of military forces. It does not prevent presidential initiative, but it requires that Congress act within 60 days to sustain or limit an undeclared war action. Interestingly, this is not mere intrusion upon the president. It means that a president must give an early accounting to Congress for military action, but it also requires Congress to render a judgment, one way or another, fulfilling its own constitutional mandate for warmaking.[2]

But one can expect legislatures to have difficulty coming to grips with issues that have cultural values at their roots. Two significant examples are problems of population and environment. If the growth of U.S. population is a long-term problem, then Congress is not a likely source of policies to deal with its implications. In addition to an absence of policy foresight in Congress, solutions threatening the traditional values concerning the goodness of growth, the sanctity of life, the encouragement of single-family life styles, and the like will be unacceptable to a majority of legislators for a long time. For similar reasons environmental protection through legislation will be enacted only gradually. The environment is endangered not simply by technology (technological correction could be accomplished through legislative regulation). The environment is threatened by American culture—the emphasis upon consuming goods and services. That emphasis is not limited to productive effort on the job, it is a major portion of leisure time activity. Traffic is not only congested at work week rush hours, it is likewise a problem on weekends and holidays. Some national parks are threatened by their very popularity. The beauty of nature is endangered by all those hurrying to "get back to the beauties of nature." Americans have learned to value efficiency in the use of man-hours, but it has been achieved at great cost in other resources. Until a new resources morality is learned, legislatures will regulate in terms of the old one.

The pace of legislative gradualism will depend upon the success that policy promoters have in advancing both programs and new cultural values. As I have previously argued, one key person in policy promotion is the president. Change will also require the leadership of social critics, interest group spokesmen, and media communicators.

CHANGING LEGISLATIVE RESPONSIVENESS TO NEW VALUES

For a political system to keep ahead of needs and to anticipate the implications of new values requires leadership. The legislative environment does not nurture leadership. Frequently the opposite is true: Congress and legislatures are institutionalized to restrict leadership, particularly policy leadership on the progressive side of cultural values. In both Congress and state legislatures, positions of leadership are encumbered with heavy expectations that those in them will perform as process managers. Party leaders have to manage the flow of legislative business—planning the calendar, calling up bills, helping sponsors and bill managers, balancing demands for deliberation and haste. In state legislatures policy specialization has been more modest. Committees are not well institutionalized; thus legislatures have not nurtured their members to achieve expertise through specialization. In Congress, on the other hand, circumstances are somewhat different. Institutionalization has encouraged expertise, but not policy promotion. In fact the emphasis is upon defeating innovation—committees "cull out," "water down," "gut," "weed out," and compromise bills. Committee chairmen known as powerful (men such as Wilbur Mills, Clarence Cannon, "Judge" Howard Smith, and Richard Russell) are those remembered for their ability to resist policy promoters from outside the Congress, particularly presidents. This style is embedded in the process for attaining leadership—that of seniority. One does not achieve leadership by success in policy promotion. Under present arrangements in the House, Democratic party nominations for committee chairmen are made by the Steering and Policy Committee. Then they must withstand challenge in the caucus in an election. In 1974–75 four turnovers occurred: Mills, obviously sick, was replaced in Ways and Means; Patman (Banking), Poage (Agriculture), and Hebert (Armed Services) were defeated in open contests. But with only one exception the chairmen named were the next most senior Democratic committee members. The seniority rule was only minimally violated in the Banking Committee. Republicans, by the way, retained their senior committee members as ranking minority members of every committee.

But consider other possible arrangements. Suppose that candidates could run for the position of chairman. One could campaign by promising to promote particular policies. Alternative candidates could promise others. In short, the competitors would be seeking opportunities to lead committees and Congress to new policy enactments. If policy promotion were a means of fulfilling office ambitions, the policy process of legislatures might well be markedly changed. Similarly committee chairmen, particularly those conspicuous for success in promoting policy in their committees, would become promising contestants for party leadership positions. If committee chairmanships were stepping stones toward the speakership, chairmen would be much more likely to be loyalists in party affairs. Their committee influence would support (and even construct) party positions rather than diminish them.

Policy promotion requires a sensitivity to contemporary values. Policy offerings of rival aspirants within the legislature are likely to test legislators' perceptions of what constituents do or do not hold dear in their value orientations. Changing the achievement criteria among legislators could meaningfully alter legislative responsiveness to changes in cultural values.

Changing the Executive-Legislative Relationship

There has been a good deal of puzzlement about how weak Congress seems by comparison with the president (although I have argued that this is more apparent than real). But even President Ford, who inherited a weakened presidency and whose congressional party took a thrashing in 1974, held a largely Democratic Congress from enacting its own slate of Democratic programs. How can this be explained, particularly after learning from Clausen that the president's impact upon congressional voting is so modest?

The answer has to do with policy promotion. An apt comparison can be drawn between the five full years of Johnson's presidency and the first five years of Nixon's (disregarding the traumatic year of 1974). By actual count President Johnson offered Congress 1902 proposals. Nixon made 882.[3] The policy process with which Congress had been comfortable since the time of Franklin D. Roosevelt and beyond was suddenly changed. Congress was habituated to discretionary policy adoption working from a presidentially set agenda. Nixon's strategy for reducing the role of the federal government in social programs was not simply to propose reduced programs; rather, he refrained from policy promotion. Without presidential proposals to stimulate changes and alternatives, policy promotion in social programming dropped off. It is not that members of Congress lacked the ideas or the political intention; rather, the existing leadership—both structurally and in the leadership styles of those in office—was not oriented toward policy promotion. The party leaders do not speak with one voice. They have not obtained the visibility to dramatize national needs and offer comprehensive solutions. Staff resources are decentralized and uncoordinated. The capacity for policy promotion simply has not been developed in the legislature. This is especially noticeable in the large majorities of congressional Democrats who have not been able to put together a set of domestic programs on social issues in the face of Nixon and Ford administration opposition.

It may be that the congressional leadership will be adapted by its members to the task of policy promotion. Some real changes have occurred in the House Democratic caucus.[4] Behind closed doors the congressional party has thrashed out and voted on some significant issues. Importantly the caucus atmosphere forces the committee chairmen to deal with the membership without their traditional prerogatives of influence. The task of nominating committee chairmen, as well as making all other committee assignments, has become the responsibility of the Democratic Steering and Policy Committee of the caucus. While the seniority rule was certainly not destroyed by the overthrow of four chairmen in 1975, chairmen were put on notice that they are no longer responsible primarily to themselves or even to their committee members; they are accountable to a majority of their fellow party members. Standing committees are specialized bodies, whose senior members often are highly experienced and knowledgeable about the substance of their jurisdiction. If the legislative parties institutionalize a selection process that encourages aspirants for committee chairmanships to assert themselves as policy promoters, the development of policy alternatives within Congress could substantially change its atmosphere. Certainly the rivalry of Congress with the president would be intensified. It is not likely that policy leadership within Congress would neutralize the president's advantages in policy promotion. His visibility and resources for putting together comprehensive packages would still be apparent. But a presidential strategy of not proposing could be met much more aggressively by a Congress which possessed leadership resources of its own to promote alternatives.

It is too early to say that the activities of the new committee chairmen are moving along the path I have outlined. It should be noted though that two of the new chairmen, Ullman and Reuss, did move rather quickly to become public men by offering and promoting their own alternatives to proposals (and nonproposals) of President Ford in the substantive jurisdictions of their committees. Neither has as yet been able to put together a program that has both passed Congress and gotten past the president. Ullman's energy tax bill did obtain House passage by mid-1975, but he conceded that he could not get all the measures he wanted in the bill passed by a majority.

Leadership in legislatures is difficult to accomplish. In American legislatures, especially Congress, the procedures and rules have brought about decentralization and specialization. Nevertheless, legislators are expected to lead. A study of opinion in 1968 reveals an interesting distribution of public views about the sources of policy leadership. Table 12.1 reports the data. Parker discovered that:

> Generally speaking, people are decisively more attentive to presidential—rather than congressional—affairs. Yet, Congress is more likely to be perceived as having "great effect" on a person's life, and three-quarters of those with a definite institutional preference believe that Congress should have the leading role in forming public policy.[5]

While the data are less than compelling, they suggest that legislators have better prospects for arousing popular support for policy promotion than they may realize. Particularly those who can achieve visibility, such as party and committee leaders, may find popular response eminently tractable.

The opportunity for policy leadership in Congress may be enhanced by some long-term trends now evident. The aggregate policy differences between the two political parties appear to have declined substantially in the last century. Table 12.2 reports this decline, indicating a partisan context in

Table 12.1   Public Prescriptions for Leadership in the Formation of Public Policy

Prescription	%
Congress	27
Presidency	9
Both about equal	64
TOTAL	100
N[a] =	1339

[a]N = number of respondents.

SOURCE: Glenn R. Parker, *Political Beliefs About the Structure of Government: Congress and the Presidency* (Beverly Hills: Sage Professional Papers in American Politics, vol. 2, no. 04–018), p. 19.

Table 12.2   The Case of the Disappearing Party: Index of Party Dissimilarity in the House, 1873–1973

Period	Congresses	Mean Index of Party Dissimilarity[a]
1873–1881	43–47	0.583
1883–1893[b]	48–50, 52–53	0.438
1895–1911	54–62	0.625
1913–1931	63–72	0.424
1933–1939	73–76	0.529
1941–1951	77–82	0.397
1953–1963	83–88	0.357
1965–1971	89–92	0.250

[a]Taken across all nonunanimous roll calls in each Congress. The higher the mean score, the more dissimilar the voting of the two parties in roll call votes. The score can range from 1.0, parties totally dissimilar, to 0.0, parties no different from one another.

[b]The index of .713 for the 51st Congress (1889–91) is abnormally high for unique reasons, and has been excluded.

SOURCE: Adapted from Walter Dean Burnham, "Insulation and Responsiveness in Congressional Elections," *Political Science Quarterly* 90, no. 3 (Fall 1975): 427.

which the conventions of partisan loyalty are increasingly weakly felt by legislators. This fits in with the recent popularity of "new politics," which is more issue- and program-oriented than partisan. Burnham, reflecting on the 1974 congressional elections, notes that:

> The entire content of the 1974 election, no less than the striking mixture of diverse movements in its result, suggests that it marks a turning point in the current crisis sequence which has been affecting American electoral politics as a whole. Moreover, it is associated with a swing in the institutional balance between president and Congress toward the latter, the first such swing in many decades. For quite deterministic reasons this will not mean the emergence of anything approximating "congressional government" even in the short term. But for some time to come, the autonomous policy importance of the legislative branch will probably be enhanced to a degree scarcely imagined by political analysts of even a few years ago.[6]

Loosened partisan ties, popular expectations that Congress should lead, and heightened regard for congressional initiatives are a context for evoking policy promotion activities from members of Congress. I expect that leadership will be institutionalized in the committee and party leaders as a concomitant to a more participatory process of selecting committee chairmen and party leaders.

This does not portend rigid partisanship or monolithic factions. The decentralization of present-day legislatures has enhanced the significance of individual members. In the absence of party-line discipline and habits of rigorous presidential support, the individual and his vote count. Members can bargain, oppose, and compromise to achieve individual objectives through policy—for constituents, interest groups, like-minded colleagues, party, and their own careers.

CONCLUDING OBSERVATIONS

American legislatures exercise real discretion in making policy. They have their own organizational flaws. Some of their members are fools and others are dishonest. They are subject to popular control. Legislative careers are sufficiently attractive for competitors to run for office and for incumbents to seek renewal of their authority from the people. Decentralization means that the legislature speaks with a cacophony of voices and is, therefore, a confusing institution, but it accommodates, moderates, and reflects competing interests in the society. It interjects parochialism into policy adoption. Its members bargain and compromise. Its outputs do resolve conflicts and legitimate actions taken elsewhere. Its openness to demands and complaints makes it a real outlet for the dissident voices of the society. Its authority over chief executives and governmental departments is the most important check upon the administering end of government. Patterns of change in and through legislatures tend to be gradual, yet the constraints of gradualism reflect the political support of citizens who participate in behalf of moderate, rather than comprehensive, social changes.

NOTES

1. David Easton, *A Systems Analysis of Political Life* (New York: John Wiley & Sons, Inc., 1965), p. 220.

2. See Alton Frye, *A Responsible Congress: The Politics of National Security* (New York: McGraw-Hill Book Company, 1975), especially pp. 212–15.

3. See *Congressional Quarterly Almanac*'s Presidential Boxscore reports for appropriate years.

4. For a concise summary, see *Congressional Quarterly Weekly Report,* May 3, 1975, p. 913.

5. Glenn R. Parker, *Political Beliefs About the Structure of Government: Congress and the Presidency* (Beverly Hills: Sage Professional Papers in American Politics, vol. 2, no. 04–018), p. 37.

6. Walter Dean Burnham, "Insulation and Responsiveness in Congressional Elections," *Political Science Quarterly* 90, no. 3 (Fall 1975): 411–35; quotation is from p. 434.

Index

Italic numbers indicate pages on which material appears in figures or tables. Boldface numbers indicate pages on which complete references occur. Numbers in parentheses indicate note numbers.